Church Laws and Ecumenism

Written by experts from within their communities, this book compares the legal regimes of Christian churches as systems of religious law.

The ecumenical movement, with its historical theological focus, has failed to date to address the role of church law in shaping relations between churches and fostering greater mutual understanding between them. In turn, theologians and jurists from the different traditions have not hitherto worked together on a fully ecumenical appreciation of the potential value of church laws to help, and sometimes to hinder, the achievement of greater Christian unity. This book seeks to correct this ecumenical church law deficit. It takes account of the recent formulation by an ecumenical panel of a *Statement of Principles of Christian Law*, which has been welcomed by Pope Francis and the Ecumenical Patriarch of Constantinople, leader of the Orthodox Church worldwide, as recognizing the importance of canon law for ecumenical dialogue. This book, therefore, not only provides the fruits of an understanding of church laws within ten Christian traditions but also critically evaluates the *Statement* against the laws of these individual ecclesial communities.

The book will be an essential resource for scholars of law and religion, theology, and sociology. It will also be of interest to those working in religious institutions and policy-makers.

Norman Doe is Professor of Law and Director of the Centre for Law and Religion at the Law School, Cardiff University. He has taught and published widely in the field of law and religion, particularly comparative church law. He has been listed in the 'top ten' law and religion scholars worldwide.

Law and Religion

The practice of religion by individuals and groups, the rise of religious diversity, and the fear of religious extremism, raise profound questions for the interaction between law and religion in society. The regulatory systems involved, the religion laws of secular government (national and international) and the religious laws of faith communities, are valuable tools for our understanding of the dynamics of mutual accommodation and the analysis and resolution of issues in such areas as: religious freedom; discrimination; the autonomy of religious organisations; doctrine, worship and religious symbols; the property and finances of religion; religion, education and public institutions; and religion, marriage and children. In this series, scholars at the forefront of law and religion contribute to the debates in this area. The books in the series are analytical with a key target audience of scholars and practitioners, including lawyers, religious leaders, and others with an interest in this rapidly developing discipline.

Titles in this series include

Law and the Christian Tradition in Italy
The Legacy of the Great Jurists
Edited by Rafael Domingo and Orazio Condorelli

Church Laws and Ecumenism
A New Path for Christian Unity
Edited by Norman Doe

For more information about this series, please visit: www.routledge.com/Law-and-Religion/book-series/LAWRELIG

Church Laws and Ecumenism

A New Path for Christian Unity

Edited by Norman Doe

Routledge
Taylor & Francis Group
LONDON AND NEW YORK

First published 2021
by Routledge
2 Park Square, Milton Park, Abingdon, Oxon OX14 4RN

and by Routledge
52 Vanderbilt Avenue, New York, NY 10017

Routledge is an imprint of the Taylor & Francis Group, an informa business

British Library Cataloguing-in-Publication Data
A catalogue record for this book is available from the British Library

Library of Congress Cataloging-in-Publication Data
Names: Doe, Norman, editor.
Title: Church laws and ecumenism : a new path for Christian unity / edited by Norman Doe.
Description: Abingdon, Oxon ; New York, NY : Routledge, 2020. | Includes bibliographical references and index.
Identifiers: LCCN 2020017540 (print) | LCCN 2020017541 (ebook) | ISBN 9780367540586 (hardback) | ISBN 9781003084273 (ebook)
Subjects: LCSH: Comparative canon law. | Ecumenical movement.
Classification: LCC KB164 .C48 2020 (print) | LCC KB164 (ebook) | DDC 262.9—dc23
LC record available at https://lccn.loc.gov/2020017540
LC ebook record available at https://lccn.loc.gov/2020017541

ISBN: 978-0-367-54058-6 (hbk)
ISBN: 978-1-003-08427-3 (ebk)

Typeset in Galliard
by Apex CoVantage, LLC

Contents

Foreword

John Witte, Jr

Law is the backbone of Christian ecclesiology and ecumenism. That is the central message of this collection of well-written and well-integrated chapters on church law by scholars of a dozen global Christian churches. And that has been the abiding message of the distinguished editor of this volume, Professor Norman Doe, founding director of the Centre for Law and Religion at Cardiff University, the leading such centre in Europe.

In a series of brilliant volumes – from his opening 1990 title *Fundamental Authority in Late Medieval English Law* to his 2013 masterwork *Christian Law: Contemporary Principles* – Professor Doe has demonstrated that church law is an important but oft-neglected foundation for principled Christian ecumenism. Despite deep theological differences that have long divided Christian churches and denominations – over the Bible, the Trinity, the sacraments, justification, clerical celibacy, women's ordination, natural law, and so much more – the church universal has always been united in its devotion to and need for church law. From the earliest instructions of St. Paul and the *Didache* to the elaborate codes of canon law and church discipline in place today, the Christian church has been structured as a legal entity. The church depends upon rules, regulations, and procedures to maintain its order, organisation, and orthodoxy; its clergy, polity, and property; its worship, liturgy, and sacraments; its discipline, missions, and diaconal work; its charity, education, and catechesis; its publications, foundations, and religious life; its property, governance, and interactions with the state and other social institutions. Still today, every church, whether an individual congregation or a global denomination, has law as its backbone, balancing its spiritual and structural dimensions and keeping it straight and strong, especially in times of crisis.

The church laws themselves, of course, vary greatly in form and function over time and across the denominations and regions of the world. Some church laws are written; others are customary. Some are codified, others more loosely promulgated. Some are mandatory, others probative or facilitative. Some are universal canons; others are local and variant. Some are drawn from the Bible; others go back to ancient Roman law and the Talmud. Some church laws deal with the essentials of the faith, others with the adiaphora. Some are internally created by the church's own government; others are externally imposed or induced by the state. Some church laws are declared by ecclesiastical hierarchies; others are democratically selected. Some churches maintain elaborate tribunals and formal procedures; other use informal and conversational methods of enforcement. But, for all this variety, church law is a common and necessary feature of church life and an essential dimension of ecclesiology and theology.

Given its universality, church law is therefore also a powerful foundation for a global principled ecumenism. 'Though dogmas may divide', Professor Doe writes in his 2013 monograph *Christian Law*, 'laws link Christians across traditions' around the world today. Indeed, 'all denominations of the faith share common principles in spite of their doctrinal divisions'. In that earlier pathbreaking volume, Doe extracted a series of common principles of church law from the written canons, constitutions, charters, codes, and cases on record in each of the major denominations, putting these principles under topics and suggesting a common global framework of church laws. Nothing on that order of detail, sweep, and systematization had been done before in the study of comparative church law.

This volume goes further, reflecting a focussed effort to foster deliberative ecumenism around church law. In a series of deliberations over the past decade, Mark Hill QC, with Norman Doe, drew together jurists, theologians, and church leaders from several of the major Christian denominations to see how much confluence of opinion there might be on a set of common principles of church law. The group included distinguished scholars from the Roman Catholic, Eastern Catholic, Orthodox, Anglican, Lutheran, Methodist, Reformed, Presbyterian, Baptist, Pentecostal, and United Churches, together with leadership from the World Council of Churches. In exemplary ecumenical earnest, the group sat together for many days over four years, quietly presenting, listening, and learning about the legal culture of each denomination, with an eye to seeing the points of conflict, convergence, and creative tension in how each conceived and constructed their church law. From this inductive exercise, they slowly worked out a *Statement of Principles of Christian Law* (Rome 2016). Some 230 common legal principles ultimately won common assent from this group of scholars and the church leaders whom they consulted.

This volume harvests the fruit of those ecumenical labours. Each of the major scholars involved in the deliberations presents here a crisp study of the origin, range, and current uses of church law within their own denomination and analyses how their denomination reflects and sometimes refracts the 230 common principles. Many readers will be more familiar with Roman Catholic, Anglican, Methodist, and Presbyterian church law, but these chapters are especially well crafted and authoritative. Many readers will be less familiar with Orthodox, Eastern Catholic, and Pentecostal church law, but here, too, the chapters provide fascinating insights into the inner legal working and thinking of these denominations. Professor Doe's own sweeping Chapter 1 sets this modern ecumenical project in a two millennia context and defends ably the concept of *regulae*, maxims, or principles as a suitable trope for building a new 'concordance of discordant canons' across the denominations.

It is worth noting that these church laws are not just arcane dusty documents for legal specialists to ponder. They are front page news these days. The Roman Catholic Church has been rocked by grave revelations of widespread paedophilia of delinquent priests and cover-ups by complicit bishops. Mainline Protestants and evangelicals now face major charges of sexual, physical, and financial abuses by their clergy. Global Methodist and Anglican communities are dividing over questions of same-sex liberty. Pentecostal churches in the Global South are facing massive resistance from local authorities. Orthodox churches have been decimated by Middle Eastern wars and a return to Soviet-style controls of their clergy. And in Western liberal lands, religious freedom has come under strong academic and political attack. All these challenges test not only the faith of the church and its capacity to repent, recompense, reconcile, resist, renew, and reform itself but also the law of the church and its capacity to hold the local and global church to its most fundamental mission of preaching the Word, administering the sacraments, catechising the young, and caring for the poor and needy in imitation of Christ.

John Witte Jr
Director, Center for the Study of Law and Religion
Emory University, Atlanta

Preface

Three factors have stimulated the production of this book. First, there is a paucity of scholarly literature in the emerging field of law and religion that compares the legal regimes of Christian churches, as systems of religious law, and that is written by persons from within these faith communities. Second, the ecumenical movement, with its historical theological focus, has failed to date to address the role of church law in shaping relations between churches and fostering greater mutual understanding between them. Third, in turn, theologians and jurists from different traditions have not to date worked together on a fully ecumenical appreciation of the potential of church law to help (and sometimes hinder) the achievement of greater Christian unity.

A book filling these gaps – and seeking to correct this ecumenical church law deficit – is timely, not least given the recent formulation by an ecumenical panel of a *Statement of Principles of Christian Law* (Rome 2016), currently being fed into the work of the World Council of Churches. In 2019, in Rome, His All-Holiness Bartholomew, Ecumenical Patriarch of Constantinople, welcomed the *Statement* 'as designed to fill the historical juridical deficit in the ecumenical enterprise', and Pope Francis pronounced, for the first time in papal history, that 'canon law is essential for ecumenical dialogue'. No book has been written thus far on these historical developments in ecumenism. This book, therefore, not only provides the fruits of an understanding of church laws within ten Christian traditions but also critically evaluates the *Statement* against the laws of these individual ecclesial communities. The ten traditions studied are Catholic (Roman and Eastern), Orthodox, Anglican, Lutheran, Methodist, Reformed, Presbyterian, Baptist, Pentecostal, and United Churches.

These themes and potentialities are summed up in the idea of 'maximising' church laws for the ecumenical enterprise of greater Christian unity. Not only do the chapters 'maximise' church laws themselves – in the sense of presenting these laws in the form of principles and maxims – but they also explore the extent to which each ecclesial tradition, through the principles of its own laws, recognises itself in the common juridical principles or maxims contained in the *Statement*, so that, together, they 'maximise' – in the sense of increase – their potential for greater Christian unity. Maximising church laws, in both senses, represents a new way for the ecumenical imagination and practice, supplementing but not supplanting theological dialogue.

It has been an enormous privilege and pleasure to edit this book. It could not have been completed without incurring debts of gratitude to a great many individuals and institutions. First, it was in 2013 that Mark Hill QC raised with me the possibility of assembling an ecumenical panel of lawyers, theologians, and church leaders from across the Christian traditions to develop a greater mutual understanding of the role of church law in the institutional lives of these traditions as part of the wider ecumenical enterprise of stimulating Christian unity. The panel members did not participate as representatives of, but rather as experts in the regulatory instruments of their own respective churches. The panel met in Rome, from 2013–2016, recognised how church law is a missing link in contemporary ecumenism, discussed whether it was possible to induce common juridical principles from the comparative study of the laws of the churches, and in 2016 agreed and issued its *Statement of Principles of Christian Law* common to the churches whose members participated in the work of this ecumenical panel. It was this work that stimulated, and that forms, a key element of the studies in this volume. To Mark Hill, who convened the panel from the start, I and all the contributors to this book owe much for his foresight and energy.

Second, all the contributors to this volume (with the exception of two) served as members of the ecumenical panel. They all took up the invitation to write without demur but with an enthusiasm and goodwill undaunted by the demanding *grille thématique* and the tight and relentless timescales involved. It was deeply rewarding to work with such a distinguished, energetic, and experienced team, and I thank each one for their industry, flexibility, and patience in responding to queries, requests for further research, and suggestions for fine-tuning. I thank Andreas Henriksen Aarflot, Adviser in the Legal Section of the National Council of the Church of Norway, and the Very Revd Aetios, Grand Ecclesiarch of the Ecumenical Patriarchate of Constantinople, for joining the team so enthusiastically towards the end of the project.

Third, we have enjoyed the support of many institutions, and we owe so much to the Venerable English and Welsh College, Rome, and its Rector, Monsignor Philip Whitmore, for hosting the meetings of the ecumenical panel for its Rome sessions; the Center for Law and Religion, Emory University, Atlanta, for providing generous financial assistance, and its distinguished director, Professor John Witte Jr for encouraging us throughout and writing the foreword to this volume; Cardiff University, which has contributed towards the expenses of some meetings; the Faith and Order Commission of the World Council of Churches and its director, Odair Pedroso Mateus, and secretary, Ani Ghazaryan Drissi, for their wisdom and inspiration at meetings in Geneva in 2017, and the John Knox Centre in Geneva for hosting the ecumenical panel; Corpus Christi College, Oxford, for hosting a roundtable to plan the book in May 2018, funded by the Emory University Center for Law and Religion; the Society for the Law of the Eastern Churches and its president, Professor Astrid Kaptijn (a member of the ecumenical panel and contributor here), for the opportunity at its fiftieth anniversary conference at Rome in September 2019 to showcase the project (likewise the Ecclesiastical Law Society at its London Lectures in July 2019); the

Colloquium of Anglican and Roman Catholic Canon Lawyers (established in 1999) for the confidence it has provided about the value of comparative church law as an ecumenical instrument; Reverend Anthony Currer of the Pontifical Council for Christian Unity at the Vatican and Archbishop Sir David Moxon, Director of the Anglican Centre, Rome, and, until June 2017, the Archbishop of Canterbury's Representative to the Holy See, for their invaluable input at the annual sessions of the ecumenical panel; the British Ambassadors to the Holy See, Their Excellencies Nigel Baker and Sally Axworthy, for hosting in Rome the panel and supporting its work; and, in September 2019, His All-Holiness Bartholomew, the Ecumenical Patriarch of Constantinople, for his public support of the work of the ecumenical panel and Pope Francis for publicly recognising, for the first time in papal history, how canon law is an essential dimension of ecumenical dialogue. To all these, I am profoundly grateful.

Norman Doe
Cardiff
January 2020

Contributors

Andreas Henriksen Aarflot (M.Phil., University of Oslo) is Adviser on Church Law to the National Council and General Synod of the Church of Norway and Lecturer in Church Law at the MF Norwegian School of Theology, Religion and Society (formerly named Menighetsfakultetet, Faculty of Congregations). He is a member of the Governing Board of the Conference of European Churches, a member of the Council on Ecumenical and International Relations of the Church of Norway, and the Vice-Chair of the Norwegian Society of Church Law.

Leon van den Broeke is Associate Professor of Church Polity and the Director of the Deddens Church Polity Centre at the Theologische Universiteit Kampen and Associate Professor of Religion, Law and Society and Chair of the Centre for Religion and Law at the Vrije Universiteit Amsterdam. He has also taught Reformed church polity at the Catholic University, Leuven, and the Centre for Law and Religion at Cardiff University Law School.

John Chalmers (The Very Revd Dr) has served as Principal Clerk (2010–2017) and as Moderator (2014–2015) of the General Assembly of the Church of Scotland. Ordained in 1979, he first served as a parish minister (1979–1995) before becoming responsible for the pastoral care, support, and development of ministers and deacons throughout the church. He was appointed as a chaplain to the Queen in Scotland in 2013. For services to the church and wider society, he was awarded an honorary Doctor of Divinity degree from Aberdeen University in 2016. He is one of the founders and is now a patron of the charity Place for Hope, which provides training and facilitation in transformational change, reconciliation, and peacebuilding. Currently, he serves the Church of Scotland as Convener of the Assembly Trustees and also chairs the Carnegie UK Trust Action Group on access to affordable credit.

Norman Doe is a professor and Director of the Centre for Law and Religion at Cardiff University Law School. A barrister, he studied at Cardiff, Cambridge, and Oxford universities. His books include studies on mediaeval law, Anglican canon law, law and religion in Europe, and Christian law. A visiting professor at Paris University, he has acted as a consultant on canon law to the Anglican Communion; served on the Lambeth Commission (2003–2004); was a visiting fellow/scholar at Trinity College, Corpus Christi College, and Jesus College Oxford (2011, 2015, and 2018) and visiting fellow at Clare Hall, Cambridge (2020); and is Chancellor of the Diocese of Bangor in the Church in Wales.

Paul Goodliff is a Baptist minister, currently serving as General Secretary of Churches Together in England, having previously held posts of local, regional, and national responsibility within the Baptist Union of Great Britain. He is a pastoral and systematic theologian and is widely published in those fields. A member of the World Council of Churches team in the WCC-Pentecostal Joint Consultative Group, he teaches ecumenics and doctrine at the University of Roehampton and both Christian spirituality and pastoral supervision at Spurgeon's College, London, where he is an associate research fellow.

John Harrod graduated from London University in sociology before reading theology at Cambridge University whilst preparing for Methodist ministry at Wesley House. He later gained a doctorate from Manchester University in moral philosophy. After some 15 years in pastoral ministry, he spent the rest of his working life in theological education, latterly as principal of Hartley Victoria College, the Methodist foundation within the ecumenical Partnership for Theological Education in Manchester. His principal publication is *Weaving the Tapestry of Moral Judgement: Christian Ethics in a Plural World* (Epworth, 2007). He also contributed to N. Doe, ed., *Christianity and Natural Law* (Cambridge, 2017). Now retired and living in Cornwall, he is married with a son and daughter and five grandchildren.

Mark Hill QC is an associate professor at Cardiff University; the University of Pretoria; King's College London; and Notre Dame University, Sydney; and a fellow of the Center for the Study of Law and Religion at Emory University. He is Chairman of the Ecclesiastical Law Society and Vice-President of the International Consortium for Law and Religion Studies. He holds various judicial appointments, including Recorder assigned to the Midland Circuit, hearing criminal, civil, and family cases, and sits as a judge in the Consistory Courts of the dioceses of Chichester and Leeds. His recent publications include the fourth edition of the practitioner text *Ecclesiastical Law* (2018) and the following edited works: *Magna Carta, Religion and the Rule of Law* (2015), *The Confluence of Law and Religion* (2016), *Great Christian Jurists in English History* (2017), *Religion, Law and Security in Africa* (2018), and *Christianity and Criminal Law* (2020).

Astrid Kaptijn is a professor of canon law and Vice-Rector at the University of Freiburg (Switzerland) and a consultant to the (Vatican) Congregation for the Eastern Churches and currently serves as the President of the Society for the Law of the Eastern Churches.

Leo J. Koffeman is Professor Emeritus of Church Polity and Ecumenism at the Protestant Theological University (Amsterdam, the Netherlands) and

Extraordinary Professor at the University of Stellenbosch and the University of Pretoria (South Africa). He served as a member of the Faith and Order Commission of the World Council of Churches (2008–2013), and he is the author of *In Order to Serve* (Zurich: LIT Verlag, 2014).

Nikos Maghioros is an associate professor at the School of Theology of the Aristotle University of Thessaloniki, where he specialises in canon and ecclesiastical law. He studied at both the Aristotle University of Thessaloniki and the Pontifical Lateran University in Rome. He teaches Orthodox canon law, sources of canon law, comparative canon law, ecclesiastical law, and church and state relations. He has organised, and has participated in, numerous conferences dealing with ecumenical dialogue between Christians, religion and state relations, human rights, and the relationship of religion to culture.

Aidan McGrath is from Banbridge, Northern Ireland. He entered the Franciscans (OFM) in 1972 and was ordained priest in 1980. From 1984–2009, he served successively as Judge and Presiding Judge of the Dublin Regional Marriage Tribunal, from 1995–2009 as President of the Canon Law Society of Great Britain and Ireland, and as Professor Invitatus in the Faculty of Canon Law at Pontifical Gregorian University, Rome. From 2009–2017, he was Secretary General of the Order of Friars Minor and is now Minister Provincial of the Franciscan Province of Ireland. He is also a consultant to many religious institutes and dioceses in different parts of the world and has written extensively on canon law topics.

Dimitrios Nikiforos, The Very Revd Aetios, studied at the Law School of the Aristotle University of Thessaloniki, New York University School of Law, and St. Vladimir's Orthodox Theological Seminary, New York. After working as a lawyer of First Instance at the Kavala Bar Association (Greece), in 2019 he was tonsured monk, ordained to the holy diaconate, and then ordained to the holy priesthood. He is the Grand Ecclesiarch of the Ecumenical Patriarchate under His All-Holiness Ecumenical Patriarch Bartholomew. He also serves as the Assistant to the Director of the First Patriarchal Office and as the Secretary of the Committee on Inter-Orthodox Matters of the Holy and Sacred Synod.

Robert Ombres is a Catholic priest and a Dominican friar. He was the Procurator General of his religious order 2004–2011. He taught canon law for the Cardiff LL.M. and the Heythrop College London MA, and he continues to teach it at Blackfriars Hall, Oxford as well as in Rome, at the Pontifical University of Saint Thomas Aquinas (The Angelicum).

Paul Rochester is the General Secretary of the Free Churches Group, which comprises 24 denominations. As General Secretary, he serves both the directors and group members, providing oversight of the organisation and its work programme. The Free Churches Group has, among other things, a public profile through Free Church chaplains in the healthcare and prisons sectors and the Free Church voice in education and the public square. Paul has been an ordained minister in the Church of God of Prophecy for over 30 years and, within it, currently pastors a church in South London and provides oversight for eight churches as the Regional Bishop. He worked in the civil service for 34 years and in 2016 was awarded the MBE for his work on small-scale renewables and community work.

John Witte Jr is Robert W. Woodruff University Professor and Director of the Center for the Study of Law and Religion at Emory University. A specialist in legal history, human rights, religious freedom, marriage and family law, and law and religion, he has published some 300 articles, 18 journal symposia, and 34 books in 15 languages, most recently *Church, State, and Family: Reconciling Traditional Teachings and Modern Liberties* (2019).

Introduction

Norman Doe

The relationship between law and religion is slowly but surely emerging as an important interdisciplinary field for the study of what has become known as 'religion law' – international and national state laws on religion – and 'religious law' – the internal regulatory systems of religious traditions and organisations. The study of secular religion law is well served by an ever-expanding literature that focusses on the regulation of religion in such important areas as individual and collective religious freedom, religious discrimination, and state-religion relations,[1] and scholars have increasingly recognised that an understanding of religious laws is useful to identify and evaluate the acceptable scope of state law on religion.[2] Similarly, whilst little attention has to date been given to religious law in the sociology of religion, some modern scholars are alert to, but only briefly recognise, the importance of religious 'self-regulation'.[3]

The study of religious law has traditionally focussed on the examination of the norms and juridical traditions of single world faiths, notably Jewish law, Islamic law, and Hindu law;[4] and Islamic law and Jewish law, for example, have themselves been compared.[5] However, with regard to Christianity, there is a growing body of scholarly and practitioner literature on the regulatory systems of separate and individual churches, such as Roman Catholic canon law, the law of the

1 Recent titles include R. Ahdar, ed., *Research Handbook on Law and Religion* (Cheltenham: Edward Elgar Publishing, 2018); J. Rivers, *The Law of Organized Religions* (Oxford: Oxford University Press, 2011); R. Sandberg, *Law and Religion* (Cambridge: Cambridge University Press, 2011); N. Doe, *Law and Religion in Europe* (Oxford: Oxford University Press, 2011).

2 See e.g. P. Edge, *Religion and Law* (Aldershot: Ashgate, 2006); P. Cane, C. Evans and Z. Robinson, eds., *Law and Religion in Theoretical and Historical Context* (Cambridge: Cambridge University Press, 2008).

3 See e.g. J.A. Beckford and J.T. Richardson, 'Religion and Regulation', in J.A. Beckford and N.J. Demerath, eds., *The Sage Handbook of the Sociology of Religion* (London: Sage, 2007) 396.

4 See e.g. J. Schacht, *An Introduction to Islamic Law* (Oxford: Clarendon Press, 1982); N.S. Hecht *et al.*, eds, *An Introduction to the History and Sources of Jewish Law* (Oxford: Oxford University Press, 1996); W.F. Menski, *Hindu Law* (Oxford: Oxford University Press, 2003).

5 E.g. J. Neusner and T. Sonn, *Comparing Religions Through Law: Judaism and Islam* (London: Routledge, 1999).

Church of England, Orthodox canon law, and Presbyterian law,[6] but there is very little on the rules of other churches, such as those of the Methodist and Baptist traditions.[7] There is also a growing body of literature on Christianity and law, but its focus is, generally, civil law.[8] Moreover, it is only relatively recently that laws of different Christian traditions have been compared, and this only from the perspective of an outsider to all (bar one) of the churches studied and, crucially, not by members of those churches themselves.[9] In turn, the recent growth in literature on 'religious law', welcome though it is, does not generally cover a wide field of Christian traditions but instead focusses on a small number.[10] Thus, comparative church law beyond such studies as these is still virtually unknown. This book fills this gap in bringing together, for the first time in a single volume, studies of the law of individual churches from ten Christian traditions, importantly written by persons from within the traditions studied.

Not only is this book intended to contribute to the ever-growing study of religious law in the academy, but it is also designed to address what might be styled the legal deficit in worldwide ecumenism. The ecumenical movement seeks to promote and achieve Christian unity through greater visible communion between the separated (or divided) institutional churches of global Christianity. The practice of ecumenism and the growing field of ecumenical theology have developed principally at the doctrinal and theological levels; that is, the level of religious belief. However, Christians and their institutional churches are prolific legislators. Yet the juridical instruments of churches have not thus far played a central role in ecumenical discourse – they are occasionally seen as the 'missing link' in ecumenism. Moreover, the Faith and Order Commission of the World Council of Churches recognises that church laws actually impede ecumenism.[11] Presenting the laws of churches together

6 See, respectively, e.g. J. Hahn, *Church Law and Modernity* (Cambridge: Cambridge University Press, 2019); M. Hill, *Ecclesiastical Law* (Oxford: Oxford University Press, 4th edition, 2018); P. Rodopoulos, *An Overview of Orthodox Canon Law* (Rollinsford, New Hampshire: Orthodox Research Institute, 2007); J.L. Weatherhead, ed., *The Constitution and Laws of the Church of Scotland* (Edinburgh: The Board of Practice and Procedure, 1997); P. Coertzen, *Church and Order: A Reformed Perspective* (Leuven: Peeters, 1998).

7 See e.g. D.C. Sparkes, *The Constitutions of the Baptist Union of Great Britain* (Didcot: Baptist Historical Society, 1996).

8 See e.g. the books in the series Cambridge Studies in Christianity and Law.

9 N. Doe, *Christian Law: Contemporary Principles* (Cambridge: Cambridge University Press, 2013).

10 See e.g. A. Huxley, ed., *Religion, Law and Tradition* (Abingdon: Routledge, 2002): this covers only Roman Catholic law: 49 (S. Ferrari, 'Canon Law as a Religious Legal System'); N. Doe and R. Sandberg, eds., *Law and Religion*, Vol. 3, *Religious Law* (Abingdon: Routledge, 2017); R. Bottoni and S. Ferrari, eds., *Routledge Handbook of Religious Laws* (Abingdon: Routledge, 2019); N. Doe, *Comparative Religious Law: Judaism, Christianity, Islam* (Cambridge: Cambridge University Press, 2018).

11 'Several union negotiations have been frustrated or delayed because the legal problems involved in uniting have not been sufficiently foreseen. It must be borne in mind that unsolved legal questions can be used by dissenting minorities as a means of frustrating union':

is important because laws should have a more prominent place in ecumenical practice and theology, not least as they tell us much about the scope of the commitment of churches to and their participation in the ecumenical enterprise. Juridical instruments define what ecclesial communion is possible and what is not, either enabling or restricting the development of greater visible communion between separated churches in the quest for Christian unity. This exercise in 'juridical ecumenism' offers a theoretical and practical framework for the global transformation of ecumenism to complement but not replace the current dominance of the doctrinal and theological focus in contemporary ecumenical method and practice,[12] especially important for ecumenism today 'at a time when its future progress sometimes seems to be slowing in this so-called "ecumenical winter" '.[13]

As such, this book provides an opportunity to re-imagine ecumenism as in part a profoundly legal matter in which church law may be used as a creative force for Christian unity. It enables the ecumenical movement to recognise the deeply shared experience of Christians in their use of regulatory instruments, their fundamental relationship with theology as applications of it, and their place in the wider context of the demands of civil law. In point of fact, today there is a growing appetite to re-invigorate ecumenism, particularly under the auspices of receptive ecumenism, and for separated churches to reflect in scholarly and practical ways on what Christians might learn from one another – in the realm of action – and come to appreciate more fully how church law may help (and sometimes hinder) the movement towards greater visible Christian unity. This appetite is nowhere more clearly evident than in the recent formulation by an ecumenical panel of a *Statement of Principles of Christian Law* (Rome 2016), currently being fed into the work of the Faith and Order Commission of the World Council of Churches.

On 16 September 2019, in Rome, the *Statement* was welcomed publicly by His All-Holiness Bartholomew, the Ecumenical Patriarch of Constantinople (and leader of the Orthodox Church worldwide); he recognised its value and spoke of it 'as designed to fill the historical juridical deficit in the ecumenical enterprise'.[14] At the Apostolic Palace in Rome, three days later, Pope Francis pronounced, for the first time in papal history, that 'canon law is essential for ecumenical

Gunther Gassman, ed., *Documentary History of Faith and Order 1963–1993* (Geneva: WCC, 1993). *The Ecumenical Movement and Church Laws* (Accra Documents 1974), Statements and Recommendations, "Mid-Stream" 9, 1970/2–3, pp. 4–12, 10.

12 N. Doe, 'Juridical Ecumenism', 14 *Ecclesiastical Law Society* (2012) 195–234.

13 P. Goodliff, 'Juridical Ecumenism', a lecture delivered to the Society for Ecumenical Studies, Westminster Abbey, 8 February 2020.

14 See www.christianunity.va/content/unitacristiani/en/dialoghi/sezione-orientale/chiese-ortodosse-di-tradizione-bizantina/relazioni-bilaterali/patriarcato-ecumenico/altri-documenti-ed-eventi/2019-conference-du-patriarche-bartholomee-a-l-occasion-du50e-ann.html.

dialogue'.[15] No book on this *Statement* has been written thus far.[16] This book, therefore, not only provides the fruits of an understanding of church laws within ten Christian traditions but also critically evaluates the *Statement* against the laws of these individual ecclesial communities. The ten traditions are Catholic (Roman and Eastern), Orthodox, Anglican, Lutheran, Methodist, Reformed, Presbyterian, Baptist, Pentecostal, and United Churches.

Following a chapter that describes the evolution of the project that led to the *Statement of Principles of Christian Law* (2016) and the historic use of 'principles of law' by jurists across the centuries, there are chapters on the regulatory systems of the Roman and Eastern Catholic, Orthodox, Anglican, Lutheran, Methodist, Reformed, Presbyterian, Baptist, Pentecostal, and United and Uniting Churches. With the exception of the chapters offering an Eastern Catholic, a Lutheran, and a Pentecostal perspective, all the authors of the other chapters were members of the ecumenical panel that produced the *Statement*. The regulatory instruments that are studied here are styled variously as law, order, or polity, depending on the tradition in question.

In terms of the methodology, each contributor was encouraged to think freely about what or what not to include in their chapter, but some core questions were offered by way of guidance. As such, first, each chapter, within the tradition, explores the sources and forms of church law/order/polity, subjects they treat, and whom they bind; the foundations of and reasons for the law (such as theology and doctrine); and the extent of the use of principles of law/order/polity in the tradition. Second, each chapter addresses the empirical process of identifying a proposition in the *Statement* as a principle of Christian law – that is, what principles prove to be unproblematic and problematic from the perspective of the tradition and why; how those principles (where appropriate) were re-drafted to accommodate (or be reconciled to) the norms of the tradition; and to what extent some principles are more important than others and why. Third, each chapter offers an evaluation of the *Statement* in terms of the extent to which the principles reflect the doctrinal or theological position of the tradition and the value of the *Statement* for the tradition and how it might be developed further. The book also contains an appendix that outlines the aborted work on church law of the Faith and Order Commission of the World Council of Churches some decades ago (in which the study of church law was seen as necessary to uncover

15 See http://press.vatican.va/content/salastampa/it/bollettino/pubblico/2019/09/19/0714/01466.html.

16 P. Goodliff, op cit: the Statement is 'a set of juridical "middle axioms". They are sufficiently broad so as to invite wide acceptance and adoption for further, more concrete, work, but are not so vague as to be virtually useless. An analogy for these middle axioms is the role played by compasses and anchors in navigation. A compass helps those at sea to get their bearings, while an anchor helps minimise drift in troubled waters. The Principles give shape to the map and provide the compass for those seeking the juridical dimension to ecumenical work, while they also provide some stability when the troubled waters of change, church fragmentation and secular societal pressures threaten to destabilise the ecumenical ship'.

'differences' between churches) and an appendix with the *Statement* itself. The conclusion offers reflections on the studies by way of a general assessment of the chapters in light of how the *Statement of Principles of Christian Law* (2016) has been received thus far by Christian leaders and its wider significance for the global ecumenical movement. In particular, it explores the extent to which each tradition might identify itself in the *Statement.*

Finally, the book is intended as a resource for practitioners; namely, church officers engaged in Christian dialogue with the state and society, interfaith dialogue, and ecumenical dialogue. At such moments when a church faces pressure from its host state(s) to adopt secular standards in its ecclesial life and practice, studies of Christian laws might provide support to that church and reinforce or underpin its position on a given matter. For the same reason, the book may assist lawyers in the practice of e.g. human rights law and discrimination law when they need to explain the juridical approaches of Christians in these contexts. Equally, access to a statement of Christian laws enables government to understand what opportunities and constraints the rules of a church place on that church in its dealings with the state and society. State courts often deal with Christian obligations in religious freedom cases, the state legislates on matters that concern Christians, and in e.g. the field of charity law, state administrative bodies need to understand the juridical standards of accountability prevailing within the churches. The book may also enable other world faiths to understand the opportunities and constraints that laws place on a church in its dealings with and policy decisions about their relations with Christians, not least how much those faiths share normatively with Christianity.

1 The evolution of the principles of Christian law

Norman Doe

In November 2013 an invited Christian Law Panel of Experts met at the Venerable English and Welsh College in Rome. It was convened by Mark Hill QC. The participants attended in their personal capacities, not as representatives of their denominations, and on the basis of their expertise in the church law, church order, or church polity of particular Christian churches; namely, Anglican, Baptist, Catholic, Lutheran, Methodist, Orthodox, Presbyterian, and Reformed.[1] Its aim was to explore critically the extent to which different Christian churches share common principles in their laws and other instruments of internal governance and the ways in which these principles and instruments may contribute creatively to ecumenism. The initiative was inspired directly by recent research on the potential of church law as a unifying force amongst Christian traditions worldwide.[2] This chapter describes, explains, and evaluates the development of the principles of the Christian Law project. It does so by examining (1) the historical antecedents – that is, the part played by *regulae iuris* and the maxims of church law from the mediaeval church in the West to beyond the Reformation of

1 The Panel of Experts: Convenor: Mark Hill QC (Professor, Cardiff University, Pretoria University, King's College, London); Members: Revd John Chalmers (Former Moderator of the General Assembly of the Church of Scotland); Professor Norman Doe (Director, Centre for Law and Religion, Cardiff University); Revd Ken Howcroft (Former President of the Conference of the Methodist Church in Great Britain); Aidan McGrath OFM (Secretary General of the Franciscan Order); Robert Ombres OP (Blackfriars Oxford, formerly Procurator General of the Dominican Order); Professor Leon van den Broeke (Vrije Universiteit, Amsterdam); Professor Leo Koffeman (Protestant Theological University, Amsterdam); Professor Nikos Maghioros (Aristotle University, Thessaloniki); Anna Tronêt (Diocesan Lawyer, Church of Sweden); Revd Dr John Weaver (Former Principal, South Wales Baptist College); Revd Paul Goodliff (Former Head of Ministry at the Baptist Union); Observers: Fr Tony Currer (Pontifical Council for the Promotion of Christian Unity, Vatican); Archbishop Sir David Moxon (Archbishop of Canterbury's Representative to the Holy See); Revd Marcus Walker (Associate Director, Anglican Centre in Rome); Tim Macquiban (Methodist Church); Revd Dr Peter Stevenson (Principal, South Wales Baptist College): Corresponding member: Mary McAleese, formerly President of Ireland.

2 N. Doe, *Christian Law: Contemporary Principles* (Cambridge: Cambridge University Press, 2013): Doe was a Panel member, as was Professor Leo J. Koffeman, author of the landmark book *In Order to Serve: An Ecumenical Introduction to Church Polity* (Zurich: LIT, 2014).

the sixteenth century; (2) models used early on by the Panel of Experts – namely, the work of the Colloquium of Anglican and Roman Catholic Canon Lawyers (established in 1999) and that of the global Anglican Communion Legal Advisers Network in a document entitled *The Principles of Canon Law Common to the Churches of the Anglican Communion* launched at the Lambeth Conference 2008; and (3) the work of the Panel of Experts, its working methods, the internal organisation of the *Statement of Principles of Christian Law* (Rome 2016), its work with the director of the Faith and Order Commission of the World Council of Churches (Geneva 2017), and the future.[3]

I The historical models: from *regulae iuris* to principles of church law

The distinguished legal historian Frederic William Maitland claimed in 1898, 'When in any century, from the thirteenth to the nineteenth, an English lawyer indulges in a Latin maxim, he is generally, though of this he may be profoundly ignorant, quoting from the Sext' (a canon law text of 1298).[4] This section seeks to make sense of this claim in the mediaeval period, from the Reformation to the Enlightenment. It does so by outlining the enduring appeal of juridical axioms to church lawyers in Europe, across almost one thousand years, and their domestication in English church law. Whilst there is continuity in the spirit of juridical axioms, there has also been change – in the terms used to signify them, in the abandonment of many axioms of the classical canon law, and in the creation of new axioms to meet ever-changing ecclesial needs.[5]

Roman law is the starting point for the mediaeval development of *regulae iuris* in the canon law of the Latin Church.[6] The last title of Justinian's Digest (50.17) is *De diversis regulis iuris antiqui*. Its *regulae* are broadly modelled on popular and literary proverbs, formulated under the influence of techniques in Greek philosophy, and represented 'traditional authority' often associated with the work of particular jurists.[7] A *regula* is 'a brief exposition of an existing state of affairs: not of such a nature that the law is derived from the rule, but the rule is established by the existing law'; *regulae* are like *causae coniectio* (the outline of a case presented to a judge at trial), and a *regula* 'ceases to function when it is vitiated in any

3 See also N. Doe, 'The Principles of Christian Law Project in Context', *Quaderni Di Diritto E Politica Ecclesiastica* (2017) 3–25.

4 F. Pollock and F.W. Maitland, *The History of English Law before the Time of Edward I* (Cambridge: Cambridge University Press, 2nd edition, 1898; reprint Liberty Fund: Indianapolis, 2010), 2 vols., 196.

5 See N. Doe and S. Pulleyn, 'The Durability of Maxims in Canon Law: From *Regulae Iuris* to Canonical Principles', in T. Harris, ed., *Studies in Canon Law and Common Law in Honor of R.H. Helmholz* (Berkeley: The Robbins Collection, 2015) 303–336.

6 For the use by canonists of Roman law sources generally, see R.H. Helmholz, *The Spirit of Classical Canon Law* (Athens and London: University of Georgia Press, 1996) Chapter 1.

7 R. Pound, 'The Maxims of Equity – I: Of Maxims Generally', 34 *Harvard Law Review* (1921) 809–836.

way'.[8] *Regulae iuris* are cited as generally recognised truths or maxims, formulated to express a point concisely, applied and interpreted as rules of law (similar to statutory rules today), understood sometimes as propositions of natural law, and deployed to interpret legislation and legal transactions – for example, in testaments we interpret the will of the testator liberally; in penal causes the milder interpretation is to be used; and, if there are different possible interpretations, the more meritorious is to be adopted.[9]

Mediaeval civil lawyers debated, for instance, whether a *regula* was derived from law or else was itself law and whether an exception constituted a separate *regula* or was implicit in the *regula* in question. In turn, the interest of the mediaeval canon lawyers of the Latin Church in *regulae* reflects their tendency 'to abstract and generalise the decision found in the Roman legal texts and to make explicit their relation with each other'.[10] In the twelfth century, this occurs in their formulation, use, and discussion of *brocards*, freestanding axioms/propositions (*generalia*) presented in legal argument and counter-argument and reconciled in the form of a solution.[11] Initially, canonists understood *regulae iuris* not as maxims but as specific rules of law. Gratian explains (c. 1140), ' "Canon" is Greek for what is called "rule" (*regula*) in Latin. . . . It is called a rule because it leads one aright and never takes one astray. But others say that it is called a rule because it rules, presents a norm for living rightly, or sets aright what is twisted or bent'; and the rule itself may admit its own exceptions.[12] Bernard of Pavia (d. 1213) included in his *Compilatio Prima* (1187–1191) a collection of papal decretals, a title *de regulis iuris*, and his later *Summa Decretalium* could be the canonists' first full discussion of *regulae*. Influenced by the civilians, he defined *regula* as a maxim as well as *constitutio canonica* (e.g. a monastic rule of life); and all *regulae* have exceptions. Similarly, Bertram Bishop of Metz (1181–1212) sees a *regula* as a 'universal proposition' and *regulae* as *causae cum causa coniunctio* – 'the joining of one principle with another' – and for him *causa* means a principle or *ratio*.[13]

Two landmarks in the development of canonical *regulae* were the *Liber Extra* (or *Gregorian Decretals*), which consists of five books produced at the direction of Pope Gregory IX (1227–1241),[14] and the *Liber Sextus*, also five books, compiled at the direction of Pope Boniface VIII (1294–1303) and promulgated

8 P. Stein, *Regulae Iuris: From Juristic Rules to Legal Maxims* (Edinburgh: Edinburgh University Press, 1966) 1–2.

9 Testator: D.50.17, 12; penal causes: D.50.17, 155, 2; interpretation: D.I, 3, 19.

10 P. Stein, op cit., 131, 145: they did not confine *regulae* to maxims described as *regulae* in the texts or in the title *de regulis* – any brief rule of law could be a *regula*.

11 G. Evans, *Law and Theology in the Middle Ages* (London: Routledge, 2002) 75; P. Stein, op cit., 131; e.g. Damasus (at Bologna) compiled his *Brocarda sive regulae canonicae* (c. 1230) with 125 maxims, which, after 1234, was revised by Bartholomew of Brescia in his *Brocardica iuris canonici*.

12 Gratian, *Decretum*, Dist. III, Part 1, c. 1 and c. 2.

13 P. Stein, op cit., 144, 147.

14 J. Brundage, *Medieval Canon Law* (London and New York: Longman, 1995) 196–197: it was the work of Raymond de Penyafort (d.1275); P. Stein, op cit., 145.

in 1298.[15] There are 11 *regulae iuris* at the end of the fifth book of the *Liber Extra* and 88 in the last title of the *Liber Sextus* (which itself may be the work of Dinus Mugellanus).[16] Scholars are in broad agreement about the nature and purposes of these *regulae*. First, they are, variously, 'moral proverbs';[17] 'judicial maxims';[18] 'fundamental laws in the form of axioms'; 'an exposition of several laws on the same subject, conclusions or deductions, rather than principles of law drawn from constitutions or decisions'; 'general rules or principles serving chiefly for the interpretation of laws';[19] and 'common sense'.[20] Second, a *regula* may be descriptive (rooted in previous cases) or prescriptive (designed to resolve new cases).[21] Third, some *regulae* apply to specific matters (e.g. benefices), others generally (e.g. 'No one can be held to the impossible'; 'Time does not heal what was invalid from the beginning'; 'What one is not permitted to do in his own name, he may not do through another');[22] and many derive from the Digest, other parts of Roman law, the *generalia*, or *brocards*.[23]

Particular use was made of *regulae* in teaching canon law, both to sum up the law and to resolve contradictions.[24] Maxims were also used to determine when a narrow or wide interpretation of law was appropriate; for example, 'It is fitting that odious things be restricted and favourable ones extended'; 'A general concession does not include those particular items which one would not likely have included'; and 'In obscure matters, the least severe solution is to be followed'.[25] The work of English canonist William Lyndwood (d. 1446) also includes maxims that have a home-spun flavour: '[l]et him who has not been punished in his pocket be punished in his body'.[26] In sum, as Roscoe Pound puts it, the canonical maxims 'help to lead the jurist from a body of hard and fast rules, authoritatively imposed, above question and subject only to interpretation, to a conception of principles of reason, discoverable by juristic theory and philosophy, of which particular positive rules were but declaratory'.[27]

15 J. Brundage, op cit., 197–198; the title is in X.5.12; it was compiled by a committee of canonists.
16 P. Stein, op cit., 149 (Sext, hereafter VI).
17 P. Stein, op cit., 145, e.g. X.5.41 reg. jur. 3: it is better to allow scandal than to abandon truth.
18 R.H. Helmholz, *The Canon Law and Ecclesiastical Jurisdiction from 597 to the 1640s*, *The Oxford History of the Laws of England*, Vol. 1 (Oxford: Oxford University Press, 2004) 154.
19 A. Meehan, '*Regulae iuris*', *The Catholic Encyclopaedia*, Vol. 12 (New York: R. Appleton, 1911).
20 G. Evans, op cit., 76.
21 M.B. Carosi, 'Some notes on the problem of *regulae iuris* in the history of law', 10 *Annuario di emeneutica giuridica* (2005) 305–312.
22 VI.1 (benefices), 6 (impossibility), 18 (time), 47 (doing in one's own name).
23 P. Stein, op cit., 145.
24 R. Pound, op cit., 817. See also D.M. Owen, *The Medieval Canon Law: Teaching, Literature and Transmission* (Cambridge: Cambridge University Press, 1990) 7.
25 J. Brundage, op cit., 169–170: VI.15; VI.81; VI.30; VI.34 (borrowed from D.50.17, 80).
26 *Provinciale*, p. 321: *qui non luit in bursa, luet in corpore*.
27 R. Pound, op cit., 819.

At the time of the Reformation, the continental civilians and canonists of the sixteenth and seventeenth centuries continued to use *regulae iuris*.[28] This 'axiomisation' of law has been understood to express a quest both for a purer and earlier understanding of law and for simplicity of method in applying and in learning the law – law students at most major European universities studied the Digest *regulae* as part of their formal training.[29] There are, in turn, commentaries on the *regulae* of canon law,[30] studies on individual *regulae*,[31] and compilations for laymen[32] as well as collections of *brocards*, sometimes presented as 'axioms' (*axioma*).[33] Various understandings of *regulae* continued. For example, for Nicolaus Everardus (d. 1532), all statements in civil and canon law that are preceded by the words *plerumque* (generally) or *semper* (always) are regarded as *regulae*;[34] and for Sebastiano Medici (1586), '[a] *regula* is a general and brief definition and statement, whereby, in a succinct communication, many similar cases are summarised, not to give expression to a special law, but to convey the *ratio* of those cases'.[35] Some jurists compared *regulae* with other legal forms; for instance, *lex*, derived from factual situations, has 'incontrovertible authority', whereas a *regula*, derived from law, has 'probable authority', i.e. as 'a formulation of the accumulated wisdom of jurists explaining and commenting on the law';[36] and some commentators equate *regulae* with, for instance, *prima principia iuris* or *axiomata*.[37]

The termination of papal jurisdiction and the establishment of the Church of England meant neither the demise of civilian learning nor the abandonment of *regulae iuris* in English ecclesiastical jurisprudence in the sixteenth and seventeenth centuries. Richard Hooker deployed 'first principles', 'maxims', and 'axioms' (many from the Sext).[38] Church court practice abounds in the use of maxims, such as statutes in derogation of the canonical *ius commune* are to be

28 For maxims in the jurisprudence of the Reformers, see J. Witte, *Law and Protestantism: The Legal Teachings of the Lutheran Reformation* (Cambridge: Cambridge University Press, 2002) 164–165.

29 D. van der Merwe, '*Regulae iuris* and the Axiomisation of the Law and in the Sixteenth and Early Seventeenth Centuries', 3 *Journal of South African Law* (1987) 286–302 at 288.

30 E.g. Petrus Peckius (1529–1589), *Ad regulas iuris canonici commentaria elaboratissima* (1570).

31 E.g. Diego Covarruvius (1512–1577), *Regulae, Peccatum. De regulis iuris libro sexto relectio* (1558), a commentary on the rule *peccatum non dimittitur, nisi restituatur ablatum* – 'a sin is not forgiven unless what has been taken away is restored' (VI.4).

32 E.g. Thomas Murner (1475-c.1534), *Utriusque iuris tituli et regulae* (1518).

33 E.g. Augustinho Barbaros (d. 1649), *Axiomatum iuris usufrequentiorum expositio* (1631).

34 *Topica legalia* (1516) – in the 1581 edition, under the title *Loci argumentorum legales*, at 72.

35 *Tractatus de regulis iuris* in his II *Tractatuum* (1586) 2 par. 10.

36 E.g. Vigelius, *Methodus regularum utriusque iuris* (1584) 9–10; Giphanius (1534–1604) *Tractatus de diversis regulis iuris antique utilissimus* (1607) 12–13.

37 D. van der Merwe, op cit., 297–298.

38 See N. Doe, 'Richard Hooker: Priest and Jurist', in M. Hill and R.H. Helmholz, eds., *Great Christian Jurists in English History* (Cambridge: Cambridge University Press, 2017) 115–137 at 123.

interpreted strictly and suit must be brought in the forum of the defendant.[39] Their use is also common in commentaries written for practitioners, such as John Godolphin's *Repertorium Canonicum or Abridgement of the Ecclesiastical Laws of this Realm* (1678), where 'material points . . . are succinctly treated' and 'rules of canon law' are set out – for instance, a vacant benefice must be filled within six months, and an archdeacon must carry out a visitation in person.[40]

In England, the eighteenth century saw publication of numerous practitioner works on the law applicable to the Church of England. Two may be noted here for their use of 'maxims'. However, there is little in many of these maxims that is proverbial or that has an obvious link with natural law or reason; most have a particularity more reminiscent of rules rather than general principles. At the start of the century, there is, for instance, Edmund Gibson and his *Codex Juris Ecclesiastici Anglicani, or, The Statutes, Constitutions, Canons, Rubrics and Articles of the Church of England* (1713); a work 'methodically digested', this was intended 'for the service of the clergy, and in support of the rights and privileges of the Church', and treats 'the Rules of Common and Canon Law'.[41] It uses 'maxims' throughout, often in Latin,[42] sometimes to support a particular 'rule',[43] across various fields of ecclesiastical law, including the royal supremacy in church affairs[44] and subjection of clergy to statute.[45] Occasionally, he presents a proposition as 'a known maxim of the canon law'[46] or 'a rule of the canon law'.[47] Toward the end of the century, there is Richard Burn and his *Ecclesiastical Law* (1763).[48] Time and again Burn uses a 'rule of law', 'general rule', or 'rule of the canon law';[49] for instance, 'the rules which the ancient canon law hath laid down' provide that the election of a cathedral chapter must be in accordance with cathedral

39 R.H. Helmholz, op cit., 280, 509–510.

40 See N. Doe and S. Pulleyn, op cit., 316.

41 Codex I, Title page and Preface, viii.

42 Codex I, xxviii: '*maxime, cum de jure communi quilibet hujusmodi ordinarius, in causarum cognitionibus committere valeat vices suas* – 'this is especially the case with the common law when any ordinary of this kind has power to depute his powers'; i.e. to commit them to what hands they please.

43 Codex I, xx: '[a]nd as to the second rule, viz., the trial of the incident matter, by that Court which hath the proper cognisance of the principal; this hath not only a plain maxim on its side'.

44 Codex I, 5: '[a]nd it is pursuant to a maxim of our laws, *Ecclesia est infra aetatem, et in custodia Domini regis, qui tenetur Jura et hareditates suas manu tenere et defendere'* – 'The Church is under age and in the custody of the Lord king, who is bound to uphold and defend its rights and inheritances'.

45 Codex I, 22: it is a 'declared maxim' that 'the Clergy are liable to all public charges imposed by Parliament, where they are not specially excepted'.

46 Codex II, 689: it is a 'known maxim of the canon law' that '[a] church is not obliged to pay tithes to [another] church'.

47 Codex II, 1116: '[t]he Rule of canon Law' – degradation may be imposed by a bishop.

48 In four volumes, this was in a 'dictionary form', arranged alphabetically.

49 Burn, *Ecclesiastical Law* (2nd edition, 1767), I.480: 'rules of law'; I.129: '[n]o person may present himself: and it is according to the rule of the canon law'.

statutes, and '[a] church once consecrated cannot be consecrated again' is a 'general rule of the canon law'.[50] These 'rules of law' Burn distinguishes from legal 'maxims', which may be found in Roman law, canon law, and common law; thus, he refers to 'a maxim in law';[51] 'a maxim in the temporal law and . . . applied to the ecclesiastical law';[52] a 'known maxim of the canon law, that the church shall not pay tithes to the church';[53] and a 'general maxim, once discharged, always discharged'.[54]

Whilst in the nineteenth century Herbert Broom published his *Legal Maxims*, some of which deal with ecclesiastical matters,[55] the canonical literature abandons explicit reference to 'maxims' in favour of 'principles'. For example, John Henry Blunt, in *The Book of Church Law* (1873), commonly uses a 'recognised principle', a 'general principle', a 'principle',[56] 'a principle of the common law',[57] or a 'general principle of the canon law', to which he may attribute great antiquity.[58] Blunt finds principles in, for example, the Thirty-Nine Articles of Religion, case law,[59] and canon law, such as can be seen in the statements 'It is a principle of the canon law that no church can be erected without the permission of the bishop of the diocese in which it is situated'[60] and, again, '[T]his plain principle of law should be strictly recognised, and access to the church obtained' through the incumbent who has a right to the church keys in the custody of the churchwardens.[61] More extensive use was made of principles by Robert Phillimore in his two-volume *Ecclesiastical Law* (1873, second edition 1895). This is treated in Chapter 5.

50 Burn, I.255: cathedrals; I.381: 'the rule of the ancient canon law'; I.307: consecration.
51 Burn I.124: 'it is a maxim in law, that the church is not full against the king, till induction'; II.427: 'yet no maxim in the law is more established, than that a subsequent contrary act virtually repeals a preceding act, so far forth as it is contrary'.
52 Burn III.298: 'resignation can only be made to a superior'.
53 Burn II.256 and III.380.
54 Burn, III.424: no tithe is payable on oak under 20 years of age; it is privileged (even if rotten).
55 H. Broom, *Legal Maxims* (London: Sweet and Maxwell, 3rd edition, 1852): e.g. p. 323: 'it is consent, not sleeping together, that makes a marriage'; adopted from D 50.17, 80.
56 Blunt, 7: '[t]he general principle . . . is, that the Crown possesses a visitatorial and corrective jurisdiction in the Church of England'; 311: '[t]hat which is so transferred to God cannot be alienated from Him without sacrilege' is a 'principle'.
57 Blunt, 358: ecclesiastical incomes are dealt with by ecclesiastical persons.
58 Blunt, 15: the canons of the Oxford Synod 1222 are 'arranged by Lyndwood on the principle adopted by Gratian in . . . the *Decretum*'; 22: the Submission of the Clergy Act 1533 contains 'the principle that convocation has no authority to pass laws except by licence from the Crown'; 38: '[a]s regards lunatics the custom is to baptize them, if . . . in danger of death, on the principle laid down in the Elviran canon'; see also 41 (baptism), 179 (suicides and burial), and 331 (tithes).
59 Blunt, 116: Article 23 states 'a principle of the Church of England' that it is not lawful to preach unless authorised; 94 and 294: principles induced from judicial decisions.
60 Blunt, 298; Canon of Westminster 1138; J. Johnson, *Collection of All Ecclesiastical Laws* (1720).
61 Blunt, 267; he cites *Lee v Matthews* (1830) 3 Hag Ecc 169.

In sum, whilst the use of axioms is constant across the history of church law, the terminology for their designation changes from period to period, as do understandings about their nature and their relationship to the details of the positive law of the church. The *regulae iuris* of mediaeval canon law, borrowed from classical Roman law, and both descriptive and prescriptive in form, were debated extensively by the canonists of the Latin Church (particularly whether they were themselves laws or derived from laws). At the Reformation and beyond, into the eighteenth century, 'maxims' were used as a vehicle to characterise axioms in the context of the law of the established Church of England, which embarked on the development and articulation of new axioms to meet the needs of ecclesial life. However, the concept of 'maxims' was displaced by the lawyers of the English church in the nineteenth century with that of 'principles' of church law, but many are indistinguishable from more detailed legal rules, and few lawyers explicitly equated such principles with natural law or reason. Nevertheless, of historic ecumenical significance is how the use of legal maxims and principles survived the schism between Rome and the English Church. It is to the modern importance of this continuity – and the unifying potential of principles of church law implicit in it – that we now turn in terms of Catholic-Anglican dialogue, inter-Anglican relations, and the wider ecumenical movement in global Christianity.

II Three modern models for juridical ecumenism

The more immediate and recent stimuli, over the past 20 or so years, behind the initiative to establish the Christian Law Panel of Experts in 2013 – and these operated in some measure as models for its work – were the work of the Colloquium of Anglican and Roman Catholic Canon Lawyers and the Anglican Communion Legal Advisers Network and scholarship on the phenomenon of 'Christian law'. Let us first discuss the Colloquium of Anglican and Roman Catholic Canon Lawyers. In 1998, the Ecclesiastical Law Society and the (Roman Catholic) Canon Law Society of Great Britain and Ireland hosted the biennial Lyndwood Lecture; it was held at St Paul's Cathedral, London. The lecture explored how the principles of canon law may serve to function as a focus of legal unity in the ecumenical dialogue between Anglicans and Roman Catholics. It examined underlying assumptions shared by both Catholics and Anglicans that there may be overarching 'principles of canon law' that have an existence independent of the individual canonical systems within both communions, but that are particularised in the norms of those systems. The lecture went on to describe their nature and foundational character; how they differ from (detailed) rules; their often theological content; their use and usefulness, location, origin, and authority; and their potential as a unifying force in dialogue between Anglicans and Catholics.[62]

62 N. Doe, 'The Principles of Canon Law: A Focus of Legal Unity in Anglican-Roman Catholic Relations', 5 *Ecclesiastical Law Journal* (1999) 221–240.

Later that year (1998) some Anglican canonists, on a visit to Rome, participated in a colloquium organised by the Faculty of Canon Law of the Pontifical University of St Thomas (Angelicum). In the course of the event, the idea was sown that it would be good to set up a similar colloquium in which Anglican and Roman Catholic canon lawyers could present for discussion their own positions on a variety of subjects. The first Colloquium took place in 1999 in Rome. It addressed ecclesiastical property. In the ten years that followed, the Colloquium met to discuss clerical discipline, initiation into the church, authority in the church, ecumenical cooperation, orders and primacy, preparation for ministry, and marriage (including mixed marriages).[63] For the Colloquium, comparison of the respective systems of canon law has a distinctive role in ecumenical dialogue by seeking to provide a stable ecumenical methodology, concrete data that embody theology, and a detailed guide to practical action for Christian life; to define the degree of achieved communion and the opportunities for and limits of future progress; to contribute to a description of the identity of membership of the church; to liberate and order the exercise of authority in decision-making that has consequences for individuals and institutions; and, in turn, to alert ecumenical partners in dialogue to the binding nature of Christian truth.[64]

The first ten years of its work were summed up by the Colloquium as having been marked by 'academic rigour, candid exchanges of views, and respectful listening'. It had been more than interesting to observe in the work of the participants what Anglicans and Roman Catholics have in common, what they do not share, and what is done simply in another way. Behind the conversations on matters canonical, there has always been a deep respect for the doctrine that often lies behind the legislation considered and for the sensitivities of each participant towards certain very delicate matters. Moreover, '[b]y making clear what is not always perceived as clear, by setting out boundaries and limits, canon law not only serves as a useful source of norms regulating ecumenical relations but can be seen as an instrument of that very same dialogue. Canon law has helped us to see where we are radically united, and where we have yet to make progress in our journey'.[65] The years that followed saw the Colloquium discussing the teaching of

63 Its proceedings were published: J. Fox OP, ed., *Render Unto Caesar: Church Property in Roman Catholic and Anglican Canon Law* (Rome: Angelicum University, 2000); M. Hill, ed., *Clergy Discipline in Anglican and Roman Catholic Canon Law* (Cardiff: Centre for Law and Religion, 2001); J. Conn, N. Doe, and J. Fox, eds., *Initiation, Membership and Authority in Anglican and Roman Catholic Canon Law* (Cardiff and Rome: Centre for Law and Religion and Angelicum University, 2005); N. Doe, ed., *The Formation and Ordination of Clergy in Anglican and Roman Catholic Canon Law* (Cardiff: Centre for Law and Religion, 2009); N. Doe, ed., *Marriage in Anglican and Roman Catholic Canon Law* (Cardiff: Centre for Law and Religion, 2009).

64 Fourth Colloquium (2003): Statement on Authority 1: see J. Conn et al., op cit., 317.

65 M. Hill, ed., 'A Decade of Ecumenical Dialogue on Canon Law, A Report on the Proceedings of the Colloquium of Anglican and Roman Catholic Canon Lawyers 1999–2009', 11 *Ecclesiastical Law Journal* (2009) 284–328.

canon law, the regulation of public and private matters in church life, governance, parishes, and bishops in canon law.[66]

Importantly, what characterised many of the meetings was the capacity of the group to articulate shared principles of canon law common to both communions. For example, its 'agreed principles' in relation to clerical formation include the following: the church has a responsibility to provide for clerical formation; clerical formation is necessary to assure the quality of ministry, which is a means by which all the faithful receive the spiritual benefits of the church; the essential end of clerical formation is to equip ordination candidates for a life of holiness, sacramental ministry, preaching, and pastoral care; the two communions share a concern to ensure that clerics are duly grounded in the doctrine and discipline of the church; clerical formation is continuing and lifelong; clerical formation should include training in canonical matters relevant to the exercise of ordained ministry; both communions acknowledge the possibility of conflict between canonical arrangements for clerical formation and civil law, such as in relation to matters of confidentiality, discrimination, psychological assessment, and employment; ecumenical collaboration as to aspects of clerical formation is desirable and growing in practice; and the polities of the communions on marriage and celibacy affect the shape of clerical formation and instruction in seminaries.[67] The work of the Colloquium has also been appraised (and commended) by non-member scholars.[68]

The second model for the principles of the Christian Law project was work of the global Anglican Communion Legal Advisers Network, which resulted in the launch at the Lambeth Conference in 2008 of a document entitled *The Principles of Canon Law Common to the Churches of the Anglican Communion*.[69] The Communion has no formal body of law applicable to its 44 member churches; each church is autonomous, with its own legal system. The Communion is held together by 'bonds of affection', shared loyalty to scripture, the creeds, baptism,

66 N. Doe, ed., *The Approaches to Public Matters and Private Matters in Anglican and Roman Catholic Canon Law* (Cardiff: Centre for Law and Religion, 2016); N. Doe, ed., *The Teaching of Canon Law in Anglicanism and the Roman Catholic Church* (Cardiff: Centre for Law and Religion, 2016); N. Doe, ed., *Counsel and Consent: Church Government in Anglican and Roman Catholic Canon Law* (Cardiff: Centre for Law and Religion, 2016); and N. Doe, ed., *Bishops in Anglican and Roman Catholic Canon Law* (Cardiff: Centre for Law and Religion, 2018).

67 The Eighth Colloquium, Rome 17–20 April 2007: N. Doe, ed., *Formation of Clergy* (2009) 156; see also ibid 155 for 'agreed principles' on ordination, e.g. elements of the rite common to both traditions; and 157: A Note to the International Anglican-Roman Catholic Commission on Unity and Mission.

68 N. Sagovsky, 'The Contribution of Canon Law to Anglican-Roman Catholic Ecumenism', 13 *Ecclesiastical Law Journal* (2011) 4–14, and B. Leahy, 'The Role of Canon Law in the Ecumenical Venture: A Roman Catholic Perspective', ibid. 15–25. Both papers were given at a Colloquium meeting in 2010.

69 *The Principles of Canon Law Common to the Churches of the Anglican Communion* (London: Anglican Communion Office, 2008).

the Eucharist, the historic episcopate, and its instruments of communion (Archbishop of Canterbury, Primates' Meeting, Lambeth Conference, and Anglican Consultative Council); but these institutions have no freestanding jurisdiction to make decisions binding on churches.[70]

Following the Lambeth Conference in 1998, global tensions in the Communion (mostly around issues of human sexuality) stimulated discussion of how the laws of churches may contribute to more visible international ecclesial unity in Anglicanism. In 2001, on the basis of a paper discussed at the event,[71] the Primates' Meeting decided to explore whether there is an unwritten common law (or *ius commune*) shared by the churches of the Communion. An Anglican Communion Legal Advisers' Consultation (the first of its type) in 2002 tested and then accepted the hypothesis. The Primates' Meeting (2002) discussed a report on the Consultation and concluded that '[t]he Primates recognized that the unwritten law common to the Churches of the Communion and expressed as shared principles of canon law may be understood to constitute a fifth "instrument of unity" '. Later in 2002, the Anglican Consultative Council welcomed the establishment of a Network of Anglican Legal Advisers to produce 'a statement of principles of Canon Law common within the Communion', and in 2003 the Primates' Meeting urged completion of the work, as did the Lambeth Commission in 2004. A Network drafting group met in 2005 and 2006, and after extensive consultation *The Principles of Canon Law Common to the Churches of the Anglican Communion* was launched at the Lambeth Conference in 2008. In 2009, the Anglican Consultative Council commended the Principles for study in all provinces, invited them to submit comments on the document, requested a report on these, and encouraged provinces to use the Network as a central resource in dealing with legal issues in those provinces.[72]

The hundred principles are arranged under eight parts (with over 600 micro-principles). Part I, 'Order in the Church', deals with the necessity for law and the sources, subjects, authority, application, and interpretation of law. Part II concerns 'The Anglican Communion', its nature, instruments of unity, provincial autonomy, and mutual respect. Principles of 'Ecclesiastical Government', in Part III, deal with, for instance, representative government, legislative competence, visitations, and courts. Part IV addresses 'Ministry': the laity, lay ministers and deacons, priests, bishops, and archbishops. Part V, 'Doctrine and Liturgy', covers the sources and development of doctrine and liturgy, public worship, and doctrinal and liturgical discipline. Principles on baptism, confirmation, Holy Communion, marriage, confession, and burial are in Part VI, 'The Rites of the Church'. Part VII, 'Church Property', treats ownership and administration, places of worship, records, funds, stipends, and pensions. Part VIII, 'Ecumenical Relations', features

70 N. Doe, *Canon Law in the Anglican Communion* (Oxford: Oxford University Press, 1998) 338.

71 N. Doe, 'Canon Law and Communion', 6 *Ecclesiastical Law Journal* (2002) 241–263.

72 ACC-14, Resolution 14.20 (5 May 2009).

ecumenical responsibilities, recognition of churches, ecumenical agreements, and admission to the Holy Communion. The principles themselves are induced from the similarities between the laws and other regulatory instruments of the churches (including normative doctrinal texts) and cast as e.g. precepts, prohibitions, permissions, exhortations, and descriptive maxims.[73]

This document is not a system of international canon law but a statement of principles of canon law that articulates the common ground between the legal systems of each of the churches of the global Communion; the document defines a 'principle of canon law' as 'a foundational proposition or maxim of general applicability which has a strong dimension of weight, is induced from the similarities of the legal systems of churches, derives from the canonical tradition or other practices of the church, expresses a basic theological truth or ethical value, and is about, is implicit in, or underlies canon law'.[74] In point of fact, many of the principles echo or equate with the traditional canonical maxims 'Laws cannot oblige a person to do the impossible';[75] 'Persons cannot give what they do not have';[76] a declaration to comply with ecclesiastical jurisdiction binds the person who makes that declaration;[77] 'bodies or persons who exercise ecclesiastical functions may delegate to others only such functions as they are not required to perform themselves';[78] the judges of church courts are 'to exercise their office impartially, without fear or favour';[79] consecrated property 'may not be used for purposes inconsistent with the uses of God for which it was set aside';[80] and church trustees are not liable for any financial loss resulting from an investment 'unless such loss is due to their own wilful default or culpable negligence'.[81] Some principles admit to their own exceptions – and they apply to the extent allowed by church law.[82]

Third, three publications added to the impetus for a wider ecumenical consideration of the potential unifying value of principles of church law.[83] The first is a

73 For the process and methodology used by the Network, see N. Doe, 'The Common Law of the Anglican Communion', 7 *Ecclesiastical Law Journal* (2003) 4–16.

74 *Principles* (2008); for background, see ibid., p. 97, N. Doe, 'The Contribution of Common Principles of Canon Law to Ecclesial Communion in Anglicanism'.

75 Principle 7.3; VI.6: '[n]o-one can be obliged to the impossible'.

76 Principle 7.4; VI.79: '[n]o one gives more right to another than what he has'.

77 Principle 5.6; VI.27: '[t]o the one who knows and approves, there is neither injury nor malice'.

78 Principle 17.4; VI.68: '[w]hatever someone can do by himself, he can do it by another (unless the power to act cannot be delegated)'.

79 Principle 24.7; VI.12: '[j]ustice should be rendered without respect to persons'.

80 Principle 81.5; VI.51: '[o]nce given to God it should not be transferred to the use of man'.

81 Principle 89.4; VI.62: '[n]o liability arises from advice given provided it was not fraudulent'.

82 E.g. Principle 41.6: '[c]lergy . . . are subject to . . . the bishop to the extent provided under the law'.

83 Whilst recent years have seen a dramatic increase in studies on law and religion (mainly on state law on religion), and on laws of individual churches, little work exists on comparative church law. However, see the prophetic article, H. Engelhardt, 'The Lawyer's Contribution to the Progress of Christian Unity', *The Ecumenical Review* (1969) 7–22: this proposed the establishment of an Ecumenical Institute of Ecclesiastical Law maintained by the World Council of Churches.

book written by Marc Reuver. This valuable study describes in parallel the laws of churches from numerous Christian traditions but focusses on the potential differences between these laws as an ecumenical problem – namely, legal differences institutionalise the separation of churches.[84] The second is a book by a Welsh (Anglican) canonist that offers a detailed comparison of the laws and other regulatory instruments of over a hundred churches across ten historic Christian traditions worldwide: Catholic, Orthodox, Anglican, Lutheran, Methodist, Reformed, Presbyterian, United, Congregational, and Baptist. From this comparison, the book proposes that all the denominations studied share common principles of law in spite of their doctrinal differences and that these principles reveal a concept of 'Christian law' and also contribute to a theological understanding of global Christian identity. It deals with the sources and purposes of church law, the faithful and ministers, church governance, discipline and dispute resolution, doctrine and worship, the rites of passage, ecumenical relations, and property and finance as well as church, state, and society. Its key message is that whilst dogmas may divide, laws link Christians across the traditions by stimulating through their norms of conduct common action – and this should feed into the global ecumenical enterprise.[85]

The third is a book by Leo J. Koffeman, a professor of church polity and ecumenism at the Protestant Theological University Amsterdam, who served on the Faith and Order Commission of the World Council of Churches. Writing mainly but not exclusively from the Reformed tradition, Koffeman observes that ecclesiology (that branch of theology that focusses on the nature of the Church universal) is at the centre of current ecumenical dialogue. However, this focus on ecclesiology does not include theological reflection on church polity (order or law). Therefore, the book seeks 'to enhance a truly ecumenical and inter-cultural approach of the theological discipline of church polity, without neglecting its juridical character'. Particularly relevant to juridical ecumenism are the following themes developed by Koffeman. First, as to 'ecumenical church polity', he proposes that, alongside unilateral norms made by a church on ecumenism and joint norm-making in inter-church agreements, ecumenical partners could develop 'a joint set of regulations in which the churches transfer specific competencies to

84 M. Reuver, *Faith and Law: Juridical Perspectives for the Ecumenical Movement* (Geneva: World Council of Churches, 2000). See upcoming discussion for WCC consideration of law.

85 N. Doe, *Christian Law: Contemporary Principles* (Cambridge: Cambridge University Press, 2013): the Appendix contains a Statement of Principles of Christian Law. The book was stimulated partly by the invitation of John Witte for a chapter on 'Modern Church Law', in J. Witte and F.S. Alexander, eds., *Christianity and Law* (Cambridge: Cambridge University Press, 2008) 271–291. For critical appraisal, see Baroness (Brenda) Hale, 'Secular Judges and Christian Law', 17 *Ecclesiastical Law Journal* (2015) 170–181 at 178; and B. Hale, 'Religious Freedom and the Law', in F. Cranmer, M. Hill, C. Kenny and R. Sandberg, eds., *The Confluence of Law and Religion: Interdisciplinary Reflections on the Work of Norman Doe* (Cambridge: Cambridge University Press, 2016) 218–232 at 229; and L. Koffeman, 'The Ecumenical Potential of Church Polity', 17 *Ecclesiastical Law Journal* (2015) 182–193 at 193.

ecumenical organisations, arbitration committees or other bodies'. Second, and critically, '[e]ach church polity system has to be challenged theologically, and each includes challenges to the other systems . . . there is no "ideal" system . . . the only option is a truly ecumenical approach' that recognises that 'each church polity system is necessarily provisional'. Third, in light of the marks of the church universal (one, holy, catholic, and apostolic), Koffeman offers four criteria to measure the moral standards of church polity: inclusivity (embracing all people), authenticity (living up to the Gospel), conciliarity (giving voice to all the faithful), and integrity (meeting the highest standards of ethical behaviour – 'not everything goes within the church. The Gospel implies limitations'. This book is a landmark not only in understanding the juridical dimension of ecclesial life but also in uncovering the value of church law/order/polity for ecumenism. Koffeman, therefore, facilitates exploration of the ways in which laws enable or restrict greater visible communion between separated churches.[86] Many of these important ideas mirror, independently, the thinking of the Roman Catholic canonist Robert Ombres OP, for whom canon law is applied ecclesiology and the missing link in global ecumenism.[87]

III The Panel of Experts and its *Principles of Christian Law* (2016)

At its first meeting in Rome in 2013, the Christian Law Panel of Experts was presented with the Anglican principles of canon law project as a possible model.[88] First, the Panel found 'broad consensus on the following general conclusions';[89] namely, (1) there are principles of church law and order common to the Catholic, Orthodox, Anglican, Lutheran, Methodist, Reformed, Presbyterian, and Baptist traditions, and their existence can be factually established by empirical observation and comparison; (2) the churches contribute through their own regulatory instruments to this store of principles; (3) the principles have a strong theological content and weight and are fundamental to the self-understanding of Christianity; (4) they have a living force and contain within themselves the possibility of further development and articulation; and (5) they demonstrate a degree of unity between churches, stimulate common Christian actions, and should be fed

86 L.J. Koffeman, *In Order to Serve* (2014), op cit: '[c]hurch polity as a theological discipline is: the systematic analysis, evaluation and development of the sum total of established rules as a legal system that governs structure and legal relations within churches . . . their mutual relations and . . . to respective states, from the perspective of ecclesiology'.

87 R. Ombres, 'Canon Law and Theology', 14 *Ecclesiastical Law Journal* (2012) 164–194.

88 At the first symposium of the Panel (see footnote 1 above for its membership), the present author presented the Anglican project in the first session. Reference was also made to the Anglican project in L.J. Koffeman, *In Order to Serve* (2014), op cit., 70.

89 That is, 'as ventured by Professor Norman Doe in his book, *Christian Law: Contemporary Principles* (Cambridge: Cambridge University Press, 2013)': Christian Law Panel of Experts: Response to the World Council of Church Faith and Order Commission Paper, *The Church: Towards a Common Vision* (2013) (December 2015) p. 3.

into the global ecumenical enterprise to enhance fuller visible unity. Second, the Panel agreed that church law and order exist to serve a church in its mission and witness to the salvific work of Christ; laws are necessary to constitute the institutional organisation of a church and facilitate and order its public activities but cannot encompass all facets and experiences of the Christian faith and life; laws are the servant of the church and must promote the mission of the church universal; theology shapes law, and law implements theological propositions in norms of conduct; and church laws should conform to, and are subject ultimately to, the law of God, as revealed in Holy Scripture and by the Holy Spirit. Third, the Panel agreed that a consideration of church law/order/polity may provide a new medium, within the context of receptive ecumenism, for the ecumenical enterprise; namely, that law (as a discrete element of the ecclesiological self-understanding of churches) should be conceived as an instrument for global ecumenism. Identifying juridical similarities and differences is likely to be important for ecumenical understanding.[90]

To test further these hypotheses, the Panel of Experts met a second time in Rome, in October 2014, to discuss how its work might feed into that of the World Council of Churches by means of a response to the WCC Faith and Order Commission Paper No 214, *The Church: Towards a Common Vision* (2013). The Panel noted that over the years there has been interest in the role of church law and church order in the ecumenical enterprise, but that this has not been developed. For example, in 1974 the Faith and Order Commission called for discussion of 'church law' on the basis that '[t]he churches differ in their order and their constitution'; 'differences in the . . . legal systems of the churches have their roots in different confessional traditions'; and these differences concern 'not only the actual order which the churches have, but also the general orientation by which their legislation is inspired'.[91] In the same year, a call was made 'to consider the role of constitutional matters', but in 1978 the director of Faith and Order reported that 'given limited resources available . . . the study will probably never get very far'; this has led to the view that 'questions and conflicts in these areas have accompanied the ecumenical movement ever since, which confirms the foresight of those earlier initiatives and the need to take them up once again'.[92]

The Panel, therefore, considered at its second meeting that a juridical response to *The Church: Towards a Common Vision* (2013) would be valuable. This was the case for two reasons. First, *Common Vision* does not consider church law or its role in ecumenism. Yet the thrust of *Common Vision* is convergence in belief (the primary stimulus for law) and in action (the primary focus of law), and its

90 Panel: Response to *Common Vision* (2013) (December 2015) pp. 3–4. These points broadly mirror those of the Anglican Communion Legal Advisers Network: see above n. 73.

91 FAOC: 'The Ecumenical Movement and Church Law', Document IV.8 (1974).

92 Also, in Louvain in 1971, the Faith and Order Commission discussed a study on 'Institution, Law and State', but this 'was not pursued further, mainly because of lack of funds': G. Gassmann, ed., *Documentary History of Faith and Order 1963–1993* (Geneva: WCC, 1993) 206–207.

language is often normative (the primary character of law). Many themes in *Common Vision* surface in church laws. Exploration of these would enable the WCC to see how church laws articulate ideas in *Common Vision*; translate these into norms of conduct; and, in turn, generate unity in common action (across the church families). Second, church laws are applied ecclesiology. They also shape the ecclesiology of churches. Third, such exploration would enable the WCC to understand how systems of church law help or hinder ecumenism. The Panel began work on drafting a response to *Common Vision*.[93]

The Panel met a third time in Rome in October 2015. It achieved three things. First, it finalised its response to *Common Vision*.[94] This indicated how comparing church laws facilitates the articulation of principles of law common to the churches, enables reconciliation of juridical difference in the form of underlying principles of law, provides a stable ecumenical methodology through its focus on concrete textual data, offers a practical guide for Christian life, and defines both achieved communion and opportunities for and limits on future progress. Moreover, '[r]e-imagining ecumenism through law, as applied ecclesiology in . . . norms of conduct, would advance *Common Vision's* idea that "common action" is 'intrinsic to the life and being of the Church'.[95]

Second, the Panel worked on a set of candidate principles, circulated to its members in advance, on two topics: Church Discipline and Church Property. In terms of method, the preparatory work asked members to agree, disagree, or agree to differ on the candidate principles. The meeting also gave the opportunity to revise principles over which there was disagreement in order to reconcile differences in the form of a common principle of law. The exercise was whether there was legal evidence that the candidate principles appear explicitly or implicitly in the regulatory instruments of the traditions in question. The exercise was *not* whether the candidate principles *ought* to be principles of Christian law. Discussion was robust. Of the 50 or so candidate principles circulated, 47 were agreed.[96] The agreed principles, with the Panel response to *Common Vision*, were submitted to WCC in December 2015, with a view 'in the longer term, towards adoption by the WCC so that the Christian Law endeavour will be of lasting value to the ecumenical movement in its quest for greater visible Christian unity'; more immediately, the Panel also invited the Faith and Order Commission itself

93 The suggestion to respond to *The Church: Towards a Common Vision* was that of L.J. Koffeman.

94 The paper (with changes) was reproduced as N. Doe, 'The Ecumenical Value of Comparative Church Law: Towards the Category of Christian Law', 17 *Ecclesiastical Law Journal* (2015) 135–169.

95 Panel: Response (2015) p. 4 (see Common Vision par. 61 for 'common action'). These points mirror those made by the Colloquium of Anglican and Roman Catholic Canon Lawyers: see above n. 64.

96 These are set out in section III of the Response (pages 26–29): for the purposes of the response, the expression 'law' was understood by the Panel to encompass a variety of regulatory instruments and norms, including constitutions, canons, covenants, books of church order, and other polity documents.

'to engage in a dialogue in which the Christian Law project can be used as an expression of institutional unity and a means of practical ecumenism'.[97] Third, the Panel agreed to continue to discern and articulate principles of law on governance, ministry, doctrine, worship, ritual, church-state relations, and ecumenism.

During the course of 2016, further candidate principles were circulated to the Panel in two batches. The first contained principles on four topics: Churches and Their Laws, the Faithful, Ministry, and Church Governance. The second contained principles on Doctrine and Worship, Rites of Churches, Ecumenism, and Church-State Relations. At its fourth symposium in Rome in September 2016, the Panel used the same method as that employed at its 2015 meeting. Once again, discussion was rigorous, rich, and robust.[98] First, occasionally, candidates were agreed without revision; for example, 'A church is autonomous in its system of governance or polity'; 'Customs may have juridical force to the extent permitted by the law of a church'; and 'A church may institute a system of ecclesiastical offences'. Second, some were agreed with minor or substantial revision; for instance, 'Laws are necessary to constitute the institutional organisation of a church and facilitate and order its public activities but cannot encompass all facets and experiences of the Christian faith and life' became 'Laws contribute to constituting the institutional organisation of a church and facilitate and order its activities'; and 'The right to exercise discipline over the faithful is based on divine and spiritual authority' became 'The right to exercise discipline has a variety of foundations including divine and spiritual authority'. Third, many were rejected; for example, 'The presence of law in a church does not mark out its doctrinal posture'; 'Laws are the servant of the church and must promote the mission of the church universal'; 'Laws cannot oblige a person to do the impossible'; 'If there is doubt about the meaning of a law, that law does not bind'; 'All the faithful share in the threefold ministry of Christ: king, prophet and priest'; 'A church may receive into its membership any person who qualifies under its law'; 'Ordination cannot be repeated'; and 'An international ecclesial institution has such functions and authority over its autonomous constituent parts as are assumed by the institutional church represented in it or conferred upon it by those churches associated with it'. Fourth, some were simply replaced; for example, 'No person in a church is above its law' was replaced with 'All members of a church are subject to its laws as are its component institutions, to the extent that the law provides'. Fifth, others, not appearing among the candidates, were added; for instance, 'All ecclesial units at each level are interdependent'.[99]

97 Panel: Response (2015) p. 5.

98 The candidate principles considered by the Panel of Experts were those as set out in N. Doe, *Christian Law: Contemporary Principles* (Cambridge University Press, 2013) Appendix, 387–398.

99 Each Panel member, needless to say, gave legal reasons for these – reception, revision, replacement, rejection, or addition. However, a description of these reasons is beyond the scope of this study. Whilst most principles are prescriptive (precepts, prohibitions, or permissions), many are descriptive; of the latter, some were placed at the opening of a Section as statements of legal fact.

At the end of the 2016 symposium, the Panel agreed to a *Statement of Principles of Christian Law*.[100] It appears in Appendix II of this volume and has ten sections: churches and their systems of law, the faithful, ordained ministry, church governance, church discipline, doctrine and worship, the rites of the church, ecumenism, church property, and church and state relations. Each section opens with a short narrative that sets out 'a number of facts based on church regulatory systems which the Panel considers relevant to the area of ecclesial life treated, but which may not in the Panel's opinion represent principles of law'.[101] The grouping of principles into these sections is conditioned by the systematisation of laws generally employed by the historic churches from whose laws they are induced. The principles are derived from various regulatory sources, including codes of canon law, statutes, constitutions, books of church order, and other policy documents. The juridical values of clarity, conciseness, and consistency govern their form, and they are cast in a variety of ways – as permissions, precepts, prohibitions, exhortations, and descriptions. Their forms, once more, mirror the laws from which they are induced.

The 2016 Rome symposium of the Panel also decided to seek a meeting in Geneva in November 2017 with the director of the WCC Faith and Order Commission, Dr Odair Mateus. This was agreed on the basis of the conviction of the Panel that ecumenical rapprochement may be served if experts in church polity, order, or law from most confessional traditions enter into an ecumenical dialogue. The meeting would also seek to evaluate what the Panel has done so far with regard to methodology, conclusions, the extent its work fosters the ecumenical movement, and the degree to which the project may be extended to other church families whose churches are members of the WCC; the meeting would also consider how the project might be received by the WCC Faith and Order Commission and fit into its wider programme over the years to come. In preparation, during 2017, Panel members were asked to address (1) the value of the definition of a 'principle of law common to the churches';[102] (2) whether all the principles may be 'factually established by empirical observation and comparison'; and (3) in what ways the Panel might continue its work and identify further objectives and next steps and how important it is to 'establish a clear link with the Faith and Order Commission'.[103]

100 Of the 250 or so candidate principles considered, 230 were accepted (in a revised or added form).

101 See also above footnote 99.

102 Namely, '[a] "principle of law" common to the churches of the Christian traditions studied here is a foundational proposition or maxim of general applicability which has substance, is induced from the similarities of the regulatory systems of churches, derives from their juridical tradition or the practices of the church universal, expresses a basic theological truth or ethical value, and is implicit in, or underlies, the juridical systems of the churches'; see also N. Doe, *Christian Law* (2013) Appendix, 388.

103 Leo Koffeman (a former Faith and Order Commission member) would arrange the meeting; he also drafted the Leading Questions. Leo Koffeman, email to Odair Mateus and Panel members 25-4-2017.

At Geneva in November 2017, suitably in the year of the 500th anniversary of the Reformation,[104] the Panel presented to Dr Mateus (Director, WCC Faith and Order Commission) a published copy of *Principles of Christian Law*,[105] the first ecumenical exercise of its type. This was received with thanks by Dr Mateus, who outlined the history of ecumenism leading to *Common Vision* (2013), the aborted WCC discussion of church law in the 1970s, and how debate on Christian law would represent a new development for WCC practice insofar as its traditional focus has been on theological dialogue, not law. Importantly, Dr Mateus also recognised the potential unifying force of law as 'an element of the true church'. Dr Ani Ghazaryan Drissi of the Faith and Order Commission Secretariat added that the Panel response (2015) to *Common Vision* had already been seen, within the Commission process examining this and other responses, as 'unique', 'profound', a 'valuable approach', and an 'alternative path'. The Panel's work is the subject of ongoing consideration by the members of the Commission. Equally important, Dr Mateus suggested that there was also scope for debate about law in other areas currently of concern to the Commission; namely, justice and peace, moral discernment, and new churches. Dr Mateus then proposed setting up an 'informal but substantial consultative partnership' between the Panel and the WCC Commission in order for them to continue working together. The Panel warmly welcomed this, and the partnership was later confirmed by an exchange of letters.[106]

The Panel next met in Rome in November 2018 with Commission members. The Panel members reported on local events agreed at Geneva 2017 to be held on the *Statement of Principles of Christian Law* (Rome 2016). Ann Tronet spoke about an event held at Uppsala, Sweden, on 28 May 2018, at which the project was welcomed as neutral and novel, but questions were raised about the definition of terms in the *Statement*. Norman Doe spoke of an event held with Churches Together in Wales at Cardiff on 10 September 2018, at which participants were initially hostile but then moved to welcome the project as useful (though questions were asked about the descriptive/prescriptive nature of the principles). Leo J. Koffeman spoke about an event held in Amsterdam on 26 September 2018 that he and Leon van den Broeke organised – a Muslim and a Baptist responded to the project, which was welcomed as 'fruitful' and 'juridically correct', but questions were raised as to what use might be made of the *Statement*. Nikos Maghioros explained that he had started work on translating the *Statement* into Greek.

Leo J. Koffeman circulated a paper about the aborted 1970s WCC project. He explained how the project would have focussed on church laws as expressing 'differences' between churches, not as about their potential for unity; that the proposed project was very much 'of its time', when organic union was a key WCC

104 It was at the John Knox Centre, 23–24 November 2017.

105 M. Hill and N. Doe, 'Principles of Christian Law', 19 *Ecclesiastical Law Journal* (2017) 138–155.

106 E.g. email: Koffeman-Druber: 11–4–2018.

focus, and legal challenges were faced by uniting churches; and that the idea was dropped because of, *inter alia*, new agendas intervening, personnel issues, and finance. The Panel agreed that a focus on difference embeds difference, and that its project focusses on the unifying potential of comparing church law with a view to articulating shared principles.

The informal partnership proposed and agreed at Geneva 2017 with the director of the Faith and Order Commission has been fruitful. Angela Berlis (Commission member) joined the Panel and contributes from Old Catholic perspectives. Susan Durber, Moderator of the Commission, attended the Rome meeting in 2018 and spoke of, and the Panel discussed, further possible activity based on the partnership with regard to (1) the Commission Study Group 1, the pilgrimage of justice and peace, focussing on churches acting together in the world; (2) Study Group 2, analysing the responses to *The Church: Towards a Common Vision* (2013), including the Panel's submission and its *Statement* (2016) (see upcoming discussion); and (3) Study Group 3, on moral discernment. Susan Durber went to the heart of the matter: (1) the perception is, in some places, that church law inhibits ecumenical advancement – it is often seen as an instrument of division – and there is also in some places an anxiety among churches that the ecumenical movement itself will call for changes to the canon law of churches; but (2) the *Statement* changes this perception, and it provides a safe space for churches to reflect on issues; (3) it would be good for the partnership to work for the mutual flourishing of the Panel and Commission; and (4) the Panel should more widely test the *Statement*, e.g. among Roman Catholics and Orthodox, for a wider recognition of the facilitative role that comparative church law offers to ecumenism – that is, in order to 'change the discourse from church law as an inhibitor to ecumenism' to seeing its potential for enabling greater visible unity.

Mark Hill summed up that the *Statement* is 'not a threat to ecumenism – neither is it a panacea – but the principles are a tool for identifying common ground ecumenically'. There was also consensus around the idea that when churches are in the process of uniting with other churches (organic union), the *Statement* could contribute usefully.

There were three sessions to 'drill down' into the principles on ecclesial discipline. The Panel was heartened by the fact that these principles stood up to rigorous testing. However, matters debated included the meaning of 'discipline' and how this was related to 'discipleship'; that discipline is perceived today as needed in light of issues about sexual abuse; that 'visitation' could be placed alternatively under 'oversight' in Principles III.4; that the phrase 'or civil law' in V.4.2 was problematic – a church could not be required by civil law to carry out an internal formal process for discipline, though a church could be required to participate in a formal process in state courts; and V.4.4, 'must secure', could include 'should ensure'. It was accepted that whilst the principles are in one sense interpretations of actual church laws, they themselves are also the object of interpretation in the light of the actual laws of churches. Susan Durber welcomed the consensus style of the Panel in its work and its confidence in the novel use of the language of prescription when articulating the principles of Christian law.

It was agreed that Phase One of the work of the Panel was complete (from 2013–2018), expressed by Leo J. Koffeman as itself in the nature of realising 'a dream'; namely, (1) agreeing on the category 'principles of Christian law', the methodology to articulate them, and their potential for ecumenism; (2) responding to the WCC *The Church: Towards a Common Vision*; (3) agreeing to the *Statement of Principles of Christian Law* (Rome 2016); (4) establishing an informal partnership with the WCC Faith and Order Commission in 2017 (at Geneva) and, in 2018, Susan Durber, Commission Moderator, participating in a Panel meeting; and (5) the introduction of national/local events to stimulate debate on the *Statement*. It was agreed that there should be no full Panel meeting in 2019. Instead, Phase Two should be for advocacy, testing, and reception of the *Statement* at national and international events. Advocacy and discussion of the *Statement* have taken place since; for example, at Melbourne and Sydney (Mark Hill, February 2019), Istanbul at a private meeting with the Ecumenical Patriarch (Norman Doe, March 2019), Rome at a meeting with Pope Francis (Norman Doe and Mark Hill presenting the *Statement*, April 2019), and London (at a meeting of Churches Together in England, Paul Goodliff, Mark Hill, and Norman Doe, July 2019). At Oslo in June 2019, Norman Doe presented the *Statement* to the Most Revd Helga Haugland Byfuglien, Presiding Bishop of the (Lutheran) Church of Norway, and addressed a meeting of ecumenists on it. Plans are also underway for a workshop to be held on the project at the World Council of Churches Assembly (which meets every eight years) meeting at Karlsruhe, Germany, in September 2022.

Conclusion

There are well-tested historic and modern models for the wider articulation today of principles of Christian law. The mediaeval western canonists used juridical maxims in the form of *regulae iuris*. This practice survived at and beyond the Reformation and continued with the move to principles of law (exemplified in English ecclesiastical law from the Enlightenment). The practice has also thrived in the modern models provided by the work of the Colloquium of Anglican and Roman Catholic Canon Lawyers, the Anglican experience with respect to its principles of canon law, and recent scholarship. When compared, there are profound similarities between the basic elements of the normative regimes of the churches across the ecclesial traditions from which jurists and theologians met for the work of the Christian Law Panel of Experts. This is not surprising: juridical unity is often based on the practice of churches to use a common source in shaping their laws (chiefly, Holy Scripture) and their adoption or adaptation of norms of the mother church, in the case of those churches within a single tradition, or at least elements of them, in the case of churches that have broken away from that tradition. From these similarities may be induced common principles of law. The existence and articulation of these in the Panel's *Principles of Christian Law* (Rome 2016) are rightly of particular interest to the World Council of Churches, its Faith and Order Commission, and its *Common Vision* project. This volume is itself both inspired by and the fruit of the partnership established by the Panel and the World Council of Churches Faith and Order Commission in Geneva 2017 – and an apt way to mark the 500th anniversary of the Reformation.

Regulatory systems of churches shape and are shaped by ecclesiology. These systems also tell us much about convergence in action, including and beyond the matters addressed in *Common Vision*, based on common norms of conduct as well as the commitment of churches to ecumenism. Whilst certain dogmas may divide churches, this does not negate those profound similarities between their norms of conduct, which produce juridical convergence. This reveals that norms of the faithful, whatever their various denominational affiliations, link Christians through their stimulation of common forms of action. As laws converge, so do actions. Whilst there are key differences, similarities between the norms of conduct of churches indicate that their faithful engage in much the same actions in the visible world as other Christians. This must count for something in the ecumenical enterprise. In turn, comparing church law/order/polity systems, themselves forms of applied ecclesiology, enables the articulation of principles of law common to the churches, enables the reconciliation of juridical difference in the form of underlying principles of law, provides a stable ecumenical methodology through a focus on concrete textual data, offers a practical guide for Christian life, and defines the degree of achieved communion as well as opportunities for and limits on future progress.

2 Roman Catholic canon law

Aidan McGrath and Robert Ombres

In the context of the *Statement of Principles of Christian Law* issued by the ecumenical panel in 2016, this chapter offers the particular perspective of one church that has a long, elaborate, and universal juridical history related to its theological self-understanding. In terms of the law of the Latin (Catholic) Church, first the sources and forms of this law will be outlined, followed by an account of how such law divides into universal, particular, and proper law, before concluding with a discussion of the scope of canon law in the life of the faithful. This having been done, the focus will be on the different kinds of laws/norms adopted and the foundations of canon law. Once the juridical system has been described on its own terms, some comments and an evaluation of the *Statement of Principles* are given based on this self-understanding.

I The law of the Latin Church

1 Sources and forms of church law

The practice of making disciplinary regulations for the faithful within the church is often traced back to the decisions of the so-called Council of Jerusalem (cf. Acts 15). As the church spread, so the need arose to regulate the behaviour of the individual Christian, and the community itself, in the light of the teachings and practices found in the biblical texts. Among those works that are seen as having had such a role are the *Didache*, the *Didascalia Apostolorum*, and the *Constitutiones Apostolorum*, which contain the so-called 85 Apostolic Canons. These testify to the felt need among the early Christians to make certain decisions that were concrete and practical, as distinct from the more significant doctrinal issues. The influential *Didache* probably dates from the end of the first century and includes instructions on baptism, fasting, prayer, the Eucharist, and how to treat apostles and prophets, bishops, and deacons. It is the earliest of the series of 'Church Orders'.

Within the universal church, the origins of canon law as such are to be found in the 20 canons that were passed at the First Council of Nicaea (325), dealing with a whole range of non-doctrinal matters concerning such topics as the clergy and conflicts of jurisdictions.[1] Subsequent ecumenical councils, often well known for the content of their doctrinal debates, also contributed to the development of norms. In addition to the more solemn norms promulgated by the ecumenical councils, many other disciplinary and regulatory norms were issued by provincial and regional councils or synods too varied and numerous to list.

During the mediaeval period, in both East and West, a movement began of gathering these decisions into a single source. This saw the creation of great collections of canonical decisions, such as the *Nomocanon*, possibly re-edited in the ninth century by Photius in the East, and the Decree of Gratian in the West (c. 1140). In the case of the Decree, no effort was made to reconcile completely the different approaches taken in a wide variety of norms, hence the title of the Decree: *Concordia discordantium canonum* (the Concordance of discordant canons). After the Great Schism, traditionally dated to 1054, East and West – already following quite a distinct line in terms of canon law – developed further their own traditions.

In the Western or Latin Church (more commonly referred to as the Roman Catholic Church in ecumenical dialogue), the move towards collecting the decisions of earlier councils and Popes continued; collections were published of the decretals, generally the authoritative responses to questions or the settling of problems by successive Popes – the so-called *Liber Extra* of Gregory IX, the *Liber Sextus* of Boniface VIII, the *Clementinae*, and the *Extravagantes.* These collections of decretals, along with the Decree of Gratian, formed the *Corpus Iuris Canonici.* As such, the *Corpus* did not have any binding force, although many of the individual decisions contained in the collection did. To this fundamental collection were added subsequent decisions of popes and ecumenical councils. Needless to say, this method of compiling collections without any attempt at harmonising or integrating the various decisions meant that the practice and study of canon law within the church became increasingly complex and complicated.

Even during the First Vatican Council (1869–1870), a small but significant number of cardinals and bishops began to call for a more simplified and streamlined approach to the law of the church. Both Pope Pius X and Pope Benedict XV acknowledged that, by the turn of the twentieth century, canon law no longer responded to the historical conditions and day-to-day demands of human life. Over the course of many centuries many laws and norms had been promulgated; several of these had been abrogated or had fallen into disuse; several others appeared to serve no useful purpose. Such a situation could not be permitted to continue. In 1904, Pope Pius X established a pontifical commission for the redaction of a single unified text of the church's universal law. After a long and exhaustive process, the fruits of the commission's work were promulgated in 1917 by

1 N. Tanner, ed., *Decrees of the Ecumenical Councils* (London: Sheed & Ward, 1990) 2 vols. This includes the original texts and translations of all the ecumenical councils, from Nicaea I to Vatican II.

Pope Benedict XV as the Code of Canon Law. This completely transformed the work of the canonist. From having to sift through historical documents containing, it was said, well in excess of 10,000 pieces of law, the Code reduced it all to 2,414 canons. Each norm was a short, succinct expression that regulated some aspect of the life of the faithful and the church community.

The Pio-Benedictine Code remained in force until 1983. However, already in 1959, when he announced the celebration of the Second Vatican Council, Pope John XXIII had promised a revision of the Code in the light of major developments within the church and in wider world society. After the end of the Council, Pope Paul VI named a commission of cardinals, bishops, and experts to undertake the work of revision. Finally, on 25 January 1983, Pope John Paul II promulgated the current Code of Canon Law for the Latin Church, which took into account many of the changes to the universal law that followed the Second Vatican Council (1962–1965). In 1990, the same Pope promulgated the Code of Canons of the Eastern Churches for those *sui iuris* churches in communion with Rome (e.g. the Maronite Church, the Syro-Malabar Church); this is considered in Chapter 3.

Since the promulgation of the two Codes, there have been several interventions by the pope as the supreme legislator to complement or update the norms of the universal law – e.g. the norms for the handling of the more serious offences against morals and against the sacraments, promulgated originally in 2001 and updated in 2010. The norms of the Codes and other norms issued by the pope govern the faithful of the whole Latin Church and of those Eastern Churches in communion with the See of Rome.

2 *Universal law, particular law, proper law*

Underpinning the work of the commissions charged with the redaction of the two Codes was the principle of subsidiarity. This meant that the broad and general norm contained in each Code for the church or churches regulated by it was to find more concrete expression in other levels of legislation. Thus, alongside the norms of universal law, there are to be found in the Catholic Church a host of other legal instruments, principally those issued by diocesan bishops or religious institutes. These depend on territorial divisions or bind only certain categories of people, of which the following are principal types.

Each bishop is a legislator in his diocese, and, therefore, has the authority to promulgate laws for those who live within his diocese. The diocesan bishop governs his particular church by the exercise of legislative, executive, and judicial power. His legislative power is exercised personally. In some cases, the bishops' conference of each nation can also issue legally binding norms for the faithful of that territory. These diocesan and national norms are generally referred to as *particular law*. They are more concrete expressions of some more general law found in the Code.

Religious institutes and Societies of Apostolic Life, groupings within the Catholic Church of men and women consecrated to God by the profession of the evangelical counsels of poverty, chastity, and obedience, or dedicated by similar bonds to the work of the apostolate, also have the authority to issue binding norms. These are generally made by the members of the institutes and societies gathered in chapters or assemblies at different levels (e.g. conventual, provincial, general). Since the laws made in this way bind only those who are formally incorporated into the institutes or societies in question, these norms are referred to as *proper law*.

Although they are not strictly speaking laws in the technical sense, the regulations governing other bodies within the Catholic Church are, nevertheless, expressions of the principle of subsidiarity and can well be considered as falling into the category of proper law. These include the internal norms of associations of the faithful, juridical persons, and all those other bodies where the Code of Canon Law remits the more precise norm to be followed in each case to 'the Statutes'. These observations about the sources and forms of law in the Latin Church are reflected in the *Statement of Principles of Christian Law* (Principles I.2.1–3).

3 The scope of canon law in the life of the faithful

The laws of the Roman Catholic Church – i.e. the Latin Church – are very extensive and comprehensive in what they deal with. The Code of 1983 is divided into seven Books; the index gives a very broad indication of just how all-encompassing ecclesiastical legislation is.

Book I is entitled 'General Norms'. The first five parts of this Book give some broad general principles concerning ecclesiastical laws and other normative measures, indicating how they are to be interpreted and applied. The remaining six sections deal with various aspects of the juridical reality of the church: physical and juridical persons, juridical acts, the power of governance, ecclesiastical offices, prescription, and the computation of time. The content of the canons found in this Book is technical but essential for the correct reading, interpretation, and application of the norms found elsewhere in the Code and in the other sources of law.

Book II bears the title 'The People of God'. The title and contents reflect the self-understanding of the church that found expression in the 1964 Dogmatic Constitution of the Second Vatican Council *Lumen Gentium*. Thus, before considering the structural elements of the church and its government, Book II provides norms regulating the obligations and rights of all the faithful – the lay faithful in particular – and then of the sacred ministers or clergy. The second part of this Book presents the norms governing the structure of the church at the universal level and at the particular or diocesan level, with a lot of attention given to the internal ordering of particular churches. The final part of the Book is devoted to those groupings of the faithful formally established as Institutes of Consecrated Life and Societies of Apostolic Life. The juridical status of these groupings – as is stated explicitly in both *Lumen Gentium* and canon 207 §2 – does 'not belong to the hierarchical structure of the Church, it nevertheless belongs to its life and holiness'.

Book III is entitled 'The Teaching Function of the Church'. This is an explicit reference to the Second Vatican Council's teaching of the sharing of the Christian faithful in the three *munera Christi* – a doctrine whose formulation owes much to the teaching of John Calvin. The canons of this Book deal with the ministry of the Word of God (preaching and catechesis); missionary activity; Catholic education in schools and institutions of higher learning; instruments of social communication, especially books; and the profession of faith.

Book IV also gets its title from the Council's teaching on the three *munera Christi*. The canons of this Book are concerned with the 'Sanctifying Function of the Church'. Here are found the norms regulating the celebration of the seven sacraments (Baptism, Confirmation, Eucharist, Penance, Anointing of the Sick, Orders, and Marriage) as well as those dealing with other acts of worship and sacred places and times.

Book V is entitled 'The Temporal Goods of the Church' and is concerned with all those norms that regulate the acquisition, possession, administration, and alienation of property by the church in all its various manifestations – i.e. the universal church, the diocese, the parish, and religious institutes in general and their internal constituent parts. The canons cover practical matters such as contracts and wills.

Book VI, 'Sanctions in the Church', covers all that relates to the application and cessation of penalties as well as a general presentation of the major offences that call for such action on the part of ecclesiastical authority. These offences are grouped into seven categories, including offences against the unity of the church and offences against human life and liberty.

Book VII is perhaps the most juridically technical section of the Code, apart from Book I. It bears the simple title 'Processes' and contains all the norms that govern procedures to be used in both administrative and judicial processes within the church, identifying the principal officers of the law (judges, defenders of the bond, promoters of justice, advocates for the parties, notaries, etc.) and highlighting the rights and obligations of the faithful who, for whatever reason, feel the need to approach a church tribunal.

It would not be an exaggeration to say that the provisions of the Code of Canon Law seek to offer a general norm that regulates the life of the faithful in almost all its dimensions, from birth to death. Indeed, given the nature of the communion that the church is in Christ, canon law has also to regulate aspects of this fellowship enduring after death. Hence, there are canons on causes of canonisation; the offering that may be made to celebrate Mass for a specific intention, including for the dead; and indulgences that may be applied by way of suffrage to the dead. The particular law of each diocese or conference of bishops seeks to give a more concrete expression to these general norms, as – within a more limited context – do the provisions of the proper law of religious institutes and societies of apostolic life. The wide scope and functions of the Roman Catholic canon law, as contrasted with, say, the Anglican position (see Chapter 5), were in fact underlined by the 1976 Report of the Anglican-Roman Catholic International Commission on marriage. The Commission noted how, for Roman Catholic Christians, insofar as their life in the church is concerned, the canon law operates as a juridical expression of the church's doctrine about itself and of its pastoral responsibility for bringing the faithful to the complete awareness of and response to the redemption once wrought for them by God in Christ: in short, for their renewal in the image of God, for the enjoyment of his presence and his glory eternally. By contrast, in their ordinary Christian living, Anglicans accept the authority of the church as a moral obligation; the sense of there being a law to keep seldom occurs to them.[2] These approaches to the scope of and matters addressed by law in the Latin Church order are echoed in the *Statement of Principles of Christian Law* (Principle I.4.1).

4 Different kinds of laws/norms

To understand better the significance of canon law in the life of the Roman Catholic Church, it is important to bear in mind that not all the canons of the Code have the same juridical or theological significance. For example, within the Code it is possible to identify the following:

> Doctrinal statements that are the basis for more properly juridical norms, e.g. canon 1055 §1: '[t]he matrimonial covenant, by which a man and a woman establish between themselves a partnership of the whole of life and which is ordered by its nature to the good of the spouses and the procreation and education of offspring, has been raised by Christ the Lord to the dignity of a sacrament between the baptized'.
>
> Exhortations addressed to the faithful that may have serious juridical consequences, e.g. canon 1446 §1: '[a]ll the Christian faithful, and especially bishops, are to strive diligently to avoid litigation among the people of God as much as possible, without prejudice to justice, and to resolve litigation peacefully as soon as possible'.
>
> Norms that are based on divine positive law, i.e. certain prescriptions specifically ordained by Christ (indicated in the following by words emphasised in italics), e.g. canon 849: '[b]aptism, the gateway to the sacraments and necessary for salvation by actual reception or at least by desire, is validly conferred only by a washing *of true water* with the proper form of words'; and canon 924: '(§1) The most holy eucharistic sacrifice must be offered *with bread and with wine*. . . . (§2) The bread must be only wheat and recently made so that there is no danger of spoiling. (§3) The wine must be natural from the fruit of the vine and not spoiled'.[3]
>
> Statements that are taken by the church to be self-evident, granted its ecclesial self-understanding, e.g. canon 1254: '[t]o pursue its proper purposes,

2 *Anglican-Roman Catholic Marriage* (London: Church Information Service, 1976) 11–12.

3 A useful list of the canons in the 1983 Code of a dogmatic nature and of the canons that declare or interpret divine law is in L. Chiappetta, *Il Codice di Diritto Canonico: Commento Giuridico-Pastorale* (Bologna: Edizione Dehoniane, 3rd edition, 2011) Vol I, 5–6.

> the Catholic Church by *innate right* is able to acquire, retain, administer, and alienate temporal goods independently from civil power'; canon 1260: '[t]he Church has *an innate right* to require from the Christian faithful those things which are necessary for the purposes proper to it"; and canon 1404: '[t]he First See is judged by no one'.
>
> Clearly, juridical norms that have no origin except in positive ecclesiastical law, i.e. norms whose content and form have been determined by ecclesiastical authority, e.g. canon 119: '[w]ith regard to collegial acts, unless the law or statutes provide otherwise: (1) if it concerns elections, when the majority of those who must be convoked are present, that which is approved by the absolute majority of those present has the force of law; after two indecisive ballots, a vote is to be taken on the two candidates who have obtained the greater number of votes or, if there are several, on the two senior in age; after the third ballot, if a tie remains, the one who is senior in age is considered elected; (2) if it concerns other affairs, when an absolute majority of those who must be convoked are present, that which is approved by the absolute majority of those present has the force of law; if after two ballots the votes are equal, the one presiding can break the tie by his or her vote'; and canon 1382: '[a] bishop who consecrates someone a bishop without a pontifical mandate and the person who receives the consecration from him incur a *latae sententiae* excommunication reserved to the Apostolic See'.

This wide variety of legal and literary genres means that changes in the law are sometimes not easily made since the content of the canon pertains more to the realm of doctrine or theology than to that of legislation in the strict sense. Some of the more recent legislative interventions by Pope Francis in the domain of the procedures for obtaining a declaration of the nullity of marriage, especially his *motu proprio Mitis Iudex Dominus Iesus* (2015),[4] have had a notable impact on the doctrine surrounding moral certainty in judicial decisions but have not touched the more fundamental teaching of the church on the indissolubility of marriage. These elements of law in the Latin Church are reflected in the *Statement of Principles of Christian Law* on the structure and effect of norms (Principles I.4.2–9).

5 *The foundations of canon law in the Church*

A fundamental starting point for a reflection on the foundations of canon law in the life of the Roman Catholic Church is faith in the presence and activity of the Holy Spirit. Since the Second Vatican Council, perhaps more than ever in the church's history, there has been a greater and more conscious awareness of the activity of the Spirit. No one would assert that the Holy Spirit is the direct author of canon law or of the juridical dimension of the church; nevertheless, the Spirit's

4 *Acta Apostolicae Sedis* 107 (2015) 958–970.

role of animating, vivifying, guiding, and directing the church finds expression in the norms that are established by the competent authorities.

Another starting point is the understanding of the term 'law'. Thomas Aquinas gave two complementary definitions of law – 'Law is a rule and measure of acts'[5] and 'Law is an ordinance of reason for the common good made by the one who has care of the community and promulgated'.[6] The English word 'law' is used to translate the two Latin words *ius* and *lex*; in that sense, the English language poses something of a problem. Traditionally, the word *ius* was used to denote the objective norm by which relationships between individual citizens is regulated, the subjective rights of the individual citizens, and justice, or that which is right. The word *lex*, by contrast, was used to denote a particular written norm by which relationships were regulated, subjective rights guaranteed, or justice protected.

Laws of some kind have been part of every human civilisation. It is an innate impulse of human beings to seek to regulate their relations in some kind of structured manner. This regulation varies from the law of the state to the internal rules of a tennis club. But what is canon law? Curiously, neither the 1917 Code of Canon Law nor its successor promulgated in 1983 offers a definition of canon law; a definition is also lacking in the Code of Canons of the Eastern Churches promulgated in 1990. But, as a working definition, for the Roman Catholic Church at least, the following might be considered: canon law is a body of norms/rules/regulations issued by the lawful and competent ecclesiastical authority for the good government of the community of the faithful. In this sense, 'canon law' differs from 'ecclesiastical laws', which are regulated in some detail by the 1983 Code of Canon Law. Canon law cannot be reduced to merely ecclesiastical laws as contingent human creations because it also embodies – sometimes explicitly – divine law. Thus, a crucial feature of any Christian legal system is the origin and nature of ecclesiastical office, and canon 145§1 of the 1983 Code of Canon Law contains the fundamental statement that an ecclesiastical office is any post that, by divine or ecclesiastical disposition, is established in a stable manner to further a spiritual purpose. To give another important example, canon 22 provides that when the law of the church remits some issue to the civil law, the latter is to be observed with the same effects in canon law insofar as it is not contrary to divine law and provided it is not otherwise stipulated in canon law. As has been pointed out earlier, for the Roman Catholic Church (the Latin Church) this canon law is to be found not only in the Code of Canon Law but also in a wide variety of other legislative measures, i.e. the decrees of bishops in their dioceses; the decrees of the bishops' conferences; the constitutions, directories, and statutes of religious institutes; societies of apostolic life; public juridical persons; associations of the faithful; etc.

A reflection on the foundation of canon law must also take into account the church's self-awareness. This has been markedly renewed in the Second Vatican

5 T. Aquinas, *Summa Theologiae* I-II q 90 a 1 (Ottawa: Commissio Piana, 1953) 1206a.
6 T. Aquinas, *Summa Theologiae* I-II q 90 a 4 (Ottawa: Commissio Piana, 1953) 1209a.

Council. Never before had such attention been devoted to reflection and discussion on the nature and mission of the church. This has had an immeasurable influence in the life of Christians in the years since. One of the keys to understanding this renewed image and self-understanding of the church is to be found in the statement in the Dogmatic Constitution on the Church, *Lumen Gentium* 4: 'the universal Church is seen to be a people brought into unity from the unity of the Father, the Son and the Holy Spirit'. Whereas in previous centuries the Roman Catholic Church had described or defined itself primarily in terms of its visible, social structure, the Council focusses first and foremost on the church's identity as a supernatural mystery. It developed this through the theology of 'communion', taking the New Testament concept of 'fellowship' as a key to understanding the mystery of the church. Useful comparisons could be made at this point with the Orthodox concepts of *koinonia* and *sobornost.*

Within the documents of the Council, it is possible to discern three dimensions to this 'communion'. The first and most radical is communion with God: fellowship with the Father, through the Son, in the Spirit, which is brought about by baptism and deepened in the other sacraments; it is best seen in the reception of the Eucharist, or Holy Communion.[7] This communion with God is not an isolated relationship between God and individuals: because of their common call all Christians are in communion with one another. Thus, a unity exists between Christians gathered together as a community and between various communities. The bond of unity is the Holy Spirit; it is made concrete in charity, and its clearest expression is found in the celebration by the community of the Eucharist.[8] This bond of fellowship between Christians finds a juridical expression in the relationship that exists between the various particular churches and the Church of Rome. This ecclesiastical communion is not to be seen as a denial or a contradiction of the other levels of communion, but rather as an external manifestation of the fullness of that communion.[9]

The third dimension of communion, whilst arising out of the other two, and whilst having Christ as its source and centre (*Unitatis Redintegratio* 20), is external, juridical, and largely disciplinary in nature; it is not always necessary or accurate as an expression of the fundamental unity of the Catholic Church, which is communion with God. Given the distinction drawn by Vatican II between the different levels or dimensions of communion within the church, it is not surprising that many see here the basis of an opposition between the institutional church and the church of charity or the charismatic church. Such a vision is not new. At the beginning of the twentieth century, Rudolf Sohm, an eminent German jurist and church historian, put forward the theory that the church was wholly spiritual, whilst law was of its nature purely secular. There was, he said, no room in the

7 See *Lumen Gentium* 7b of 1964; *Unitatis Redintegratio* 2b; 15a of 1964; *Ad Gentes* 39a of 1965.

8 See *Lumen Gentium* 7b; *Unitatis Redintegratio* 7c; 14a; 15a.

9 See *Lumen Gentium* 13c; *Unitatis Redintegratio* 3a; 13b; 19a; 20.

church for law of any kind. One can see the appeal of such a theory in a church that had become so full of norms and laws that all freedom appeared to have been taken away. However, the theory itself was not accepted widely among academics. Adolf Harnack, another German, also an historian but, more importantly, the greatest patristic scholar of his day, was one of the first to refute Sohm's thesis. He showed that the early church, from its beginnings, responded to its innate need as the new 'people of God' to find appropriate structures, taking them from its Jewish heritage as well as from the secular society in which it found itself.[10]

Vatican II offered its own reflections on the subject of the relationship between the external, juridically organised church and the mystery of supernatural communion. The key to this relationship is the famous analogy between the mystery of the Incarnate Word and the mystery of the church: 'as the assumed nature, inseparably united to him, serves the divine Word as a living organ of salvation, so, *in a somewhat similar way*, does the social structure of the Church serve the Spirit of Christ who vivifies it, in the building up of the body'.[11] In this way, the spiritual community of those sharing in supernatural communion with God and the visible community are not to be considered as two separate realities or entities; rather, 'they form one complex reality which comes together from a human and divine element'.[12] In the eyes of the Council, there is no contradiction between the basic mystery of the church as a communion with the Father and the Son in the Spirit and its external and often very human juridical structure. Far from seeing any problem between these two very different aspects of the church, the Council presents them in terms of a sacrament: the church as a visible, ordered community is a sign of the invisible, supernatural life of grace, of communion with the Trinity.[13]

This renewed vision of the church as fundamentally a supernatural fellowship on many levels had an enormous influence on those who worked in the two decades after the Council preparing the revised Code of Canon Law. On several occasions, in his annual address to the Roman Rota, Pope Paul VI spoke of the nature of law in the church and its relationship to the Spirit:

> The sacramentality of the Church ensures its union with God, its supernatural effectiveness, its sense of Christ. What is more, it is animated by the Spirit who builds up and animates the Mystical Body of Christ, the People of God. It is the Spirit who transforms human beings into glorious sons and daughters of God and secures for them the liberty of God's children. It is the Spirit who induces them to pray the prayer of Jesus and is active in their apostolate. Every apostolate is an activity of Christ that can only be exercised

10 R. Sohm, *Kirkenrecht I: Die geschictlichen Grundlagen* (Leipzig: Duncker & Humboldt, 1892) 22–23, 51–56; A. von Harnack, *The Constitution and Law of the Church in the First Two Centuries* (London: Williams & Norgate, 1910) 176–257.

11 Emphasis added: *Lumen Gentium* 8.

12 Ibid.

13 *Lumen Gentium* 1.

> under the impetus of the Spirit. The Spirit searches the depths of God and knows what pleases the Lord. So he stirs up in us an ineffable prayer and carries on Christ's salvific activity through the activities of Christ's members. . . . If canon law has its foundation in Christ, the Word Incarnate, and hence serves as a sign and instrument of salvation, it does so only because of the work of the Holy Spirit, who imbues it with power and strength. Thus canon law must express the life of the Spirit, produce the fruits of the Spirit, and reveal the image of Christ. That is why it is a hierarchical law, a bond of communion, a missionary law, an instrument of grace, a law of the Church. These qualities are exigencies of the Spirit who vivifies and guides the Church, uniting it with Christ and leading it to God and to fellow humans in one and the same loving impulse.

Moreover, therefore, '[t]he Church's law has an authentically spiritual character – it must be informed by the Spirit of Christ, the Holy Spirit. Guided by reason, the Council demanded that the Church's law be truly an instrument of her spiritual life and rejected any separation between Spirit and law or between, as they say, the spiritual Church and the institutional Church. The hierarchically ordered institution, with its various levels in the People of God, is part of the very mystery of the Church'.[14]

For Pope Paul VI, the spiritual and social dimensions of the church were complementary, not in opposition. As can be seen from these references, he had a very exalted concept of law and great expectations of what it might achieve. Yet he was not blind to the shortcomings of law:

> It is unfortunately true that the Church, in the exercise of her power, whether judicial (procedural) or coercive (penal), has in the course of the centuries borrowed from civil legislations certain serious imperfections, even methods which were unjust in the true and proper sense, at least objectively speaking.

Pope John Paul II also spoke on the theme of the nature of church law:

> It is sufficiently clear that the purpose of the Code is not in any way to replace faith, grace, charisms and above all charity in the life of the Church or of Christ's faithful. On the contrary, the Code rather looks towards the achievement of order in the ecclesial society, such that while attributing a primacy to love, grace and the charisms, it facilitates at the same time an orderly development in the life both of the ecclesial society and of the individual persons who belong to it. And in fact a Code of Canon Law is absolutely necessary for the Church. Since the Church is established in the form of a social and

14 Paul VI, *Addresses to the Roman Rota* in 1973, 1976 and 1971: W Woestman, *Papal Allocutions to the Roman Rota 1939–2002* (Ottawa: St Paul University, 2002) 117, 139, and 109, respectively.

> visible unit, it needs rules, so that its hierarchical and organic structure may be visible; that its exercise of power and of the administration of the sacraments, is properly ordered; that the mutual relationships of Christ's faithful are reconciled in justice based on charity, with the rights of each safeguarded and defined; and lastly, that the common initiatives which are undertaken so that Christian life may be ever more perfectly carried out, are supported, strengthened and promoted by canonical laws.[15]

Underlying the words of both popes is the awareness that the church lives and works only under the guidance and inspiration of the Holy Spirit. One needs constantly to reflect on the radically mysterious nature of the church; only in that context does any consideration of its juridical structures make sense. It is within such a perspective that canon 276 §1 of the Code says of clerics that they are stewards of the mysteries of God in the service of his people. A brief reflection on the beginnings of canon law and its evolution in the church will be useful.

The communion of individuals with God, with one another in community, and between communities, gives rise to a whole series of obligations and rights. For example, as people chosen by God to share his divine life, Christians have the ***right*** to all the necessary aids for achieving that end; as people called to come to God not just as individuals but in communion at various levels with others, they have a ***duty*** to do all they can to preserve the bonds that unite them. From this concern to exercise rights and fulfil obligations there grew up a juridical framework sanctioned by those called to be leaders in the church. This framework also served to preserve intact the Good News received from Jesus Christ and provided a context in which it could be applied or read. At first this framework was very simple and uncomplicated. We can see the image of the early church in Acts 2: sharing everything in common, remaining faithful to the breaking of bread, to the fellowship and to the prayers, whilst meeting in one another's houses. Yet in Acts 6, we see the seven deacons being appointed by the community to exercise the service the apostles could no longer fulfil, leaving them free to devote themselves to the ministry of the Word. The decisions of the Council of Jerusalem in Acts 15 are a testimony to the early church's awareness of the human frailty of its members: henceforth the demands of the Jewish law were not to be imposed as an additional burden on Gentile Christians. In the letters of St Paul, we encounter further examples of this attention to the details of everyday life and the problems deriving from it. Thus, in 1 Corinthians 5–6, he resolves a very thorny question concerning the immoral behaviour of certain members of the community.

These decisions cannot be called 'law' in the strict sense. Nevertheless, they manifest a desire among the first Christians to establish some non-subjective

15 John Paul II, *Sacrae Disciplinae Leges*. This Apostolic Constitution promulgating the 1983 Code of Canon Law, together with the Code, in Latin and in translation is conveniently found in E. Caparros and H. Aubé, eds., *Code of Canon Law Annotated* (Montréal: Wilson & Lafleur Limitée, 2nd edition, 2004).

criterion for making decisions and resolving problems. As the centuries went by and the implications of Christian living came to be appreciated more fully, the framework protecting the Christian's rights and helping the individual fulfil his or her duties became fuller. As we have seen in the first section of this chapter, gradually, it developed into what we know now as canon law. The church has never existed as isolated, scattered communities, but rather as a communion of local communities, of particular churches, a communion of the faithful that was really a form of networking. This led to one community sharing with others how it had come to resolve a particular situation – a concrete expression of communion.

These developments took place in a church always under the influence and guidance of the Holy Spirit, a church that is, at the same time, a supernatural communion, rooted in charity and a visible, structured, all-too-human society. Very early in the process for the revision of the Code of Canon Law, following Vatican II, the commission responsible drew up guidelines for the work. One of these gives an insight into the true nature and purpose of canon law and its relationship with the Spirit in the church:

> For law, in the mystery of the Church, takes on the nature of a sacrament or sign of the supernatural life of the Christian faithful; it signifies that life and promotes it. Of course, not all the juridic norms are aimed directly toward a supernatural end or at directly promoting pastoral care. Yet it is necessary that the Church's law be in harmony with the attainment of the supernatural end by all men. Hence, the laws of the Code of Canon Law must shine forth with the spirit of charity, temperance, humaneness, and moderation, which as so many supernatural virtues distinguish the laws of the Church from every human or profane law.[16]

Insofar as it assists the faithful in living the Gospel and responding to the promptings of the Spirit, canon law within the Roman Catholic Church can be seen to be what some canonists have already called it, 'the minimum of charity', since, when viewed in the perspective of communion, canon law is the framework by which Christians are enabled to exercise their rights and fulfil their obligations. Along these lines, canon 223 §1 of the 1983 Code of Canon Law directs that in exercising their rights, Christ's faithful, both individually and in associations, must take account of the common good of the church as well as the rights of others and their own duties to others. These ideas about the purposes of law in the Latin Church are summed up the *Statement of Principles of Christian Law* (Principles I.3.1–4).

16 Pontifical Commission for the Revision of the Code of Canon Law, 'Principles Which Govern the Revision of the Code of Canon Law', *Communicationes* 2 (1969) 79; English translation in J. Hite and D. Ward, eds., *Readings, Cases, Materials in Canon Law: A Textbook for Ministerial Students* (Collegeville, Minnesota: The Liturgical Press, revised edition, 1990) 86.

II The principles of Christian law: comments and evaluation

It is with the history, origins, scope, and understanding of canon law and its role and function within the life of the Catholic Church that the following comments are offered concerning the project to elaborate a *Statement of Principles of Christian Law*. This project, evidenced in part in the text of a joint article published in 2017,[17] like so many others in the domain of ecumenical endeavour, is the fruit of several years of reflecting and listening. It is a project that is solidly based on the experience of life within many communities of the faithful following different ecclesial and ecclesiastical traditions; it is a project solidly based on the practice of the faithful within those communities. As is often the case, the project has its limitations, as will be seen later. Nevertheless, it marks a significant step forward in ecumenical study and dialogue since, for the first time, it has been possible to identify some of the basic principles that underpin the day-to-day life of the faithful in the different churches as well as the systems of governance within each church.

In this work, the (unpublished) definition of what is understood by a 'principle', clearly pivotal to the whole enterprise, is comprehensive and valuable, i.e. 'a foundational proposition or maxim of general applicability which has substance, is induced from the similarities of the regulatory systems of churches, derives from their juridical tradition or the practices of the church universal, expresses a basic theological truth or ethical value, and is implicit in, or underlies, the juridical systems of the churches'.[18] Perhaps of equal importance are the succinct narratives that come before each of the ten sections of the *Statement*. These narratives set out a number of relevant facts based on church regulatory systems, yet these narratives may not represent principles of law. In the preparatory work on the *Statement*, there was a constant awareness of the thin line that can separate a statement of fact from a principle. This thin line will merit further reflection because it is basic to the nature of the whole ecumenical juridical enterprise undertaken and would give greater precision to the conceptual rather than the simply empirical.

The published 2017 joint article 'Principles of Christian Law' does state some vital presuppositions about the project of the ecumenical panel. Drawing on the pioneering work of Professor Norman Doe, the Panel formed the view that there are principles of Christian law and church order common to the Catholic, Orthodox, Anglican, Lutheran, Methodist, Reformed, Presbyterian, and Baptist traditions and that their existence can be factually established by empirical observation and comparison. Each Christian tradition contributes through its regulatory

17 M. Hill and N. Doe, 'Principles of Christian Law', 19 *Ecclesiastical Law Journal* (2017) 138–155.

18 As agreed by the Panel at their Geneva meeting in 2017, this now reads: '[a] foundational proposition of general applicability; is induced from the similarities of the regulatory systems of the churches studied; is derived from their juridical tradition; and may reflect their theological understanding'.

instruments to this store of principles, which have a strongly theological content and are fundamental to their ecclesiological self-understanding. They have a living force and contain within themselves the possibility of further development and articulation. Cumulatively, they demonstrate a degree of unity between the churches and may be deployed in the ecumenical endeavour to enhance fuller visible unity.

Another area for further reflection as ecumenical partners debate the project is the use of the phrase 'in accordance with the law' and similar expressions. It needs to be emphasised that to subject a principle to legal provisions may be too positivistic an account of the nature of law, especially of Christian law. Some principles cannot be abolished or contradicted by the vagaries of what happens to be a church's positive law at any given time, unless it is accepted that the term 'law' is to be understood as always including divine positive law and natural law, where applicable. An illustration from the operation of current canon law would be canon 1163 §2 of the 1983 Code of Canon Law, stating that a marriage that is invalid because of an impediment of the natural law or of the divine positive law can be validated retroactively only after the impediment has ceased. In the *Statement* (I.3.4) it is asserted that '[c]hurch laws should conform to the law of God, as revealed in Holy Scripture and by the Holy Spirit'. Elsewhere, it is stated, 'A system of government used by a church reflects its conception of divine law' (IV.1.2).

This relationship between positive legal norms and divine positive/natural law, as conceived in each Christian community, is something that will bear and indeed require a lot of further reflection. An example will serve to illustrate this need. In the *Statement*, it is said that 'the Eucharist is presided over by such persons as are lawfully authorised' (VII.3.5). Empirically this is obviously true as a statement of fact, yet it presupposes a certain understanding of 'Eucharist' and how far an individual denomination can regulate what others take to be part of divine law. In the context of the bearing of divine law on human law, further reflection is needed on the contribution the Scriptures have made, make, and should make to the various forms and contents of canon law. In the Apostolic Constitution *Sacrae Disciplinae Leges* promulgating the 1983 Code of Canon Law, Pope John Paul II asked and answered a fundamental question: what is the Code? He continued by saying that for an accurate answer to this question, it is necessary to remind ourselves of that distant heritage of law contained in the books of the Old and New Testaments. It is from this, as from its first source, that the whole juridical and legislative tradition of the church derives. An ecumenical panel is well placed to make an important contribution because it would indicate in a detailed and wide-ranging way the resort actually made to biblical texts.

When taken as statements of fact – always bearing in mind the different understandings of certain terms – many of the principles identified in the *Statement* are not fundamentally problematic from the point of view of the Roman Catholic canonical tradition. Examples include the idea of law in service to the church and its activities (I.3.1–4); the structure, effect, and relaxation of norms (I.4.1–10); the functions of the laity (II.3.1–5); ecclesiastical offices (III.2.1–6); ecclesial discipline (V.1.1–5); church courts and tribunals (V.3.1–5); due process (V.4.1–5); the ownership of property (IX.1.1–5); and the control of finances (IX.3.1–5).

Other principles identified in the *Statement* are problematic to a certain degree, not necessarily because of their substance or even their desirability but because they are phrased more as aspirations than as either statements of fact or principles in the strict sense, e.g. 'a church should have institutions to legislate, administer and adjudicate for its own governance' (IV.1.3); 'the faithful should respect, honour and uphold the doctrine of their church' (VI.3.2); 'each church should promote visible unity amongst the separated churches' (VIII.2.1); and 'a church should promote social justice' (X.3.1).

The more radically problematic nature of some of the principles emerges when it comes to the section concerning the sacraments/ordinances, which has been placed under the general heading of 'the rites of the Church'. One of the main challenges is how to present such a central sphere of church life, identifying common principles whilst respecting the wide theological and doctrinal divergences between the different churches. For example, in the Roman Catholic Church tradition, the omission of the sacrament anointing of the sick is the omission of one of the seven sacraments; is it really not possible to identify a principle that touches on an important moment in the lives of Christians? The principle that 'marriage is for the well-being of the spouses' (VII.4.3) is also very problematic from the Roman Catholic perspective; as it is stated, it is obviously true as both a principle and a statement of fact. But, in its wording, it is not associated with procreation and the upbringing of children, something that has explicit expression in the canons of the Code of Canon Law and in the centuries-old theology and jurisprudence of the Catholic Church. This was a matter that was discussed explicitly in arriving at the final formulation. Nonetheless, it raises a fundamental question for all involved: to what extent can what has been identified as a shared principle of law be for some only a (very) partial account of their beliefs? Indeed, to what extent can the law at any given moment fully express beliefs?

It must be acknowledged that this is a factor in all agreed theological statements of an ecumenical character; indeed, in some sense, no ecumenical agreed statement can ever express the totality of what each of the denominations participating actually believes. Such agreed statements partake of the provisional dynamic of ecumenism as it strives under God's grace towards full unity. Church law, and its equivalent terms as expressed in the *Statement* (p. 1), whilst respecting what is immutable, needs to be provisional in the sense of being temporary and in the sense of exhibiting foresight. This will go some way towards alleviating the risk of canon law becoming in itself an obstacle to ecumenism.[19]

19 R. Ombres, 'Ecclesiology, Ecumenism and Canon Law', in N. Doe, M. Hill and R. Ombres, eds., *English Canon Law* (Cardiff: University of Wales Press, 1998) 48–59, especially 55–59, on canon law as provisional.

III The value of the *Statement of Principles of Christian Law*

The tension just highlighted between a general statement of a principle of law and a complete statement of the belief and practice of one of the churches illustrates well one of the weaknesses of the methodology adopted, i.e. the empirical approach. Nevertheless, the emergence of such tensions does not undermine the enormous value of this approach. To the degree that the *Statement of Principles of Christian Law* is based on reality and offers some reflection of the actual practice of a variety of Christian churches, it must be considered both adequate and appropriate. As they stand, the principles that have been identified are descriptive and are not in any sense prescriptive in the sense of binding upon all Christians – they are not laws – though they may be prescriptive in form when the laws from which they are drawn are prescriptive in form. As has been noted, the *Statement* constitutes a major step forward in ecumenical dialogue, not only on account of the text that has emerged but also on account of the process that was used: the respectful, courteous, and attentive listening to each of the traditions, outlining the structures, practices, and institutions that help us as individuals and communities to respond to the demands of the Gospel. It is imperative to get to know the positions of separated fellow Christians, and, as Vatican II noted,[20] study is necessarily required. This must be pursued in fidelity to the truth and with goodwill. Reflecting on the divisions, Eastern and Western, the Council concluded that these various divisions differ greatly by reason of their origins, place, and time but still more in serious matters concerning belief and the structures of the church. Significantly, the Council mentioned that from the beginning the churches of the East have had a treasury from which the Western church has drawn extensively: in liturgical practice, spiritual tradition, and legal order.

The principal value of the *Statement* is that it demonstrates how important structure of some kind is in the life of a Christian community, whether it is called law, order, or polity. The significance of this serves to highlight the basic anthropology that underlies much of Roman Catholic canon law and ecclesiology; i.e. human relationships (including our relationships with God) need the support of some kind of basic structure.

Conclusion

The joint project undertaken over some years by the Ecumenical Panel, and not yet concluded, has been a novel and pioneering experience for everyone involved. By means of this collaborative exploration, the members of each church have

20 *Unitatis Redintegratio* 9.

come to a deeper understanding of their own individual tradition in a comparative light, whilst at the same time they have sought to identify and express a substantial number of the principles of law shared with other Christians in what must be an unprecedented survey and synthesis. This chapter and the others add a wide range of individual juridical perspectives to the published *Statement of Principles.*

3 The Eastern Catholic Churches

Astrid Kaptijn

Twenty-two Eastern Catholic Churches are recognised as distinct entities within the Catholic Church.[1] They are designated by the expression 'Church *sui iuris*'. This expression allows us to distinguish each of these churches from the other and to accentuate the fact that they have a certain power of self-government in respect to the supreme authority of the Catholic Church. For a church to be defined as *sui iuris*, it is required that there should be a group of Christian faithful joined together by a hierarchy according to the norm of law; as well as these material aspects, a formal aspect is needed – namely, that the supreme authority recognises the church as being *sui iuris*.[2] Sometimes, *sui iuris* is translated as 'autonomy'. However, 'autonomy' can lead to misunderstandings if it is understood in relation to the status of the Orthodox churches. The common feature between those Orthodox churches having the status of autonomous churches and the Eastern Catholic Churches is that they both depend to a certain degree on another church (i.e. an 'autocephalous' church in orthodoxy) or other church authority (e.g. the supreme authority in the Catholic Church, which means the Roman pontiff or the College of Bishops). The dependence of the autonomous churches on the autocephalous church is limited to three points of detail; namely, (1) after election, the primate/head of an autonomous church needs confirmation by the head

1 The directory of the Catholic Church, the *Annuario Pontificio*, updated each year, contains a list of these Eastern Catholic Churches in the rubric concerning the rites in the church. Some of them have their origins in the Near, Middle, or Far East, such as the Syro-Malabar or Syro-Malankar Church (both in India) and the Maronite, Greek-Melkite, Syriac, Armenian, Coptic, or Chaldean Church. Several others originated in Eastern European countries, like the Ukrainian, Romanian, Hungarian, Slovak, or Bulgarian Church. They differ in terms of numbers of faithful.

2 Code of Canons of the Eastern Churches (in Latin, *Codex Canonum Ecclesiarum Orientalium*, abbreviated as CCEO), c.27. According to A. Valiyavilayil, the definition is defective since it can also be applied to e.g. the diocese that is a church – more precisely a particular church. So, the definition does not describe exactly what is a church *sui iuris*. See A. Valiyavilayil, 'The Notion of *sui iuris* Church', in J. Chiramel and K. Bharanikulangara, eds., *The Code of Canons of the Eastern Churches: A Study and Interpretation, Essays in Honour of Joseph Cardinal Parecattil* (Alwaye: St. Thomas Academy for Research, 1992) 57–90 (esp. 60, footnote 9).

of the autocephalous church on which it depends; (2) conflicts between bishops and the primate of the autonomous church are resolved by the autocephalous church; (3) the autonomous church receives the Holy Myron – the oil used in the celebration of several sacraments – from the autocephalous church since it is the head of this church that fabricates and consecrates it.[3] In the Catholic Church, other matters are also involved, and the 'autonomy' of the Eastern Catholic Churches is always related to the supreme authority of the church. Autonomy does not mean independence or sovereignty; it means self-rule but in the framework of the norms of a higher law and in respect to a higher authority.[4]

The designation as a church *sui iuris* is not enough, however – a further juridical status should be attributed to an Eastern Catholic Church. Eastern church law provides for four different categories: patriarchal churches, major archiepiscopal churches, metropolitan churches *sui iuris*, and others. The last is a category so heterogeneous that no specific designation could be appropriate. These categories determine different juridical statuses, from the largest degree of 'autonomy' in respect to the supreme authority of the Catholic Church, attributed to the patriarchal churches, to the smallest degree for the 'other' churches *sui iuris.*

I The law of the Eastern Catholic Churches

1 Sources, forms, and subject matter of church law

The Eastern Catholic Churches *sui iuris* share a common code of church law, *Codex Canonum Ecclesiarum Orientalium* (CCEO), or Code of Canons of the Eastern Churches. Promulgated in 1990, it came into force 1 October 1991. As its title indicates, the official language of the Code is Latin because no single language is shared by all 22 Eastern Churches.

The word 'canons' in the title does not simply designate the individual provisions in the Code (though they are indeed called canons) but refers principally to the canons of the first millennium. Here we come to the question of the sources of the law in the Eastern Catholic Churches. The Holy See and the drafters of the Code understood that the Eastern Catholic Churches share a common heritage in the canons of the first millennium. They all more or less recognise the sources canonised by each ecumenical council and listed by the Council in Trullo (690–691); namely, the disciplinary canons of the earlier ecumenical councils (and added later were the disciplinary canons of Nicaea II, 787) and a number of regional synods held in the period from 314 to 419, canons of two synods convoked in the ninth century, the disciplinary canons

3 D. Salachas, 'Autocéphalie ou autonomie des Eglises orthodoxes et status « sui iuris » des Eglises orientales catholiques', in R. Coppola, ed., *Incontro fra canoni d'Oriente e d'Occidente. Proceedings of the International Congress "The Meeting of Eastern and Western Canons"*, Vol. I (Bari: Cacucci Editore, 1994) 369–392 at 372–379.

4 See A. Valiyavilayil, op cit., 81–90.

of Greek Church fathers, and the 85 canons of the apostles. It is precisely because of this common heritage that the drafters thought it was possible to prepare a common code for all the Eastern Catholic Churches despite their different traditions and rites.[5]

These differences among the Eastern traditions and disciplinary heritage can be reflected in 'particular law'.[6] Each church *sui iuris* exercises, to a variable extent, legislative power, normally through its synods of bishops, when these exist. This means that the synods are able to issue norms of particular law that may themselves be inspired by the legal traditions of the church in question. Eparchial (equivalent to diocesan) bishops also have the power to legislate for their own eparchies. Customs, statutes, and other norms can also be sources of particular law whenever they do not concern the entire Catholic Church or all of the Eastern Churches.[7]

The notion of 'proper law' is also used in the Code. It speaks, for instance, of the proper marriage law of a church or ecclesial community to which non-Catholic–baptised persons belong.[8] In a more general way, the canon law tradition designates by the expression 'proper law' the law that concerns only a specific category of faithful in the Catholic Church.[9] Canon law also speaks of 'special law' in cases in which circumstances oblige the church authorities

5 This hypothesis has been criticised by e.g. D. Schon, *Der* Codex Canonum Ecclesiarum Orientalium *und das authentische Recht im christlichen Orient: eine Untersuchung zur Tradition des Kirchenrechts in sechs katholischen Ostkirchen* (Würzburg: Augustinus Verlag, 1999) (Das östliche Christentum, Neue Folge, Bd.47).

6 For a systematic presentation see S. Kokkaravalayil, 'Particular Law. Possibilities and Limits', in J. Faris and J. Abbass, eds., *A Practical Commentary to the Code of Canons of the Eastern Churches* (Chambly (Qc), Canada: Wilson and Lafleur. 2019) cxli–clv.

7 CCEO, c.1493 §2. It is difficult to access particular laws of these churches since they are normally in the language of the church. Also, often, several editions have been published since the promulgation of the CCEO in 1990, but it is not always easy to find the most recent on the internet. For example, the minimum age for marriage is fixed by the CCEO at 16 for men and 14 for women, but a higher age may be set by particular law. Several churches refer in their particular law to civil law of the place on this matter. In the Syro-Malabar Church in India, it is 21 for men and 18 for women: 2003 law, art. 181: www.smcim.org//files/portal/news/attach1_1389.pdf. This church also has particular law on permanent deacons (ibid. art.53–84), under CCEO c.327; the minor orders (ibid. art. 29–31); and 'palliyogam', a form of parish council with laity: see 'Palliyogam – Procedure Rules', ibid. pp. 53–77. Another example concerns the office of Patriarch or Major Archbishop. For these offices, candidates must fulfil the CCEO requirements for candidature to the episcopate. However, particular law can specify other requirements. For instance, under CCEO c.180, the minimum age to become bishop is 35, with 5 years' experience as a priest. But in the Ukrainian Church the minimum age is 40 to be elected head of that church, with at least 10 years' experience as a priest: Canons, art.2: http://archeparchy.ca/wcm-docs/docs/Particular_Law_Canons.pdf.

8 CCEO, c.781 §2,1°.

9 CCEO, c.387, e.g., which deals with the attire of clerics, is an example of proper law since no categories of faithful other than clerics are treated by it. However, the canon does not use the expression *proper law* and refers to particular law to detail what type of attire clerics should wear.

to adapt universal norms. Very often this implies derogations from those universal norms.[10]

Furthermore, Pope John Paul II stated, in the Apostolic Constitution by which he promulgated the Code, that this common heritage of the first millennium is also shared by those Eastern churches that are not yet in full communion with the Catholic Church.[11] Therefore, the pope reminds us, quoting the decree on the Eastern Churches issued by the second Vatican Council,[12] that the Eastern Churches, in full communion with the Apostolic See, have a special task of fostering the unity of all Christians, particularly those of the Eastern Churches. For the pope, the new Code is not an obstacle but a great help to realise the perfect unity of the entire Church of Christ.

The role of these ancient sources of law is also mentioned by the pope: 'this Code . . . must be considered to be assessed most of all according to the ancient law of the Eastern Churches'.[13] This corresponds to canon 2 of the Code, treating its relationship to the ancient law of the Eastern Churches.[14] Commentators, in line with Vatican Council II, which wished for a return of the Eastern Catholic Churches to the ancestral traditions, to the extent that they had deviated from them,[15] underline that canon 2 advocates continuity between the ancient and the actual law. The 'ancient law' is not the law as it has been received, adapted, or interpreted across the centuries, and especially during the first codification (see below, p. 51), but the original proper law of the first centuries. It is the main criterion for the evaluation and interpretation of the canons of the Code.

One reference to the ancient law is found in canon 1501 of the Code, which establishes how to resolve a case when a prescript of law is lacking. The first criterion to be used is the canons of the synods and holy fathers, and the second criterion is legitimate custom. In turn, canon 1506 provides that a custom may obtain the force of law (legitimacy) insofar as it corresponds to the action of the Holy Spirit in the ecclesial body. Even though the canon does not name ancient law explicitly, it does so implicitly because the Holy Spirit is considered to have been active in the councils and synods of the first centuries. It is on the basis of this inspiration of the Holy Spirit with respect to the bishops gathered in these

10 Examples can be found in former Czechoslovakia concerning the ordination of Catholic priests or in the Catholic Church in China, where special faculties have been issued to the bishops and priests. See Benedict XVI, Letter to the Bishops, Priests, Consecrated Persons and Lay Faithful of the Catholic Church in the People's Republic of China, 27 May 2007, www.vatican.va/content/benedict-xvi/en/letters/2007/documents/hf_ben-xvi_let_20070527_china.html.

11 John Paul II, *Sacri Canones*, 18 October 1990, *Code of Canons of the Eastern Churches*, Latin-English Edition (Washington, DC: Canon Law Society of America, 1995) xxi–xxviii (esp. xxii).

12 Decree, *Orientalium Ecclesiarum* (hereafter OE) n.24.

13 John Paul II, op cit., xxiii.

14 CCEO, c. 2: '[t]he canons of the Code, in which the ancient law of the Eastern Churches has been mostly received or adapted, are to be assessed chiefly by that law'.

15 OE, n. 6.

assemblies, or to those who were later designated as the church fathers, that the canons of the first millennium are called 'sacred'.[16]

One of the canons on the rites in the Eastern Catholic Churches describes them as 'the patrimony of the whole Church of Christ in which shines forth the tradition coming down from the Apostles, through the Fathers'.[17] Since rites consist not only of the liturgical heritage but also the theological, spiritual, and disciplinary heritage, we might stress the continuity between this patrimony and actual rites and norms. In general, tradition and the ancient law play a more important role in the law of Eastern Catholic Churches than in Latin church law, in which it is not absent but has a more secondary or auxiliary place. In this sense, the Eastern Catholic Churches are closer to the Orthodox Church, where the ancient canons are the principal sources of law.[18]

The subjects treated by church law are the rights and obligations of the faithful, the hierarchical constitution of the church and its institutions, the religious life, associations of the faithful, the ecclesiastical magisterium, sacraments, temporal goods, trials and sanctions, and the exercise of legislative and executive power. Unlike the Latin Code, the Eastern Code is divided into titles. This scheme echoes the different Byzantine collections called Nomocanons, which gathered the imperial law about the church and the canons of the church itself. The Nomocanons were organised in titles.[19] The Eastern Code of Canons has 30 titles.

According to the first canon, the Code concerns all and only the Eastern Catholic Churches. However, there are exceptions. The same canon also provides that things may be expressly established otherwise with regard to relations with the Latin Church. Indeed, about ten canons explicitly mention the Latin Church and so also bind the Latin faithful concerned.[20] According to the Pontifical Council for Legislative Texts, in 2011, concerning this first canon, whenever the Code uses the expression 'Church *sui iuris*' in the context of relations between the faithful who belong to different churches *sui iuris*, the expression applies to the Latin Church as well.[21]

16 See John Paul II, Apostolic Constitution *Sacri Canones*, 18 October 1990, in Code of Canons of the Eastern Churches. Latin-English Edition. New English Translation, Washington, Canon Law Society of America, 2001, xxi. See also, Dimitrios Salachas, Commentary on c.2, in *A Practical Commentary to the Code of Canons of the Eastern Churches*, op.cit., 51–52.

17 CCEO, c. 39.

18 See Chapter 4.

19 For instance, the Nomocanon in 14 titles or the Nomocanon in 50 titles. These collections were composed from the sixth century onwards and appeared in several editions. See W. Hartmann and K. Pennington, eds., *The History of Byzantine and Eastern Canon Law to 1500* (Washington, DC: The Catholic University of America Press, 2012).

20 Two examples: c.207 establishes that an eparchial bishop, even of the Latin Church, is to inform the Apostolic See in his quinquennial report about the state and the needs of the faithful ascribed in another church *sui iuris* but committed to his care; c.830 §1, about celebration of marriage: the local hierarch (ordinary) and the local pastor may give a faculty to bless a determined marriage to priests of any church *sui iuris*, even of the Latin Church.

21 Pontifical Council for Legislative Texts, *Nota explicativa quoad* can. 1 CCEO, 8 December 2011, in *Communicationes*, XLII (2011) 315–316.

The Code is the product of what is called the second process of codification. A first tentative codification started in the 1930s, when the decision was taken to prepare one common Code for all Eastern Catholic Churches. Two commissions were set up: one to harvest sources and another to draft the Code. The former was charged with gathering the sources of church law according to the different Eastern traditions; its work resulted in 50 volumes of sources. The latter commission submitted a draft Code in 1945 to Pope Pius XII, but he did not promulgate it. According to some, the pope considered the project too much influenced by the Latin Code of 1917. Indeed, many draft canons were copies of the Latin canons. However, the pope decided to promulgate one part of the project in 1949 – the canons on marriage. In 1950 followed the canons on trials, in 1952 those on religious life and temporal goods, and, finally, in 1957 those on persons and rites (including the hierarchical constitution of the churches). In December 1958, the commission proposed to Pope John XXIII that he promulgate the canons on sacraments, but he declined to do so. One month later, he announced the convocation of a general council and the revision of all the canon law of the Catholic Church, Latin and Eastern. Therefore, on the eve of Vatican II, the Eastern Catholic Churches did not have a complete code, only partial legislation. They had to wait until after the end of the Council, when, in 1974, a new commission was constituted to draft a new code. Here the second process of codification starts, ending with promulgation of the CCEO in 1990.

2 *Foundations and reasons for the law*

Eastern canon law has theological foundations. As Pope John Paul II stated, when promulgating the Code, the salvation of the souls is the ultimate goal of all the laws in the church.[22] Several canons of the Code also refer to this supernatural goal.[23] The theological foundations are also connected with divine law. A distinction is made between positive divine law and natural law.

Positive divine law may be found in the New Testament and Apostolic tradition. It obviously does not present itself in the form of juridical norms, but concerns elements of Christian faith that are considered to reflect the Lord's will and are therefore essential for Christian faith and identity. Because divine law is reflected in writing, it is called 'positive'. By way of contrast, divine natural law does not need to be put in writing since it is inherent to human nature; it can be identified by human intelligence. Consequently, divine natural law applies to all humans, whilst positive divine law has mandatory force in respect of Christians only. Therefore, within the Catholic Church, divine law is the same for the faithful of the Latin Church *sui iuris* and for those belonging to the Eastern Catholic Churches. The Catholic Church even applies it to other Christians whenever they

22 John Paul II, op cit., xxiv.
23 See for instance CCEO, c.595 §2; 727; 1397; 1519 §1; 873 §2; 1000 §2 and 1110 §1.

establish a relationship to the Catholic Church.[24] The interpretation of both types of divine law, however, depends on the doctrine of the church. The ecclesiastical magisterium 'discovers' and declares what is of divine law – it does not establish norms of divine law in the sense that it cannot be the author of divine law. Divine law, so far as concerns its interpretation and its content, is more relevant to the ecclesiastical magisterium than to the canon law. The latter adopts magisterial interpretations as the foundations of its own norms.

Divine law is considered to be immutable. Its content does not change – it remains the same since its revelation. The only changes in respect to divine law derive from our human understanding of it. Because human knowledge progresses, our understanding of divine law might also develop. On the basis of this notion of divine law, the Catholic Church in general speaks of canon law in respect to its legislative system and not just of church law or discipline since divine law is part of canonical legislation. Indeed, the canon law of the Catholic Church has its grounds in the doctrine of the church, whilst church law or discipline, mainly as understood in the churches of the Protestant traditions, finds its reason of existence in the need to organise the life of the group or community.[25] The expression 'Church law' can easily be misunderstood when associated with norms established by the church itself, thus stressing their human origin. In the Catholic Church, this could apply only partly to the norms of canon law. Some are of purely human origin, are called ecclesiastical law, and can be changed; others are of divine law.

Divine law also establishes a hierarchy among the norms of canon law. Norms that are of divine law are the most important and stable norms within the canonical system. Some authors are even of the opinion that all the norms of canon law derive from divine law, that they may have a very close or else a somewhat looser relation to divine law, but each norm in a certain sense finds its origin in divine law. This view seems to be a way to stress the sacred character of canon law as well as its difference from civil law systems.

Two notions are crucial in canon law, Latin and Eastern; namely, validity and liceity. Validity concerns the elements necessary for a juridical act (e.g. a sacrament) to be recognised as genuine. Liceity, by contrast, cannot affect the existence of an act, but it translates and stresses its theological aspect. The sacrament of baptism is an example. Necessary for its validity are the use of natural water and the Trinitarian formula – that is, the invocation of the name of God the Father, Son, and Holy Spirit[26] – but the norm that baptism should be ordinarily celebrated in a parish church concerns only its liceity. However, this does not

24 An example is the sacramentality of marriage. A valid marriage contract concluded by two baptised persons is a sacrament. The Catholic Church applies this to all baptised, irrespective whether they are baptised in the Catholic Church. This will have some importance only when a baptised non-Catholic addresses themselves to the Catholic Church – for instance after a first marriage in view of a new marriage celebration with a Catholic person.

25 See P. Valdrini, 'Discipline ecclésiastique', in Jean-Yves Lacoste, ed., *Dictionnaire critique de théologie* (Paris: Quadrige-PUF, 2002) 338.

26 CCEO, c.675 §1.

mean that it is completely optional. The church expresses a preference for this norm because of its theological meaning: the norm stresses the connexion of administering baptism with a concrete community of the faithful in which the baptised person is received and incorporated. Yet this norm does not have the same strength as that concerning the validity of the sacrament of baptism.

The second Vatican Council also prescribes that there should be a relationship between canon law and theology; as such, the teaching of canon law should take into account the mystery of the church according to the Dogmatic Constitution on the Church issued by the Council.[27]

The connexion between theology and canon law may also be found in the reasons for particular norms of canon law. The reasons why a concrete norm has been issued by the ecclesiastical authority have to do with what is called the *mens legislatoris* – the mind of the legislator. The underlying idea is that the legislator wants to achieve a certain goal with a norm or to bring the faithful to realise certain values. Considering this goal and the needs of the community, the legislator issues a specific norm. Therefore, identifying the mind of the legislator discloses the reason for the norm in question (which may include theological reasons). Consequently, evidence of the legislative intent may be found in the process involved in drafting the norm.[28]

Moreover, the *rationabilitas*, or rationality, of the law characterises in a more general way the canon law of the Catholic Church. Patrick Valdrini describes the different views in the history of canon law concerning the definition of the law. St Thomas Aquinas highlighted the rational character of the content of the law since it is promulgated for the common good of the church, whilst Suarez stressed the fact that the law is the result of the work of the legislator who finds its force in the act of promulgation. Both views and definitions are complementary.[29] Valdrini explains that canon law wanted to go beyond the principle '*Quod principi placuit, legis habet vigorem*' (what pleases the prince has force of law). The rational character of the law has to do with the scope of the law, which is the promotion of the common good of the church.[30] It therefore attributes an

27 Decree, *Optatam Totius*, 28 October 1965, n. 16.

28 Traditionally, *mens legislatoris* is a key for understanding the norm even if used only as a second step. See CCEO, c.1498 and its equivalent in CIC, c.17. Canon law as a law system to which one chooses to adhere, since there is no obligation to do this, appeals to the conscience of the faithful in view of the respect of the laws. In church life, *mens legislatoris* helps to make a norm more understandable and acceptable. It is easier to convince the faithful to observe a norm when they understand the reason for its existence. This has to do with the rational character of the law (see upcoming discussion) as well as respect of the faithful, who are intelligent and educated people. We are not anymore in a model of authority where some dictate what has to be done and others just have to execute the orders.

29 P. Valdrini, 'La réception de la loi en droit canonique: pertinence et signification', 50 *L'année canonique* (2008) 11–30 at 15.

30 P. Valdrini, *Leçons de droit canonique. Communautés, personnes, gouvernement* (Paris: Editions Salvator, 2017) 444.

important role to the community.[31] The rational character of the law, stressing the common good of the community, also has in mind the promotion of unity and communion in the church, as well as justice, in the sense of righteousness, of the decisions that are taken. Consequently, it is closely linked to the exercise of power in the church.[32] The rational character has to be kept in mind during the legislative process and in other decisions. Thus, canon law puts into practice mechanisms of consultation, motivation, and synodality.[33]

3 *Principles of law in the traditions of the Eastern Catholic Churches*

The category 'general principles of canon law' is used in the juristic traditions of the Eastern Catholic Churches. It is found in canon 1501 of the Code, which prescribes how to resolve a case when an express prescript of law is lacking.[34] Interestingly, the category is designated general principles of canon law, not simply 'law' in general.[35] Therefore, there is a limit on the field in which juridical principles can be sought. We might even ask whether the category includes the general principles of Roman law contained in the famous *regulae iuris*. For several reasons, we are inclined to respond positively to this question. First, one canon in earlier Eastern Catholic legislation included Roman law as a source that could be used to resolve a *lacuna legis*; it was mentioned quite separately from the general principles of canon law.[36] From this distinction, as well as the fact that Roman law is not now specified in canon 1501, we might conclude that no importance is now attached to Roman law as such or to its principles expressed in the *regulae iuris*. However, since canon 1501 prescribes that the general principles of canon law have to be applied with equity, this category could include equity as understood in Roman law, which in turn might include the *regulae iuris* or even any other type of law.[37] Moreover, one edition of the Code includes, when it lists the sources of canon 1501, the Digests of Justinian (which contain *regulae iuris*).[38]

31 P. Valdrini, 'La réception' (2008), op cit., 25.
32 P. Valdrini, *Leçons* (2017), op cit., 23.
33 Ibid., 96, 98, 172, 368, 400, 439–440, 444, 446 and 496.
34 CCEO, c.1501.
35 As is the case in the CIC, c.19.
36 The text was planned for the canon that corresponds to our current c.1501. It is part of the canons that never have been promulgated and, thus, remained in the archives. We know about it since the periodical *Nuntia* 2 (1976) 68 mentions, under the '*Testi iniziali*', can.16: '*[s]i certa de re desit expressum praescriptum legis sive universalis sive particularis, norma sumenda est, nisi lex ipsa aliud expresse statuat, a legibus latis in similibus, a canonibus Patrum, a generalibus principiis primum iuris canonici, dein, aequitate canonica servata, iuris romani, a communi constantique sententia doctorum*'.
37 See V. De Paolis, commentary on canon 1501, in G. Nedungatt, ed., *A Guide to the Eastern Code: A Commentary on the Code of Canons of the Eastern Churches* (Rome: Pontificio Istituto Orientale, 2002) (*Kanonika*, 10), 824.
38 See the edition with the sources of CCEO. As to c. 1501, the sources mentioned are D.1, 3, 4–6, 12–13, and 32.

The sources of many other canons also refer to the Digests. Further study should be undertaken to examine whether these references concern the *regulae iuris*. Even if references to these sources do not have any official authority, they nevertheless have been established by the person responsible for drafting the Code from the beginning – the secretary of the commission.[39] One special reference can be found in a canon on processes since it expressly quotes one of the *regulae iuris*. This canon provides that litigation begins with the legitimate citation of the parties or when they have appeared before the judge to pursue the case, and that, therefore, the principle 'while litigation is pending, nothing is to be innovated' takes effect immediately.[40] There are also other notions with respect to the implementation and application of the law. Generally, notions like the salvation of souls, the public good of the church or common benefit, human dignity and the fundamental rights of the human person, justice, equity, necessity, utility, or advantage to the church appear frequently in norms and should guide their interpretation and application.[41]

4 Unity of faith and diversity of law

The compatibility of unity of faith and diversity of law or disciplines is particularly clear in Catholic canon law. Since the nineteenth century, with the statements of Pope Leo XIII, the Catholic Church has adhered to the idea that diversity of disciplines is not prejudicial to the unity of faith. What is more, diversity confirms the unity of faith.[42] This has also been repeated by the Second Vatican Council in its decree on the Eastern Churches.[43] Moreover, the decree on ecumenism highlights the variety of laws and customs as well as the variety in the theological

39 Pontificium Consilium de Legum Textibus Interpretandis, *Codex Canonum Ecclesiarum Orientalium, auctoritate Ioannis Pauli PP.II promulgatus. Fontium annotatione auctus*, Libreria Editrice Vaticana, 1995. The presentation drafted by the president of this pontifical council, Archbishop Iulius Herranz, mentions that the edition has been prepared by Father Ivan Žužek S.J., undersecretary of the pontifical council and formerly secretary of the pontifical commission for the revision of the Code of Eastern Canon Law.

40 CCEO, c.1191, 5°. The source referred to is D.11, 6.1.

41 The salvation of souls appears e.g. in c. 1397 on the transfer of pastors. The eparchial bishop should take into account the good of souls or the necessity of the church when taking his decision. In the procedure for issuing extra-judicial decrees, the salvation of souls and the public good should be kept in mind, observing the laws and legitimate customs, but also justice and equity: c.1519 §1. Equity plays an important role in several fields, especially where the good of a person is at stake: e.g. the canons concerning a person who leaves a monastery, an order, or a congregation legitimately or who is dismissed from the institute. The person cannot request anything for the work he or she has accomplished, but the institute is to observe equity and charity towards the separated member: cc.503, 553 and 562. The same applies in cases of an imposed exclaustration: cc. 490 and 548 §2.

42 CCEO, c.39 speaking about the rites in the Church of Christ. See above, n. 14.

43 *Orientalium Ecclesiarum*, 21 November 1964, 1–2: 'the variety within the Church in no way harms its unity; rather it manifests it, for it is the mind of the Catholic Church that each individual Church or Rite should retain its traditions whole and entire and likewise that it should adapt its way of life to the different needs of time and place'.

expressions of doctrine. For example, as to theological diversity, the decree stresses the complementarity rather than conflicts among them.[44] In my opinion, this might also apply to laws and customs. If expressions of shared theology may differ in terms of their form,[45] so laws and customs inspired by them or by other motivations might also adopt different legal forms.

5 *Impact of civil law as a force of change in church law*

It is well known that, historically, several Eastern Churches depended in many ways on the Byzantine emperor. One of the clearest early examples of the impact of civil law concerns the form for the celebration of marriage. Emperor Leo VI introduced in 893 the requirement of a sacred rite for a marriage to be recognised as civilly and religiously valid.[46] The sacred rite specifically required the blessing of the spouses (coronation) by a priest or bishop. This entered the legislation of churches of the Byzantine tradition, and it has been adopted by churches of other traditions. A sacred rite is still mandatory in the law of the Eastern Catholic Churches.

In general, the Catholic Church has been reluctant to accept civil influences as a stimulus to change its canon law on the basis of its long-standing insistence upon its own sovereignty.[47] However, the codifications in the Catholic Church were directly based on the adoption of the civil codes of Napoleon in the early

44 *Unitatis Redintegratio*, 21 November 1964, 16: '[f]ar from being an obstacle to the Church's unity, a certain diversity of customs and observances only adds to her splendor, and is of great help in carrying out her mission . . . this holy Council solemnly declares that the Churches of the East, while remembering the necessary unity of the whole Church, have the power to govern themselves according to the disciplines proper to them, since these are better suited to the character of their faithful, and more for the good of their souls. The perfect observance of this traditional principle not always indeed carried out in practice, is one of the essential prerequisites for any restoration of unity'; and 17 continues: '[i]n the study of revelation East and West have followed different methods, and have developed differently their understanding and confession of God's truth. It is hardly surprising, then, if from time to time one tradition has come nearer to a full appreciation of some aspects of a mystery of revelation than the other, or has expressed it to better advantage. In such cases, these various theological expressions are . . . mutually complementary rather than conflicting'. What is stated here as to the Eastern churches has no equivalent in the same decree regarding the churches in the West. However, the declaration on religious freedom, *Dignitatis humanae*, 7 December 1965, recognises that they have the freedom to govern themselves according to their own norms (see no. 4).

45 Examples of recognition of sharing the same faith in spite of differences in theological expression can be found in common declarations made by the head of the Catholic Church and those of Oriental Orthodox churches in past decades. See common declarations concluded in 1971, 1973, 1984, and 1996: www.vatican.va/roman_curia/pontifical_councils/chrstuni/sub-index/index_ancient-oriental-ch_it.htm.

46 Leo VI, Novella 89. See P. Noailles-A. Dain, *Les Novelles de Léon le Sage* (Paris: Belles Lettres, 1944) 295.

47 See M. Zimmerman, *Structure sociale et Eglise. Doctrines et praxis des rapports Eglise-Etat du XVIIIe* siècle à Jean-Paul II (Strasbourg: Cerdic Publications, 1983) 2.

nineteenth century. Within the Catholic Church, the change in juristic technique from compilations to codifications was not purely ecclesial in stimulus.[48]

II Challenges in the articulation of principles of Christian law

Whilst not having taken part in the formulation of the *Statement of Principles of Christian Law* (2016),[49] the following expresses my thoughts about the methodology used and the content of the principles. I shall seek to evaluate in what ways the principles are or might be problematic from the distinct perspective of the canon law of the Eastern Catholic Churches.

1 Unproblematic principles

Most of the sections and the principles they contain are unproblematic. That is so, for instance, with Section I on the systems of laws and polity; Sections VIII-X on ecumenism, church property, and church-state relations; and large parts of Section V on ecclesial discipline. With respect to ecumenism, however, the principle that 'the purpose of ecumenism' is 'greater ecclesial communion'[50] represents, from the Eastern Catholic perspective, merely one stage in the wider understanding of ecumenism in the Code: the 'reestablishment' or 'restoration of unity'.[51] However, this nuance, important though it is, must be balanced against the principles of law of the church universal,[52] which are broadly shared by Eastern Catholic Churches.[53]

Similarly, whilst the principle that church laws 'principally deal with ministry, government, doctrine, worship, rites, admonition and discipline, and property'[54] is consistent with the Eastern Catholic Code, it is also a principle in that Code

48 See J. Gaudemet, 'Collections canoniques et codifications', XXXIII *Revue de Droit Canonique* (1983) 2, 81–109 (esp.97–109) and O. Echappé, 'Histoire des sources du droit canonique', in P. Valdrini, J-P. Durand, O. Echappé et J. Vernay, eds., *Droit canonique* (Paris: Editions Dalloz, 1999) 13–15.

49 I joined the Panel in 2017 for its meeting with the WCC Faith and Order Commission in Geneva.

50 *Statement of Principles of Christian Law* (2016) (hereafter SPCL): VIII.2.3.

51 CCEO, c.902. The CCEO contains a whole chapter on ecumenism (cc. 902–908).

52 SPCL VIII.1.1–4.

53 If we set aside the question of terminology – the SPCL speak of 'the Church universal', a reality indicated in the CCEO by the expression 'Church of Christ' – we can conclude that the Eastern Catholic Churches share the substance of these principles of law of the church universal. C.177 §1 describes the relationship between a particular church (for instance an eparchy) and the one, holy, catholic, and apostolic Church of Christ that exists and is operative in the particular church. Since the Second Vatican Council, the terminology used ('Churches who do not have full communion with the Catholic Church'; see c.671 §3) indicates that there is already a degree of communion with the other churches and ecclesial communities, but for the moment it is an imperfect communion.

54 SPCL I.4.1.

that church law deals with church membership and the rights and obligations of the faithful; it may be that this is captured by the word 'ministry' in the principle of law cited earlier – and, indeed, the principle that 'the law of a church should generally set out the basic rights and duties of all of its members'[55] is an assumption underlying the Code in its articulation of these.[56]

Principles that are almost identical to norms of the CCEO can be found all over the *Statement*. SPCL II.1 corresponds to the CCEO, stating that, through baptism, the faithful are constituted as the people of God.[57] Since this text is the opening canon of the title on rights and obligations of all the faithful, it is clear that these are generated by baptism. The equal dignity *and activity* of the faithful are expressed in another canon of this title.[58] Implicitly, it is clear that these norms concern the faithful, independent of the fact that they are laypeople or ordained, since other canons detail specific rights and obligations of these two categories of faithful.[59]

The principle that ordained ministry is divine in origin and that persons are set apart for it corresponds to different norms of the CCEO. A key canon in this context is the one describing sacred ordination that implies at the same time different types of ordained ministers.[60] The norm concerning the power of governance, stating that it exists in the church by divine institution and that those who are constituted in sacred orders are qualified for its exercise, also stresses the divine character of ministry in the Eastern Catholic Churches.[61]

SPCL V.5.3–5, on discipline, corresponds pretty well to the CCEO. It prescribes, for instance, 'Since God employs every means to bring back the erring sheep, those who have received from Him the power to loose and to bind are to apply suitable medicine to the sickness of those who have committed delicts, reproving, imploring and rebuking them with the greatest patience and teaching. Indeed, they are even to impose penalties in order to heal the wounds caused by the delict, so that those who commit delicts are not driven to the depth of despair nor are restraints relaxed unto a dissoluteness of life and contempt of the law'. This norm expresses well the healing character of penal law and underlines that the first reaction should not be to punish immediately but to have recourse to other means of mediation. The lawful character of trials and sanctions is part of

55 SPCL II.23.1.

56 See CCEO, Title I. The Rights and Obligations of all the Christian Faithful, cc.7–26. In this title are listed the fundamental rights and obligations of each of the faithful. More precise rights and duties, in conformity with the statute of the faithful in the church, are detailed in other parts of the CCEO.

57 CCEO, c.7 §1.

58 CCEO, c.11, which also is part of Title I.

59 See CCEO, cc.367–393 concerning clerics and cc.399–409 with regard to laypeople.

60 CCEO, c.743: through sacramental ordination performed by the bishop, sacred ministers are constituted by the working of the power of the Holy Spirit; they are endowed with and share in varying degrees in the task and power entrusted by Christ to his apostles to announce the gospel, to shepherd and sanctify the people of God.

61 See CCEO, c.979 §1.

the charter of rights and obligations of all the faithful.[62] They find further application in norms detailing the procedure to impose them by way of a penal trial or by extra-judicial decree.[63] Removal from office and excommunication are part of the sanctions under the CCEO,[64] which also deals with the removal of sanctions.[65]

SPCL VI.2, on proclamation of the faith, corresponds to CCEO norms on the rights and obligations of the faithful; the rights and obligations of laypeople; the teaching function of the church; and preaching by bishops, priests, and deacons.[66] SPCL VII.3, with its different aspects of the celebration of the Eucharist, corresponds well to the norms of the CCEO on this topic.[67]

2 *Problematic principles*

There are, very often, in the *Statement* principles of law that are somewhat problematic for the Eastern Catholic Churches. Section II, on the faithful, contains a principle that names of persons belonging to a church may be removed from rolls or registers of membership 'in accordance with the law' of the church.[68] This latter requirement to remove a name 'in accordance with the law' leaves space for different modalities. The CCEO has no prescriptions for rolls or registers for those who attend a local congregation. This seems to be more of a practical question, depending on local circumstances and relationships with civil authorities, which communicate the names and addresses of those Eastern Catholics who live in the territory of a particular parish to the church authorities. These lists have to be updated regularly.[69] For Eastern Catholic Churches, the principle *semel catholicus, semper catholicus* is very strong.[70] Moreover, if a person cannot lose his status as a member of the Catholic faithful and, as a consequence, be exempted from

62 CCEO, c.24 §2: 'if they are summoned to a trial by the competent authority, the Christian faithful also have the right to be judged according to the prescripts of the law, to be applied with equity'. And §3: '[t]he Christian faithful have the right not to be punished with canonical penalties except in accord with the norm of law'.

63 CCEO, c.1402.

64 See CCEO, cc.1431–1434. With respect to canon 1433, demotion of a cleric to a lower grade (e.g. a priest is demoted to the grade of deacon), deposition from the clerical state, removal, or better losing one's office is more implicit since it is a consequence of these sanctions.

65 See CCEO, cc.1420–1425.

66 See CCEO, cc.10 and 14; c.406; c.595 §1; cc.608–610.

67 CCEO, cc.698–717.

68 SPCL II.2.5.

69 The question of a kind of congregation roll, on the one hand, has to do with the financial support the faithful might give to the church. In many countries, this support is optional. On the other hand, it might have a connexion with, for instance, the parish bulletin/newssheet. The faithful can subscribe to it.

70 E.g. CCEO never recognised the possibility for one of the faithful to leave the church by a formal act. See CIC, cc. 1086 §1; 1117 and 1124. The *motu proprio* of Pope Benedict XVI, *Omnium in mentem*, 26 October 2009, abolished the exemption for Catholics who left the church by a formal act in respect to certain marriage laws.

obedience to certain purely ecclesiastical laws, this does not mean that religious freedom is denied by the Code. Nevertheless, as is also the case in the Latin Code, the Eastern Code seems to recognise religious freedom mainly in the choice to adopt the Catholic faith, i.e. to become a member of the church. Yet the freedom to adopt another faith or other religious convictions is not foreseen in Catholic doctrine. All humans are bound to seek the truth, especially concerning God and his church, and to hold fast to that truth.[71] Since the one true religion subsists in the Catholic and Apostolic Church, it is inconceivable that those who have been incorporated into it could leave the church.[72]

Section II also distinguishes the function of the laity and public ministry exercised by laypersons.[73] As to the Catholic Church, both its Latin and Eastern elements, it may be preferable to speak of the 'roles' of the laity instead of 'functions' because certain tasks or activities belong to all the faithful on the basis of baptism. No special appointment or mandate is given in this sense. For this same reason, there is an important distinction with public ministry exercised by laypersons because this always requires a special mission or mandate. However, the *Statement* recognises that '[b]aptism generates duties and rights for the faithful'.[74] These points concern terminology rather than substantive difference: the Catholic Church does not easily use the word 'ministry' with respect to laypeople and prefers to speak of 'functions'.[75] The *Statement* also provides that ordained ministers may engage in such other occupations, including offices held beyond the local church, as are not forbidden by church law or competent authority.[76] Eastern Catholic canon law indeed forbids clerics to participate in the exercise of civil power by means of holding public offices.[77]

An ecclesiological problem arises with regard to the expressions 'local church' and 'regional church structures'.[78] The *Statement* refers to the most localised level of church life. However, in Catholic ecclesiology, Latin and Eastern, 'local church' refers to the diocese and, eventually, the structures assimilated to it, e.g.

71 See *Dignitatis humanae*, 1.

72 Baptism cannot be taken away; it imprints an indelible, permanent character. Baptismal registers testify of an historical event that took place when the person was baptised. If names could be removed from these registers, the church would be a kind of association where one could choose to become a member and step out, according to one's desire – a fully subjective decision.

73 SPCL II.4: 'functions' of the laity (including 'the rights and duties of all . . . members'); III.3: 'functions of ordained ministers'.

74 SPCL II.1.3.

75 See CCEO, cc.407–408, speaking of functions and services of laypeople.

76 SPCL III.3.5.

77 See CCEO, c.384 §2, which does not allow clerics to have an active role in political parties or in the direction of labour unions unless the protection of the rights of the church or the promotion of the common good requires it, according to the judgement of the competent church authorities. Similarly, c. 385, §2 forbids clerics to exercise any commerce or business affairs except with the permission of the competent church authority.

78 SPCL IV.5.

an apostolic vicariate or prefecture or a territorial prelature or abbacy.[79] In turn, regional bodies in the Eastern Catholic Churches are the ecclesiastical provinces and metropolitan synods, not the eparchies. However, conceptually, 'regional' and 'local', as treated in SPCL IV.41–2 and IV.5.2, are more or less equivalent to eparchies and parishes under the CCEO.

The problem concerning sacrament and ordinances has been mentioned already in Chapter 2. It would be the same for the Eastern Catholic Churches and their law. In the same way, SPCL VII.4.3, in stating that marriage is for the well-being of the spouses, omits completely the CCEO norms on procreation and the upbringing of children and so seems an incomplete view of marriage.

To summarise, those principles that are more 'technical' (e.g. on forms of law or courts) are unproblematic. However, where doctrine and/or theology is concerned, reservations have to be made. This, probably, also explains why several observations concern the Latin Church in the same way as the Eastern Catholic Churches: they touch the doctrine shared by both of them.

3 A hierarchy of principles

The *Statement* does not explicitly present the principles hierarchically. That is, it does not tell us whether some principles are more important than others. Instead, the document gives the impression that all the principles are of equal importance. However, their hierarchy is at best implicit. For example, a hierarchy could be detected in the section on the rites of the church, where a fundamental statement is followed by principles concerning the celebration of a 'rite' or the conditions to be fulfilled for admission to it. SPCL VII.1.1, 3–4 seem to be more fundamental than 5–7 concerning the celebration of baptism and allowing for flexibility in the form and place of the celebration. In the Catholic Church, a similar difference is indicated with the notion of validity on the one hand and liceity on the other. Concerning the exercise of oversight, SPCL III.4.1 contains a principle that is fundamental and acceptable to all churches: oversight is an essential element of ecclesial order. SPCL III.4.2, however, the exercise of oversight as designated by the law, leaves room for diversity (as does SPCL III.4.3–7). For this reason, these principles do not have the same weight and could be differentiated.

4 The elements or terms of a principle

The terms or elements of principles seem to put more accent on their formal aspects than on actual content in the law of the different churches. This is especially so with the expression 'in accordance with law'. Stated otherwise,

79 The discussion on terminology (local church versus particular church) has not yet come to a final conclusion. To simplify, we could say the first notion is mainly used by ecclesiologists, whilst the second one belongs to the vocabulary of canon law. Unlike the CIC, the CCEO does not employ the expression 'particular Church'. See, for instance, the description of the eparchy in c. 177 §1.

their concretisation in church law is not part of the definition and, therefore, the principle satisfies itself with observing a formal, external similarity among the churches. One could wonder if it would be possible to go further, more in-depth.

However, the formula 'in accordance with law' also could imply that several principles do not exactly underlie or inspire the law, but that they are limited by the law because they adopt a typical determination or interpretation according to the law of the church in which they are observed. And if this would mean that what is asserted in the principle is true, as well as its contrary, whenever the law of a church claims this, what value is this principle invested with?[80]

The verb 'may' is often used in the *Statement*. This seems to weaken the strength of a principle. This is particularly so when the word is used in the general part of the principle since it suggests that the opposite also can be true. Does the use of the verb 'may' mean that not all the ecclesial traditions involved in formulating the principles can subscribe to the principle mentioned?

The situation is rather different when the verb 'may' conditions the second part or further determination of a principle. For instance, 'An ecclesial institution must comply with its law' is the major statement. Further determination follows with a double 'may': 'and may be subject in the exercise of its functions to such substantive and procedural limitations as may be prescribed by the law'.[81] The formula suggests that an ecclesial institution can be restricted in its activities by the law itself, so it highlights the double aspect of law: it can attribute rights and powers but can also contain limitations. In this last case the verb 'may' seems justified.

5 *The distinctively Christian character of the principles*

The principles in the *Statement* that are closely related to the specific Christian character of church law, referring to ecclesiology, sacraments, ministry, etc., are obviously clearly distinguished from principles of civil law because they are the result of specific theological and/or doctrinal views. Many of the principles deal with the functioning of laws and their interpretation or with topics that also are of importance in civil society, such as property or confidentiality/secrecy attached to the profession.[82] The CCEO refers regularly to civil law in its canons on temporal goods.[83] Confidentiality is required by the CCEO with respect to the judges and tribunal personnel and also for those exercising a function in the eparchial curia.[84]

80 Also, most of these references are to the law; only once are doctrine and law mentioned. See SPCL IV.2.2.

81 SPCL IV.1.5.

82 SPCL VII, 5,3.

83 See CCEO, cc.1027–1040.

84 CCEO, cc.1113; 1115; 244 §2,2°.

III The value of the *Statement of Principles of Christian Law*

Whilst different methods and approaches have been used traditionally in ecumenism to date, canon law has played only a minor (mostly background) role in official ecumenical dialogues and documents. However, in the Catholic Church, there are those who focus on how their own tradition deals with whether the progress of and possibilities offered by doctrine are sufficiently reflected in law[85] or whether law is able to foster the restoration of unity among Christians.[86]

Avery Dulles offers a somewhat different approach by exploring the extent to which concepts of divine law can be an obstacle to Christian unity. He distinguishes different categories of divine law: that which is necessary for the essence/existence of the church (*ad esse Ecclesiae*), that which is necessary for its full or integral existence (*ad plene esse Ecclesiae*), and that which is necessary for its well-being or good health (*ad bene esse Ecclesiae*).[87] In the context of ecumenism, introducing a hierarchy of divine law categories could indeed help to create space for flexibility and acceptance of other conceptions of the same element. We could imagine that there should be consensus on the elements that are considered necessary for the essence, the fundamental mission of the church. According to Dulles, this concerns, for instance, the apostolic ministry assuring the authority of the Lord, baptism initiating individuals into the community, and the Eucharistic meal acting as anamnesis and anticipation of the eschatological banquet as well as the church's duty to show God's forgiveness. These represent Christ's irrevocable gift to the church.[88] On the level of the full existence of the church are institutional characteristics that appeared only after the apostolic age but that could be traced to a biblical basis and were considered to express the very nature of the church. The creeds and the canon of the Scripture could be part of this category.[89] On the level of the well-being of the church, there could be divinely instituted elements that are not of apostolic origin. Examples could be a less juridical and more consensual form of leadership or a greater participation of each individual as well as more dialogue.[90] With respect to this last category, we could say that there is more room for different forms of structures, probably because they also are related to culture and mentalities.

The project that has resulted in the *Statement of Principles of Christian Law* adopts a different starting point. It begins with what the ecclesial traditions

85 See the work of Myriam Wijlens, such as *Sharing the Eucharist: A Theological Evaluation of the Post-Conciliar Legislation* (Lanham-New York-Oxford: University Press of America, 2000).

86 Walter Cardinal Kasper, 'Canon Law and Ecumenism', 69 *The Jurist* (2009) 171–189.

87 See A. Dulles, '*Ius divinum* as an Ecumenical Problem', 38 *Theological Studies* (1977) 681–708.

88 Ibid., 700–701.

89 Ibid., 701–702.

90 Ibid., 703–704.

involved have in common. The results are surprising – they demonstrate that we have more in common than perhaps could have been imagined before this project. At the same time, a study of the *Statement* gives the impression that those principles of law that concern human organisation, or perhaps even human nature, natural law, or anthropology, and the maxim *ubi societas, ibi ius* are easily identified as common to all. When theology or doctrine is involved, it is more difficult to discern common principles of law.

From the perspective of the Eastern Catholic Churches, it is submitted that the principles are perhaps not sufficiently detailed. A lack of detail may lead to only a partial reception of the *Statement*. One example is visitation. Its aim is described as to monitor, affirm, and improve the life and discipline of the entity visited.[91] Eastern canon law, however, distinguishes pastoral and canonical visitation. The latter implies control – for instance in respect to clerical discipline or the administration of church property – and it can lead to disciplinary measures. A pastoral visitation aims more at gathering information for the authority carrying out the visitation.[92] Another example concerns ecclesial discipline. Traditionally, Eastern (and Latin) canon law recognises that one of the essential purposes of ecclesial discipline is to repair scandal and/or harm.[93] The *Statement* does not include this in its principle on purposes of church discipline, though the Eastern tradition of seeing sanctions as remedial or medicinal is reflected in SPCL.[94]

Conclusion

The law of the Eastern Catholic Churches is a complex body of norms, which, for its essentials, can be presented in the form of fundamental principles. Indeed, CCEO itself provides that if there is a *lacuna legis*, recourse may be had to 'the general principles of canon law' (c. 1501). The *Statement of Principles of Christian Law* is an important initiative. It is possible to recognise the fundamentals of the CCEO in most of the *Statement*. However, a critical review of the *Statement* suggests that further refinement is needed. The initiative cannot avoid greater exploration of the theological as well as historical foundations of church law. Since several principles seem to be closely connected to facts on the one hand and organisational functioning on the other, the principles would gain in importance and relevance if their biblical foundations were indicated in the text of the *Statement* itself. This could be done, for instance, with respect to the sacraments and the foundations of disciplinary authority or sanctions. At the same time, this would help to establish some hierarchy among the principles themselves. If we consider that a definition or description of a sacrament, for instance, is more important or foundational than the conditions of admission to it or the way in

91 SPCL V.2.5.
92 This distinction is not in the Codes.
93 CCEO reference.
94 SPCL V.1.4.

which it is celebrated, and if we happen to identify the description as having biblical roots, it would help to distinguish better between essentials and incidentals. It also seems necessary to enter into details and to make the principles somewhat more concrete. This could be linked to the historical, cultural, and social circumstances in which they originated, whilst at the same time fundamentally expressing the same basic faith and seeing what is possible with a deepening of the principles.

4 The Orthodox canonical tradition

Nikos Maghioros

The study of the law of the different Christian traditions in a comparative way is a very complex task that needs to be carried out through different research methods and hermeneutical approaches. This complexity is not really surprising given the very nature of the church as a theanthropic institution, visible and invisible, shared between heaven and earth.[1] The church, as a community of the people of God, can be traced in historically different political and cultural contexts. Despite the fact that its vision is eschatological, as it is not limited to this perishable world, it still defines different aspects of the lives of the faithful in terms of their being both individuals and members of the Christian community. This visible dimension of the church needs an organisational structure capable of ensuring its unity and proper functioning so that it cannot only function within historical space and time but also achieve its salvific work. Eutaxia (εὐταξία) is the need for order and thoroughness in managing issues of daily ecclesiastical life. This orderliness is reflected in the law of the Orthodox Church in the form of its holy canons and is an integral part of its very existence; together with the church's theology, worship, and spirituality, it bears witness to the church's unity at a local and ecumenical level.

The law of the Orthodox Church has some features that distinguish it significantly from other Christian juridical traditions. The polycentric organisation of the different autocephalous churches; the territorial, chronological, and qualitative diversity of the legal sources; the quantity of the regulations and lack of a codification; and the provisions of different state laws on ecclesiastical issues, even the concept of *oikonomia*, make it difficult to adopt a common and up-to-date approach to the law of the Orthodox churches. At the same time, this

1 'The Church of Christ exists in the world, but is not of the world' (cf. Jn 17:11, 14–15). The Church as the Body of the incarnate Logos of God (John Chrysostom, *Homily before Exile*, 2 PG 52, 429) constitutes the living 'presence' as the sign and image of the Kingdom of the Triune God in history, and proclaims the good news of a new creation (II Cor 5:17), of new heavens and a new earth in which righteousness dwells (II Pt 3:13): Holy and Great Council of the Orthodox Church, *The Mission of the Orthodox Church in Today's World*, 2016. See www.holycouncil.org/official-documents/-/asset_publisher/VA0WE2pZ4Y0I/content/mission-orthodox-church-todays-world?_101_INSTANCE_.

legal polymorphy reflects the variety of the canonical traditions of the early church, supports the idea of the autonomy of the local churches, and, in particular, underlines the extreme necessity and importance of local and pan-Orthodox synods in the present day. The Holy and Great Synod that took place in Crete in June 2016,[2] after many years of preparation and numerous difficulties, some of which had their roots in the past, laid the foundations for meaningful inter-Orthodox communication, defining a democratic synodical framework, which could be the starting point for a permanent inter-Orthodox dialogue with the modern world.

In the Orthodox world it is evident that ecclesiastical affairs are not limited to a local level, but rather go beyond local Orthodox churches, for the reason that the borders of the different ecclesiastical jurisdictions continue to transcend the frontiers of the 'Orthodox' states. Ecclesiastical issues are affected by a hotchpotch of ideologies, national and international political aims, and economic and geostrategic interests. These are historically intertwined with a variety of critical pursuits of a religious and secular nature, such as the establishment of national identities and languages, the development of relations with the rest of Christendom and the modern world, and the attainment of a prestigious place among the Orthodox churches.

In Orthodox canon law, the principle according to which 'ecclesiastical affairs follow political ones' was revealed immediately after Emperor Constantine's acceptance of Christianity.[3] This idea evolved and became firmly established during the Christian Roman-Byzantine Empire and was thereafter (fifteenth cent.) transplanted to the Ottoman state, now operating in a non-Christian environment. It seems to be a time-resilient, yet flexible, theory that is able to overcome political systems and socio-religious conditions, be adapted appropriately into history, and contribute, under certain circumstances, to the harmonious coexistence of the church and the state. The rule was tested under new conditions after the gradual partition of the Ottoman Empire and the parallel formation of the nation-states in the Balkans. In this new reality, the principle was no longer applied on the level of the Orthodox church-empire, but mainly on that of the autocephalous Orthodox churches and independent states. The same principle with the necessary modern revisions seems to be valid even today, following an evolutionary and unpredictable course of development.

The earlier mentioned historical course led to the idea of the existence of different 'national canons and ecclesiastical laws' of the Orthodox churches, which are active in the various 'Orthodox' nation-states. This approach reflects the difficulty of determining the limits and relations of the two legal systems and, by extension,

2 See www.holycouncil.org.

3 See IV Ecumenical Council Can. 17 (451), Quinisext Council Can. 39 (691/2), and Photius, *Letter 290*, 1. 407. B. Laourdas and L. G. Westerink, *Photii patriarchae Constantinopolitani Epistulae et Amphilochia*, Vol. 3 (Leipzig: Bibliotheca scriptorum Graecorum et Romanorum Teubneriana, 1985).

the difference between the terms 'canon' and 'ecclesiastical law'. For example, the majority of the manuals of ecclesiastical law include among the sources of Greek ecclesiastical law the Holy Bible and the Holy Tradition. This kind of identification of the sources of canon and ecclesiastical law could be justified in the context of the church-state relationship formed during the Byzantine era, when the canons of the church acquired general legislative force and the imperial law on ecclesiastical issues became the internal law of the church.[4] Moreover, this contrasts with the modern distinction between canon and ecclesiastical law, which presupposes some form of separation between church and state and the coexistence of two autonomous legal systems that, however, can communicate and cooperate if they wish to.[5]

I Law and theology

Canon law is produced as an internal law mainly by the church and has its own particular characteristics and aims. The term 'canon law' derives from the word 'canon' (κανών). The redactors of 'Pedalion' (The Rudder), basing their argument on that of the Byzantine canon lawyer John Zonaras (twelfth cent.), explain that a 'canon' is a piece of wood, commonly called a 'ruler', used by craftsmen to straighten wood and stones. In a metaphorical sense, canons are 'the decisions of the Apostles, the Ecumenical and Local Councils and some Holy Fathers to drive out all disorders and moral distortions from clergymen and laymen and bring about orderliness and straightness in their ecclesiastical and Christian condition and virtue'.[6] The canon is like the rudder of a boat that is absolutely necessary to steer the church throughout the difficulties of the world. Holy Scripture, the holy canons, holy tradition, and the church's customs are the fundamental sources of canon law. The law of the church has theological foundations and a spiritual dimension and deals with human beings who were created in the image and likeness of God and baptised in the name of the Holy Trinity and who live a sacramental and spiritual life as members of the church. Its final objective is the 'the cure of souls and the healing of disorders'.[7]

The church's doctrine and spirituality are embodied in the historical forms of its ecclesiastical life; to put it another way, the historical existence of the church

4 S. Troianos, 'Θεσπίζομεν τοίνυν, τάξιν νόμον ἐπέχειν τοὺς ἁγίους ἐκκλησιαστικούς κανόνας . . .', 13 *Byzantina* (1985) 1193–1200 (in Greek).

5 N. Maghioros, 'Autonomy, Individual Rights and the Law of the Church', 13 *Nomokanonika* (2015) 154–155 (in Greek).

6 Agapius a Hieromonk and Nicodemus a Monk, Πηδάλιον τῆς νοητῆς νηός τῆς Μιᾶς, Ἁγίας, Καθολικῆς καί Ἀποστολικῆς τῶν Ὀρθοδόξων Ἐκκλησίας [. . .] Athens 1886. (The Rudder of the Metaphorical Ship of the Orthodox Christians of the One Holy Catholic and Apostolic Church [. . .]). Translated by Denver Cummings (Chicago: Orthodox Christian Education Society, 1957).

7 Quinisext Council Can. 102.

is the form in which its essence is intertwined with history.[8] The organisational structure of the church rests on its charismatic and sacramental life and is manifested as part of the spirituality of the faithful, laypeople, and clergy. The canons were defined by people who were all ***enlightened by one and the same spirit for our best interest.***[9] For the church fathers and members of the councils, the presence of the Holy Spirit was and is unquestionable, and the canons derive from the inspiration of the Holy Spirit and are established by His guidance for the benefit of the church.[10] The canons are produced by the church and exist and function for the church; they are founded on the Holy Bible and Holy Tradition. It is for this reason that they are called 'holy'. They are part of the ongoing two-dimensional struggle of the ecclesiastical community against the forces of decay and destruction and for the edification and internal renewal that take place through the energies of the Holy Spirit. It is the functional and charismatic unity of the church, throughout its dramatic history, that experiences successive moments of decline and renewal.[11] According to John Scholasticus (sixth cent.), the application of the canons is a spiritual act (πράξις) that requires wisdom (σοφία) and art (τέχνη) on the part of the person who is called upon to practice them. He who holds the spiritual sword – the spiritual father – should be able to properly assess the type and extent of the disease and to measure the level of receptivity of the person to whom the rule or the treatment is to be applied, always with respect for the freedom and dignity of the sufferer.[12]

The last canon (102) of the Quinisext Council recapitulates the purpose of the law of the church and explains its disciplinary system as a procedure for curing any illness afflicting the soul as a result of sin. It is worth reciting the canon *in extenso*:

> It behoves those who have received from God the power to loose and bind to consider the quality of the sin and the readiness of the sinner for conversion, and to apply medicine suitable for the disease, lest if he is injudicious in each of these respects he should fail in regard to the healing of the sick man. For the disease of sin is not simple, but various and multiform, and it germinates many mischievous offshoots, from which much evil is diffused, and it proceeds further until it is checked by the power of the physician. Wherefore he who professes the science of spiritual medicine ought first of all to consider the disposition of him who has sinned, and to see whether he

8 N. Afanasiev, 'The Canons of the Church: Changeable or Unchangeable?', 11 *St. Vladimir's Theological Quarterly* (1967) 54–68 at 57ff.

9 VII Ecumenical Council, Can. 1 (787).

10 Quinisext Council, Can. 1, Council of Carthage, Can. 66 (419).

11 N. Maghioros, 'Diritto e spiritualità nella tradizione dei canoni dei concili orientali (Evo antico)', 73 *Studia et Documenta Historiae et Iuris* (2007) 487–496.

12 See the preface of *Synagoge of Ecclesiastical Canons Divided into 50 Titles* in V. Beneševč, ed., *Ioannis Scolastici Synagoga L titulorum*, Tom. 1 (München: Verl. d. Bayer. Akad. d. Wiss. 1937).

> tends to health or (on the contrary) provokes to himself disease by his own behaviour, and to look how he can care for his manner of life during the interval. And if he does not resist the physician, and if the ulcer of the soul is increased by the application of the imposed medicaments, then let him mete out mercy to him according as he is worthy of it. For the whole account is between God and him to whom the pastoral rule has been delivered, to lead back the wandering sheep and to cure that which is wounded by the serpent; and that he may neither cast them down into the precipices of despair, nor loosen the bridle towards dissolution or contempt of life; but in some way or other, either by means of sternness and astringency, or by greater softness and mild medicines, to resist this sickness and exert himself for the healing of the ulcer, now examining the fruits of his repentance and wisely managing the man who is called to higher illumination. For we ought to know two things, to wit, the things which belong to strictness and those which belong to custom, and to follow the traditional form in the case of those who are not fitted for the highest things, as holy Basil teaches us.[13]

In the same framework, ecclesiastic *oikonomia* describes a greater flexibility in canonical matters. In the canonical tradition, *oikonomia* was usually perceived to apply to 'the management of canonical matters' relating to the canonical order through the taking of specific decisions. The bishop or a suitably appointed presbyter has the right, in a spirit of philanthropy, not to make a strict application of a canonical rule but to evaluate the special circumstances of each case and decide in a 'just' and more 'flexible' way. The term started to acquire a different context in the eighteenth century, particularly when the Ecumenical Patriarchate of Constantinople attempted to boost inter-Orthodox and inter-Christian relations. The strengthening of the unity of the Ecumenical Church, as well as the issue of the acceptance of the heterodox, paved the way for a systematic study of the question of canonical *oikonomia* not only in the Greek-speaking but also in the Slavic-speaking Orthodox world. In practice, *oikonomia* presupposes the existence of a problem that can cause, maintain, or exacerbate heresies or schisms. The unity of the church – peace in the church – is the highest good and is protected by more relaxed, moderate, and realistic choices. The calculation of profit and loss in this particular case determines the reasoned way of applying *oikonomia* to pathogenic conditions for which there may or may not be a normal provision.[14]

This idea of *oikonomia*, which has a theological content and practical application, is reflected in the *Statement of Principles of Christian Law*.[15] According

13 P. Shaff's translation in NPNF2–14. (The Seven Ecumenical Councils, 752).

14 A. Alivizatos, *Η Οικονομία κατά το Κανονικόν Δίκαιον της Ορθοδόξου Εκκλησίας* (Oikonomia according to the Canon Law of the Orthodox Church) (Athens: Astir, 1949) 41, 49, 51; N. Maghioros, 'The Concept of Oikonomia in Inter-Orthodox Relations. The Preparatory Phase: 1902–1904', 24 *Kanon* (2016) 84–97.

15 M. Hill and N. Doe, 'Principles of Christian Law', 19 *Ecclesiastical Law Journal* (2017) 138–155.

to Principle I.4.9, '[a] law may be relaxed, by competent ecclesial authority, by means of dispensation, economy or other form of equity for the spiritual good of the individual and the common good of the ecclesial community'. Relevant also is Principle I.5.3: '[f]or the interpretation of law, recourse may be had to the purposes of the law, the mind of the legislator, and the faith and practice of the church'; as well as Principle I.3.3: '[t]heology may shape law and law may realise certain theological propositions in norms of conduct and behaviour'; and Principle I.3.4: '[c]hurch laws should conform to the law of God, as revealed in Holy Scripture and by the Holy Spirit', reflect the way that the Orthodox Tradition face the issue of the relation between Theology and Law.

II The main sources of church law and institutions

The canons are a kind of interpretation of true and unaltered faith at the specific moment of the historical existence of the church.[16] The doctrinal truth they carry cannot change, but the way in which this truth is expressed in a particular historical form of ecclesiastical life can be revised. This means that the canons are not unchangeable. It is a constant challenge for the community to understand the social changes taking place in the course of the divine economy and the economy of salvation and to incorporate the eternal truths of the faith into the new conditions. The purpose of the canons is practical, aiming at solving immediate and existing, not future, problems. It seems that the church was reluctant to formulate *a priori* an elaborate canonical framework. The canons did not establish general principles of ecclesiastical organisation or a system of positive law. Orthodox canon law is casuistic and has a confessional character. It aims to define the way of life of the faithful as individuals and members of the church, reflecting biblical and moral perceptions. The structure of Eastern canonical collections confirms this view.[17]

The first three Christian centuries represent the period in which the institutions and organisational structures of the early church were created and formed. The Apostles of Christ were at the centre of this process. Their teachings on Christian life and ecclesiastical order were preserved in the Scriptures and spread as oral teachings from community to community, thus forming a primordial tradition. In particular, the New Testament contains not only the testimony of the faith of the ancient church but also moral and organisational principles that regulate aspects of ecclesiastical life, such as the mission of the Apostles in the world; the character of their office and authority; the relationships between them; the system of collective decision-making; the ordination of the elders, together with their qualifications and duties; ecclesiastical jurisdiction; baptism; the Holy Eucharist

16 J. Meyendorff, 'Contemporary Problems of Orthodox Canon Law', 17 *The Greek Orthodox Theological Review* (1972) 41–50 at 43.

17 N. Maghioros, 'Diritto e spiritualità nella tradizione dei canoni dei concili orientali', op cit., 494.

and marriage; the relationships between Christians; the role of woman in the community; and the attitude towards the governing political power.

This early tradition, which drew its authenticity from the Scriptures and its 'apostolic' origins, served as a kind of informal internal 'law' for the first Christian communities. Its application was customary since it never evolved into a corpus of written law. Yet, from the first centuries, disagreements arose among Christians, some of which have led to heresies and schisms. So different communities felt the need to capture various aspects of their lives and give them a special prestige by referring to the authentic Christian tradition. The authors of the few works that have survived, such as the *Didache* (The Lord's Teaching Through the Twelve Apostles to the Nations, first to second cent.), *Traditio Apostolica* (The Apostolic Tradition of St. Hyppolytus, third cent.), *Didaskalia Apostolorum* (The Teaching of the Twelve Apostles and the Holy Disciples of Our Saviour, third cent.), *Canones Ecclesiastici Sanctorum Apostolorum* (Church Canons of the Holy Apostles, third to fourth cent.), and *Constitutiones Sanctorum Apostolorum* (Constitutions of the Holy Apostles, fourth cent.), tried to link the lives of their communities with the authority of the teaching of the Apostles and their successors. Their prestige was based on their apostolic origins, and their provisions were based on the Scriptures and the tradition – that is to say, the praxis of the early church. These texts focussed on issues like order, worship, and teaching, and their aim was more pastoral than legal.[18]

The ever-growing Christian communities faced the need to define the right faith, to strengthen their organisational structure, and to regulate the relations of their members. It was a slow process towards the establishment of hierarchically structured communities with the bishop as a central leading figure and exponent of the Orthodox faith, which was based on the previous oral apostolic tradition. The recording of this apostolic tradition continued until the fourth century and favoured the production of a series of pseudo-apostolic works, with an obvious influence from the Old Testament. These texts had a significant effect on the subsequent collections of canon law and contributed to the formation of perceptions about and principles on the organisation and administration of the church.

The rise of Constantine the Great (AD 306–337) to the imperial throne and the radical change in his religious policy favoured the rapid expansion of Christianity. Constantine not only acknowledged the power of the ecclesiastical councils to freely decide on ecclesiastical matters, but he also placed the administrative mechanisms of the state at the disposal of the church, facilitating the settlement of issues of common interest that could potentially threaten the unity of the empire itself. However, neither the institution of the synods of bishops nor the respect for the decisions of imperial collective organs had its roots in the beginning of the fourth century. The church applied a collective system of administration very

18 S. Wessel, 'The Formation of Ecclesiastical Law in the Early Church', in W. Hartmann and K. Pennington, eds., *The History of Byzantine and Eastern Canon Law to 1500* (Washington, DC: The Catholic University of America Press, 2012) 1–23.

early on and expanded it gradually, whilst the Roman Emperor had the experience of the Roman Senate. The new element, which emerged during the first few years of Constantine's reign, was the establishment of a specific model of relations between the emperor and the church that, during the following centuries, gradually revealed its effectiveness with the convening of the ecumenical councils.

Eusebius of Caesarea stated that whenever a dispute arose in the empire, Constantine 'summoned the synod of the servants of God, as if he was placed as a general bishop from God'.[19] In the Christian emperor, Eusebius recognised the coincidence of the imitation of Christ the Word with the Father's image. As a person the emperor imitated Christ in governing all terrestrial matters. The empire identified itself with the church as an image of the Father's kingdom, the archetype, and carried out the salvific plan of Christ, which is the beginning and the end.[20] At the same time the emperor was the absolute legislator. He had the power to legislate after hearing his legal advisers to avoid any arbitration. He was the living (incarnate) law (ἔμψυχος νόμος) on Earth.[21] As he was above the law, in cases of conflict between law and justice he had the right to decide. The emperor was the follower of the legal tradition of his predecessors and the supporter of the idea of the continuation of the *imperium romanum*. In the framework of the continuity of law and values, piety, faith, justice, philanthropy, generosity, care for the public interest, and respect for the divine were values recognized as *sine qua non* for the security, unity, and peace of the empire.[22]

The cornerstone of Byzantium's political theory was the unity between Rome's law and that of Constantinople. Constantine sought to introduce the church into the Roman legal order through the gradual strengthening of the legal relations that connected the church and the empire. This fundamental development strengthened the synodical institution, dramatically boosted the production of church laws, brought different canonical traditions more closely together, and established canonical communication and communion. This institution was called upon to maintain the balance between the fullness of the local church, the church in the world drafting its ecclesiology, and the need to enhance the communication and the unity of the Christian communities. The church is not the sum of the local churches. Each local Christian community experiences the catholicity of the church by operating in communion with all the other local churches. The head of

19 Eusebius, *Εἰς τὸν Βίον τοῦ μακαρίου Κωνσταντίνου βασιλέως (Vita Constantini)*, 1, 44 and Τριακονταετηρικός *(Oratio de Laudibus Constatnini)*, 10, 5, ed. I. Heikel, Eusebius Caesariensis: Eusebius Werke. Band 1. Über das Leben Constantins. Constantins Rede an die Heilige Versammlung. Tricennatsrede an Constantin, in *Die griechischen christlichen Schriftsteller der ersten drei Jahrhunderte* (Leipzig: J. C. Hinrichs'sche Buchhandlung, 1902).

20 Eusebius, *Τριακονταετηρικός* 1, 6. P. Agapetus diaconus, *Exposition of Articles of Advice* (*Ἔκθεσις*), PG 86/1, 1163–1186.

21 Justinian, Novel 105, II, 4.

22 G. Crifò, 'La Chiesa e l'Impero nella storia di diritto da Costantino a Giustiniano', in *Cristianesimo e istituzioni politiche da Costantino a Giustiniano*, a cura di E. dal Covolo e R. Uglione (Roma: LAS, 1997) 194–196.

the church is exclusively Jesus Christ. The bishops of every province, according to the thirty-fourth canon of the Holy Apostles, must 'acknowledge the one who is first among them and account him as their head, and do nothing of consequence without his consent; but each may do only those things which concern his own parish, and the country places which belong to it. But neither let him (who is the first) do anything without the consent of all; for so there will be unanimity, and God will be glorified through the Lord in the Holy Spirit'.

Regarding their content, the resolutions of the councils are distinguished into doctrinal and legislative ones. The decisions on matters of faith are called 'rules' (ὅροι), whilst the provisions relevant to the organisation, administration, life, and action of the church are called 'holy canons' (Ἱεροὶ κανόνες). Thus, the corpus of the holy canons, which is common to all autocephalous Orthodox churches, includes norms that have been adopted, ratified, or recognised by ecumenical or local synods. In particular, Canon 1 of the Ecumenical Council of Chalcedon (451), Canon 2 of the Quinisext (in Trullo 691/2), and Canon 1 of the Ecumenical Council of Nicaea II (787) are considered fundamental, as they define the content of the ancient Orthodox canon law. Canon 2 of the Quinisext 'codified' and reconfirmed the canons of the apostles, the canons of the ecumenical and local councils, and the canons of the church fathers.

The Orthodox Church recognises seven ecumenical councils, convened between 325 and 787. Only five of these councils – namely, the First Council of Nicaea (325), the first Council of Constantinople (381), the Council of Ephesus (431), the Council of Chalcedon (451), and the Second Council of Nicaea (787) – had a legislative output. In 691/692 another synod was held in Constantinople, the council in Trullo, that is, held in the domed hall (*τροῦλλος*) in the imperial palace, which was intended to carry out legislative work, thereby completing the legislative work of the Second and Third Councils of Constantinople (553, 680–681). That is why this council is known as the 'Trullanun' or 'Quinisext'.

The canons of the six ecumenical councils cover the period from the first 20 years of the fourth century until the end of the eighth century (325–787). The legislative work of the ecumenical councils includes:

1 20 canons of the First Ecumenical Council of Nicaea (325)
2 Seven canons of the Second Ecumenical Council of Constantinople (381)
3 Eight canons of the Third Ecumenical Council of Ephesus (431)
4 30 canons of the Fourth Ecumenical Council of Chalcedon (451)
5 102 canons of the Quinisext Ecumenical Council of Constantinople (691/692)
6 22 canons of the Seventh Ecumenical Council of Nicaea (787)

The canons of the nine local councils cover the period from the mid-third to the beginning of the fifth century (251–419). It is important to note that not all canons compiled by all local councils in the Roman Empire during this period are included – only the canons of the local synods that were recognised or validated by Canon 2 of the Quinisext. The legislative work of the local councils includes:

1 25 canons of the Council of Ancyra (314) dealing with the problem of the lapsed Christians (lapsi)
2 15 canons of the Council of Neocaesarea (314–319 or 315) on issues of moral and ecclesiastical order and discipline
3 21 canons of the Council of Gangra (340) against the heretical teaching of Bishop Eustathius of Sebastia, who praised ascetic life and condemned marriage
4 25 canons of the Council of Antioch (341) on matters of ecclesiastical order and discipline
5 21 canons of the Council of Sardica (343) regulating matters of ecclesiastical order and discipline
6 60 canons of the Council of Laodicea (343–381) dealing with moral, liturgical, and administrative issues
7 the decision of the Council of Constantinople (394) on the dispute between Bishops Agapius and Vagadius
8 133 canons of the Council of Carthage (419), which codified the earlier canonical output of the African Church and introduced some new canons on matters of discipline and order
9 One canon of the Council of Carthage (251 or 255–256) that was held under the presidency of Cyprian on the question of the baptism of heretics

The second canon of the Quinisext recognised also the canons of certain fathers of the church. These texts were based on the letters of these ecclesiastical leaders that either addressed solutions to specific ecclesiastical problems or answered questions. The responses of the fathers were given the form of canons and contributed effectively to filling the gaps in the ecclesiastical regulations, although they had been customarily accepted by the Christian community before receiving wider conciliar authority. The canons of the 12 church fathers cover the period from the middle of the third century to the middle of the fifth century. The *Canons of the Fathers*, in chronological order, are as follows:

1 Four canons of Dionysius of Alexandria (+265)
2 11 canons of Gregory of Neocaesarea, Taumaturgus (+270)
3 15 canons of Peter of Alexandria (+311)
4 Three canons of Athanasius of Alexandria (+373)
5 92 canons of Basilius of Caesarea (+379)
6 18 responses of Timotheus of Alexandria (+385)
7 34 verses from the poem of Gregory of Nazianzius (+389/390)
8 69 verses from the poem of Amphilochius, Bishop of Iconium (+395)
9 Eight canons of Gregory of Nyssa (+395)
10 14 canons of Theophilus of Alexandria (+412)
11 Five canons of Cyril of Alexandria (+444)
12 a circular letter of Gennadius, patriarch of Constantinople (459)

The second canon of the Quinisext as well as the first canon of the Council of Nicaea II ratified the so-called Canons of the Holy Apostles. These 85 'apostolic' canons are included in the forty-seventh chapter of the eighth book of the Apostolic Constitutions. This is a falsely entitled (pseudepigraphical) compilation that was probably written in Antioch in Syria around 380. The Quinisext attributes the work to Clement of Rome and rejects it (except for the canons) as material that was unauthentic and alien to the Orthodox faith that had been introduced by heretics. The canons refer to the ordination, discipline, and abstinence of the clergy as well as worship, ecclesiastical justice, and property. The canons share common features with those of previous synods, such as those of Nicaea, Antioch, Neocaesarea, and Laodicea. Regardless of their precise dating, the 'apostolic' canons reflect the ecclesiastical reality of the early fourth century.

In the canonical collections, there are also some canons that, even though they have not been included in the second canon of the Quinisext Council, are considered sources of canon law:

1 The canons of the Protodeutera Council (861) and Council of Hagia Sophia (879–880), despite the fact that these councils have not been recognised as ecumenical, acquired a pan-Orthodox authority. The Protodeutera Council was convened in Constantinople, in the Church of the Holy Apostles, under Emperor Michael III to put an end to the iconoclast sect. The council recognised the canonical election of Patriarch Photius to the See of Constantinople and issued 17 canons dealing with monastic life, church order, and worship. This meeting was attended by many bishops of the Eastern Church as well as envoys of Pope Nicholas I. The Council of Hagia Sophia in Constantinople was assembled under Emperor Basil I to ensure peace between the Eastern and Western churches. Representatives of Pope John VIII and other patriarchs also attended the synod. Photius was re-established as the canonical archbishop of Constantinople, and three canons were issued dealing with the mutual recognition of the canonical sanctions applied by the pope and the patriarch to laymen or clerics under their jurisdiction as well as the status of the bishops.

2 The monastic rules of Pachomius (+346–48), as well as the 'Greater Monastic Rules' of Basil the Great (*Regute fusius tractata*, Migne, PG, XXXI, 889–1052) and the 'Lesser [twelfth cent.] Rules' (*Regula, brevius tractatae*, ibid, 1051–1306) of Basil the Great (+378), were very important sources for the monastic liturgical life and order, together with the later monastic rules *(typika)*.

3 The pseudepigraphical canons of John IV Nesteutes, patriarch of Constantinople (582–595), which form part of his work entitled *Kanonikon*; the letter that was sent by Tarasius, patriarch of Constantinople (784–806), to Pope Adrian on the subject of simony; the *responsa* of Nicephorus I of Constantinople (806–815) and Nicholas III Grammaticus of Constantinople (1086–1111); and the canons of Theodore the Studite (759–826) dealing with ecclesiastical discipline.

4 The synodical acts and decisions of the ecumenical patriarchate from the ninth century to today, as the 'mother church', which has historically acquired great prestige among the Orthodox churches. The synods of the patriarchate have issued a variety of legislative norms in different forms. *Patriarchal and Synodical Tomoi* and *Synodical Acts* deal mainly with the organisation and administration of the church.

5 The legal opinions, decisions, and interpretations of the canons by ecclesiastical leaders or well-known canon lawyers (eleventh to twelfth cent.). These take the form of canonical *responsa* and canonical treatises. They provide answers on different issues concerning the liturgical and moral life of the church. The interpretations and comments on the canons of the three canonists of the twelfth century, Alexius Aristinus, John Zonaras, and Theodore Balsamon, are fundamental to Orthodox canon law. Later important works on canon and imperial law are the *Syntagma* of Matthew Blastares (1335); the *Hexabiblus* of Constantine Armenopoulos (1344/1345); the *Nomokanon* of Manuel Malaxus (1561); the *Vaktiria* of Iakovos (1645); the *Procheiron Nomikon* of Theophilos, bishop of Campania (before 1793); the *Pedalion* of Agapios and Nikodemos (1800); and *The Syntagma of Holy and Sacred Canons* of Rallis and Potlis (1852–1859).

The emperors of the East issued an ever-increasing number of decrees on ecclesiastical issues. In the Justinian Code (534), for example, imperial legislation on ecclesiastical issues covers the 13 chapters of the first book. As has been pointed out, this part of the code far exceeds the entire *corpus canonum* in size. In this legislation a large number of the *Novels* Justinian issued after 534 have been added to regulate church issues. The *Pandects* (Digest) and the *Institutes* contain a smaller quantity of church law. Other important imperial legal texts relating to the church are the *Ecloga* of the iconoclast emperors Leo III (717–741) and Constantine V (741–775), dealing mainly with marriage, patrimonial, and penal law; the *Eisagoge* of Basil I (885/886), which includes the ideas of Patriarch Photius, who describes in a more separatist perspective the power of the emperor and the patriarch; the several *Novellae* of Leo VI the Wise and his successors on ecclesiastical matters; the *Procheiros Nomos* (907); and the *Basilika*, 60 books published under Constantine VIII (1025–1028) and used by Theodore Balsamon in his canonical-hermeneutic work.

The constantly growing canonical output of the church, as well as the codification work of Justinian, led to the search for more practical methods of recording and organising the canons and laws. Since the sixth century the law of the church had coexisted in canonical collections alongside state law. At first these systematic collections contained ecclesiastical canons and laws attached in the form of a supplement or appendix. Towards the end of the sixth and early seventh centuries, Byzantine canonists combined these two sources under the same thematic areas, calling the new collections *Nomokanones*. The main feature of these collections is the gradual integration of the canons of the apostles, the canons of the fathers, and the canons of the African Church (*Codex canonum Ecclesiae Africanae*), in their Greek translations, into older collections of the canons of the councils. As far as their structure is concerned, the collections are divided into titles, chapters, and canons-laws. The most sophisticated collection of this type is the *Nomokanon in 14 titles* (612–629), which became the basis for all subsequent collective endeavours.

A *Nomokanon* is composed by regulatory instruments – that is, laws and canons – and constitutes a form of ecclesial regulation. This variety of legal instruments and forms is easily reflected in Principle I.2.1: '[l]aws are found in a variety of formal sources including codes of canon law, charters and statutes, constitutions and bylaws, and books of church order'; as well as in Principle I.4.2: '[c]hurch laws consist of various juridical formulae, such as precepts, prohibitions, and permissions, and may be cast as principles and rules, rights and duties, functions and powers'.

III Unity in diversity

From the study of the development of the Byzantine collections of canons and laws, we can draw important information concerning the liturgical and sacramental life of the church as well as church order and discipline. More particularly, we can learn about the origins and evolution of ecclesiastical institutions, the limits of episcopal power, the operation of the synodical system, and the relationship between the local and the universal church, liturgical rites, ecclesiastical sanctions, and church property. These are issues that are still of concern today and often provoke conflicts. Moreover, the canonical collections reflect the evolution of the relationships between the church and the state as well as church law and state law. Although the ecclesiastical laws of Byzantine emperors have a purely historical significance today, the ancient canonical tradition has contributed to the creation of a canonical conscience in the Orthodox Church on the fundamental role of the state and its legislation on internal ecclesiastical matters. The canon law of the Orthodox Church (or churches) cannot be perceived without state laws or court judgements, regardless of whether these provisions agree with or oppose the canonical tradition and order. Constitutional provisions, international conventions, EU legislation, laws, decrees or ministerial decisions, decisions of national and European courts, and church regulations and statutes are necessary not only to understand but also to implement Orthodox canon law.[23] It is evident that although the Orthodox churches are united in faith and there is a canonical communion among them, the sources of

23 The autocephalous Church of Greece, for example, exercises a conferred administrative power, implementing as a public legal entity the provisions of state legislation. The administrative acts issued by the competent ecclesiastical institutions, such as the synods of bishops, dioceses, parish councils, and ecclesiastical courts, could be reviewed by the Council of State, the supreme administrative court. Ch. Papastathis, 'Greece: A Faithful Orthodox Christian State, The Orthodox Church in the Hellenic Republic', 339–375 at 353–355: www.iclrs.org/content/blurb/files/Greece.2.pdf.

law are different. The common corpus of ancient holy canons remains intact – but the more recent legislation of each autocephalous church has introduced changes, influencing the level of its autonomy. In other words, there is unity in diversity manifested in various areas, such as the number and composition of the local synods; the process for appointment of bishops, priests, and deacons; the participation of laypeople in administrative offices; and relations with other Christians.

The immense number of canons and ecclesiastical laws makes it necessary and imperative to impose a codification. Although this idea was among the first priorities in the attempts made to organise a pan-Orthodox synod in the early twentieth century and later, the plan was abandoned. A critical approach to the canons is still necessary to redefine their mutable and outdated historical components and to re-emphasise the unalterable and eternal message of Orthodox teaching. In this way the substance of the local legal traditions can be preserved without harming the canonical unity of the Orthodox Church as a whole. The church can reform its internal law by taking into account local social needs, the national and international legal framework, and particularly the concept of human rights.

It seems that the idea of a principle of canon law is not self-evident at first glance, nor does it arise from a systematic theoretical approach. This does not mean that there are no principles of law in the Orthodox Church. Specific research into the various legal sources is necessary to reveal and categorise these principles. Indicatively, mention can be made of the principles of synodality, autocephaly, identification of personal and territorial jurisdiction, and doctrinal unity in legal diversity. Relevant principles in the *Statement of Principles of Christian Law* are I.1.1: '[a] church as an institution may define itself by its autonomy, polity, and objects'; I.1.4: '[a] church is autonomous in its system of governance or polity'; IV.1.6: '[e]cclesial institutions may be organised at international, national, regional, and/or local level'; and IV.3.3: '[t]he autonomy and functions of a national ecclesial entity, and its conference, synod, council, or other form of central assembly, may include the authority to legislate, administer, and adjudicate on matters within its competence'.

IV Church organisation and administration

According to Orthodox theology, the hierarchical structure of the church is based on God's grace and the sacramental life, and it manifests itself in the functions of its charismatic institutions, both lay and priestly. The variety of charisms of the members of the undivided body of Christ constitutes the gift, the precondition, and the means for the human encounter with God, who as the sovereign of Creation reveals Himself in various ways (I Cor 12, 5–7). The experience of the diversity of charisms manifests the spirituality of the local community under the form of liturgical unity, the communion of agape among the faithful. This unity in diversity also extends into the area of ecclesiastical order since one of the main aims of canonical norms is to safeguard communitarian life, to repress the tendencies towards a love of power (φιλαρχία), and to guarantee an ecclesiastical administrative system that can preserve the variety of the charisms.[24]

During the nineteenth and twentieth centuries, the form of organisation and self-government of a local church was determined by its degree of independence from the ecumenical patriarchate under whose jurisdiction it lay. The ecumenical patriarchate used to recognise the full independence of a local church through a patriarchal and synodical tomos (a document promulgated by the Holy and Sacred Synod presided over by the ecumenical patriarch), declaring its self-governance and administration by the synod of the bishops and the primate according to the holy canons, internal statutes, and norms as well as state law. An autocephalous church is recognised as a 'sister church' and, together with the former 'mother church' and the other autocephalous 'sister churches', remains united in doctrinal, spiritual, and canonical communion. It is important to underline that doctrinal and canonical bonds between the different local Orthodox churches, as well as between the collective (conciliar) and single-person (clerical) administrative organs, guarantee the visible unity of ecumenical orthodoxy and its structural order. The establishment of autocephalous churches is related mainly to political conditions. Usually, when part of a certain state breaks away and forms a new political territory, the new sovereign state, together with the faithful, demands the establishment of an autocephalous church. The synod of the church, under whose jurisdiction the geographical area in question lay up to that point, decides to recognise the autocephalous status of the new local church.

The hierarchical organisational framework of the Orthodox Church includes (1) the ancient patriarchates, established during the period of the ecumenical councils – namely, the ecumenical patriarchate of Constantinople and the patriarchates of Alexandria, Antioch, and Jerusalem;[25] (2) the new patriarchates – namely, the patriarchates of Russia (1589), Serbia (1920), Romania (1925), Bulgaria (1961), and Georgia (1990); and (3) the autocephalous churches

24 This, among others, is the aim of the canons that recognise the bishop's power to administer all the issues of his diocese and to ordain the clerics or of the canons that forbid the bishop to extend his jurisdiction beyond the limits of his own diocese or to move to other dioceses without the invitation of the local ordinary or of the canons that regulate the role of the council of a province, make obligatory the observance of its decisions, and regulate the relationships of the bishops among themselves and with the metropolitan. See Can. 4, 6, 15, 16 of the First Ecumenical Council; Can. 9, 11, 14, 16, 19, 20, 21, 22, 23 of the Council of Antioch; Can. 1, 3, 4, 5 6, 10 of the Council of Sardica; Can. 12 of the Council of Laodicea; Can. 17, 18, 23, 49, 50, 53, 56, 98, 99 of the Council of Carthage.

25 'Renewing the laws made by the one hundred and fifty Holy Fathers who assembled in this God-guarded imperial capital city, and by the six hundred and thirty of those who assembled in Chalcedon, we decree that the throne of Constantinople shall enjoy equal seniorities (or priorities) with the throne of older Rome, and in ecclesiastical matters shall be magnified like the latter, coming second after the latter; after which the throne of the great city of the Alexandrians shall come next, then that of Antioch, and after this the throne of the city of the Jerusalemites': Can. 36 of the Quinisext.

of Cyprus (431), Greece (1850), Poland (1924), Albania (1937), the Czech Republic and Slovakia (1998), and Ukraine (2019). The autonomous churches depend on the 'mother church'. Usually, the primate of an autonomous church is elected or ratified by the synod of the bishops of the mother church. The archdioceses of Finland and the Church of Estonia, for example, were recognised as autonomous by the ecumenical patriarchate of Constantinople. There are also autonomous churches under the churches of Antioch, Jerusalem, Russia, Serbia, and Romania.

Ecumenical councils hold the highest authority in the church, as they represent ecumenical orthodoxy. They are convened to deal with important issues that concern the whole church and decide both doctrinal and canonical issues. The decisions are binding on every self-governing local church. There are many reasons why the convocation of an ecumenical council of the Orthodox Church seems very difficult nowadays. This is not only because of the relations existing between the local Orthodox churches and the corresponding political powers but also because of the fact that the synods of the autocephalous churches have absolute authority and will resolve most administrative and disciplinary issues themselves. The assembly of the bishops of an autocephalous church under the primate constitutes the highest administrative, legislative, and juridical authority of a local church, one that governs independently of any other ecclesiastical authority in accordance with internal canon (and civil) law.

All members of the church have rights and obligations according to their role in the ecclesiastical organisation. A person becomes a member of the Orthodox Church through the sacrament of baptism, administered by a priest or a bishop according to Orthodox liturgical praxis in the name of the Holy Trinity. The people of God are composed of the clergy and the laity. During the historical evolution of ecclesiastical life, the movement of monasticism appeared. Monks and nuns are devoted to a radical Christian life, alone or in communion with others. After a long period of probation and training, the novice makes solemn vows of chastity, obedience, and poverty during a special ceremony. No member of the church has a superior position or predominance over the other members. The clergy have the right to administer church issues as a *diakonia* according to the law and in collaboration with laypeople.

The priesthood is a charism related to the ecclesiastical body and is activated only within this body. Its 'power' is not dominant, autonomous, or legal but charismatic and liturgical. Spirituality is the precondition for the exercise of ecclesiastical 'power' and is realised through therapeutic canons. The regulation of the relations between the primate and the other bishops confirms unity and unanimity. It does not mean submission in a pyramidal hierarchical form but a relationship of love and mutual dependency. The bishops are equal among each other, administer their dioceses independently, discuss general issues of ecclesiastical organisation, and decide collectively. The three major orders of priesthood are the deacon, the presbyter (priest), and the bishop. The Orthodox clergy is composed only of men who, through the sacrament of ordination celebrated during the Divine Liturgy by the bishop, enter the priesthood. Deacons and priests can get married before their ordination or remain celibate. Only celibate priests can become bishops.

The bishops, like the apostles, are all *pares* (equals). It was the importance of the city that gave prestige to the episcopal see and especially the capitals of the empire, Rome and New Rome. The metropolitan and the patriarch are recognised as *primus inter pares* – members of the synods of bishops – without any superior rights. The bishops run their own dioceses independently, but they discuss and decide on issues of common interest collectively. Depending on the importance of the issues and the number of local churches that are represented, synods can be local or ecumenical. The bishop is the clergyman who administers his diocese, under the authority of the local synod, assisted by the clergy and the laypeople. Bishops are elected by the synod of the bishops or an electoral body according to the electoral system applied in the local church, with wider or less participation of the laity. The priests, as heads of the parishes, become parishioners by election of the parish and ordination and appointment by the bishop. They represent the bishop in their pastoral, liturgical, and administrative work within the boundaries of their parish, assisted by the deacons. There are also three lower orders, the sub-deacons, the readers, and the cantors, who acquire this capacity through the 'laying on of hands' – a blessing. These individuals have simple and very limited liturgical duties. In the Orthodox tradition, the clergy cannot perform sacraments without the presence of laypeople. Laypeople have the right to participate in the sacramental life, worship, and administration of the church. They participate in the administration of the church as members of the parish and diocese councils as well as in the election of the clergy.

The earlier mentioned system of church governance is reflected in Principles IV.1.3: '[a] church should have institutions to legislate, administer, and adjudicate for its own governance'; IV.1.4: '[a]n ecclesial institution has such power, authority, or jurisdiction as is assigned to it by law'; IV.1.6: '[e]cclesial institutions may be organised at international, national, regional, and/or local level'; IV.3.2: '[a] church or other ecclesial community organised at national level may have such institutional structure as is prescribed by the regulatory instruments applicable to it'; III.2.1: '[a]n ecclesiastical office is a position constituted by law'; III.2.4: '[a]n ecclesiastical office may be held by a person or persons with such qualifications as are prescribed by law'; and III.1.4: '[v]ocation to and suitability for ordained ministry are tested by the church through a process of selection, examination, and training by competent authority'.

V The *Statement of Principles of Christian Law*: comments and evaluation

This project aims to reveal the particular institutional relations created between the variety of local religious communities. It can be considered pioneering and innovative, as for the first time experts in the law of the churches belonging to the World Council for Churches, under the coordination of Professors Norman Doe and Mark Hill, gathered in order to seek common principles of Christian law in the traditions of said churches. In the Orthodox context, as far as I know, there have been no relevant collective research efforts or individual works of such extent. In my opinion, this project offers a new dimension and perspective to the research on Orthodox canon law, as there are no publications dealing with principles in the Orthodox canonical tradition. Few attempts have been made to highlight the importance of canon law as a tool for enhancing the ecumenical approach of Christians. The method followed by the group working on the project was empirical and comparative. The participation of specialists from different Christian traditions and ecclesiological backgrounds in their personal capacities, and not as representatives of their churches, lent more flexibility to the attempts to identify similarities and differences among the various legal ecclesiastical systems. The dialogue on the nature, sources, and content of church law has revealed the importance of such a dialogue to the ecumenical approach and understanding. Although history has gradually led Christian traditions to diverge, canon law can contribute to an ecumenical rapprochement where other theological endeavours have not achieved the desired results.

The initial affirmation that all churches have a variety of regulatory instruments demonstrates their importance for the Christian communities, whether these norms are called law, order, or polity (Principle I.1.2). This is self-evident for canonists but not necessary for theologians. It is not rare in the Orthodox context to hear the opinion that other Christian traditions, especially Protestants, have no law, or, even, that the law of the Orthodox Church is mainly *oikonomia e philanthropia*. Similar perceptions on the usefulness of law for the church or ecumenical dialogue probably exist in other ecclesiastical traditions as well. One of the very positive outcomes of this project will be to help eliminate these kinds of concerns and misunderstandings and to enable reflection on the well-known debate between grace and institution, the difference between the soteriological dimension, and the formal observance of the norms.

Obviously, there have been several difficulties during these years, such as the struggle to distinguish the term 'principle of law' in relation to a simple description of fact, a theological concept, or ethical reference. During our meetings, we often had to discuss what constitutes a principle and what is merely a simple description of reality. I think that kind of debate will continue, as it is connected with the task of finding out if there are any external similarities in the regulatory systems of churches or profound common principles of law based potentially on common theological backgrounds. This kind of tension is related to the empirical methodology that was adopted, although this was probably the best solution that could have been adopted to achieve as many results as possible within a short period of time.

It seems that the more principles are formulated in a general way, the easier and more widely they become accepted. The majority of the principles in the *Statement* are unproblematic from the point of view of the Orthodox canonical tradition, which is based on the holy canons and recent ecclesiastical legislation – for example the church as an autonomous institution in its system of governance or polity (Principles I.1.1–4); the servant law, that is to say, the law in service to the mission and its witness to the salvific work of Christ (I.3.1–4); the structure, effect, and relaxation of norms (I.4.1–10); the interpretation of law (I.1.1–5); the functions of the laity (II.3.1–5); ecclesiastical offices (III.2.1–6); national church structures (IV.3.1–4); ecclesial discipline (V.1.1–5); due process (V.4.1–5); ecumenism (Section VIII); and church property (Section IX). Other principles could be problematic, not directly as a result of the way in which they are phrased but because of the way they can be interpreted and applied in the Orthodox context – for example issues relating to ordination and women (III.1.5), the exercise of oversight and the territorial jurisdiction of a local church (III.4), the rites of the church (Section VII), and church and state relations (Section X).

Conclusion

The study of the law of the churches, rather than opening up the inherent difficulties, opens up new horizons in the knowledge and understanding of ecclesiastical traditions. It reveals various aspects of the lives of Christian communities, which, despite the fact that they coexist locally, have little knowledge of or communication with each other. The process of shaping their institutional organisation, the way they interpret history and view the future, their perceptions of their role in today's multicultural society, their relationship with politics, and their attitude towards the state are issues imprinted on their internal law and demonstrate their willingness to adopt an ecumenical approach, reconciliation, and friendship. Seeking points of commonality between the laws of different Christian traditions is a process that will benefit each individual church, as such a search could become an instrument for an internal dialogue with theology and ecclesiology. Moreover, such a search can facilitate the ecumenical understanding of other Christian traditions and the dialogue with civil society and also generate ideas for further academic research in the area of theology and law. Finally, this project opens up new perspectives for the study of the rich Orthodox canonical tradition. The efforts to explore and reveal diachronic principles of law could contribute to the codification and renewal of Orthodox canon law, the strengthening of inter-Orthodox communication, and the effectiveness of the ecumenical dialogue with the other churches. It could also contribute to the harmonisation of church and state law to safeguard and enhance ecclesiastical autonomy.

5 The Anglican canonical tradition

Mark Hill

Effective ecumenism has its foundations in self-understandings of the nature of church.[1] The law and polity of different Christian traditions have been the subject of empirical study, led by Professor Norman Doe at the Centre for Law and Religion at Cardiff University, which has identified certain universal principles of Christian law.[2] These, wisely deployed, can give greater traction to the ecumenical endeavour.[3] The purpose of the law for Christian communities is much the same today as it was in the days of the early church: to regulate the functioning of the faith community and the conduct of its members by a combination of commands, prohibitions, and permissions.[4] Ombres indicates that canon law, as applied ecclesiology, contributes to sustaining and expressing the freedom of the children of God.[5] What follows explores the laws of Anglican churches, summed up in *The Principles of Canon Law Common to the Churches of the Anglican Communion* (2008), in terms of their sources and forms; scope and purposes; and structure, effect, and enforcement. This chapter also discusses the extent to which the principles of Anglican canon law are reflected in the *Statement of Principles of Christian Law* (2016). It does so by offering examples of clear convergence but also of how, in relation to some matters, a more nuanced or generous interpretation of the latter is required to establish as full a degree of congruity as possible

1 For the place of canon law in ministerial training, see M. Hill, 'Canon Law: The Discipline of Teaching and the Teaching of the Discipline', in T Harris, ed., *Studies in Canon Law and Common Law in Honor of R H Helmholz* (Berkeley: Robbins Collection, 2015) 337–353.

2 N. Doe, *Christian Law: Contemporary Principles* (Cambridge: Cambridge University Press, 2013).

3 See in particular, N. Doe, 'The Ecumenical Value of Comparative Church Law: Towards the Category of Christian Law', 17 *Ecclesiastical Law Journal* (2015) 135–169.

4 M. Hill, 'The Regulation of Christian Churches: Ecclesiology, Law and Polity' (2016) *Theological Studies* 72(1).

5 R. Ombres, 'Why then the Law?', 55 *New Blackfriars* (1974) 296–304. Attempts at an Anglican articulation of the interface between canon law and theology are to be found in N. Doe, 'Towards a Critique of the Role of Theology in English Ecclesiastical and Canon Law', 2 *Ecclesiastical Law Journal* (1992) 328–346; and M. Hill, 'Gospel and Order', 4 *Ecclesiastical Law Journal* (1997) 659–663.

between the principles of Anglican law and the principles of Christian law as articulated in the *Statement*.

I The sources and forms of Anglican law

At the international level, the Anglican Communion has no formal body of law applicable globally to its 46 churches in communion with the See of Canterbury; each church is autonomous and has its own legal system. The Communion is held together by 'bonds of affection'; namely, shared loyalty to scripture, creeds, baptism, Eucharist, and historic episcopate and its institutional instruments of communion – the archbishop of Canterbury, Primates' Meeting, Lambeth Conference, and Anglican Consultative Council – but these cannot make decisions binding on churches unless incorporated in the laws of those churches.[6] However, as we have seen in Chapter 1, *The Principles of Canon Law Common to the Churches of the Anglican Communion* (2008)[7] is a statement of principles induced from the similarities between the laws of the churches.[8]

At the national level, 'law' is understood as 'a binding public instrument created within a church by a duly constituted lawful authority of that church, that is, a species of human law as distinct from the will or law of God'.[9] Within each church,[10] general law, typically provincial, is created by a synod or other assembly representative of bishops, clergy, and laity, and laws made at more localised levels (such as diocesan law created by the diocesan synod of bishop, clergy, and laity) must be consistent with the general law.[11] Some churches have a code of canons only. Most have a constitution, canons, and other regulatory instruments, including rules and regulations, ordinances, resolutions, and liturgical rubrics found in the service books. Alongside written laws are less formal and sometimes unwritten sources: customs or tradition, the decisions of church courts, the English

6 See, generally, N. Doe, *Canon Law in the Anglican Communion* (Oxford: The Clarendon Press, 1998).

7 *Principles of Canon Law Common to the Churches of the Anglican Communion*, Anglican Communion Legal Advisers Network (London: Anglican Communion Office, 2008) (hereafter *Principles*).

8 *Principles*, 17: (1) there are principles of canon law common to the churches of the Anglican Communion; (2) their existence can be factually established; (3) each province or church contributes through its own legal system to the principles of canon law common within the Communion; (4) these principles have strong persuasive authority and are fundamental to the self-understanding of each of the member churches; (5) these principles have a living force and contain within themselves the possibility for further development; and (6) the existence of the principles both demonstrates and promotes unity in the Communion.

9 *Principles*, Definitions, 95.

10 *Principles*, Definitions, 95: '[a] "church" means an autonomous member church, national, regional, provincial, or extra-provincial, of the Anglican Communion'.

11 *Principles*, Definitions, 95: '[t]he expression "general law of a church" means the law of that body which has competent jurisdiction over that church, as distinct from laws of units within a church such as a diocese'.

Canons Ecclesiastical 1603, or pre-Reformation Roman canon law.[12] In addition to formal laws, churches today increasingly use quasi-legislation, or 'soft law' – informal administrative rules designed to supplement formal laws (to clarify or implement them); these resemble laws (with prescriptive language), but there is dubiety as to their binding force.[13]

Consequently, the Anglican *Principles of Canon Law* (2008) deal with the sources and forms of law within churches of the Communion.[14] Scripture, reason, and tradition are fundamental authoritative sources of church law.[15] Laws exist in a variety of formal sources that should be identifiable, including constitutions, canons, rules, regulations, and other instruments. Historical sources recognised as such in the canonical tradition, including custom, have such status in a church as may be prescribed by its law. Laws contain principles, norms, standards, policies, directions, rules, precepts, prohibitions, powers, freedoms, discretions, rights, entitlements, duties, obligations, privileges, and other juridical concepts. Laws should be short, clear, and simple to the extent that is consistent with their purpose, meaning, and comprehensiveness.[16] With the exception of the last proposition, these Anglican ideas are broadly mirrored in the *Principles of Christian Law* (Principles I.2.1–2), but the latter, unlike the former, deals explicitly with the entity of ecclesiastical quasi-legislation (Principle I.2.3).

II The scope and purpose of Anglican law

There is considerable but not exact convergence between Anglican churches as to the subjects treated by their regulatory instruments. What differs is the instrument by which subjects are treated. Typically, *constitutions* treat matters of faith and doctrine; territorial, governmental, and institutional organisation (legislative, administrative, judicial); appointment of bishops; discipline; and property. *Canons*, by contrast, address functions of ordained and lay ministers as well as liturgical and sacramental matters.[17] In turn, the Anglican *Principles of Canon Law* recognise that laws of churches deal with church order, government, ministry,

12 N. Doe, *Canon Law in the Anglican Communion* (1998), op cit., Chapter 1.

13 See N. Doe, 'Ecclesiastical Quasi-legislation', in N. Doe, M. Hill and R. Ombres, eds., *English Canon Law* (Cardiff: University of Wales Press, 1998) 93–103.

14 *Principles*, Definitions, 95: a 'principle of canon law' is 'a foundational proposition or maxim of general applicability which is induced from the similarities of the legal systems of churches, derives from the canonical tradition or other practices of the church, expresses a basic theological truth or ethical value, and is about, is implicit in, or underlies canon law'.

15 See the seminal work of Richard Hooker in this regard, discussed from a juridical perspective in N. Doe, 'Richard Hooker: Priest and Jurist', in M. Hill and R.H. Helmholz, eds., *Great Christian Jurists in English History* (Cambridge: Cambridge University Press, 2017) 115–137.

16 *Principles*, Principle 4.

17 N. Doe, *Canon Law in the Anglican Communion* (1998), op cit., 21–22.

doctrine, liturgy, rites, property, and ecumenism.[18] These subjects are mirrored in the *Principles of Christian Law* (Principle I.4.1). However, the Anglican principles also recognise 'the limits of law': laws should reflect but cannot change Christian truths; laws cannot encompass all facets of ecclesial life; laws cannot prescribe the fullness of ecclesial life, ministry, and mission; laws function predominantly in the public sphere of church life; and some laws articulate immutable truths and values.[19] Yet the *Principles of Christian Law* is silent on the matter of the scope and limits of church law.

In Anglicanism, the purposes of law are shaped by the understandings each church has about the nature of the church universal and about itself as an institutional church. First, at a national level, the principal purposes of laws are to facilitate and to order the life and mission of that church; typically, law exists 'to serve the sacramental integrity and good order of the Church and to assist its mission and its witness to the Lord Jesus Christ'.[20] Therefore, the *Principles of Canon Law* (2008) provide that law exists to assist a church in its mission and witness to Jesus Christ; a church needs within it laws to order, and so facilitate, its public life and to regulate its own affairs for the common good; and the law is not an end in itself.[21] These are reflected directly in the *Principles of Christian Law* on 'the servant law' (Principles I.3.1–2).

Second, Anglicans recognise a close relationship between church law and theology: law should reflect the revealed will of God; law has a historical basis and a theological foundation, rationale, and end; law is intended to express publicly the theological self-understanding and practical policies of a church; and law in a church exists to uphold the integrity of the faith, sacraments, and mission and to provide good order, to support communion amongst the faithful, to put into action Christian values, and to prevent and resolve conflict.[22] With the exception of the last proposition (about communion, values, and conflict), these, too, are generally echoed in the *Principles of Christian Law*, which adds, more fully than does Anglicanism, that 'law may realise certain theological propositions in norms of conduct and behaviour' (Principle I.3.3).

III The effect and structure of Anglican laws

In Anglicanism, the extent to which, and the ways in which, regulatory instruments are binding vary as between the different churches. At a national level, in some churches the laws bind only ordained ministers, but in others they bind both ordained and laypersons.[23] Often laws provide for undertakings to be made by church members to assent to or comply with the law (though the *Principles*

18 These subjects are treated, respectively, in the eight parts of the *Principles*: see Chapter 1.
19 *Principles*, Principle 3.1–4, 6; 3.5.
20 Church in Wales, Con., Prefatory Note.
21 *Principles*, Principle 1.
22 *Principles*, Principle 2.
23 Compare the Church of England and the Church in Wales: Doe (1998) 23.

of Christian Law is silent on this matter).[24] The administration and enforcement of Anglican law are assigned to a variety of institutions. On the one hand, compliance is effected by means of executive or quasi-judicial authority, typically on the basis of the doctrine of canonical obedience – clergy must obey the lawful and honest directions of their bishops.[25] On the other hand, churches provide for formal judicial law enforcement and resolution of conflict: courts/tribunals are ordered hierarchically and their subject matter jurisdictions are prescribed in laws.[26] Failure to comply with law may result in proceedings for offences and imposition of sanctions (typically conceived as medicinal and corrective, such as rebuke, suspension, and exclusion).[27] In turn, the principles of Anglican canon law recognise the binding effect of laws: the law binds the bishops, clergy, and lay officers; the laws may bind laypeople who do not hold office; no one shall be above the law; all institutions and persons in positions of authority or office must act in accordance with the law; laws, rights, and duties are enforceable within a church by its own ecclesiastical authorities through executive action or by judicial process; any person or body injured by a violation of law should be able to obtain a remedy before a competent ecclesiastical authority in accordance with the law; and a voluntary declaration or other form of assent prescribed by law to comply with ecclesiastical jurisdiction binds the person making that declaration.[28] The *Principles of Christian Law* is much less detailed on these matters – it simply provides that 'laws may be binding or exhortatory' and that members of a church 'are subject to its laws as are its competent institutions to the extent that the law provides' (Principles I.4.3 and 4). Nevertheless, all of the elaborate Anglican principles on church discipline, informal dispute resolution, visitation, and due judicial process in church courts/tribunals[29] are echoed directly in the Christian law principles and in largely comparable detail, with the exception of those on the nature of ecclesial discipline itself (Principles V.1–4).

There are also parallels between the Anglican laws and the principles of Christian law with regard to the creation, interpretation, and dispensation of church law. The Anglican principles provide that later laws abrogate earlier laws, that laws are prospective and should not be retrospective unless this is clearly provided for in the laws themselves, and that laws may be dispensed with in their application to particular cases on the basis of legitimate necessity provided authority to dispense is clearly given by the law,[30] and all find a place in the *Principles of Christian Law* (Principles I.4.5, 6, and 9). Likewise, Anglican principles deal with the

24 Scottish Episcopal Church, Can. 58: 'I will give all due obedience to the Code of Canons'.

25 E.g. Church of England, Can. C14: 'I will pay true and canonical obedience to the Lord Bishop of C and his successors in all things lawful and honest'.

26 See N. Doe, *Canon Law in the Anglican Communion* (1998) 80–88.

27 Ibid., 80–85.

28 *Principles*, Principle 5.1–6.

29 *Principles*, Principle 23: visitation; and Principle 23: due judicial process.

30 *Principles*, Principle 7.1–6.

interpretation of law,[31] though these are much more detailed than their equivalents in the *Principles of Christian Law* (Principles I.5.1–3). The basic juridical presumptions that appear in the Anglican text, however, find no parallel in the *Principles of Christian Law*.[32]

IV Church membership

Anglicans use the concept of church 'member'. Whilst a church 'should serve all who seek its ministry, membership in a church' may be based on any or all of the following: baptism; baptism and confirmation; baptism, confirmation, and communicant status; or regular attendance at public worship. In turn, there are various classes of member: a communicant is a person who has received Holy Communion at such frequency and on such occasions as may be set by law, and a communicant in good standing is one who for a prescribed period has been faithful in worship and has supported the work and mission of the church. Names may be entered on a parish roll or other register, subject to any conditions as prescribed by law, enabling eligibility for selection to participate in governance and other functions and offices; but names may be removed only in accordance with the law, justice, and equity. Membership of a church implicitly involves profession of the faith; acceptance of its doctrine, government, law, and discipline; and enjoyment of fundamental and other rights and duties.[33] All the faithful, lay, and ordained are responsible for church life and witness and should regularly attend public worship, especially at Holy Communion; practise daily devotion, private prayer, Bible reading, and self-discipline; bring the example of Christ into everyday life; uphold Christian values; be of personal service to church and community; and assist the church financially. Two types of rights are envisioned, inherent rights and acquired rights: 'all persons, equal in dignity before God, have inherent rights and duties inseparable from their dignity as human beings created in the image and likeness of God and called to salvation

31 *Principles*, Principle 8.1–4: laws should be interpreted by reference to their text and context; laws are to be understood according to the proper meaning of their words; authoritative interpretations of law may be issued by church courts or tribunals, or by commissions or other bodies designated to interpret the law, in such cases, in such manner and with such effect as may be prescribed by the law; and if in a church the meaning of laws remains in doubt recourse may be had to analogous texts, the purposes and circumstances of the law, the mind of the legislator, the jurisprudence of church courts and tribunals, the opinion of jurists, the principles of canon law and theology, the common good, and the practice and tradition of that church and of the church universal.

32 *Principles*, Principle, 9.1–3: validity is acquired by full conformity to the will of God and is presumed by conformity to law; ordained ministries, validly conferred according to the gospel, the catholic tradition and the law of a church, are given by God as instruments of grace and possess not only the inward call of the Spirit, but also the commission of Christ through his body, the church universal; episcopal ministry, personal and collegial, is maintained, embodied and exercised in a variety of forms, under law, in continuity of apostolic life and mission.

33 *Principles*, Principle 27.

through Jesus Christ'; however, baptism is the foundation of Christian rights and duties, and a church should respect both sets of rights and duties. Also, the faithful enjoy such rights to government, ministry, teaching, worship, sacraments, rites, and property as may flow from their human dignity, baptism, the duties of others, 'and the law of that church'. There is to be no unlawful denial of equal rights, status, or access to the life, membership, government, ministry, worship, rites, and property of a church on grounds of race; colour; ethnic, tribal, or national origin; marital status; sex; sexual orientation; disability; or age.[34] All the faithful, as appropriate to their state, participate in teaching, governing, and sanctifying; laypersons exercise authority in church life according to, and are subject to discipline to the extent prescribed by, law.[35] These Anglican ideas are all broadly echoed in the *Principles of Christian Law* applicable to the faithful (Principles II.1–4).

V Ordained ministers

For Anglicanism, the holy orders are bishops, priests, and deacons – the 'threefold ordained ministry'.[36] No person is to be a priest or deacon unless called, tried, examined, and admitted according to the rite of ordination, and the diocesan bishop has a special responsibility, assisted by the faithful, to provide sufficient priests and deacons and to foster vocations to ordained ministry. The normal age for the diaconate is 23 and that for the priesthood 24. There is no right to ordination. Baptism and confirmation are necessary qualifications, and the authority to determine suitability of a candidate rests with the bishop, who must be satisfied the candidate has the necessary spiritual, moral, physical, and mental qualities. Both men and women may be ordained to the extent permitted by law. A candidate must assent to church doctrine, use only lawful forms of service, obey the lawful and honest directions of the bishop, and comply with the law. Progression from diaconate to priesthood is not automatic. Normally, a deacon may not be ordained priest for at least one year, unless the bishop has good cause to ordain earlier. Laws provide for training and the production of prescribed documents prior to ordination. The ordination must be in accordance with the ordinal or other authorised form of service, and it must be administered episcopally under the authority of the diocesan bishop. Valid ordination consists in fulfilment of what the church universal intends, with the free consent of the candidate, through the imposition of hands by a validly consecrated bishop, with the invocation of the Holy Spirit to give grace for the work of a priest/deacon, whichever is bestowed. Ordination cannot be repeated; orders are indelible.[37]

34 *Principles*, Principle 26.
35 *Principles*, Principle 25.1.
36 *Principles*, Principle 31. See e.g. England: Can. C1.1.
37 *Principles*, Principle 32. See e.g. England: Can. C7. Ordinations usually take place in a cathedral: see N. Doe, *The Legal Architecture of English Cathedrals* (Abingdon: Routledge, 2017) Chapter 1.

There is nothing problematic in the *Principles of Christian Law* (Principle III.1) in terms of all of these Anglican norms.

In Anglican churches, to exercise public ordained ministry within a diocese, prior authorisation must be obtained from the diocesan bishop.[38] The bishop may confer authority to minister publicly by means of appointment to a particular office (such as that of a parish priest), licence, written permission, or such other process prescribed by law. The laity, or their representatives, may participate in the appointment of clergy to an office or other public ministry in such manner, and to such extent, as may be prescribed by law. Authorisation to exercise public ministry in a diocese may be refused only on grounds provided for in the law. No bishop, priest, or deacon coming from another diocese may exercise public ministry in the host diocese without the prior permission of the host diocesan bishop. Before permitted by the bishop to minister in the diocese, clergy from another diocese must produce to the host bishop such evidence of ordination and good standing as is lawfully required.[39] Once more, these norms are reflected well in the *Principles of Christian Law* on ecclesial offices (Principle III.2)

In Anglicanism ministry is service, a gift of God, and the public ministry of ordained persons is exercised under Episcopal authority in various forms, including parish ministry,[40] to which, like all offices, prescribed functions attach.[41] First, all clergy (1) should fashion themselves after the example of Christ and should not engage in any occupations, habits, or recreations inconsistent with their sacred calling but lead a disciplined way of life appropriate to their clerical state; (2) must be diligent in liturgical life, particularly the Eucharist, personal prayer, self-examination, and study, especially Holy Scripture; (3) must not engage in any secular employment or other occupation without permission from the diocesan bishop; (4) must reside within the territory of the ecclesiastical unit to which they are assigned unless the bishop permits otherwise; (5) are subject to the jurisdiction of their diocesan bishop and must comply with that bishop's lawful and honest directions; and (5) should dress in a manner suitable to the performance of their ministry as may be a sign and mark of their calling both to those within their charge and to society at large.[42] Second, a deacon must care for people in

38 *Principles*, Principle 42.1; 34.1: charge of a parish; 34.2: assistant clergy.

39 *Principles*, Principle 42.1–6. See e.g. England: Can. C10 and Patronage (Benefices) Measure 1986: appointment is by (1) presentation/nomination by the patron (e.g. bishop) consulting parish representatives (with appeal against refusal to the archbishop); (2) admission/institution by the bishop, and (3) induction.

40 *Principles*, Principle 28: the exercise of ministry is structured, authorised, representative, and accountable.

41 *Principles*, Principle 29; 29.1: ecclesiastical offices include the offices of primate, archbishop, bishop, dean, archdeacon, and parish priest; ecclesiastical office (its meaning and admission to it).

42 *Principles*, Principle 41: clerical discipleship. See e.g. England: Can. C26.1: personal prayer, self-examination, and study; Can. C14.3: 'I swear by Almighty God that I will pay true and canonical obedience to the Lord Bishop of C and his successors in all things lawful and honest'; Scotland: Can. 19: secular employment without the permission of the bishop; Wales: Con. VII.48–51: residence.

need and assist the priest (subject to the priest's direction) but must not exercise functions reserved to the order of priests.[43] Third, working with the bishop, a priest is to: (1) proclaim the Gospel through preaching and teaching, administer the sacraments, and provide pastoral care; (2) preside at the Eucharist, pronounce the absolution; (3) visit those within their charge for spiritual consultation and advice, prepare candidates for baptism and confirmation and reception, and instruct children within their care in the Christian faith.[44] Fourth, a parish priest has the primary authority and responsibility for the care of souls, exercised under the general authority, oversight, and pastoral direction of the diocesan bishop.[45] Fifth, in the exercise of their ministry, clergy must uphold the professional ethic of public ministry (e.g. honesty, integrity, and efficiency) and standards in the delivery of pastoral care, respect for colleagues, and confidentiality.[46] Moreover, an archdeacon assists the diocesan bishop in governance within the archdeaconries of a diocese, and an area dean must report to the bishop any matter in a parish within the deanery that it may be necessary or useful for the bishop to know (e.g. illness).[47] The diocesan bishop exercises a ministry of oversight as chief pastor of the diocese.[48] All of these arrangements in Anglican law are echoed adequately in the *Principles of Christian Law* as to the functions of ordained ministers and exercise of oversight (Principles III.3 and 4).

VI The institutions of church governance

An Anglican church consists of one or more province(s). The central organ of government is the national assembly, styled typically the general synod, composed of bishops, clergy, and laity. The archbishop or primate convenes and presides at meetings held each year – and there are complex procedures for the transaction of business. The principal functions of central assemblies are law-making, policy-making, and, to a lesser extent, administration over a wide range of prescribed subjects of common concern to the whole of the church. The central assembly also has various committees, commissions, boards, and other administrative bodies.[49]

In addition, the territory of each Anglican church is divided into dioceses; a diocese is a territory under the oversight of a diocesan bishop and assisted by a representative assembly (typically a synod or conference). The creation, division,

43 *Principles*, Principle 33.1–3.
44 *Principles*, Principle 33.4–6.
45 *Principles*, Principle 34; see e.g. Scotland: Cans. 17.3 and 38.4.
46 *Principles*, Principle 43: trust; 44: accessibility; 45: respect for custom; 46: disclosure of confidential information received outside confession may be subject to disciplinary process.
47 *Principles*, Principle 33.6. See e.g. Ireland: Con. II.38–42: Wales: Con. VII.2.
48 *Principles*, Principle 35 (admission to the order of bishop), 36 (admission to office), 37 (functions).
49 See *Principles*, Part III.

amalgamation, and dissolution of a diocese are usually in the keeping of the central national church assembly.[50] The diocesan assembly consists of houses composed of the bishop and elected representatives of the clergy and laity; meetings are convened and presided over by the bishop and are usually annual.[51] It may have competence to legislate for the diocese in prescribed matters and jurisdiction over its more localised ecclesiastical units (such as parishes); the diocesan assembly must also consider any matter referred by the central assembly and implement the lawful directions of the latter to which it must make an annual report.[52] The diocesan assembly has an executive organ (its standing or executive committee) that acts with the authority of the assembly between its sessions, advises the bishop, and discharges other functions assigned to it by the assembly; the diocesan assembly may also establish a variety of committees, boards, commissions, and other bodies, such as on ministry, liturgy, and finance, under the control of the diocesan assembly.[53]

An Anglican diocese consists of more localised ecclesial units, such as archdeaconries, and deaneries, and within these, parishes, the territorial organisation of which is usually in the keeping of the diocesan assembly.[54] Each parish is governed by an assembly (typically a parochial church council) consisting of clergy and representatives of the laity elected at an annual meeting; the assembly is usually under the chairmanship of the minister in charge of the unit, and elaborate rules cover meetings, quorum, and decision-making.[55] The council and minister must cooperate in exercising spiritual, governmental, and administrative functions. Typically, the assembly must promote the whole mission of the church, pastoral, evangelistic, social, and ecumenical; report to the diocesan assembly; elect officers; implement matters refereed to it by the diocesan bishop or assembly; administer property; and cooperate at visitations.[56] All of these arrangements, at their various territorial levels, reflect the *Principles of Christian Law*, as does the institutional organisation of the instruments of communion in the worldwide Anglican Communion, with their non-coercive jurisdictions (Principles IV.1–5).

50 *Principles*, Principle 20: a diocese consists of the faithful in a territory overseen by a bishop.

51 See e.g. England: Synodical Government Measure 1969, s. 4; Scotland: Can. 50; Wales: Con. IV.

52 *Principles*, Principle 20: the bishop may give/withhold consent to proposed legislation if allowed, but may not legislate unilaterally; see e.g. Wales: Con. IV.43: Acts of the Diocesan Conference.

53 For executive committees, see e.g. Wales: Con. IV.16; for boards, etc., see e.g. England: Diocesan Boards of Finance Measure 1925, s. 1–3: the board must comply with synod directions.

54 For archdeacons and deaneries see e.g. Ireland: Con., II.42; England: Synodical Government Measure 1969, s. 3: a deanery has a synod (an archdeaconry, divided into deaneries, does not).

55 E.g. Wales: Con. VI.24: meetings, etc., of the parochial church council.

56 E.g. Wales: Con. VI.22: mission. See also *Principles*, Principle 21.

VII Doctrine, worship, and ritual

For Anglicans, doctrine is the teaching of the church on any matter of faith that a church receives, believes, and represents anew from generation to generation by virtue of its belonging to the one, holy, catholic, and apostolic church;[57] thus, 'The faith of Our Lord Jesus Christ is taught in the Holy Scriptures, summed up in the Creeds, and affirmed by the ancient Fathers and undisputed General Councils'; Holy Scriptures contain 'all things necessary to salvation and are the rule and ultimate standard of faith', the Apostles' Creed represents 'the Baptismal Symbol', and the Nicene Creed is recognised as 'the sufficient statement of the Christian faith'. Moreover, the Thirty-Nine Articles of Religion, the Book of Common Prayer, and the Ordinal 1662 of the Church of England, 'grounded in the Holy Scriptures, and in such teachings of the ancient Fathers and Councils . . . as are agreeable to the Holy Scriptures', represent the historic sources of lawful doctrine for a church in the Anglican Communion.[58] Furthermore, each church must maintain 'the Faith, Doctrine, Sacraments and Discipline of the One, Holy, Catholic and Apostolic Church, and its own doctrinal formularies shall be compatible with the faith revealed in Holy Scripture, summed up in the Creeds, and received, practised and held by the church universal in the light of tradition and reason'. Yet a church may draw up its own doctrinal formularies in terms suitable to the present day and needs of its people and circumstances so that the faith may be presented loyally and intelligibly from generation to generation.[59] Competence to develop, reformulate, or alter doctrinal formulae vests only in the national/provincial assemblies of a church subject to substantive limitations and procedural requirements as may be prescribed by its law to ensure the protection of the faith of the church universal. No new doctrinal formulae may be approved by a central church assembly without the consent of the House of Bishops or equivalent.[60] The laws of Anglican churches also make provision for the maintenance of doctrinal discipline.[61] There is nothing problematic in the *Principles of Christian Law* from the perspective of these Anglican norms (Principles VI.1–3).

Norms in service books provide for order and decorum in liturgy; enable the community to participate fully in worship; and ensure adaptability to meet local circumstances, practices, and needs.[62] All the faithful should keep the Lord's Day, commonly called Sunday, by regular participation in corporate public worship, hearing the Word of God read and taught, acts of devotion and charity, godly and

57 *Principles*, Principle 48.1.

58 *Principles*, Principle 49.1. See e.g. England: Can. A2–5.

59 *Principles*, Principle 50.1–2.

60 *Principles*, Principle 50.3–6. See e.g. Wales: Con. II.34–43: the Governing Body.

61 *Principles*, Principle 53.

62 *Principles*, Principle 54.1–5. See e.g. Ireland: Alternative Prayer Book, 1984: 'liturgy becomes worship when the people . . . make the prayers their own prayers, and turn in faith to God'.

sober conversation, and abstention from all unnecessary labour and business.[63] Clergy must provide instruction in the faith for those entrusted to their charge,[64] especially children and young persons, who are to be instructed in the doctrine, sacraments, and discipline of Christ, as the Lord has commanded and as found in Holy Scripture, and in church teaching and catechism.[65] Again, these Anglican laws are echoed in the *Principles of Christian Law* applicable to the nature, forms, and administration of worship (Principles VI.4 and 5).

The sacrament of baptism, instituted by Christ, is a sign of new birth by which those who receive it are incorporated into the Church of Christ.[66] Valid baptism is administered with water, by pouring, sprinkling, immersion, submersion, or other similar means, simultaneously with the words 'I baptize you in the name of the Father and of the Son and of the Holy Spirit'.[67] Baptism by ordained ministers is the norm, but it may be administered by a layperson in an emergency. Baptism should be administered publicly in the presence of the congregation but may be administered privately if permitted by law. Baptisms must be recorded. Valid baptism is indelible and cannot be repeated.[68] The number of godparents (or other sponsors) is customarily two – at least one should be of the same sex as the candidate – and both of an age prescribed by law. Parents or guardians may be sponsors. Subject to any permitted dispensations, sponsors must be baptised persons and should be communicants.[69] They are to help the baptised person grow in the knowledge and love of God and fellowship of the church. Parents and sponsors of infants must receive instruction prior to the baptism as to the sacrament itself and the Christian life entered by it, as must adults or others able to answer for themselves. No minister may without lawful cause refuse or unduly delay baptism of a child if the parents desire baptism. However, a minister may postpone it until the parents and sponsors are instructed and able to undertake their obligations. A minister should not baptise a child without parental consent. If a minister refuses or unduly delays to baptise a child, parents may apply to the bishop for directions. A minister refusing to baptise without lawful cause may be subject to discipline. When adults are baptised, they should be presented to the bishop for confirmation at the same

63 *Principles*, Principle 54.6: attendance; 7: Sunday.

64 *Principles*, Principle 48.2–4.

65 *Principles*, Principle 48.8. See e.g. Ireland: Con. IX.27.

66 *Principles*, Principles 61.1 and 61.3; see also AR, Arts. 25, 27: a dominical sacrament, baptism is 'a sign of Regeneration or new Birth, whereby . . . they that receive [it] are grafted into the Church'; by it the promises of forgiveness of sin and adoption as sons of God by the Holy Spirit are signed and sealed: '[f]aith is confirmed, and Grace increased by . . . prayer unto God'.

67 *Principles*, Principle 61.2.

68 *Principles*, Principle 61.5–10; 5. See e.g. Scotland: Can. 27.3: public and private baptism.

69 *Principles*, Principle 62.1–4. See e.g. Scotland: Can. 27.2: in 'cases of necessity', one sponsor 'shall be deemed sufficient'; England: Can. B23: this requires three godparents but also allows dispensation.

time or as soon as possible.[70] If there is an uncertainty or reasonable doubt as to whether a candidate has been baptised previously, such person may be baptised conditionally.[71] These Anglican norms are mirrored directly in the *Principles of Christian Law* (Principle VII.1).

For Anglicans, the Holy Communion, Eucharist, or Lord's Supper, is a sacrament instituted by Christ, the central act of worship, and an act of the whole church – and it must be maintained and duly administered by each church. Every confirmed person should receive it frequently and regularly. It should be administered in a church building, except for the communion of the sick or housebound, or in other cases with the consent of the bishop. The elements consecrated for Holy Communion are bread and wine, received in both kinds. Presidency at the Holy Communion is reserved to a priest or bishop; a deacon or authorised lay minister may assist to distribute the elements. The sacrament may be reserved for the sick, housebound, dying, or those in special need and for devotional services, if the bishop so permits. To receive, normally, a person must be baptised and, if required by law, confirmed or ready and desirous of being confirmed.[72] No minister shall without lawful cause deny the Holy Communion to a baptised Christian who devoutly and humbly desires it. However, a person, in the absence of repentance and amendment of life, may be denied Holy Communion for living openly in grievous sin or contention, causing scandal to the congregation, or bringing the church into disrepute.[73] These Anglican norms are all broadly echoed in the *Principles of Christian Law* (Principles VII.2–3).

For Anglicans, marriage is an honourable estate instituted by God, an exclusive lifelong union, signifying the mystical union that is between Christ and his church. It is constituted on the free exchange of consents between one man and one woman joined together by God as husband and wife and lasting until the death of one spouse. Marriage is a creative relationship to share life together in the spirit of Christ for the development of their personalities; procreation and nurturing of children; right use of the natural instincts and affections; mutual society, help, and comfort that the one ought to have for the other, in prosperity and adversity; and establishment of a home and family life.[74] Ministers must comply with civil law as to the formation of marriage and church law as to its solemnisation.[75] An ecclesiastical marriage is presumed valid if both parties have a right under civil law to contract it; freely and knowingly consent to marry,

70 *Principles*, Principle 62–63. See e.g. England: Can. B22.4: '[n]o minister shall refuse or . . . delay to baptize any infant within his cure that is brought to the church to be baptized' (*Bland v Archdeacon of Cheltenham* [1972] 1 All ER 1012).

71 *Principles*, Principle 64.

72 *Principles*, Principle 66, 67 and 68. See e.g. England: Can. B15 and B15A and B17.

73 *Principles*, Principle 69. See e.g. England: Can. B16: summary exclusion to prevent e.g. scandal; Scotland: Can. 26: 'it is the inherent right of a Bishop . . . to repel offenders from Communion'.

74 *Principles*, Principle 70; see also AR, Art. 25. See e.g. England: Can. B30.1.

75 *Principles*, Principle 71.1; 71.2: '[t]he parties to a marriage must satisfy the civil and ecclesiastical requirements for a valid marriage. Otherwise the minister should refuse solemnisation'.

without fraud, coercion, or mistake as to the identity or mental condition of the other party; do not fall within the prohibited degrees of relationship; have attained the required age; and, in the case of minors, have obtained the consent of their parents or guardians.[76] A church is free to impose for spiritual purposes such conditions for admission to ecclesiastical marriage as are prescribed by its law. Although a Christian marriage is one between baptised persons, the law may provide for marriage where the normal requirement of baptism is not met. Generally, a minister may refuse to solemnise a marriage for such cause, which may include conscientious objection, as is provided by the law.[77] A minister should instruct the parties in the nature, significance, purpose, and responsibilities of marriage. Lawful notice of the date of the marriage must be given to the minister, who must establish that no impediment obstructs its valid celebration under canon law and civil law; if any impediment is alleged, marriage should be deferred until the truth is established.[78] The ordinary minister is a priest or bishop, but the man and woman may also be understood as both recipients and ministers of marriage; deacons, too, may be authorised to solemnise marriage. The liturgical books must be used. A marriage is created by the free, competent, and open consent of the parties in the presence of at least two witnesses. The marriage is recorded in registers maintained in the church for this purpose. A civil marriage may be followed by a blessing of it in the church.[79] The *Principles of Christian Law* on marriage (Principle VII.4) is considerably less detailed than but in its essentials reflects succinctly the fundamentals of these Anglican principles.

In Anglicanism, the matrimonial bond is intended to be dissolved only by the death of one spouse. When this occurs, the surviving spouse is free to marry in church. However, when marital unity is imperilled, before recourse to civil law, the spouses are to approach the church, which should labour that they may be reconciled. If a harmonious or even tolerable relationship has in fact ceased to exist, a church may hold that whilst divorce is undesirable it may be preferable to the continuance of a destructive relationship.[80] After the civil dissolution of a marriage, a church may permit a person whose former spouse is still alive to be married in church and may stipulate conditions required for the solemnisation of such a marriage that it judges necessary to safeguard the holiness of marriage and

76 *Principles*, Principle 71.3. See e.g. England: Can. B31–32.

77 *Principles*, Principle 71: a church may relax baptismal requirements for marriage by way of e.g. dispensation of a bishop; a person, being a member of, associated with, or resident in a parish of, a church, may be entitled to a church marriage. See e.g. Church of England Marriage Measure 2008: the common law right of parish residents extends to persons with a 'qualifying connection' to the parish.

78 *Principles*, Principle 72.1–6; 72.4: it may be solemnised following e.g. publication of banns.

79 *Principles*, Principle 73. For England, see e.g. M. Hill, *Ecclesiastical Law* (Oxford: Oxford University Press, 4th edition, 2018) par. 5.26–5.52. The Scottish Episcopal Church and the Episcopal Church USA permit same-sex marriages; the other Anglican churches do not.

80 *Principles*, Principle 75.1–4. Principle 74: this deals with annulment; however, no provision is made for annulment within the church in the Church of England, Church in Wales, or Scottish Episcopal Church.

the respect due to it. An ordained minister may refuse for reasons of conscience or other lawful cause to solemnise the marriage of a divorced person whose former spouse is still alive. A church may provide that the decision to solemnise such a marriage is to be made by a member of the clergy, as the case may be, either alone or in consultation with the bishop or with the consent of the bishop or such other competent authority prescribed by law. A person who has a civil divorce should not by virtue of that fact alone be excluded from Holy Communion. Persons who remarry during the lifetime of a former spouse and those married to them may receive Holy Communion subject to conditions operative under the law.[81] The basic Anglican position is summed up accurately in the principle of Christian law that a marriage is ended by the death of one of the spouses and may be dissolved when so determined by competent authority (Principle VII.4.7). However, neither the Anglican nor the Christian principles of law reflect the fact that some Anglican churches (e.g. the Scottish Episcopal Church and the Episcopal Church USA) now permit the solemnisation of same-sex marriage.

VIII Church property

It is a principle of Anglican law that churches should satisfy the rules of civil law that apply to the acquisition, ownership, administration, and alienation of church property, both real and personal; property is held by those authorities within a church that enjoy legal personality as trustees or other entities of a fiduciary nature under civil law and competence under church law.[82] Ecclesiastical authorities are the stewards of church property, which they hold and administer to advance the mission of a church and for the benefit and use of its members in accordance with church law.[83] As property is held in trust for a church, it should not be alienated or encumbered without such consents as may be prescribed by church law; church trustees may sell, purchase, and exchange property as authorised by that law.[84] A central assembly of a church, or other designated body, may frame laws for the management and use of property.[85] Management and day-to-day administration of church property at the local level vest in parish assemblies

81 *Principles*, Principle 75.5–9; 10: lack of parity of religion is not of itself a reason for seeking divorce. See e.g. Scotland: College of Bishops Guidelines (1981): no priest is 'required to officiate . . . contrary to his conscience'; Ireland: Con. IX.31.3–6: the cleric consults the bishop.

82 *Principles*, Principle 80.1–2. See e.g. Wales: Con. II.56, III.2–5, 17, 20–21, 26: the representative body is incorporated by royal charter and holds property as trustees at the provincial level.

83 *Principles*, Principle 80.3–4.

84 *Principles*, Principle 80.5–6. See e.g. Ireland: Con. XI.11: the representative body holds property subject to the control of the General Synod; it may lease or sell property in a diocese with the consent of the diocesan council; X.11: movables used in services vest in it 'subject to any trusts affecting' them.

85 *Principles*, Principle 80.7.

or other entities subject to such rights of the clergy as may be provided by law.[86] National, regional, provincial, diocesan, parish, or other trustees function under the order and control of the appropriate assembly to which church law renders them accountable.[87] These norms are broadly reflected in the *Principles of Christian Law* (Principles IX.1.1–5).

For Anglicans, buildings may be designated as places of public worship that, with places for Christian burial, may be set aside for the purposes of God by consecration or dedication customarily performed by a bishop.[88] Such property may not be used for purposes inconsistent with the uses of God for which it is set aside; wardens or other stewards must not allow churches to be profaned by any temporal use inconsistent with the sanctity of the place and sound doctrine.[89] The day-to-day control, direction, and administration of places of worship vests in the parish council or other local assembly, which must ensure that proper care is taken of them and their contents and endeavour to keep them decent, clean, and in good repair.[90] Episcopal or other lawful consent, whether executive or judicial, must be obtained to alter or add to or remove property from places of worship to such extent and in such manner, and subject to such appeals, as may be prescribed by law.[91] An inventory should be kept of the contents of churches, and a church authority should inspect them and their contents at such regular intervals as may be prescribed by law.[92] There are also norms on the maintenance of and access to records.[93] Moreover, provision is to be made for clergy to have appropriate accommodation, which should be inspected periodically and whose occupation may be terminated or restricted only in accordance with law.[94] The *Principles of Christian Law* on sacred places and objects (Principle VII.4) is considerably less detailed but in its essentials reflects succinctly the fundamentals of these general principles of Anglican law.

The principle of 'financial stewardship' is equally pivotal in Anglicanism. A church should be financially independent and self-supporting, and each unit within it should be entrusted with a share in the responsibilities for,

86 *Principles*, Principle 80.9. E.g. in the Church of England each bishop, archdeacon, and incumbent is a corporation sole in civil law, and a parochial church council is a corporation aggregate; nationally, the church commissioners hold a wide range of properties.

87 *Principles*, Principle 80.10.

88 *Principles*, Principle 81.1–3. See e.g. Ireland: Con. IX.36: '[a]s often as churches are newly built or rebuilt, or churchyards are appointed for burial, they shall be dedicated and consecrated' by the bishop.

89 *Principles*, Principle 81.5–6. See e.g. Ireland: Con. IX.27.

90 *Principles*, Principle 81.7. See e.g. Scotland; Can. 35.3.

91 *Principles*, Principle 81.8. See e.g. Wales: Rules of the Diocesan Courts: the diocesan chancellor deals with such matters under the faculty jurisdiction.

92 *Principles*, Principle 81. See e.g. England: Can. F17: inventory.

93 *Principles*, Principle 83. See e.g. Scotland: Can. 42, Res. 1: inspection of registers every four years.

94 *Principles*, Principle 82; e.g. Ireland: Con. IV.51.5: a vicar has a right to a 'free residence'.

and control and direction of, the finances in that church. An ecclesiastical organisation must comply with such financial procedures and controls as are prescribed by church law, keep financial accounts, and submit an annual report with the audited accounts to the appropriate church assembly in order for that assembly to review the financial management and affairs of that organisation.[95] Also, ministers must exercise propriety in financial matters.[96] Oversight of finance in an ecclesiastical unit in a church resides in its assembly, and day-to-day administration of funds by a lawfully constituted financial executive is under the general direction and control of the relevant assembly (such as a parish council). The bishop has no unilateral general control over diocesan finance. Funds must be used according to the terms of any gift by which they are acquired, and investigation of complaints of financial mismanagement should be carried out by an independent body, with an appeal lying to an appropriate ecclesiastical authority.[97] Once more, there is a general congruity between these laws and the *Principles of Christian Law* on property and finance (Principles IX.3–5).

IX The ecumenical laws of Anglican churches

According to the principles of Anglican canon law, 'the "church universal" means the One, Holy, Catholic and Apostolic Church'; it is the indivisible body of Christ. Also, 'the Anglican Communion is a [worldwide] fellowship of churches within the One, Holy, Catholic and Apostolic Church', and each church affirms 'its communion in the one, holy, catholic, and apostolic Church' as well as its commitment to 'the catholic and apostolic faith'.[98] Anglican churches recognise 'the divided Christians of the world' in 'separated churches' – 'parts of the Church of Christ' but nevertheless 'other churches'.[99] The church universal is indivisible, and it is the will of God that separated churches should share a more visible communion than exists one with another. The mission of a church is part of the wider mission of all Christians.[100] These principles accord very closely with those in the *Principles of Christian Law* on the church universal and the nature of ecumenism and the ecumenical obligation on all Christians (Principles VIII.1–2).

95 *Principles*, Principle 84.

96 *Principles*, Principle 85.1–5: a minister must: ensure the highest standards, of honesty and care, in financial activities (e.g. keep separate church and personal finances).

97 *Principles*, Principle 86. See e.g. Wales: Con. VI.23: parish finance.

98 *Principles*, Principle 10.1; see also Definitions, 95.

99 Principle 94.1; 95: the category 'non-member church'; 98.1: 'faith communities of other Christian traditions'; West Indies: Can. 33: 'other Churches'.

100 *Principles*, Principle 93.3; Korea: Con., Fundamental Declaration of Faith and Rites: the duty to 'strive' for unity; Lusitania: Can. X.

For Anglicans, ecclesial communion between two or more churches exists when a relationship is established in which each church believes the other to hold the essentials of the Christian faith and recognises the apostolicity of the other. Full communion involves 'the recognition of unity in faith, sacramental sharing, the mutual recognition and inter-changeability of ministries, and the reciprocal enjoyment of shared spiritual, pastoral, liturgical and collegial resources'. In turn, intercommunion is 'an ecclesial relationship in which at least one but not all of the elements of full communion is present. Churches in communion become interdependent but remain autonomous'. But communion does not require 'the acceptance of all theological opinion, sacramental devotion or liturgical practice characteristic of another church'.[101] These are echoed almost verbatim in the preamble to Section VIII of the *Principles of Christian Law*.

An Anglican church is free to establish relations of ecclesial communion with other churches if permitted by the discipline of each ecumenical partner. It is for a church in agreement with its ecumenical partner to determine when dialogue reaches a stage that allows establishment of ecclesial communion. If an Anglican church enters a relation of ecclesial communion with a non-Anglican church, this effects a relationship between such non-Anglican church and other Anglican churches only to the extent provided in their own laws and the regulatory instruments of the non-Anglican church.[102] In accordance with Anglican systems of synodical government (representative of bishops, clergy, and laity), ecumenical relations may be authorised centrally (but administered locally); the authority to recognise a non-Anglican church (for ecumenical relations) vests in the central assembly or other lawfully designated body of a church. A church should establish commissions with such membership and functions as may be prescribed under its law to enable ecumenism by stages or other process, and central assemblies often have a standing commission on ecumenical relations.[103] Ministers, too, should seek to foster and participate in ecumenical partnership with faith communities of other Christian traditions, especially those with which their church already has formal relations.[104] With the exception of the last, these norms are echoed in the *Principles of Christian Law* on institutional structures for ecumenism, although the Christian law principle that a church 'should provide for the ecumenical formation of the faithful' has no equivalent in Anglicanism (Principle VIII.3.3).

With regard to ecumenical agreements, therefore, in Anglicanism, the extent and terms of ecclesial communion or other relationship between a church and a church not in the Anglican Communion may be set out in a constitutional

101 *Principles*, Principle 94.
102 *Principles*, Principle 95.1–3.
103 *Principles*, Principle 96.3; 21.6: the parish council must promote the 'ecumenical' mission of the church.
104 *Principles*, Principle 98.1.

union, concordat, covenant, or other instrument agreed between the participant churches. A church may incorporate in its own law an ecumenical instrument to which it is party in order to implement the terms of ministerial, liturgical, or sacramental communion or other form of reciprocity as agreed by the participant churches. A parish may enter a local ecumenical project to provide for shared ministerial, liturgical, or sacramental communion or other form of reciprocity agreed by the participant churches in the manner and to the extent authorised by law.[105] With the exception of the last, these norms also appear in the *Principles of Christian Law* (Principle VII, preamble and 5).

Anglican laws also provide for reception into an Anglican church of persons whose baptism was administered in a non-Anglican church. Moreover, communicant members of an Anglican church may receive Holy Communion in a church outside the Anglican Communion that subscribes to the doctrine of the Holy Trinity and upholds the apostolic faith in such circumstances permitted by the discipline both of their own church and of the host church; conversely, there may be admitted to the Holy Communion in an Anglican church, to the extent permitted by its discipline, baptised persons who are communicants of good standing in a church outside the Anglican Communion that upholds the apostolic faith and subscribes to the doctrine of the Holy Trinity.[106] These arrangements are in form more specific applications of *Principles of Christian Law* on ecclesial, ministerial, and sacramental communion (Principle VIII.4); once more, there is nothing in these principles that is inconsistent with Anglican norms.

X Church-state relations

The *Principles of Christian Law*, with regard to church and state relations (Principle X.1), clearly accommodates the position of Anglicans, their view of the state,[107] cooperation with it, the applicability of civil law,[108] recourse to state courts in disputes between the faithful, and deference to the state in its domain.[109] For example, the Church of England is the established church in England. As a result, the monarch is its titular head, takes an oath to uphold it, and appoints its bishops (who may sit in Parliament in the House of Lords);

105 *Principles*, Principle 97. See N. Doe, *Christian Law* (Cambridge: Cambridge University Press, 2013) 304.

106 *Principles*, Principle 99.

107 See AR, Art. 37: Of the Civil Magistrates: the monarch has 'the chief Government of all estates . . . Ecclesiastical or Civil' but does not administer God's Word or the sacraments.

108 *Principles*, Principle 46.2–3: processing data; 71–75: civil marriage; 77.5–7: civil law on disclosure of information in breach of the seal of the confessional; 80.1–2: trustees must comply with civil law.

109 Ireland: Con. VIII.26.4: the Court of General Synod hears no matter that 'in the opinion of the lay judges, is within the jurisdiction and more proper to be submitted to the . . . decision of a civil tribunal'.

measures of the general synod must be approved by the sovereign in Parliament, and canons receive royal assent; but generally its institutions are legally separate and distinct from those of the state. Indeed, the Church of England in Wales was disestablished in 1920, and the Church in Wales today exists on the basis of a statutory contract.[110] The Scottish Episcopal Church and Church of Ireland, as it serves in Northern Ireland, are also institutionally separate from the state.[111] Finally, other than the established Church of England,[112] most Anglican churches, such as the Church in Wales,[113] function in civil law as voluntary associations, and their internal regulatory instruments have the status in civil law of terms of a contract entered into by the members and are enforceable in matters of property in state courts.[114] These different Anglican experiences on church-state relations are aptly articulated in the *Principles of Christian Law* (Principle X.1).

Conclusion

In 2009, the Anglican Consultative Council expressed its gratitude to the Anglican Communion Network of Legal Advisers for its work compiling the *Principles of Canon Law Common to the Churches of the Anglican Communion* and commended them for study in every Anglican province, inviting each of them to submit comments on the document.[115] The underlying idea is not revolutionary. The principles are simply a statement of common factual data derived from the convergences of Anglican legal systems. This Anglican *ius commune* is not a 'top-down' binding global legal system imposed and administered by a universal Anglican authority (there is none competent to) but a 'grass-roots' development growing from the functioning in each province of their own autonomous legal system. The principles show how much Anglicans share, using their laws as the medium for so doing. They are themselves a product of the exercise of the autonomy and the promotion of communion in contributing to the common statement in which they are articulated. Provinces remain free legally to depart from or to add to them. That legal systems converge in shared principles of canon law is a concrete expression of the very character of Anglicanism and its commitment to the values presented in them, and, insofar as each and every province contributes to them, they are collectively responsible for shaping and maintaining Anglican identity. The principles may also be a useful resource for provinces to reform and revise their canon law. They were invoked in a property dispute

110 Welsh Church Act 1914, which disestablished the Church of England in Wales (as from 1920).

111 See e.g. M. Hill, R. Sandberg, and N. Doe, *Religion and Law in the United Kingdom* (Alphen aan den Rijn, Netherlands: Wolters Kluwer, 2nd edition, 2014) 46, 47, and 53.

112 See M. Hill, *Ecclesiastical Law* (Oxford: Oxford University Press, 4th edition, 2018) Ch. 1.

113 See N. Doe, *The Law of the Church in Wales* (Cardiff: University of Wales Press, 2002) Ch. 1.

114 See N. Doe, *Canon Law in the Anglican Communion* (Oxford: Clarendon, 1998) Ch. 1.

115 ACC-14, Resolution 14.20 (5 May 2009).

by the Supreme Court of British Columbia,[116] and there is express reference to the principles in the statement of the Anglican Roman Catholic International Commission (ARCIC). The Commission commends 'the further development of canons, or commonly accepted canonical principles' and suggests that Anglicans across the Communion could formally receive them.[117]

116 *Bentley v Anglican Synod of the Diocese of New Westminster* [2009] BCSC 1608.
117 *Walking Together on the Way: Learning to be the Church – Local, Regional and Universal* (2018) para 145, recommendation VI.C.

6 A Lutheran perspective

Andreas Henriksen Aarflot

This chapter offers a Lutheran perspective on the sources, subjects, and purposes of law in Lutheran churches using the (Evangelical Lutheran) Church of Norway as a case study whilst at the same time drawing on examples from other Lutheran churches, especially the Nordic churches. First, the roots of Lutheran church law will be outlined, followed by the subjects treated by law, using the disposition of the *Statement of Principles of Christian Law* (2016) as a basis. Finally, the value of the *Statement* will be assessed from a Lutheran perspective.

I The law in Lutheran churches

1 The roots of Lutheran church law

Martin Luther famously burned the books of canon law on 5 December 1520 in front of the faculty of Wittenberg.[1] Whilst this was partly an expression of his break with Rome, it also serves to illustrate Luther's view on the laws of the church. Luther argued that canon law fostered papal tyranny – it was abusive and self-serving, it was an instrument of greed and exploitation, and it was devoid of authority.[2] Luther's attack on canon law also led to an attack on law in general, but he eventually realised that law was necessary to avoid anarchy.[3]

According to Luther's two-kingdoms theory, God has ordained two kingdoms or realms in which humanity is destined to live: the earthly kingdom and the heavenly kingdom. The earthly kingdom is the realm of creation, of natural and

1 J. Witte, *Law and Protestantism: The Legal Teachings of the Lutheran Reformation* (Cambridge: Cambridge University Press, 2002) 53; this book provides a detailed discussion on the impact of the Lutheran reformation on law. See also H.J. Berman, *Law and Revolution II: The Impact of the Protestant Reformations on the Western Legal Tradition* (Cambridge, MA: Belknap Press Harvard University, 2003), and J. Habermas, *Auch eine Geschichte der Philosophie: Band 2. Vernunftige Freiheit. Spuren des Diskurses über Glauben und Wissen.* (Frankfurt: Suhrkamp, 2019) 62–70.

2 J. Witte, op cit., 55–59.

3 H. Berman, op cit., 62–63.

civil life, where a person operates primarily through reason and law, whilst the heavenly kingdom is the realm of redemption, of spiritual and eternal life, where a person operates primarily by faith and love. Christians are citizens of both kingdoms at once. As a heavenly citizen, the Christian remains free in his or her conscience, called to live fully by the light of the Word of God, but as an earthly citizen, the Christian is bound by law and called to obey the orders and offices that God had ordained and maintained for the governance of this earthly kingdom.[4] Furthermore, God had ordained three forms of authority in the earthly life: domestic authority (the family), ecclesiastical authority (the church), and political authority (the state). All three offices stand equal before God and before each other in discharging their natural callings; but, according to Luther, only the state held legal authority, the authority of the sword, to pass and enforce positive laws for the governance of the earthly kingdom.[5] Thus, one of the cardinal teachings of the Lutheran Reformation was that law was the province of the state, not of the church.[6]

For Luther and his followers, law was primarily instrumental.[7] The civil or political use of law, according to Luther, was to restrain people from sinful conduct by threat of punishment. The theological use of law was to make people conscious of their duty to give themselves completely to God whilst at the same time making them aware of their inability to fulfil this duty without seeking grace with divine help.[8] Finally, the third use of law, which Luther touched lightly on and which was further developed by Melanchthon, was the educational use of law: to teach the faithful the higher spiritual morality that is appropriate to Christians.[9]

To implement the new evangelical Lutheran teachings, the civil magistrates of cities, duchies, kingdoms, and other territories promulgated or commissioned Lutheran Reformation laws.[10] These laws came in various forms and were labelled 'reformations, ordinances, acts, statutes, mandates, articles, edicts, decrees, instructions and even occasionally as decretals'.[11] Whilst law-making was transferred from the church to the state, many of the provisions in the new reformation laws were drawn from the older canon law, with the difference that they were now to be administered by secular authorities and enforced in the secular courts.[12]

The process of promulgating new Lutheran laws can be illustrated by the decisions made in the Kingdom of Sweden and the Kingdom of Denmark and

4 This summary is based on the summary by J. Witte in *Law and Protestantism*, op cit., 5–9.
5 Ibid., 7.
6 Ibid., 179.
7 J. Habermas, op cit., 63.
8 J. Witte, op cit., 102–103.
9 Ibid., 103–104, 127–128.
10 Ibid., 182–195.
11 Ibid., 182.
12 H. Berman, op cit., 64.

Norway to introduce the Lutheran Reformation. In Sweden, the Lutheran Duke Charles convened a church synod in Uppsala in 1593, where the Augsburg Confession was adopted by the Swedish Church and it was decided that Sweden would be a Lutheran country, with the Lutheran church as a state church.[13] This important decision was adopted by a synod of the Swedish Church, not by Parliament. Duke Charles had intended to call a meeting of the national parliament but was dissuaded by the council on the ground that this was a royal prerogative his interim government could not assume. So, Charles called a church synod instead.[14] As the bishops supported the king in the wars during the time of the Reformation, the internal, hierarchical administrative structure of the Church of Sweden, including the archbishop and the chapters, was maintained.[15]

In the kingdoms of Denmark and Norway, the Lutheran Reformation was adopted by royal decree under the principle *cuius regio eius religio*. Duke Christian of Schleswig-Holstein, son of King Frederic I of Denmark, was present at the Diet of Worms and had become an ardent Lutheran after hearing Luther make his famous defence of the Gospel.[16] After the death of his father, the rural nobility elected him king in 1534, but the council of the realm, with its Catholic bishops, opposed his election. A civil war followed. Duke Christian was victorious, crowned as Lutheran king, and with the help of Johannes Bugenhagen (reformer and confessor of Luther) issued a new church order: the *Ordinatio ecclesiastica regnorum Daniae et Norwegiae et ducatuum Sleswicensis Holtsatiae etc.*, published in Latin in 1537 and in Danish in 1539.[17] In contrast to that of Sweden, the Danish reformation meant a break with the internal church structure. The archbishop of Nidaros in Norway was forced to flee to the Netherlands, and the bishops were arrested, removed, and later replaced by 'superintendents' charged with visiting and supervising the clergy on behalf of the king.[18]

Whilst Lutheran churches across the globe today have a variety of different church orders and legal systems, from state churches, through corporations under public law, to private associations,[19] the Lutheran Reformation and its legal teachings serve as an important starting point for understanding the law of Lutheran

13 L. Friedner, 'Church and State in Sweden', in G. Robbers, ed., *State and Church in the European Union* (Baden-Baden: Nomos, 3rd edition, 2019) 641–656, L. Friedner, 'Sweden', in *Encyclopedia of Law and Religion* (Leiden: Brill, 2015): https://referenceworks.brillonline.com:443/entries/encyclopedia-of-law-and-religion/sweden-COM_00000106 and T.R. Skarsten, 'The Reception of the Augsburg Confession in Scandinavia', 11 *The Sixteenth Century Journal* (1980) 87–98.

14 T.R. Skarsten, op cit., 93.

15 L. Christoffersen, 'Church Autonomy in Nordic Law', in L. Christoffersen, K. Å Modéer and S. Andersen, eds., *Law & Religion in the 21st Century – Nordic Perspectives* (Copenhagen: DJØF Publishing, 2010) 563–592, 577.

16 T.R. Skarsten, op cit., 95.

17 N.V. Vinding, 'State and Church in Denmark', in G. Robbers, ed., *State and Church*, op cit., 87–108 at 88.

18 Ibid., 88–89.

19 N. Doe, *Christian Law: Contemporary Principles* (Cambridge: Cambridge University Press, 2013): this book studies a variety of different ecclesiastical instruments – see 406–407.

churches, especially for those churches that became established in Germany and Scandinavia.

2 *Church law*

For Lutherans, 'canon law' is traditionally understood as the law of the Roman Catholic Church. It is therefore common to say that 'canon law' was abolished or rejected with the Lutheran Reformation.[20] As just explained, the Lutheran Reformation had the impact that the state took over as the principal lawmaker, including for ecclesiastical affairs. As Lisbet Christoffersen explains, in the Nordic countries 'ecclesiastical law has been understood as a branch of public administrative law'.[21] In this context, 'ecclesiastical law', or rather 'church law', which is the most direct translation,[22] has traditionally been understood as follows:

> The Church is according to the Evangelical [Lutheran] tradition both a spiritual community of faith and a society of law. In the spiritual sense the Church includes everyone who professes the Christian faith. In the world the Church appears as an organised society of people, whose activities presuppose certain forms and rules. The norms that apply in that regard for the individual church denomination, make up the church law (*kirkeretten*).[23]

In the Norwegian context, it would make little sense, at least historically, to exclude the law made by the state for the church, as that would make up most of the law regulating the Church of Norway. Thus, according to this definition, 'church law' encompasses both 'religion law' and 'religious law'. For the purposes of this chapter, drawing on the definition (in the English Anglican context) of 'ecclesiastical law' that Mark Hill uses in his book of the same title, the term 'church law' is used to denote the law of the Church of Norway and that of other Lutheran churches, howsoever created.[24] This is to ensure that not only the law made by the church itself ('religious law') but also law made by the state for the church ('religion law') is included by the definition.[25] This is in line with the understanding of Principle I.2.1 in the *Statement of Principles of Christian Law*

20 L. Christoffersen, 'The Argument for a Narrow Conception of 'Religious Autonomy', 4 *Oxford Journal of Law and Religion* (2015) 278–302 at 279.

21 Ibid., 278. For Norway, this traditional understanding is confirmed in Andreas Aarflot, 'Jus in sacra', 4 *Lov og Rett* (1983) 75, 200–212 at 200 and Arne Fliflet, 'Den norske kirkes private autonomi', 6 *Lov og Rett* (2001) 40, 323–345 at 324.

22 'Church law' is the translation I use for 'kirkerett' (Norwegian), 'kirkeret' (Danish), and 'kyrkorätt' (Swedish).

23 K. Hansson, *Norsk kirkerett* (Oslo: Aschehoug, 2nd edition, 1957) 13 (my translation).

24 M. Hill, *Ecclesiastical Law* (Oxford: Oxford University Press, 4th edition, 2018) 2.

25 R. Sandberg, *Law and Religion* (Cambridge: Cambridge University Press, 2011) 6.

(2016), where ecclesiastical regulations are found in a variety of formal sources, including statutes (in whose creation the state may be involved).[26]

The use of 'church law' as the term for law pertaining to churches is also employed by the German scholar Munsonius in a publication of the Lutheran World Federation and in some of the texts of Norman Doe,[27] who (in the English Anglican context) uses 'church law' to cover both internal church-made law and secular state-made law.[28] In the following, on the basis of the outline of the *Statement of Principles of Christian Law*,[29] I will describe the systems of law, order, and polity within Lutheran churches and the subjects treated by the law.

3 Systems of law, order, and polity – sources of law

Having defined 'church law' as the law of Lutheran churches, howsoever created, the sources of law in the Lutheran tradition take on various forms. In the Nordic countries, they include constitutional provisions, statutes, and secondary legislation made by the state as well as ecclesiastical ordinances or other rules made by the relevant church. According to the Norwegian Constitution of 1814, as amended in 2012, 'The Church of Norway, an Evangelical-Lutheran church, will remain the Folk Church of Norway and will as such be supported by the State. Further provisions as to its system will be laid down by law.'[30]

Denmark,[31] Finland,[32] and Iceland[33] have somewhat similar provisions in their constitutions, whilst the Swedish Instrument of Government 1973 states that legal provisions relating to the Church of Sweden, as well as to other religious communities in Sweden, should be decided through Acts of Parliament.[34] The Instrument of Government 1809 and the Act on Succession to the Throne 1810 also contain provisions stating that the king and heirs to the throne must confess the 'pure evangelical doctrine, as it is approved and explained in the unaltered confession of Augsburg and the decision of the Uppsala meeting in 1593'.[35]

26 'Laws are found in a variety of formal sources including codes of canon law, charters and statutes, constitutions and bylaws, and books of church order', in M. Hill and N. Doe, 'Principles of Christian Law', 19 *Ecclesiastical Law Journal* (2017) 138–155 at 140.

27 H. Munsonius, 'The Church and Its Law: An Introduction', in F. Hübner and H. Müller, eds., *What is Lutheran? Introductions to Theology, Worship, Congregation, Ecumenism and Church Law* (Leipzig: Evangelische Verlagsanstalt, 2019) 172–203 at 177–183, N. Doe, *The Legal Framework of the Church of England* (Oxford: Clarendon Press, 1996, Upso ed) 16 and N. Doe, 'Modern Church Law', in J. Witte, Jr. and F.S. Alexander, eds., *Christianity and Law – An Introduction* (Cambridge: Cambridge University Press, 2008) 271–291.

28 N. Doe, *The Legal Framework of the Church of England*, op cit., 16.

29 M. Hill and N. Doe, op cit.

30 The Constitution of the Kingdom of Norway 1814, Article 16.

31 The Constitutional Act of Denmark 1849, s. 4 and s. 66.

32 The Constitution of Finland 1999, s. 76.

33 The Constitution of the Republic of Iceland 1944, Article 62

34 The Instrument of Government 1974 (Sweden), Chapter 8, Article 2(4).

35 L. Friedner, 'Church and State in Sweden', op cit., 643. The Instrument of Government 1809 (Sweden), Article 2 and The Act of Succession 1810 (Sweden), Article 4.

Acts of Parliament are also an important source of law in the Nordic countries – that is, civil law adopted by the respective parliaments. In Norway, there is still an Act of Parliament in force, the Church of Norway Act of 1996 (with the short title, the Church Act), which contains provisions mainly on the organisation of the Church of Norway.[36] In Sweden, the Church of Sweden Act 1998 contains 14 short sections that include norms on the Church of Sweden's 'definition as a religious community with a legal personality; parochial and diocesan structure; the church fee; a general direction on property and assets; custody of and access to archives; and the obligation to provide information'.[37] There is also a Church Act in Finland – this act can only be amended on the initiative of the General Synod of the Evangelical Lutheran Church of Finland, and the Finnish Parliament has authority only to accept or reject the church-proposed amendments.[38] In Iceland, there is the Act on the Position, Administration and Procedures of the National Church governing the Church of Iceland. Even though the Danish Constitution states that the Constitution of the Evangelical Lutheran Church of Denmark is regulated by law, such law has not yet been enacted. The Danish Parliament has not passed any comprehensive 'Church Act', as has occurred in the other countries, but it has made several acts on specific topics, e.g. Act on the Appointment of Bishops, Act on Parochial Church Councils, and Act on Finances of the Established Church.[39]

In addition to the Acts of Parliament, some of the Nordic Lutheran churches make ecclesiastical instruments styled a 'Church Order' or 'Church Ordinance' (*kirkeordning* or *kyrkoordning*). With the disestablishment of the Church of Sweden, the General Synod of the Church of Sweden adopted a church order that came into force on 1 January 2000.[40] Similarly, the General Synod of the Evangelical Lutheran Church of Finland adopted in 1993 a church order pursuant to Chapter 2, s. 1 of the Church Act.[41] These church orders generally contain the doctrinal basis as well as the organisational structure of the churches.

Currently, Norway illustrates the historical move from a situation in which the state regulated the Nordic Lutheran churches by Acts of Parliament to a situation in which the state recognises that the church should be able to regulate itself. On 21 June 2019, the Norwegian government submitted a bill to Parliament with a proposal

36 The Church of Norway Act 1996 is expected to be repealed as of 1 January 2021 if and when the Norwegian Parliament adopts a bill that is currently before Parliament, with a new proposal for an act on faith and life stance communities (Prop. 130 L [2018–2019]. Lov om tros- og livssynssamfunn [Bill no. 130 {2018–2019} Act on Faith and Life Stance Communities]).

37 F. Cranmer, 'The Church of Sweden and the Unravelling of Establishment', 5 *Ecclesiastical Law Journal* (2000) 417–430 at 426 and the Church of Sweden Act 1998.

38 The Church Act 1993 (Finland), Ch. 2, s. 2.

39 L. Christoffersen, 'State, Church and Religion in Denmark', in L. Christoffersen, K. Å Modéer and S. Andersen, eds., *Law & Religion in the 21st Century – Nordic Perspectives* (Copenhagen: DJØF Publishing, 2010) 145–161 at 150.

40 The Church Order of the Church of Sweden 1999.

41 The Church Order of the Evangelical Lutheran Church of Finland 1993.

for a new Act on faith and life stance communities.[42] It provides a scheme to repeal the Church of Norway Act, to treat the Church of Norway on a more equal footing with other faith and life stance communities, and to function as an enabling act that will enable the general synod to adopt the Church of Norway's own church order for the Church of Norway, which can replace the regulations that were previously in the Church of Norway Act. At its meeting in 2019, the General Synod of the Church of Norway adopted conditionally the Church Order of 2019, subject to adoption of the bill repealing the Church of Norway Act. The church order will come into force when the new Act on faith and life stance communities comes into force.

In some countries, like Norway, some of the laws of the general synod will be considered as secondary legislation and part of the law of the land, with full legal effect; they can be enforced in secular courts if necessary. An example is the Parochial Church Council and Joint Council Governance Rules 1996, containing rules of procedure, which are binding for all the parochial church councils and joint councils.[43] If these procedural rules are not followed, decisions may be deemed unlawful and set aside by secular courts. The General Synod of the Church of Norway also makes some rules and regulations that do not have the status of general secondary legislation, but rather rules and/or regulations only binding for internal bodies or employees – for instance its Standing Orders or rules that an employer may make in its function as employer based on the principle of private autonomy. Liturgical law adopted by the general synod is not law in the strict sense – it is not legally binding at the level of the law of the land – but it nevertheless binds clergy through the agreement clergy make with the church by virtue of their ordination and appointment as such.[44]

In addition to the formal ecclesiastical regulation mentioned earlier, Lutheran churches also make so-called quasi-legislation in the form of codes of conduct, guidance, handbooks, circulars, etc., to complement formal law. This quasi-legislation consists of rules that are nevertheless prescriptive in form and generate the expectation of compliance (as is envisaged in the *Statement of Principles of Christian Law* (2016), Principle I.2.3). When adopting its regulation on the use of church buildings in 2015, the General Synod of the Church of Norway also decided to instruct the national council to prepare revised guidance relating to the regulation.[45] The national council also provides handbooks for church elections and for parochial church councils and joint parochial church councils.

42 Prop. 130 L (2018–2019). Lov om tros- og livssynssamfunn (Bill no. 130 [2018–2019] Act on Faith and Life Stance Communities).

43 Regler om formene for menighetsrådets og kirkelig fellesråds virksomhet (The Parochial Church Council and Joint Council Governance Rules) 1996.

44 This is clearly expressed in a consultation paper dated 15 February 2019 from the Ministry of Culture to the General Synod of the Church of Norway 2019: *Special provisions regarding the Church of Norway in the common law on faith and life stance communities: Consultation paper from the Ministry of Culture to the General Synod* (2019) 60.

45 Regulations on the use of church buildings (2015). The decision to instruct the National Council to prepare a revised guidance was made by resolution KM 16/15, see *Report of Proceedings of the General Synod* 2015, 170.

In addition, as church law in Norway has traditionally been understood as part of the public administrative law and the law of the land, the traditional sources of law employed by the Norwegian legal system in general are also employed when interpreting church law. As such, changes in civil law are naturally a force for ecclesial change, as they generally affect the Church of Norway. For example, church bodies must by law follow the rules of the Public Administration Act and the Freedom of Information Act.[46] In addition, the general synod has at times found it expedient to copy and adapt provisions from the public administration as a basis for its own procedures. For example, the Standing Orders of the General Synod are inspired by the Rules of Procedure of the Norwegian Parliament, and the rules of procedure for the parochial church councils, joint councils, diocesan councils, and national council are inspired by similar rules for municipal bodies laid down in the civil Municipality Act.

4 The people of God – the members of the church

Drawing on the Lutheran concept of the priesthood of all believers, the 'People of God', from the perspective of the Church of Norway, includes all who are baptised, the members of the church (*Statement*, Principles II.1 and II.2). At the same time, there is a distinction between lay and ordained (cf. Principle II.1.4). For the Church of Norway, this is expressed indirectly in the relevant legislation.[47] By contrast, the Church of Sweden elaborates the differences between the calling to all the people of God and those especially commissioned to service as ordained ministers in its preamble to Chapter 7 of the church order.

The Church of Norway Act states that 'anyone who has not previously been baptized must be baptized according to the ritual of the Church of Norway in order to become a member of the Church'.[48] Likewise, a child who is affiliated with the church becomes a member upon being baptised.[49] There is a statutory obligation to keep a record of the members in the Church of Norway's membership register.[50] When church elections are held, the information from the membership register is used to produce an electoral roll for the parish in question.

The law of the Church of Norway sets out some basic rights and duties of its members that echo those in the *Statement of Principles of Christian Law* (Principle II.3.1). In particular, the right to vote in church elections and the right to be eligible for election, as well as the duty to take up office if elected, are set out in the Church of Norway Act, s. 4 and s. 6. By contrast, the law does not give the members of the church a right as such to have their child baptised or to

46 The Church of Norway Act, s. 38.
47 Especially through the fact that lay members and priests (ordained) are elected to the diocesan council (The Church of Norway Act, s. 23) and the General Synod (The Church of Norway Act, s. 24).
48 Ibid., s. 3(7).
49 Ibid., s. 3(5)
50 Ibid., s. 37, cf. s. 3.

receive holy communion.[51] This area is more indirectly regulated by assigning to the priests the duty to conduct services and to administer the sacraments as prescribed by law.[52] For example, a regulation adopted by the general synod called the Order on the Ministry of Parish Priests contains a provision stating:

> The priest does not have the duty to conduct services or administer sacraments for persons that are not members of the Church of Norway, except when this follows from an agreement made between the Church of Norway and another church.[53]

The implication is that the priest must conduct services and administer sacraments for those who *are* members of the Church of Norway; but if a priest does not do so, this is a neglect of duty for the priest, not a breach of the right of the member in question. The liturgical law of the Church of Norway also contains some *expectations*, rather than *duties*. For instance, '[t]he Church of Norway expects that members of the Church will put their child forward for baptism';[54] and the 'church expects that all who are baptized as children, will be brought into the Church's Christian education and take part in the fixed order of confirmation'.[55]

Part of the reason for not setting down many duties for members of the church was that liturgical law was adopted by the king in the council of state ecclesiastical as an ecclesiastical ordinance pursuant to the former Article 16 of the Constitution; and the ecclesiastical ordinances could not, according to constitutional theory, establish rights and duties for private persons – this had to be done by a statute. In addition, some writers argue that it would be problematic, both theologically and legally, to speak of a right to be baptised, a right to receive holy communion, etc.[56] An argument for this is that if something was considered a legal right and was infringed, the private person could sue the church. The consequence could then be that a secular court would have to hear the case and perhaps even order the church to fulfil its duties, which may not be appropriate for a secular court to do.

In addition, part of the reason is connected with the Church of Norway's self-understanding as a 'folk church'. This self-understanding, which is expressed, among other places, in the preparatory work of the new Church Order of 2019, underlines that there should not be any other requirements for church membership than baptism.[57] By contrast, in the Evangelical Lutheran Church in Amer-

51 P.O. Gullaksen, *Stat og kirke i Norge: kirkerett mellom teologi og politikk* (Oslo: Verbum, 2000) 93–94.
52 Ibid.
53 Tjenesteordning for menighetsprester (The Order on the Ministry of Parish Priests) 2016, s. 11.
54 Alminnelige bestemmelser for dåp (General Provisions for Baptism) 2011, s. 2.
55 Alminnelige bestemmelser for konfirmasjon (General Provisions for Confirmation) 2002, s. 2.
56 P.O. Gullaksen, op cit., 93–94.
57 KM 06/19 – Kirkeordning for Den norske kirke (Church Order of the Church of Norway. Paper from the National Council to the General Synod) 2019.

ica it is the 'privilege and duty' of members to 'make regular use of the means of grace, both Word and Sacraments'; to 'live a Christian life in accordance with the Word of God and the teachings of the Lutheran church'; and to 'support the work of [the] congregation, the synod, and the church-wide organization of the [ELCA] through contributions of their time, abilities, and financial support as biblical stewards'.[58] Such provisions would not be considered acceptable for the Church of Norway – indeed, when discussing the proposed new church order in 2019, the general synod underlined that baptism is in principle the only requirement for church membership in the Church of Norway.

5 *Ordained ministry and other ecclesiastical ministries*

Lutherans understand the office of ordained ministry essentially as one, and the episcopal office is seen as an extension of the one office of ordained ministry into a wider field of responsibility.[59] In the Church of Norway, there is a requirement to be ordained to take up the office of priest after having been called to the office. This is in line with Article XIV of the Augsburg Confession that 'no one should teach publicly in the Church or administer the Sacraments unless he been called in a proper and normal way', and it is in line with Principle III.1.3.[60] According to church regulations, after 'having found the candidates suitable for the service', the diocesan bishop decides on ordination to the ministry of priests and the ordination of other ministries.[61] The bishops' conference has established a programme – The Road to Ordained Ministry – under which candidates follow a selection process to help the bishop decide whether candidates are suitable for ordination (cf. Principle III.1.4).

The Church of Norway has commissioned priests, bishops, deacons, catechists, and cantors as different categories of ministry. Deacons are responsible for directing the diaconal service in a parish, catechists are directors of Christian education there, and cantors are specialised church musicians and directors of music. Only priests and bishops are considered part of the ministry of teaching the Gospel and administering the sacraments in the sense of Article V of the Augsburg Confession; however, deacons, catechists, and cantors are all consecrated by the laying of hands by the bishop after having been found suitable for service. The general synod passed a resolution in 2011 stating: '[t]he ministry of the deacon is an independent and necessary ministry within the framework of the fellowship of ministries of the Church of Norway'; 'the ministry of the deacon is based on an independent theological foundation and is primarily understood as a caring ministry'; 'the ministry of the deacon is a consecrated ministry'; and 'consecration in

58 ELCA: Model Constitution for Congregations, Ch. 8.04–8.05.

59 A. Aarflot, 'The Collegiality of Bishops: A Lutheran Perspective', 48 *Jurist* (1988) 359–375 at 361.

60 Tjenesteordning for menighetsprester (The Order on the Ministry of Parish Priests), s. 5.

61 Tjenesteordning for biskoper (The Order on the Ministry of Bishops), s. 8.

the Church of Norway is a consecration to a distinct ministry. Moving from one ministry to another leads to a new consecration to the new ministry'.[62]

In the liturgies of the Church of Norway, 'ordination' is used only in relation to becoming a priest, and 'consecration' is used for bishops, deacons, catechists, and cantors. In a statement issued prior to the general synod decision of 2011, the bishops' conference underlined that 'theologically there is no fundamental difference between consecration and ordination. The term ordination has traditionally been used for the ministry of priests, and the Bishops' Conference see no need to change this.'[63] This decision highlighted the fact that there is a fellowship of ministries in the Church of Norway. Though not all ministries are considered as belonging to the *ministerium ecclesiasticum/das Predigtamt* in the sense of the Augsburg Confession, Article V, they are all consecrated and independent ministries within the framework of ministries of the Church of Norway. As the bishops' conference sees no basic theological difference between consecration and ordination, one could argue that consecrated ministries are part of the ordained ministry; and so the Church of Norway distinguishes different types of ordained minister (as provided in the ecumenical *Statement*, Principle III.1.2). However, according to the Church of Norway Act, s. 23, deacons, catechists, and cantors are all considered 'lay church employees' when it comes to electing representatives to the diocesan council, general synod, and national council.[64] This suggests that whilst these ministries may have been recognised theologically as part of the ordained ministry, the implementation of this recognition in the law of the Church of Norway is not yet complete. By contrast, the Church of Sweden operates the three offices of bishops, priests, and deacons.[65]

In addition to the permanent ministries that require consecration, there are also offices open to lay members in the Church of Norway. These include parish teachers, Christian educators, vergers, organists, secretaries, administrators, and churchwardens. The latter are employed by a joint council to fulfil the daily management of the joint council, including functioning as the line manager of lay church employees as well as deacons, catechists, and cantors. Generally, there is a requirement to be a member of the Church of Norway to be employed by the church,[66] but dispensation for non-members is generally given – except in

62 Report of Proceedings of the General Synod 2011 p. 264. For a further analysis of the decision of the General Synod in 2011, see O. Fanuelsen, 'A Distinct and Independent Ministry – the Deacon's Ministry in the Church of Norway: Answers and Questions on the General Synod's Decision (2011)', 13 *International Journal for the Study of the Christian Church* (2013) 312–326. Fanuelsen translates 'vigslet tjeneste' as 'ordained ministry', whereas I translate it as 'consecrated ministry'; see p. 312.

63 Bispemøtet, *Diakontjenesten i kirkens tjenestemønster (The Diaconal Ministry in the Framework of the Minisistries of the Church». Statement from the Bishops' Conference BM 03/10)* (2010) p. 3

64 The Church of Norway Act, s. 23, cf. 24 and Kirkevalgreglene 2018 (The Church Elections Rules 2018), s. 2–3, cf. s. 3–4.

65 The Church Order of the Church of Sweden 1999, preamble to part 7.

66 The Church of Norway Act, s. 29.

cases where a person's membership constitutes a genuine, legitimate, and justified occupational requirement.

As already mentioned, the internal structure of the Swedish Church was continued with the introduction of the Reformation at the Uppsala meeting in 1593. A consequence is that the Nordic eastern countries of Sweden and Finland still have the office of archbishop. In Denmark, Norway, and Iceland, there are no archbishops, something that can also be traced back to the introduction of the Reformation, where the archbishop and bishops were deposed. Historically, the bishop of Oslo was considered the *primus inter pares* of the bishops in Norway and elected presiding bishop by the bishops' conference. In 2011 a new full-time presiding bishop was appointed by the king to strengthen the episcopal leadership in the Church of Norway. The presiding bishop has episcopal oversight, with one deanery in the diocese of Nidaros, whilst the bishop of Nidaros has episcopal oversight over the rest of the deaneries in the diocese. In Denmark, the bishop of Copenhagen is considered the *primus inter pares* of the bishops' conference of the Evangelical Lutheran Church of Denmark.

6 Church governance and discipline

The Augsburg Confession VII states:

> For true unity in the church, it is enough to agree about the teaching of the gospel and the use of sacraments. It is not necessary that human traditions, that is, rituals or church ceremonies that have been set up by humans, should be the same everywhere.[67]

As church order and governance have been understood as part of human traditions, so, too, have they been considered *adiaphora* according to Lutheran tradition. An *adiaphoron* can be defined as 'a matter where there is no clear biblical guidance, and where matters therefore can and should be ordered according to what seems reasonable, according to time and space'.[68] Consequently, Lutheran churches are pragmatic in matters of governance; and, in turn, historical context has been important for the development of church governance.

In Norway, the king and the state had historically significant powers to regulate the church. With the King's Law of 1665 (*Lex Regia*), the king's role was defined as follows:

> The King also has the sole authority over the whole clergy, from the highest to the lowest, to order and arrange for all public church and liturgical

67 The Augsburg Confession Article VII (CA VII).

68 *Kirkens embete & råd: hvem skal bestemme hva – og hvorfor?: utredning fra en arbeidsgruppe oppnevnt av Kirkerådet (The Church's Ministry and Council: Who Shall Decide – and why? Report from a working group appointed by the National Council)* (Oslo: Kirkerådet, 1987) 15.

> service, all meetings and assemblies concerning religious matters, to allow or prohibit according to his judgement.[69]

With the new Constitution of the Kingdom of Norway of 1814, the royal supremacy was continued as the basis for church law even though the principle of absolute monarchy was abandoned and gave way to the principle of the sovereignty of the people.[70]

Gradually, in a step-by-step-approach, the king and, later, Parliament established bodies of the church on a local, regional, and national level. A bill for a proposed law on parochial church meetings was in 1873 defeated in Parliament, but the Norwegian government found a way to establish such meetings anyway through a royal decree pursuant to the Constitution Article 16.[71] The primary purpose for the establishment of parochial church meetings was to regulate a procedure for the adoption of the psalm book in the parishes.[72] The first bishops' conference was convened in 1917. This was followed by the adoption of the Act on Parochial Church Councils and Parochial Church Meetings of 1920, establishing parochial church councils consisting of the priest and members elected by the church members in the parish. This was followed by the establishment of diocesan councils with the Act on Diocesan Councils of the Church of Norway in 1933 – they were responsible for nominating bishops – and the decision to establish a national council in 1969.[73] This was followed by a decision to establish the General Synod of the Church of Norway as well as diocesan synods in every diocese in 1984.[74] Diocesan synods were never popular, and they were changed from a mandatory to a voluntary body with the Church of Norway Act in 1996.[75] The same year, joint parochial church councils (or joint councils) were established at the level of the municipality as a second body of the parish.[76] Joint councils were responsible for employing church employees and handling finances, administration of church property, and burials on behalf of the parish, whereas the parochial church council would have the residual powers that were not given to any other body in or pursuant to law.[77] Consequently, it is true also for

69 The King's Law 1665, Article VI.

70 See A. Aarflot, 'Motifs and Perspectives in the Reform Process of the Church of Norway', in H. Askeland and U. Schmidt, eds., *Church Reform and Leadership of Change* (Eugene, OR: Pickwick Publications, 2015) 18–37 at 21.

71 A. Aarflot, 'Rettslig handleevne lokalt og sentralt i Den norske kirke; refleksjoner over rettssituasjonen etter den siste revisjon av kirkeloven', 56 *Lov og rett* (2017) 195–214 at 196.

72 Ibid., 196.

73 Act on Parochial Church Councils and Parochial Church Meetings of 1920, Act on Diocesan Councils of the Church of Norway 1933, and the Act relating to the Organisation of the Church of Norway (Amending) Act 1969.

74 The Act relating to the Organisation of the Church of Norway (Amending) Act 1984.

75 The Church of Norway Act, s. 23.

76 Ibid., s. 5, s. 12, s. 13, s. 14, and s. 15.

77 Ibid., s. 5.

the Church of Norway that there are national, regional, and local church structures (see Principle IV.3–5).

The general synod currently consists of 116 members, including the 12 bishops, 11 priests elected by the clergy, 11 lay church employees elected by lay church employees (including deacons, catechists, and cantors), 77 lay members elected by lay members of the church, four Sami representatives, and one representative of deaf congregations. With the exception of one of the Sami representatives, the moderator of the Sami church council, the members of the general synod also make up the diocesan council. Upon election, the elected members become members of both the diocesan council and the general synod. The general synod is the highest representative body in the Church of Norway, with power to legislate certain church laws and administer and organise the activities of the legal entity of the Church of Norway (Principle IV.3.1). As we will see, the exercise of the general synod's power in doctrinal matters has to follow set procedures that involve the bishops' conference.

The way the general synod in Lutheran churches is elected illustrates how church structure can be understood as an *adiaphoron*. In Sweden and Norway, respectively, the members and lay members of the general synod are elected by a popular election where all baptised members generally have the right to vote. In well-developed democracies like Sweden and Norway in the twenty-first century, a system of direct church elections is seen as a reasonable system for church governance. The Evangelical Lutheran Church in Württemberg is another example of a Lutheran church with direct elections to its synod. By contrast, in Finland the lay members of the general synod are elected by the lay members of parochial church councils and the clergy members by the members of the clergy.[78] The Evangelical Lutheran Church of Denmark does not have a synod as such, but some would argue that the Danish Parliament acts as the synod of the church.[79] It is also in line with Principles IV.3.4 and IV.4.5.

7 *Doctrine, worship, and rites*

The Lutheran World Federation has the following doctrinal basis:

> The Lutheran World Federation confesses the Holy Scriptures of the Old and New Testaments to be the only source and norm of its doctrine, life and service. It sees in the three Ecumenical Creeds and in the Confessions of the Lutheran Church, especially in the unaltered Augsburg Confession and the Small Catechism of Martin Luther, a pure exposition of the Word of God.[80]

78 The Church Act 1993 (Finland), Ch. 23, s. 14.

79 H.R. Iversen, 'Det folkekirkelige i den danske folkekirke – organisation, baggrund, egenart og pejlemærke', in E. Berggren and M. Eckerdal, eds., *Ecclesiologica & alia: studia in honorem Sven-Erik Brodd* (Stockholm: Artos & Norma Bokförlag, Bibliotheca Theologiae Practicae, 2016) 125–140.

80 Constitution of the Lutheran World Federation, Article II.

Only churches that 'accept the doctrinal basis set forth in Article II' of the Constitution of the Lutheran World Federation can become member churches.[81] Whilst the Lutheran World Federation has the legal status of a non-profit association and consists of autonomous churches,[82] the expression of its doctrinal basis in its constitution mirrors the doctrinal basis of its member churches as expressed in their laws. For example, the doctrinal basis of the Church of Norway is found in King Christian V's Norwegian Code of 1687, the oldest statute still in force in Norway today. Here 'the Holy Biblical Scripture, the Apostolic, Nicaean and Athanasian Creeds, and the Unaltered Augsburg Confession of 1530, and Luther's small Catechism' are listed as the doctrinal basis of the church.[83] For Denmark, King Christian V's Danish Code of 1683 contained similar provisions for the Evangelical Lutheran Church in Denmark.[84] The Church of Sweden has made provisions about its doctrinal basis in its church order (Chapter 1, Article 1).[85] Similarly, the Evangelical Lutheran Church of Finland keeps its provisions regarding its doctrinal basis in the first section of its church order.[86]

Returning to Norway, it is expected that the government will put forward a proposal to repeal the relevant provisions of the Norwegian Code of 1687 when the General Synod of the Church of Norway has adopted its own church order containing its doctrinal basis once the Church of Norway Act is repealed (see previous discussion).[87] However, historically, before the constitutional changes in 2012, the king had the formal responsibility to 'at all times profess the Evangelical-Lutheran religion, uphold and protect the same' as well as to ordain all public church services and religious worship, all meetings and assemblies dealing with religious matters, and ensure that public teachers of Religion follow the norms prescribed for them'.[88] In the Norwegian constitutional tradition, with a constitutional monarchy, the king in these provisions would mainly be understood as the king-in-council; that is, the Norwegian Council of State. There was also a requirement that more than half the members of the council of state had to profess the official religion of the state.[89] When dealing with ecclesiastical ordinances or other cases pertaining strictly to the Church of Norway, the councillors of state that were not members of the church would not take part. For the purpose of

81 Ibid., Article V.1
82 Bylaws of the Lutheran World Federation, Article 1.1. and Constitution of the Lutheran World Federation, Article IV.
83 Kong Christian den Femtis Norske Lov 1687 (King Christian V's Norwegian Code of 1687), Book 2 Chapter 1.
84 Kong Christian den Femtis Danske Lov 1683 (King Christian V's Danish Code of 1683), Book 2 Chapter 1.
85 The Church Order of the Church of Sweden 1999, Ch. 1, s. 1.
86 The Church Order of the Evangelical Lutheran Church of Finland 1993, s. 1
87 Prop. 130 L (2018–2019). Lov om tros- og livssynssamfunn (Bill no. 130 [2018–2019] Act on Faith and Life Stance Communities) p. 227.
88 The Constitution of the Kingdom of Norway 1814, Articles 4 and 16, respectively, before the amendments in 2012.
89 The Constitution of the Kingdom of Norway 1814, Article 12.

dealing with ecclesiastical matters, the council of state would be called what can be translated as the council of state ecclesiastical (*kirkelig statsråd*). The king in the council of state ecclesiastical was considered constitutionally to be the highest body of the Church of Norway.[90] The council of state ecclesiastical had the responsibility to appoint bishops and deans (including area/rural deans) as well as pass 'ecclesiastical ordinances' by royal decree.

A typical 'ecclesiastical ordinance' was to approve liturgy books. The power to make ecclesiastical ordinances was considered part of the king's prerogative powers, which the Norwegian Parliament could not infringe.[91] By royal decree 26 October 1990, the king delegated the authority to adopt liturgies for use in the church to its general synod.[92]

The Norwegian Constitution, Article 16, was changed 21 May 2012; it abolished the king's role in ecclesiastical affairs, although, according to King Harald V's own wish,[93] the king would still be required to 'at all times profess the Evangelical-Lutheran religion'.[94] At the same time, by an amendment of the Church of Norway Act, the general synod was recognised as 'the highest representative body in the Church of Norway' and, as such, responsible for 'deciding on all books of services (liturgies, rituals, etc.) to be used in the Church'. The preparatory works of the amendment of the Church Act stated that 'the provision aims at clarifying and recognising that the general synod possesses this authority *by virtue* of its role as the faith community the Church of Norway's highest representative body'.[95] Christoffersen argues that 'the 2012 change of the Church law did not clearly enough answer the question of whether this piece of legislation was *delegation by law* or whether it was a confirmation of a *sui generis status according to FROB*' whilst at the same time discussing many sub-arguments for the *sui generis* argument.[96] In the bill on faith and life stance communities in Norway, the responsible ministry states that the provision from 2012

> is designed in such a way that the liturgical authority is not assigned to the General Synod from the Parliament. The liturgies are expressions of the

90 St. meld. nr. 17 (2007 2008) *Staten og Den norske kirke (White Paper no. 17 (2007 2008) The State and the Church of Norway)* p. 22 and the NOU 2006: 2 *Staten og Den norske kirke (Norwegian Official Report no. 2 (2006) The State and the Church of Norway)* 17.

91 This was affirmed by the Supreme Court in a case from 1987, *Rt. 1987 s. 473* (cited according to the Norwegian citation style).

92 Royal decree 26 October 1990.

93 I. Vik and C. Endresen, 'Norway, Religion and the United Nations', in A. Stensvold, ed., *Religion, State and the United Nations: Value Politics* (Abingdon: Routledge, 2017) 170–184 at 173.

94 The Constitution of the Kingdom of Norway 1814, Article 4.

95 Prop. 71 L (2011–2012). Endringer i kirkeloven m.m. (Bill no. 71 L (2011–2012) The Church of Norway (Amending) Act etc.) p. 34.

96 L. Christoffersen, 'Towards Re-Sacralisation of Nordic Law?', in M.T. Mjaaland, ed., *Formatting Religion: Across Politics, Education, Media, and Law* (Abindgon: Routledge, 2019) 175–204 at 184 and 193–194.

> Church's doctrine, and the Parliament can hardly regulate such internal affairs in the faith community of the Church of Norway, nor by assigning competence in such matters to an ecclesiastical body.[97]

Based on this, the liturgical authority of the general synod should be considered inherent, as the highest representative body of the Church of Norway. The Church of Norway is a faith community, and it would have been an infringement of the Church of Norway's collective religious freedom under the European Convention on Human Rights, Article 9, and the United Nations International Covenant of Civil and Political Rights, Article 12, if the state had regulated such affairs after the king in the council of state ecclesiastical was abolished in 2012.

Whilst it is the general synod that is responsible for making liturgical and doctrinal decisions, the episcopal ministry has an important role of oversight in doctrinal matters through the bishops' conference. As with all matters before the general synod, the national council is responsible for preparing the decisions of the general synod, including those on liturgical and doctrinal matters; but the Standing Orders of the General Synod, s. 2–4, state:

> Matters of a doctrinal character shall be referred to the Bishops' Conference before the General Synod considers them. Matters concerning the church's liturgy and psalm book, shall be prepared according to the rules of procedure in liturgical matters before final consideration. If a 2/3 majority of the Bishops' Conference recommends a motion, and the motion is not passed by the General Synod, the motion shall be referred back to the Bishops' Conference. If the General Synod wants to take a decision which is not in accordance with the last recommendation from the Bishops' Conference, the decision requires a 2/3 majority of the members of General Synod.[98]

In addition to the special procedure with the bishops' conference, liturgical matters are prepared with the help of the Liturgical Commission of the Church of Norway.

When it comes to doctrinal discipline, the bishops' conference must consider complaints against bishops, priests, and others to assess whether they are teaching or acting against the confession of the Church of Norway. Although the bishops' conference is not a court, the respondent has a right to be represented by counsel.[99] This corresponds with Principle V.4.5. Based on the deliberations in the bishops' conference, the bishops' conference will issue a statement. If the bishops' conference finds that there are grounds for disciplinary action, the

97 Prop. 130 L (2018–2019). Lov om tros- og livssynssamfunn (Bill no. 130 [2018–2019] Act on Faith and Life Stance Communities) p. 209.

98 Standing Orders of the General Synod, s. 2–4, my translation.

99 Regulation on the procedure for complaints on doctrinal matters in the bishops' conference, s. 2.

statement is sent to the body responsible for taking disciplinary action, with a copy to the respondent.[100] It is then up to the responsible body to take action. For instance, if the bishops' conference finds that a bishop has been teaching against the confession of the Church of Norway, it is up to the Church of Norway Appeals Tribunal to consider whether to suspend or remove the bishop from office.

8 Ecumenism

Lutheran churches consider themselves part of the one, holy, catholic, and apostolic church.[101] For the Church of Norway, ecumenism is only to a limited degree regulated by law. The Church of Norway Act 1996, s. 24, states that the general synod shall take care of 'the Church of Norway's international and ecumenical tasks' (cf. Principle VIII.3.1).[102] The general synod has also adopted rules for the Council on Ecumenical and International Relations of the Church of Norway (cf. Principle VIII.3.2). This council was previously established pursuant to s. 24 of the Church of Norway Act, but with an amendment of the Church Act in 2016 abrogating the relevant subsection of s. 24, it should now be considered a body established on the basis of the Church of Norway's private autonomy. The council is responsible for coordinating and promoting contact between the Church of Norway and churches around the world, for maintaining close relations with international church bodies, and for dialogue and cooperation with other churches and faith communities in Norway.[103]

The Church of Norway promotes visible unity through its active participation as a member of the Lutheran World Federation, the World Council of Churches, the Conference of European Churches, the Community of Protestant Churches in Europe, and the Christian Council of Norway (cf. Principle VIII.1.1). In addition, the Church of Norway is part of the Porvoo Communion and has a made covenant, The Community of Grace, with the United Methodist Church in Norway, establishing communion between the two churches.

Whilst the membership in the ecumenical movement and the agreements on Communion in themselves have been adopted by the decision of the relevant ecclesiastical body (namely, after its establishment in 1984, the general synod), they have not been directly incorporated in the law of the church. However, the agreements have indirectly led to amendments of several provisions. After the Porvoo Declaration had been adopted by the churches, there was a need to clarify the legal consequences of the declaration. Church lawyers from the Porvoo

100 Ibid., s. 9.
101 CA VII.
102 The Church of Norway Act, s. 24.
103 Statutter for Mellomkirkelig råd (Rules on the Council on Ecumenical and International Relations), s. 2.

Communion met in Westminster, England, 16–17 January 1998 and issued a legal commentary to the Porvoo Declaration, stating, among other things, that

> The Porvoo Declaration is not itself legally binding (except in a church which has incorporated it into its law). However, the churches which have approved the Declaration are morally bound to implement the commitments which it contains.[104]

For the Church of Norway, such implementation was effected through changes made to the Order on the Ministry of Parish Priests, s. 3, and Order on the Ministry of Bishops, s. 8, ss. 11 and 12.[105] Whilst the church lawyers' meeting in January 1998 clarified several questions as to the understanding of the Porvoo Declaration, it also helped shed light on similar questions with regard to the other ecumenical agreements the Church of Norway had entered.[106]

9 Church property and church and state relations

As mentioned already, the Norwegian Constitution stipulates that the Church of Norway, as the Folk Church of Norway, will be supported by the state. The current financial system is that the state provides one third of the church's finances and the municipalities provide two thirds. The state provides a grant with the purpose of financing the activities of the national and diocesan level of the church, including the clergy.[107] The municipalities' functions are especially linked to financing the church buildings, graveyards, joint councils, and parochial church councils as well as church employees (with the exception of clergy).[108] The Lutheran churches in Sweden, Finland, and Denmark are financed by a church tax, as are German Lutheran churches.[109] The Church of Iceland follows a similar system to that in Norway.[110]

104 B. Fagerli, L. Nathaniel and T. Karttunen, eds., *Towards Closer Unity: Communion of the Provoo Churches 20 Years* (Helsinki: Porvoo Communion of Churches, 2016) 384. The whole commentary from the church lawyers' meeting of January 1998 can be found on pages 384–387.

105 The provisions are found in the current Tjenesteordning for menighetsprester (The Order on the Ministry of Parish Priests), s. 3, and Tjenesteordning for biskoper (The Order on the Ministry of Bishops), s. 8, s. 11, s. 11a, and s. 12.

106 The National Council of the Church of Norway discussed a paper in September 2001 on the status of 'Church Law Consequences of the Ecumenical Agreements – Status' (KR 61/01).

107 The Church of Norway Act, s. 2a.

108 Ibid., s. 15.

109 S. Kjems, 'The Significance of Church Tax – The Historical Background, the Concept and the Significance of Church Tax: The Case of the Established Church in Denmark' (Copenhagen: University of Copenhagen, 2018) and G. Robbers, 'State and Church in Germany', in G. Robbers, ed., *State and Church*, op cit., 109–124 at 120.

110 Ibid. – e.g. it is financed by the state via general taxes.

Church property was previously administered in Norway by the municipalities, but when the Church of Norway Act 1996 came into effect in 1997, church properties were transferred from the municipalities to the church parishes, which had just been recognised as legal entities separate from the municipalities. The church buildings are owned by the parish, unless alternative arrangements are provided on a special legal basis.[111] There are various restrictions on the leasing the church buildings as well as closing or selling those buildings.[112]

Currently, the municipalities are obliged to fund the construction of new churches.[113] However, the ministry responsible for religious and life stance affairs[114] has the power to make exceptions from these obligations in special cases.[115] In practice, the construction of new churches is quite dependent on whether or not there is a will in the municipality to fund a new church. With the new bill before Parliament – on a new act on faith and life stance communities – the legal obligation on the municipality to continue to fund new churches is preserved, but without giving any precise guidance as to how large such grants should be.[116]

One could argue that the Church of Norway is no longer a state church, but remains a church established by law.[117] In any event, the particular legal relationship of the Church of Norway to the state may be characterised as a system of cooperation on the basis of 'the establishment of, or other formal relationship between, a church and the State' (see Principle X.1.3[1]).

II The value of the *Principles of Christian Law*

Due to the Lutheran emphasis on church law as mainly an issue of *adiaphora*, most of the principles in the *Statement of Principles of Christian Law* (2016) are unproblematic in terms of the Lutheran tradition. As shown earlier, Article VII of the Augsburg Confession underlines that it is enough to agree about the teaching of the Gospel and the use of sacraments for true unity, whilst questions of

111 The Church of Norway Act, s. 17.

112 Ibid., s. 18.

113 Ibid., s. 21.

114 As the responsible minister for church affairs was obliged to be a member of the Church of Norway according to the Church Act, s. 38, the ministerial department responsible for church affairs had historically been transferred from ministry to ministry when the prime minister wanted to install a minister who was not a member of the Church of Norway (changes occurred in 1989, 1991, 2001, 2010, and 2013). Whilst the requirement was abolished in 2012, the responsibility for religious and life stance affairs still transferred from the Ministry of Culture to the Ministry of Children and Families in 2019. This was linked to the fact that the new minister of Children and Families was the leader of the Christian Democratic Party in Norway. The current ministry responsible for religious and life stance affairs is therefore the Ministry of Children and Families.

115 The Church of Norway Act, s. 21.

116 Prop. 130 L (2018–2019). Lov om tros- og livssynssamfunn (Bill no. 130 [2018–2019] Act on Faith and Life Stance Communities) pp. 262–263.

117 See L. Christoffersen, 'Towards Re-Sacralisation of Nordic Law?' (2019), op cit., 193–194.

church order and church law are generally considered issues of adiaphora status. From this pragmatic Lutheran starting point, the use in the *Statement* of the formula 'may' is helpful. For instance, when Principle I.3.3 states that 'theology may shape law and law may realise certain theological propositions in norms of conduct and behaviour', it is true that certain provisions from a Lutheran perspective may have a theological basis; however, that may not necessarily be so, as in relation to all aspects of property and finance, for example.

Principle VII.4.1, that 'the foundation of marriage is a lifelong union between one man and one woman', might, at first reading, present a challenge to those Lutheran churches that allow same-sex marriage. In 2016, the General Synod of the Church of Norway adopted a resolution stating, in summary, that the disagreement on the issue of same-sex marriage is not an issue that needs to divide the church, that there are two views on the matter in the church, and that both views will be expressed in the church's liturgical law, education, and teaching.[118] This was implemented in the liturgical law of the Church of Norway in January 2017. Similarly, the Church of Sweden, the Evangelical Lutheran Church of Iceland, and the Evangelical Lutheran Church of Denmark have all approved ceremonies for same-sex marriage. There are still different views on this issue in other Lutheran churches, including the Evangelical Lutheran Church of Finland. In light of the fact that some churches have adopted positions where they approve of same-sex marriage, this might be a problematic principle for some churches. By contrast, on a more careful reading, it is possible to understand the principle as a statement of the original *foundation* of marriage, without saying that it rules out the possibility for the law of the church to accept marriage *also* as a lifelong union between two persons of the same sex. With such a nuanced reading, the principle might still be acceptable, although it is only a half-truth for some Lutheran churches.

With reference to the Augsburg Confession, Article VII, Harald Hegstad argues that 'to be Lutheran is to be ecumenical'.[119] He considers that Lutheran churches can make a special contribution to ecumenism through highlighting the central contents of the Gospel, whilst at the same time being open to a great variety of Christians and Christian expressions.[120] As Lutherans are ecumenically minded, and pragmatists when it comes to church law, I would argue that the value of the *Principles*, from a Lutheran perspective, lies with its ecumenical potential. By using church laws to induce shared principles, comparative church law becomes an instrument of ecumenism. The Christian Law Panel has shown through their contribution to the World Council of Churches' consultation on

118 Report of Proceedings of the General Synod 2016 p. 176.

119 H. Hegstad, 'Å være luthersk er å være økumenisk (To be Lutheran is to be Ecumenical)' (The General Synod of the Church of Norway 2011).

120 Ibid. Hegstad elaborates this argument in H. Hegstad, 'Evangelisk-luthersk kirke i en økumenisk kontekst', in S. Dietrich, T.S. Dokka, Trond Skard and H. Hegstad, eds., *Kirke nå – Den norske kirke som evangelisk-luthersk folkekirke* (Trondheim: Tapir Akademisk Forlag, 2011) 11–27.

the document *The Church – Towards a Common Vision* that it can also give input to genuine ecumenical reception processes.[121]

Conclusion

The *Statement of Principles of Christian Law* can, from a Lutheran perspective, be seen as an important ecumenical instrument, which can, in the words of the Most Revd Helga Haugland Byfuglien, presiding bishop of the Bishops' Conference of the Church of Norway, be 'welcomed [. . .] in fostering collaboration between divided Christians worldwide'. From a Lutheran perspective, the principles are so carefully formulated that they are, as we have seen, in general unproblematic, especially as church law is considered an *adiaphoron*. Yet, for Lutheran churches, certain principles on marriage require careful interpretation. In general, though, the *Statement* represents a fresh new ecumenical initiative with great potential.

The ecumenical movement follows the commission 'That they all may be one; even as thou, Father, art in me, and I in thee, that they also may be in us, so that the world may believe that thou hast sent me',[122] thus calling 'one another to visible unity in one faith and in one Eucharistic fellowship'.[123] The *Statement* has an impact in changing ecumenical practice to recognise and appreciate the role of law in following this commission through developing greater visible unity between churches. The *Statement* is significant because it is the first time in the history of Christianity that common principles of church law can and have been articulated; it develops ecumenical practice by introducing church law to ecumenical dialogue, so moving that practice beyond theological dialogue; it also provides an instrument for ecumenism, enabling Christians to understand what they share legally and so recognise that they share in the realm of Christian action stimulated by church law. In doing so, it can function as a link between the ecumenical movement's branch of common Christian action on the one side and theological dialogue on the other since common Christian action can be stimulated by common principles of Christian law.

121 Christian Law Panel of Experts, *Response to the World Council of Churches Faith and Order Commission Paper, The Church: Towards a Common Vision (2013)* (December 2015).

122 John 17:21.

123 The Constitution of the World Council of Churches, Article III, states: '[t]he primary purpose of the fellowship of churches in the World Council of Churches is to call one another to visible unity in one faith and in one Eucharistic fellowship, expressed in worship and common life in Christ, through witness and service to the world, and to advance towards that unity in order that the world may believe'.

7 Methodist law and discipline

John A. Harrod

The British Methodist Church 'claims and cherishes its place within the Holy Catholic Church which is the Body of Christ'.[1] That said, Methodism, which began as a society within the Church of England whilst also attracting many from outside, manifested some characteristics which, whilst by no means exclusive to early Methodism, nonetheless in the eighteenth century contrasted with the kind of conventional conformity represented, say, by Coggan in Hardy's novel.[2] John Wesley preached a faith that invites a 'heart strangely warmed', a personal appropriation of faith, a desire to share it, and a commitment to growth in love. Moreover, Methodism's fervent Arminianism encouraged an inclusiveness and served as a social leveller. Wesley employed lay preachers, often the 'self-taught' whose faith encouraged their educational betterment, and gathered people into 'classes' for fellowship and mutual support, with lay leaders, some of whom were women. The class leader in the chapel might have in their class someone who was their foreman at work. Methodists were expected to take their faith seriously and to take themselves seriously as 'forgiven, loved and free'.[3] Of course, this quick portrait is perhaps too cheerful, but it captures something of Methodism at its best even if the reality was often more complicated and less cheery. And other less complimentary portraits – such as that offered by John Kent – are not necessarily more accurate.[4]

Can there be a causal link, or at least a coherence, between such a theology and spirituality and a church that moved, be it only slowly, to become an inclusive structure of governance with a belief in the 'ministry of the whole people of God'?[5] This is one of the questions pursued in this chapter – a question encouraged by the proposition in the *Principles of Christian Law* that theology may

1 Methodist Church in Great Britain, Deed of Union, Paragraph 4.

2 Thomas Hardy, *Far From the Madding Crowd* (London: Folio Society, 1985), Ch. 42, 292; the book was first published by Smith, Elder and Co. in 1874.

3 For an analysis of these themes in Wesley's theology, see R.L. Maddox, *Responsible Grace* (Nashville, TN: Abingdon Press, 1994).

4 J. Kent, *Wesley and the Wesleyans* (Cambridge: Cambridge University Press, 2002) 189ff.

5 The phrase is the title of a major report, adopted by the Methodist conference in the 1980s.

shape law.[6] It is argued in particular that 'connexionalism' and a 'corporate episcope' are rooted in Methodism's theological emphases, being also basic principles informing Methodist law. As such they represent a 'hierarchy of principles'.

A word of caution is necessary at the outset. There are many forms of Methodism. British Methodism is diverse enough in itself. The World Methodist Council represents many national Methodist churches, and the Methodist Church in the USA has grown far larger than its British roots. In this chapter, however, our focus will be on the Methodist Church in mainland Great Britain. This restriction is regrettable but justified on account of limitation in space, the author's own experiences, and the fact that the world Methodist churches all have their ultimate origin in British Methodism even if, for some, by way of the United States.

I The purpose and practice of Methodist law

The expression 'canon law' is rarely used in British Methodism; but laws, procedures, rules, and regulations there are in abundance, as indeed might be expected of Method-*ists*. The law of the Methodist Church in Great Britain is found in its *Constitutional Practice and Discipline*.[7] This instrument includes the 'Deed of Union' – the basis for bringing together into the one British Methodist Church the Wesleyan, Primitive, and United Methodist Churches in 1932. Included also is the Methodist Church Act of 1976, a statute enacted by the UK parliament.

Theology is a principal guide for, and informs the *purpose* of, Methodist law. Law serves the life and well-being of the church, its faithfulness to its calling, and the furthering of its mission.[8] By the same token, all existing law must be subject to theological critique, ultimately by the annual conference, the highest constitutional authority in the church (see upcoming discussion). For example, underpinning much Methodist law is the theological conviction that we play our part in responding to God's judgement and grace. There is thus much emphasis upon the church's responsibility to maintain the 'means of grace' – primarily provision for worship, the sacraments, pastoral care, and fellowship. The concept of 'being a member' implies this responsibility.[9] One tangible expression of this is that each year the presbyter in pastoral charge of each congregation writes a membership ticket for each member, the ticket outlining the basic 'duties of membership', under the headings of Worship, Learning and Caring, Service, and Evangelism. Church law also lays down the expectations of local churches with respect to maintaining up-to-date membership lists and the pastoral care of members.[10] Along with the presbyter in pastoral charge, 'pastoral visitors' and

6 *Statement of Principles of Christian Law* (Rome 2016) I.3.3. (Henceforth SPCL).

7 The book of this title is published every year with its annual amendments after the summer Methodist conference. It is referred to in this chapter as '*CPD*'. It contains the 'Standing Orders' of the conference. All references are to the 2019 edition.

8 Consistent with SPCL I.1.3.

9 *Deed of Union*, Clause 9.

10 Consistent with SPCL II.2.4–5. *CPD* Standing Order 054–5.

church stewards are among those fulfilling the church's responsibilities, as mentioned earlier.[11] Churches in a locality are grouped into 'circuits', and the circuit meeting is described as being 'the focal point of the working fellowship of the churches . . . overseeing their pastoral, training and evangelistic work.'[12] All this is but one example of the Methodist outworking of the principle that theology shapes law.

In this way Methodist law is 'enabling'. However, in other ways law may seek to maintain the order and integrity of the church. Thus, only those Methodists 'accredited' and under the church's discipline may lead worship and preach.[13] Anyone who is not accredited by Methodism must be approved by the circuit superintendent. Pastoral visitors must be appointed by the local church council, receive some training, and be accountable, likewise those working with young people. Only those authorised to do so may preside at the sacrament of the Lord's Supper – this means presbyters by virtue of their ordination or, in order to meet a need in a large circuit, suitable laypeople to whom has been granted a 'dispensation' by the conference.[14] Likewise, the law forbidding the managing trustees of local congregations from 'sponsoring meetings in support of a political party' seeks to maintain the integrity of the church as not aligning itself to a particular party, as is also the law that states it is 'not permitted to submit resolutions, or to take votes, on political matters during . . . religious worship.'[15] None of this, of course, precludes informed discussion of public issues.[16]

Methodist law is also related to theology insofar as it approves theology expressed in liturgical texts. For example, the 1846 Marriage Service of the Wesleyan Church follows essentially the *Book of Common Prayer* (1662) of the Church of England, although omitting the prayer book's second purpose for which matrimony was ordained – namely, as a 'remedy against sin to avoid fornication'. This is probably on account of Victorian sensitivities over the blunt Elizabethan language used in the 1662 text rather than because pious Methodists are not needful of such a warning! The 1936 Methodist *Book of Offices*, by contrast, is, for its day, quite innovatory. The 1662 prayer book's third purpose, the 'mutual society' of the spouses, becomes the primary purpose of marriage for Methodism, whilst still being ordained that 'children might be brought up in the knowledge and love of God'. For Methodism, marriage becomes primarily a covenant relationship between the spouses rather than primarily an institution for the nurture of children. Also, in the 1936 rite, the earlier pledge made of the

11 *CPD*, Standing Orders 630–637.

12 *CPD*, Standing Order 515.

13 The 'accredited' comprise ordained presbyters, local preachers – connexionally accredited after a process of training – and worship leaders accredited by the circuit, likewise after a process of training. *CPD*, Standing Orders 560–569.

14 *CPD*, Standing Order 1011.

15 *CPD*, Standing Order 921(2).

16 Note SPCL X.1.2, which allows the faithful to participate in politics unless prohibited by church law.

bride to 'obey' her husband is removed. The vows of both parties are identical. These changes are sustained in the 1975 *Methodist Service Book* and its successor, the 1980 *Methodist Worship Book*.

There remains a certain fluidity in Methodism over how Methodist 'law' in fact operates. The annual Methodist conference is the supreme governing body that makes the law, but a church does not operate like a sovereign state with wide coercive and punitive powers. There are indeed procedures for the discipline of its ordained ministers and other office-holders, but sanctions are elusive save for the ultimate one, that of a required resignation after due process as defined by Standing Orders.[17] Much Methodist law in practice is 'soft', in that it relies for its implementation upon consent and persuasiveness, and this resonates with an ecclesiology of a 'corporate episcope' (about which more later). In line with this, the church's initial response to disputes, complaints, and disciplinary matters is pastoral, seeking first a resolution based on mediation and reconciliation, formal legal proceedings, as laid out in Standing Orders, being followed only if such mediation fails. This expresses a theological conviction about the primacy of reconciliation within a Christian community.[18] Similarly, Methodist law urges members to accept certain obligations, but a local pastoral committee is usually reluctant to declare a member as 'ceased to meet' without the strongest of reasons.[19] Moreover, the conference may make 'soft' law that is advisory or exhortatory but not binding. For instance, total abstinence from alcohol has never been binding upon members, but it was a 'recommendation' until the 1970s, when a number of conference resolutions spoke more cautiously, commending instead 'responsible attitudes' in drinking. Likewise, the conference may sometimes commend reports for study, issue 'guidance', or encourage 'good practice'. Examples include guidelines on confidentiality and the support of those 'with impairment'.[20]

All that said, the culture of British Methodism is generally one of willing compliance. A mutual commitment to proper order is widely evident, and it is facilitated by a conference that is unlikely to enact a law that does not command the general consent of the church. The law forbidding alcohol on Methodist premises invariably holds, although some churches carried out raffles before the rule forbidding all gambling was relaxed.[21] And, frankly, beyond exhortation and appeal for compliance, there was little a circuit superintendent could do if the rule was ignored. Matters are tighter when it comes to complying with civil law when this impacts on church affairs, such as in relation to employment contracts, management of property and finance, or safeguarding procedures. This is partly echoed in the Christian law principles.[22]

17 *CPD*, Standing Orders 1100 following.
18 *CPD*, Standing Order 110(2); 1100(3.ii).
19 *Deed of Union*, Section 10(a) and *CPD*, Standing Order 054(11).
20 This is consistent with SPCL I.2.3 (on ecclesiastical quasi-legislation).
21 *CPD*, Standing Order 924.2.
22 See e.g. SPCL IX.3.2 on compliance with civil law in matters of finance.

II The Methodist principle of connexionalism

British Methodism – as Methodists never tire of pointing out, sometimes to the irritation of ecumenical friends – is a connexional church. Local churches are 'connected' together. In Britain the older spelling with an 'x' is retained. This is a fundamental guiding principle of Methodist law. Of course, it would be difficult to find any local church that did not claim to be part of and thus 'connected' to the one catholic church of Christ. Belonging together is part of being a Christian. All traditions within Christendom are to that extent 'connexional', including old dissenting traditions with a more congregational ecclesiology, as are more recent 'community' churches. Congregations within an episcopal church will be connected to and through their bishop. But Methodist connexionalism has its own distinctive flavour, which is not to say, of course, that it is in any way qualitatively superior. It has a major root in early Methodism's character as a 'society' within the Church of England. It was part of the genius of Wesley to recognise that it was irresponsible to be a 'hit and run' evangelist. Those who responded to evangelism he gathered into connected 'societies'.[23] Even to this day Methodists might still speak of a local church as a 'society', and the beginning of Methodism as a 'connexion' of societies continues to be reflected in its church law.

In their eighteenth-century beginnings the 'societies' were ruled – and that is the appropriate word – by the dominant personality of Wesley. In the present day, indicative of this connexionalism, the supreme governing body of the Methodist Church is the annual conference. In legal and constitutional terms, the whole church is governed by the conference, which alone has final authority. Save a few exceptions, all Methodist property is vested in connexional custodial trustees. The conference is restricted by the terms of the Methodist Church Act 1976 and Deed of Union, but the conference may amend the latter, though subject to stringent procedural safeguards.[24]

To be more specific, Methodist 'connexionalism' has at least three aspects. First, it is about culture and ethos. There is a sense of mutual belonging among Methodists and a sense of mutual trust that is a positive feature of Methodist culture even if to outsiders it may sometimes feel somewhat exclusivist and 'precious'. An example of this is that Methodist Evangelicals Together – a group within Methodism seeking to represent an 'evangelical' position – tend to be loyal to the connexion. They are, for instance, overwhelmingly supportive of the mutual partnership of women and men at every level of the church's life. Methodism has avoided dividing into parties. This may be partly because the church is not strong enough to afford this luxury, if luxury it be. But it is surely due in part also to the sense of mutual trust and belonging that a connexional culture nourishes.

23 See, for one of many accounts, H. Rack, *Reasonable Enthusiast* (London: Epworth Press, 1989) 237ff.

24 The procedures are laid out in the Methodist Church Act 1976, s. 5.

Second, connexionalism is signally operative in both the formulation of Methodist law and the exercise of jurisdiction within the church. The salient fact is that church law is made and amended by the conference and the conference alone, and its jurisdiction is that of the whole connexion. The result is a certain commonality about what may be expected in any local Methodist church, circuit, or district. There is a commonality about the structures of governance and also about certain expectations. For instance, parents may expect a Methodist church to be open to the baptism of their child since it is a conference requirement that all ministers be willing to baptise infants 'in appropriate circumstances',[25] likewise the practice of welcoming children to receive the elements in a Communion service. Those whose previous marriage has been dissolved can expect a sympathetic hearing if they wish to remarry in church, subject to a pastoral judgement that it is appropriate in the particular case. A minister who is unwilling on principle is required to refer to a colleague who might be so willing. Connexionalism allows there to be a nationally recognised office of lay preachers (called 'Local Preachers'), an office validated by a nationally recognised and overseen training programme, held for life, and connexionally recognised. 'Fully Accredited Local Preachers' may carry their position with them if they move to another area in the country. Connexionalism has also facilitated a nationwide network of support for specific Methodist charities – for example Action for Children, Methodist Homes, and All We Can (formerly Methodist Relief and Development Fund). This has allowed every church and circuit to follow the same safeguarding policy. Probably no other church in the United Kingdom has been ahead of the Methodist church in putting its house in order in this respect, and this is because its connexional system provided the necessary structure. The same is the case with respect to statutory compliance. There is also common practice with respect to the management of property and finance.[26]

Third, connexionalism is about a culture of mutual support. A circuit is a network of mutual support. Whilst it is usual for each church to have one of the presbyters as 'their own minister', all the ministers are still ministers of the circuit together. Moreover, in the circuit a stronger church may support the weaker financially and in other ways. Ministers are financially supported by the circuit, not by local churches, and to the circuit fund individual churches contribute in amounts locally negotiated and related to their 'ability to pay'. Grants to circuits and to building schemes are administered impartially and local churches will likewise give to connexional funds – and for the good of the wider church there are levies on local proceeds of sales unless hypothecated for local approved property schemes. Mutual support is evidenced also in the district, constituted by a group of circuits, of which there are currently some 35 in British Methodism. Districts have officers and committees to support the circuits, coordinated by the chair of

25 *CPD*, Standing Order 520(3).

26 See e.g. *CPD*, Standing Orders 532, 635–636, 650–653, 900–985. Note SPCL Section X on church-state relations.

district. In all, a fairly complicated structure is in place that allows, in all kinds of ways, a structure of mutual support across the connexion. In this way the Methodist Church reflects the principle in the *Statement of Principles of Christian Law* (2016) that states: '[a] local church and other entities may be required by competent authority to make a financial contribution to meet the wider institutional costs and needs of the church' (IX.4.4).

Similarly, Methodist law regarding ordained ministry, its procedures for selection, training, ordination, discipline, and deployment, fits like a glove a connexional ecclesiology. The British Methodist Church has two 'orders' of ordained ministry, the presbyterate and the diaconate, the latter normally characterised as a ministry of service, with a community focus, but without special responsibility for the 'pastoral charge' of congregations and without a specific focus on 'Word and Sacrament'. Deacons are required to be recognised worship leaders but need not be accredited local preachers, although some are. In this chapter, unless 'presbyters' and 'deacons' are specified, the word 'minister' will be used generically to speak of both orders.[27]

There is one day each year – and this is at the annual conference – for the ordination of both presbyters and deacons. Each ordination service is presided over by the president or an ex-president. Ordination is declared to be into the church of God, but on the same day, also at the conference, ordinands are 'received into full connexion'. This expresses a mutual commitment between church and minister. Being 'in full connexion' ministers are recognised by the whole church, an understanding expressed powerfully by the fact that all ordinations are at the annual conference. When ministers take up a new appointment they are officially 'welcomed' but not 'inducted' since it is the conference that 'stations' ministers, the circuit's role being that of merely 'welcoming'. Ministers have authorisation to exercise a ministry anywhere in the connexion. Whilst there is no specific standing order forbidding this, no circuit or church would be allowed to object to the stationing of, say, a woman or ethnic minority minister – and indeed there is no evidence any circuit would wish to do so. This would be incompatible with both connexionalism and the church's rejection of any such discrimination. But to conclude, there is nothing in the *Statement of Principles of Christian Law* (III.1) from which Methodists might demur, and Methodist understandings and processes concur fully with this section.

The British Methodist system for deploying (or 'stationing') its ministers has been many times overhauled but only marginally. Its basic philosophy remains and is so familiar to Methodists as to have developed its own analgesic. It may strike some outsiders as bizarre, but again, it fits like a glove Methodist connexionalism. All ministers are 'stationed' by the conference. Indeed, legally each station is for one year only, until the next conference. In reality, the conference usually ratifies existing arrangements where a minster is not due to move, but the conference has the right to 'pull a minister out' for another appointment. The

27 *CPD*, Standing Order 005.

'adoption of the stations' is one of the final acts of the conference and is agreed in some solemnity by a standing vote. All ministers 'in full connexion' are under the authority of stationing – and enjoy its security. If a minister wishes to serve outside the church – say, in teaching, chaplaincy, social work, or the charity sector – they must have permission by the church's due process. A minister even needs 'permission' to retire, although this is a formality if the prescribed criteria are fulfilled.[28] Moreover, that ministers belong to a single order serving the 'connexion' is further indicated by the fact that there are common terms of service. There is essentially the same stipend for all. There are no increments for years of service and only modest extra allowances for those with 'additional responsibilities.' Despite these characteristically Methodist arrangements, there is nothing in the *Statement of Principles of Christian Law*, Principles III.2 and 3.5, from which Methodists might demur, apart from expressing a strong conviction that the judgement that a person be 'worthy to be ordained' should be made by 'the whole people of God' by due process rather than by the episcopate.

To fill in the details, presbyters are appointed to a circuit for an initial period of five years, and this may be extended by mutual agreement between circuit and minister.[29] For both initial and subsequent periods, there is a mutual commitment to stay the course, unless there is a termination by due process. This has the advantage of stability and of preventing their looking for a 'better' appointment, but it also means that in any one year only about 12% of presbyters are available for vacancies. This is hardly a system designed to find the right people for each position. How many ideal matches fail to be secured because either presbyter or circuit appointment is not free that year? These concerns might be lessened to a degree by the fact that the church does have a right to move a minister before any term of service has been completed; any such move, however, is seen only as a last resort on account of pressing need.

Presbyters have only limited say over where they will be stationed, and circuits have only limited say over whom they will get. Circuits seeking a presbyter, and presbyters available, will complete profiles, outlining, respectively, the nature of the appointment and the kind of ministry offered. These are made available, and circuits and presbyter will be invited to submit a short list of five preferences – on the basis of the profile only. It is strictly forbidden for minsters and circuits to negotiate or indeed to be in contact at this stage. A 'Stationing Matching Group', appointed by the conference, then 'matches' circuit to presbyter, district chairs often being involved as advisors. And, to lubricate the system, all new appointments commence on 1 September each year. Once a provisional match has been made, the parties to this arranged marriage meet, and if love at first sight fails to sparkle, or if realism and pragmatism fail to prevail, both circuit and presbyter go into the 'second round'; but in so doing they understand that the options will

28 *CPD*, Standing Order 790.

29 Ministers serving in some other capacity likewise serve an initial appointment, subject to review.

be reduced. That said, within a general framework of 'law' the detail of practice is under constant review.[30] The system for stationing deacons is broadly similar, although more directive in character.

A minister, therefore, must submit to the 'discipline of stationing', allowing the church to decide not only their appointment but also with whom they will work, the manse in which they will live,[31] and, by implication, the employment opportunities for their spouse and educational options for their children. Anecdotal evidence suggests the church has lost fine ministers, both potential and actual, who wish more freedom in their lives.[32] Those controlling the system claim they struggle to accommodate individual preferences, and no doubt this is widely true, and chairs of districts invariably defer to the best interests of the church and do not compete for a minister for their district. Moreover, the minister is guaranteed a job and stipend until retirement, followed by a defined benefit pension[33] and, indeed, a modest house in retirement on a subsidised rent for those with 'limited means'.[34] Controlling and paternalistic it may be, but it is a secure and benevolent paternalism. Moreover, the Methodist Church may justly claim to honour the obligations placed upon it stated in the *Statement* (Principles IX.5.2 and 3).

The system is generally defended on the grounds that the 'needs of the church' have priority over individual preferences, supported by the insistence that the current system ensures that less attractive circuits and localities are adequately served. There may be some truth in this latter claim, but it is by no means obvious that the current system better serves the church than a system whereby circuits may advertise and short list and ministers apply – albeit probably only after serving a minimum period in an existing appointment to allow continuity. Curiously, chairs of districts are appointed on the basis of application,[35] shortlisting, and interview, but that option is not permitted for any circuit appointment – even for superintendents of large circuits. The claim, however, that this system of connexional stationing is adopted because it best serves the needs of the church, whilst having some cogency, is in danger of being perceived as being disingenuous. In reality, it serves best the security of 'employment' for its ministers. Suppose

30 *CPD*, Standing Orders 780–785 set out the legal framework.

31 A minister is not required to live in the manse provided, but the church refuses the offer of an accommodation allowance in lieu of a manse.

32 'Anecdotal evidence' refers here and elsewhere to what the present writer has picked up over 50 years serving the Methodist Church in various capacities. But it has to be acknowledged that in these areas survey evidence based on professionally competent research is not available.

33 *CPD* Standing Orders 800–807 set out the terms of service.

34 Since its inception in the mid-1940s the Methodist Ministers Housing Society – legally an independent charity but *de facto* part of the church – has acquired some 950 properties. Entitlement is means-tested, and rents are about one third of what the market would command. About 35% of retired ministers are accommodated and, happily, the society has sufficient resources to meet demand.

35 Technically, those interested cannot 'apply', although they may 'express an interest' or ask a friend to 'nominate' them. See *CPD*, Standing Order 423 (4).

circuits were to advertise, short list, and interview? Would some ministers fail to secure an appointment? In this case would there be a residual stationing for circuits no minister wants to serve and for ministers no circuit wants to have? By intention or not that scenario is avoided by the present system. The connexional church accepts responsibility for all ministers in 'full connexion'. A station is guaranteed. And if no station is available one will be created or even, *in extremis*, a manse and stipend provided. The system serves the security of its ministers, and anecdotal evidence suggests the stationing process gives priority to a minister's personal preferences (sometimes not unreasonable, family commitments and so forth) over the needs of circuits. But whilst no circuit is required to offer a station, once one is offered there is certainly in some quarters disquiet over a stationing process that allows a circuit very little say in whom they will get.[36]

A further feature of being 'in full connexion' is that ministers are not legally 'employed' by the church and thus have neither the protection of employment rights nor tenancy rights with respect to their manse.[37] In some respects, they have more protection – the church accepts responsibility for a minister for life. But in others perhaps less so. For instance, there are connexional standard requirements regarding the size and maintenance of the manse, and manses are inspected every five years or so. However, a minister remains vulnerable if a circuit fails to honour its responsibilities, and manse inspections have no power beyond exhortation.[38] And to be fair, circuits, the bodies owning the manse, have no legal redress if a minister wrecks the place, apart from lodging a formal complaint, which could result in the minister being required to pay compensation. The culture is very much one of a reliance upon mutual obligation and goodwill; but, alas, this sometimes fail. And, more generally, it is incredible that there are no 'Grievance Procedures' for ministers.

Moreover, if there are difficult issues to resolve (e.g. complaints, discipline) ministers are dependent on the church's processes independent of civil law. This can become especially messy if a case involves both a minister and a lay employee, who may rely on employment rights. On paper, church law is impressive in terms of defining due process and honouring natural justice. British Methodism may justly claim to be compliant with respect to the principles outlined in the *Statement*, Principles V.3 and 4. It is, however, a fundamental principle of British justice not only that justice be done but that it be *seen* to be done. This makes possible a public scrutiny that holds the system and its functionaries to account. In Methodism, however, there is no such scrutiny since everything is conducted confidentially. The church is an imperfect institution run by fallible human beings. Sometimes there are alarming leaks of

36 See footnote 32 previously.

37 Note here the Supreme Court upheld the church's claim that a Methodist minister in not an employee: *President of the Methodist Conference v Preston (formerly Moore)* [2011] EWCA Civ. 1581.

38 See *CPD*, Standing Order 965.4, which speaks simply of offering 'advice' to the circuit if the inspection adjudges 'inadequacy'.

incompetence and a failure to exemplify best practice and due process, followed by an alarming tendency for the church's executive to insist on marking its own homework. After all, although those adjudicating cases are given some training, *ad hoc* panels comprise those for whom this kind of work is not their main responsibility and expertise. That said, it is reasonable to believe such instances are in the minority and that the church more usually acts fairly and with compassion. Certainly, the culture of Methodism is generally compassionate and inclusive rather than readily judgemental. And the church probably has more reason to complain at the inadequacy of some of its ministers than ministers have to complain about their treatment.

III The Methodist principle of corporate episcope

Along with connexionalism, Methodist law expresses another fundamental principle, 'corporate episcope' – lay and ordained persons acting together collegially. The British Methodist Church does not have bishops in the sense of a separate 'order of ministry' in which bishops enable an orderly succession of ministry through ordination, have special responsibility for the integrity and catholicity of the church, and usually claim to be in communion with other bishops within an historic episcope. The American Methodist Church has bishops, as have other churches originating from American missions, but such bishops are generally 'presiding bishops' or 'bishops in Synod', synodical authority limiting the personal authority of the bishop.[39] British Methodism did not rebel against the historic episcopate. After all, Wesley remained a loyal Anglican to his dying day. Rather, it broke loose, partly out of practical necessity and partly because such a departure was deemed theologically permissible. The early Methodists, being a society within the established Church of England, were expected to attend worship in their parish church and to share in its sacraments. Increasingly, however, there was pressure to celebrate Holy Communion in their own meetings. Moreover, for many in the expanding towns a parish church was not within reasonable travelling distance. The poor, after all, had to walk. Perhaps more pressing, after American independence, many Anglican clergy returned to Britain, more so than Methodist preachers, who were more sympathetic to independence.[40] A number of times Wesley appealed to bishops to ordain some of his preachers, but he was always refused, notoriously by the bishop of London with respect to America, in whose diocese the former colony belonged. So much for practical necessity. As for theological expediency, Wesley had become convinced by reading Peter King's work on the primitive church (1691) that ordination was within his own presbyteral competence. Consequently, in 1784 he ordained three of his preachers for work in America. This was some 40 years after being persuaded by reading King, but loyalty to the order of the Church of England prevented him from

39 See J.E. Kirby, *The Episcopacy in American Methodism* (Nashville: Kingswood, 2000).
40 According to R.E. Davies, *Methodism* (Harmondsworth: Penguin, 1963) 127–128.

acting until it was of such a pressing practical necessity. Historically, this was the decisive step in the Methodist societies becoming a separate church.[41]

Since then, Methodist law has developed and now exemplifies a 'corporate episcope'. Oversight and governance are the responsibility of the 'whole people of God' by a process of Christians 'conferring together'.[42] The increasing use of the word 'episcope'[43] has value in placing Methodist law within a broad ecumenical framework. The Deed of Union states that the Methodist Church in Great Britain 'holds to the doctrine of the "priesthood of all believers"'.[44] The idea was developed in a report adopted by the conference in 1988: *The Ministry of the Whole People of God*. Some may worry that the use of the word 'ministry' might encourage clericalizing the whole church. That, however, is a point about language, not substance.

Semantics aside, the Deed of Union provides that whilst ministers are ordained to the 'sole occupation' of being 'stewards in the household of God and shepherds of his flock', having 'a principal and directing part in these great duties', nonetheless they 'hold no priesthood differing in kind from that which is common to the Lord's people, and they have no exclusive title to the preaching of the gospel and the care of souls. These ministries are shared with them by others to whom also the Spirit divides his gifts severally as he wills'.[45] This foundation statement of the Deed of Union points towards a corporate episcope whilst of course also allowing a crucial role for a 'personal' and 'collegial' episcope exercised by ordained ministers. The careful wording seeks to accommodate a 'high', or even exclusivist, understanding of the prerogative of the pastoral office found in nineteenth-century Wesleyan Methodism and the stronger commitment to lay participation within the Primitive and United Methodist churches; as noted earlier, all three traditions united to form the Methodist Church in Great Britain in 1932.

To give the basic outline of how this theology is expressed in law, local Methodist churches are grouped together into 'circuits' – there are over 600 of them in the three nations of mainland Britain. Circuits are grouped into some 35 or so districts. Then there is the supreme national governing body, the conference, which meets annually. To begin with each local church and then to build outwards, the 'General Church Meeting' – comprising members and adherents – elects

41 Many accounts include R.E. Davis and E.G. Rupp, *A History of the Methodist Church in Great Britain*, Vol. I (London: Epworth Press, 1965) 69ff; R. Maddox and J.E. Vickers, *The Cambridge Companion to John Wesley* (Cambridge: Cambridge University Press, 2010) 235; H. Rack, op cit., 506fff; according to Rupp 'it does not seem' that Wesley ever read William Sclater's 1717 critique of Peter King: E.G. Rupp, *Religion in England 1688–1791* (Oxford: Clarendon Press, 1986) 439.

42 Consistent with SPCL III.4.1

43 As noted by B.E. Beck. Paper 'Conference Episcope', in M. Davies, ed., *A Thankful Heart and a Discerning Mind* (Lonely Scribe, 2010) 110.

44 *Deed of Union* 1932, Section 2. Paragraph 4.

45 *Deed of Union*, Ibid.

church stewards and representatives to the 'Church Council', which serves as the managing trustees and decision-making body for the local church. Members are formally enrolled. 'Adherents' are not so enrolled, the name referring to any deemed to have links with, or belonging to, the local church community. Obviously, the church council is predominately 'lay', although an ordained presbyter must chair the meeting. The church council elects representatives to the 'Circuit Meeting', which elects representatives to the 'District Synod',[46] bodies chaired by the superintendent minister of the circuit and the chair of district – a presbyter – respectively. Then the district synod elects representatives to the annual conference. In these various ways Methodist structures fit within the parameters defined by the *Statement of Principles of Christian Law* (Principles IV.4 and 5).

This outline makes clear the thrust of Methodist governance and oversight, which is the responsibility of the church as a whole – shared by both lay and ordained. This principle is expressed powerfully in the fact that the membership of the conference is more or less half lay and half ordained. And the conference votes as one body – not in separate 'houses' like the General Synod of the Church of England. The conference is chaired by its president or vice-president. These are presbyteral and lay offices, respectively, and the partnership symbolises and exemplifies the partnership between ordained and lay. These offices are held for one year only. They have representative, pastoral, and leadership roles but have very little executive authority to make decisions. They are president and vice-presidents *of the conference*, and decision-making arises out of Christians 'conferring' together. The very fact that presidents and vice-presidents hold office for one year only is itself an expression of a corporate episcope. Historically, the limitation of the office to one year had its origin in a desire never to have 'another King in Israel' after the autocratic style of Wesley![47] Whilst the secretary of the conference – always a presbyter – is an executive position held for a longer term and the holder has significant influence, if not much formal power, the Methodist Church does not have a single 'leader.' Instead, the role of president, the closest to a single 'leader', is passed round, allowing different people with different skills and contributions to play their part. With respect to the *Statement of Principles of Christian Law* (Principles IV.2 and 3), all this applies to the British Methodist Church as a national church, autonomous from other national churches even if in many ways there may be partnership and cooperation, such partnership and cooperation often existing in relationship with the World Methodist Council.

Some may be surprised or even alarmed that even matters of doctrine are decided by such a conference. Is the Word of God subject to a democratic vote?

46 The district synod is the weakest link in the Methodist constitution. Meeting twice a year, it has limited power, tending to be more a forum for debate and for building some sense of a belonging to a wider church. Its principal formal responsibility is that of electing representatives to the annual conference.

47 See J.M. Turner, *Conflict and Reconciliation: Studies in Methodism and Ecumenism* (London: Epworth, 1965) 85.

It is not, however, quite like that. On all major matters, the conference will be guided by reports of the church's expert committees and working parties, all of course comprising both 'lay' and 'ministerial' members. Half the conference comprises laypeople, providing their own rich expertise in a whole range of areas, together with their varied life experiences. That half comprising the ordained offers a corporate contribution with its own distinctive experience, expertise, and vocational responsibility. A 'corporate episcope' does not mean that everything is decided by plebiscite. Neither does a 'corporate' episcope exclude the 'personal' episcope exercised by the ordained. But it is always accountable to the whole church, and all major decisions are made corporately by due process by 'conferring together'.[48]

A further expression of a corporate episcope is how synods and circuits may raise questions or make suggestions that the conference must by law address. A national committee considers these and advises the conference as to its response; such proposed and considered responses are on the conference's agenda. At worst the response can feel condescendingly dismissive – but not always. Significant action has resulted from these 'memorials' and 'suggestions'.[49]

The majority of conference members in any one year are there for the first and often only time. However, there is some continuity in membership – e.g. district chairs are members *ex officio*. Further continuity is given by a body of 'Conference elected' representatives, who serve for more than one year.[50] Even so, this is not an ideal model for informed and coherent governance, although the difficulty is mitigated somewhat by the fact that districts normally convene briefing meetings of their representatives before the conference, and lay members tend to be retired or over-representative of those whose work or financial position allows attendance.

Methodists are likely to resist any insinuation that such a process for oversight and governance should be on the defensive, claiming that a process of discernment, employing the wisdom of the whole people of God, is, to say the least, no more fallible than processes based on more hierarchical models.[51] Methodists would accept Principle III.4.1 of the *Statement*, and the permissive and inclusive tone of Principle III.4.2.6 and 7 is consistent with Methodism's 'corporate episcope'.

It was noted earlier that all ordinations take place at the annual conference and that this is an expression of a 'connexional' church. Similarly, the procedure for selection mirrors Methodism's 'corporate episcope' since the whole church – by due process – is involved in attesting the 'gifts and graces' and authenticity

48 This procedure outlines how Methodism responds to the subject raised in SPCL VI.3.6.

49 The 'Daily Record' of each annual conference, on the church's website, records all 'Memorials' and 'Suggestions' and the conference's response.

50 See *Deed of Union*, paragraph 14(5).

51 Note A. Shier-Jones, 'Conferring as a Theological Method', in C. Marsh and B.E. Beck, eds., *Unmasking Methodist Theology* (New York: Continuum, 2004) 82ff.

of vocation of those offering for ministry.[52] Candidates have to be commended to the process by the circuit meeting. Selection panels at both the district and national level comprise both lay and ordained. During the process of training, probation, and the final recommendation that they be ordained, oversight and recommendations are made by panels served by both lay and ordained. The final acceptance of candidates for training and the subsequent decision that a person be ordained are both made at the representative session of the conference on the recommendation of the presbyteral session.[53] When, therefore, the liturgical cry 'They are worthy' is heard at ordination, the congregation is expressing faith in a process of discernment in which the whole church is engaged.[54]

None of this is inconsistent with Principle III.1 of the *Statement*, even if these principles are consistent with differing arrangements and procedures in other churches. Most Methodists would not be so bold as to claim their systems of governance and oversight are superior, merely that a particular church order and pattern of governance is not an essential part of faith, even if it may be guided by theology. Episcopacy is one form among others, and as with all forms of church order it has its strengths and its weaknesses. British Methodism in 1969 agreed to 'take episcopacy into its system', subject to qualifications, when it agreed to a union scheme with the Church of England. But a recent exploration of the possibility of Methodism adopting episcopacy, without being a constituent of such a unity scheme, did not attract strong support.[55] Methodists are likely to feel patronised or even insulted, rather than reassured, by the claim that, whilst not belonging to the 'essence' of the church, episcopacy nonetheless serves the church's 'fullness' – the *plene esse*.[56] Yet this is all about Methodists claiming full legitimacy for their 'corporate episcope'. In no way does it prevent Methodists from honouring what episcopacy brings to other traditions, and, surely, they will wish to honour and support the particular place the bishops of the established church in England have in national affairs.

All this, however, is a description of what Methodism had become in the twentieth and twenty-first centuries, but it took time for these structures to develop. British Methodism has in fact seen a gradual development from a fairly autocratic structure of governance, controlled by the small body of the presbyterate, to the 'corporate episcope' of today.[57] But how much of this

52 See also N. Doe, *Christian Law: Contemporary Principles* (Cambridge: Cambridge University Press, 2013) 81ff.

53 The very limited powers of the presbyteral session are set out in the *Deed of Union*, paragraph 15.

54 The process is set out in *CPD*, Standing Orders 320–321, 450–453.

55 Methodist Conference Report, '*What Sort of Bishop?*' (2007).

56 The argument of essays in J. Carey, ed., *The Historic Episcopate* (London: Longman and Green, 1947).

57 One accessible history of this development may be found in R.E. David and E.G. Rupp, op cit., Vol. II.

is owed to the characteristic Methodist theology outlined at the beginning of this chapter? This is impossible to answer with precision and certainty. Causal relationships in history are often elusive to the historian, especially when we seek to trace the influence of ideas. There can be little doubt that the Methodist Church was prompted to became more 'democratic' as franchise in the wider society was, step by step, extended. The development of a more inclusive and participatory structure of oversight and governance was almost certainly influenced by these wider social trends. And Methodist theology did not prevent Wesleyan Methodism from at least being conservative politically. It was not a vanguard of social reform, and this may have been partly due to the legacy of an anxiety that it be accused of being revolutionary and seditious. The French Revolution and Napoleonic wars were not, after all, fully settled. The antagonistic proposals of Lord Sidmouth's bill in 1811, which sought to require Methodist lay preachers to obtain licences, although defeated, gave Methodists reason to proceed cautiously even if they had wanted to make greater haste.

That said, ideas take time to have their full effect. Methodist theology encouraged people to take seriously the personal appropriation of faith. Faith is not a matter of social conformity, obedience to ecclesiastical authority, or a semi-detached participation in the rites of the church. Their faith demanded 'growth in holiness', which for many issued in self-education, self-discipline, thrift, and industry, resulting in economic and social betterment. Above all it gave people self-respect, a sense they were loved by God. There is a resonance at least, and very probably a causal link, between a people so formed and a participatory structure of governance.

All that said, Methodism does not claim that these principles and details of law and governance have 'scriptural foundations', if by that we mean they are 'required' by Scripture. Methodists take the general Protestant position that we do not look to Scripture for the specifics regarding church order and governance. Whilst not required by Scripture, it may be claimed that there are many broad resonances. The New Testament envisages a 'universal' church, and the epistles tend to assume 'all the faithful should be equal' (e.g. 1 Cor. 12). Moreover, the New Testament generally speaks of faith issuing in transformed lives (e.g. Romans 12). Methodists may claim their 'corporate episcope' and 'connexionalism' do no violence to the New Testament. That said, the mistakes of the past – when appeal to Scripture has been made to support the divine right of kings, slavery, and the marginalisation of Jews (as well as even stringent opposition to kneeling when receiving the elements)[58] – should counsel caution and humility in claiming 'biblical foundations' for church law for a very different church in a very different world.

58 J. Dawson, *John Knox* (New Haven, CT: Yale University Press, 2015) 72ff.

IV Evaluating the *Statement of Principles of Christian Law*

1 A Methodist perspective

Many of the Christian law principles will find warm agreement amongst Methodists, and many indeed reflect Methodist law. To the examples already given, the following may be added. With respect to churches and their systems of law, the Methodist Church is a national entity, has a distinct membership, agrees that 'theology may shape law', and has laws that are both 'binding and exhortatory' (Principles I.1.1–2 and 3). The same applies to the principles on church membership (such as Principles II.2.4–5) and to the relaxation of law (Principle I.2.9); for example the Methodist Church may 'relax' the normal restriction of Eucharistic presidency to the ordained by granting a 'dispensation' to preside to suitable laypeople so as to avoid deprivation to serve the 'common good of the ecclesial community'. Methodist Arminian theology has also encouraged a strong profession on the part of Methodists to serve the well-being of all and not just the gathered congregation (Principle II.2.3). Likewise, Methodism has a strong commitment to the partnership between ordained and laypeople (Principle II.4.3). Moreover, the analysis given previously of Methodist polity clearly expresses the principles on national and regional church structures (Principles IV.3–4). The focus Methodist law places upon reconciliation and restoration in its complaints and discipline procedure resonates with the principle on due process (Principle V.4). Under its code of practice, the strong *prima facie* duty of confidentiality may be overridden by a higher obligation, although best practice expects the reason to be explained to the owner of the confidence (Principle VII.5.3). Similarly, Methodism has always had a strong ecumenical commitment, summed up in the principles on ecumenism (Principles X.2.1–2); but Methodists are likely to be part of a general tendency to see ecumenism as a wider and richer issue than simply 'organic' institutional unity, even having reservations about the latter as an ideal.[59]

There are, however, some areas where Methodists may demur, even if it is sometimes only over the drafting, rather than the substance, of principles. For example, the spirit of the principle that ministers are to preach the Word of God, teach the faith, administer the sacraments, and provide pastoral care (Principle III.3.2) will command the support of Methodists because of the centrality of preaching in the church's tradition. That said, the church now has 'two orders' of ordained ministry, and those ordained to the diaconate are not required to be authorised preachers; some are, but it is not a requirement inherent to this order. The same might be said of the principle that church law *should* (rather than *may*) require public worship to follow an 'authorized form of service'

59 Note an earlier defence of this perspective in J. Macquarrie, *Christian Unity and Christian Diversity* (London: SCM Press, 1975).

(Principle V.5.2). The British Methodist Church has an authorised hymn book, *Singing the Faith* (2011), and an authorised Methodist worship book (1985); these are offered as standards and resources. However, Methodism has a tradition of *extempore* prayer, and worship leaders are free to use other resources as judged appropriate. Moreover, Methodist law places the emphasis on the authorisation of the *person* leading worship, their training and accountability, rather than the 'form of service'; this may be partly because of the traditional emphasis on preaching. Bad preaching is more serious than reading from the wrong prayer book. Of course, the use of *extempore* prayer and other resources may be said to be part of an 'authorized' form in the Methodist tradition; if so, perhaps the principle would be better expressed less ambiguously as, for example, 'Church law will prescribe what are acceptable forms of worship within its tradition'. In a similar vein, as noted earlier, the Methodist Church has a strong commitment to the participation of the whole church in governance and oversight. Laypeople serve on all committees, working parties, and such, and roughly 50% of the conference comprises laypeople. The whole section in the *Statement* on 'The Faithful' does little more than hint at this, and indeed the choice of the word 'faithful' might even suggest a clergy-dominated church patronising a compliant laity. It may be noted that in Methodist culture and documentation the term 'the faithful' is used very rarely, if at all, no doubt for this reason.

2 The generality of the principles

Because of diversity among churches, and consequently of church law, the principles work at a level of generality, which means that commonality identified is often of limited significance.[60] The generality of the principles is apparent in repeated statements of what churches 'may' do rather than what they do. The formula used in the *Statement* that conduct is regulated 'in the manner prescribed by law' (see e.g. Principle VI.1.2 on the interpretation of doctrine) achieves an inclusivity and generality that will vary enormously among different Christian traditions. In particular, the principles on ordination (Principles III.1.1–6) do not fully capture debates about different 'orders' of ministry and the differences between churches claiming the historic episcopate and those that do not, though the principle that a church may distinguish between different types of ordained minister may be pertinent to this debate (Principle III.1.2). By contrast, the principles are inclusive of those Christian bodies that do not practice baptism (Principle II.2.3) and of those that 'lawfully authorize' to preside at the Eucharist those who are not ordained (Principle VII.3.5).

At this level of generality, and with this level of generous inclusivity, contentious issues in ecumenical relationships are thus sidestepped. Moreover, in some churches women may not hold certain offices; but the issue is sidestepped by the

60 Examples are SPCL II.2.1 and 3, III.1.2 and 4, III.3.1, IV.1.6, and others.

use of gender-inclusive language in the formula that 'lay persons may' perform prescribed acts (Principle II 4.3). The question of the ordination of women is likewise sidestepped. The principles are thus silent on one of the most pressing issues of the day. Indeed, some descriptive principles verge on platitude. Given that a church is a social institution embodying a community and owning property, some of the principles verge on sociological inevitability given the kind of entity a church is.[61] Some 'principles' are simply bald statements of theological belief.[62] Presumably such statements are deemed 'principles of law' because law must determine what legal prescriptions derive from them; and they are deemed to be normative because they express a wide or universal theological consensus. Others express liturgical or missiological principles, or expectations of the 'faithful', and may be principles of law only in the general sense that they are exhortatory.[63]

Again, the principles that churches should 'defend human rights' and 'promote social justice' (Principles X.2.2 and X.3.1), stated at this level of generality, would be difficult to disagree with; but the 'devil is in the detail'. For example, what specifically are the 'rights' of humans?

In stark contrast, however, other principles appear to be normative and as such are more likely to attract dissent. For instance, whilst the dominant stance of the principles is one of generous inclusivity, some appear to exclude some traditions if they are to be read as being prescriptive. As drafted, they appear to be prescriptive. If they are intended merely as descriptive of the stance of most churches, this is not stated. Those on the Eucharist, Holy Communion, or the Lord's Supper, for instance (Principles VII.3.2–5), seem to exclude Salvationists and the Society of Friends. Indeed, the principle that the Eucharist should be celebrated in an authorised place (Principle VII.3.6) is surprisingly mandatory. Should it not be phrased in a more permissive manner, such as 'A church *may* restrict the celebration . . . to authorised places'? The principle appears to forbid the celebration in, say, a conference centre as well as in a private home, nursing home, or hospital on the occasion of a pastoral visit by an ordained or otherwise properly authorised person. None of this is forbidden by Methodist law, even if 'reserved sacrament' or 'extended communion' might be encouraged. The principles on the functions of ordained ministers and the exercise of oversight (Principles III.3–4) may attract the same criticism of a similar prescription in the *Lima Report*[64] since they appear to exclude those traditions for which the importance of the Eucharist is expressed in a less frequent participation. Of course, the word used is 'regularly' and not 'frequently'. If 'regularly' means 'at constant intervals', then a faithful yearly celebration is regular! But without clarification the two words are easily understood as synonymous. These principles also exclude a significant number of Christians in mainstream churches who find the whole

61 E.g. the whole of the groups in SPCL IX.1, 2, and 3.

62 E.g. SPCL VII.1.1, VII.3.1, and VII.4.

63 E.g. SPCL VII.3.2 and 4, X.2.2, and X.3.1–2.

64 *Baptism, Eucharist, Ministry* (Geneva: WCC, 1982) Section three on Eucharist. 'The Eucharist should be celebrated frequently . . . at least every Sunday'.

ritual strange and distracting and yet who claim – like those within the Society of Friends – to 'feed really and indeed'.

3 The problem of ambiguity

A reader might wonder if some of the principles suffer from ambiguity in drafting. There is a principle that 'to be married validly in the eyes of the church' couples must satisfy church law and be properly instructed (Principle VII.4.4). This appears to state that the church cannot recognise as 'validly married' those who have 'only' a civil marriage, or indeed even church marriages where there has been a pastoral failing in not ensuring the parties are properly 'instructed'. It appears to reject the Lutheran principle that marriage is a gift to humankind as a whole and not a sacrament or rite in the gift of the church. And how does it square with the principle that the consent of the couple is the prime constituent of marriage? For the Methodist Church, those married in church are validly married if the requirements of civil law are satisfied, however grave and regrettable might be pastoral failings or a failure to observe any 'church law' regarding preparation for and the conduct of the ceremony. A further ambiguity is the principle 'Marriage is for the well-being of the spouses' (Principle VII.4.3). What meaning is to be attached to the simple word 'for'? If it means that marriage *should serve* the well-being of the spouses, then it is unlikely to attract dissent. If, by contrast, it is saying the *prime purpose* of marriage is the spouses' well-being, it ignores those churches that maintain procreation is at least a complementary purpose, or even the prime purpose, thus imposing the obligation upon couples to be open to procreation. Indeed, given the complexity of the whole subject of marriage in Christian tradition it is unclear why these seven and only these seven principles have been offered. Why, for instance, does Principle VII.4.7 speak only of dissolution and not of the annulment in Roman Catholic canon law?

4 Further issues

Some Methodists might baulk – on account of 'corporate episcope' – at the nuances and focus of such statements as 'The faithful should be taught' and 'should respect' church doctrine (Principles VI.3.2 and 4); they might be read as savouring too much of a hierarchical distinction between the 'Church teaching' and the 'Church taught'. These principles perhaps imply too strong an emphasis upon assent to fixed theological propositions, in contrast to a faith that is at times tentative and exploratory. Moreover, there is no acknowledgement that the 'faithful' might have their own insights to contribute, not least from their expertise (e.g. in science or education or medicine), which encourage and inform a critical and creative reflection on received 'church doctrine'. Despite the reference to developing doctrine 'afresh' (Principle VI.1.2), the 'feel' of this section of the principles, on doctrine and worship (Principles VI.1–5), is that of the citadel rather than the pilgrimage.[65]

5 *Omissions*

Finally, the principles can appear in places to be a little dated on account of a failure to acknowledge some more contemporary issues. These could easily be accommodated if others are addressed more economically. The following may be offered as examples. First, the principle that the foundation of marriage is a lifelong union between one man and one woman (Principle VII.4.1) ignores the live issue of same-sex marriage, which appears to be by this principle excluded. The British Methodist Conference in 2019 provisionally adopted – subject to further consultation throughout the connexion – a proposal that same-sex partnerships and marriages may be blessed or solemnised in a Methodist church, provided the local church council accepts this as part of its mission, and subject also to a 'conscience clause' protecting those ministers who feel unable to preside.[66] Second, in view of the media attention given to the church's failings in the past, abuse of power, and priority sometimes given to institutional reputation, the cruciality of law concerning the safeguarding of children and vulnerable adults might warrant more explicit treatment than the principle that the purpose of discipline includes safeguarding the vulnerable (Principle V.1.4). Moreover, partly because of the need to be statutory compliant, this is an area where church law has latterly been significantly developed. The British Methodist Church has developed a rigorous safeguarding policy that is mandatory throughout the connexion.[67] Third, there is a laudable focus on the church's responsibility for the human community but no reference to its responsibility regarding environmental issues. The 2017 report *Caring for Creation in the Face of Climate Change*, adopted by the Methodist conference, is an early example of the church's engagement with this issue.

Fourth, the principles on vocation for ordained ministry, the ordination itself, and its administration seem to admit of no exception (Principles III.1.4–6); these principles can appear a little 'dated' in their exclusive focus upon selection and training, followed by ordination. The increasing recognition of the importance of continued oversight, supervision, appraisal, and continuing development receives no mention. Currently, the British Methodist Church is developing the practice of regular supervision for all its ordained minsters.[68] Fifth, there is a principle on the 'ecumenical formation of the faithful' (Principle VIII.3.3), but there is no acknowledgement of what some have called the 'wider ecumenism' of relationship with other faiths, especially perhaps the Abrahamic ones. This is a question

65 Likewise, SPCL VI.2.2., speaking of the right and duty of a church to 'instruct' the faithful; those who adopt a more Socratic and participatory approach to learning and theological exploration might object to the nuances of the word 'instruct'.

66 Methodist Conference 2019: *God in Love Unites Us.*

67 See Methodist Church Website.

68 See Methodist Church Website.

explored by some Methodist writers,[69] and no doubt it receives some encouragement from an Arminian theological perspective. At this point it is relevant to question the principle that the Christian faithful constitute the people of God (Principle II.1.1): are not Jews and Muslims – for instance – rightly called the 'people of God'? The most significant 'official' stance of the British Methodist Church is the 2004 document *Faith Meeting Faith*. Alas, because of budgetary constraints the church no longer has a full-time interfaith relations secretary, the position last occupied by Dr Elizabeth Harris.

Conclusion

The *Statement of Principles of Christian Law* certainly has value in serving as a 'check list' of the issues that any church law should or might address and may also serve as a frame of reference for ecumenical conversation. From a Methodist perspective, the principles are indeed 'meaningfully articulated' whilst 'honouring differences'. Some are uncontentious but act as stringent challenges to the church lest they be neglected. The principles, however, tend to be articulated at such a level of generality that there is often little from which to dissent. The critical reflections offered earlier leave most of the principles uncontested mainly for this reason. Because of this level of generality – examples of which have been given previously – it is difficult to see how their articulation might significantly further ecumenical dialogue and cooperation since the differences are found in specifics that are overlooked in these generalities.

69 E.g. Methodist writers M. Forward, 'Wither a Wider Ecumenism', in M. Davies, op cit., and K. Cracknell, *Towards a New Relationship* (London: Epworth, 1986).

8 Reformed church order

Leon van den Broeke

This chapter focusses on the system of church order in the Reformed tradition in light of the *Statement of Principles of Christian Law* (2016). The first section of the chapter deals with Reformed church polity. It deals with the sources and forms of Reformed church polity, the subjects addressed by church order, the question of whom the church order binds, the foundations and purposes of church order, and the use of principles of law in the Reformed Church tradition. The second section is devoted to the *Statement of Principles of Christian Law* and the empirical process behind it. It addresses those principles that are not problematic for Reformed church order, the revision of draft principles to accommodate the Reformed church order, principles in the *Statement* that remain problematic for the Reformed tradition, and the question of whether some principles are more important than others. The third section is on the value of the *Statement* from a Reformed Church perspective and in the wider ecumenical context.

I Reformed church polity

1 Sources and forms of Reformed church polity

Reformed church polity aims and claims to be both a scriptural and a confessional church polity.[1] However, from the Reformed perspective, 'there is no such thing as *the* New Testament Church order', as the Swiss New Testament scholar Eduard

1 Apart from the studies mentioned in the footnotes that follow, general use has been made of Johannes Calvijn, *Institutie of onderwijzing in de christelijke godsdienst*, translated by A. Sizoo, 3 vols. (Delft, 1949); J. Jansen, *Korte verklaring van de kerkorde* [Short Explanation of Church Order] (Kampen: Kok, 3rd edition, 1952); E. Wolf, *Ordnung der Kirche: Lehr- und Handbuch des Kirchenrechts auf ökumenischer Basis* [Order of the Church: Text and Handbook of Church Polity on an Ecumenical Basis] (Frankfurt am Main: Vittorio Klostermann Verlag, 1961); Hans Frhr. von Campenhausen, *Kirchliches Amt und geistliche Vollmacht in den ersten drei Jahrhunderten* [Ecclesiastical Office and Spiritual Authority in the First Three Centuries] (Tübingen: Mohr, 1963); H. Dombois, *Das Recht der Gnade: Ökumenisches Kirchenrecht* [The Right of Mercy: Ecumenical Church Polity], 3 vols. (Bielefeld: Luther-Verlag, 1961–1983); L.J. Koffeman, *In Order to Serve: An Ecumenical Introduction to Church Polity* (Zürich: Lit Verlag, 2014) (*Church Polity and Ecumenism* 1).

Schweizer (1913–2006) stated.[2] Indeed, in line with a body of New Testament scholarship, many Reformed theologians are convinced of the ecclesiological pluralism that exists in the New Testament and that the New Testament does not provide the church with an ecclesiological blueprint.[3] Nonetheless, all agree that the Word of God is fundamental for Reformed church polity, but opinions diverge regarding in what way the Holy Scripture is the main source of Reformed church polity. Schweizer wrote:

> The New Testament's pronouncements on Church order are to be read as a gospel – that is, Church order is to be regarded as a part of the proclamation in which the Church's witness is expressed, as it is in its preaching . . . we are not concerned only with the purely historical question of events recorded in the New Testament, as if by doing so we should then have in our hands the material for building up a present-day church. We are concerned with the much more difficult question of recognizing in the actual ordering of the New Testament Church, and in what is said about it, the theological concerns that caused it to take that form and no other. So, when we ask about the Church's order, we must also try to understand the Church's essential nature.[4]

No system of polity, governance, or church order can be cut and pasted from the Word of God to the present-day church. Nonetheless, some biblical passages are important for Reformed Church governance; for example 1 Corinthians 14:40: all things in the church need to be done decently and in order. This biblical text is to be found in the first article of the Dort Church Order of 1619 (see upcoming discussion). Although not mentioned expressly, the same idea is implicit in 1 Corinthians 14:33: God is not the author of confusion but of peace and order. Moreover, in the Reformed tradition, the church is *creatura Verbi*, a creature of the Word.[5] Therefore, Reformed church polity is about peace and order in a pragmatic way, and it is rooted in the church as *creatura Verbi*.

Reformed church polity is also confessional. The Reformed Church confession has what are called the Three Forms of Unity: the Belgic Confession of 1561, the Heidelberg Catechism of 1563, and the Canons of Dort of 1618/1619. The book of church order of Reformed denominations around the globe is usually thin because it is a practical elaboration of the confession, and what is already in the confession does not need to be repeated.

2 E. Schweizer, *Church Order in the New Testament*, translated by F. Clarke (London: SCM Press Ltd, 3rd edition, 1979) 13.

3 H.N. Ridderbos, *Paulus: Ontwerp van zijn theologie* (Kampen: Kok, 1966).

4 E. Schweizer, op cit., 14–15.

5 C. Schwöbel, 'The Creature of the Word: Recovering the Ecclesiology of the Reformers', in C.E. Gunton and D.W. Hardy, eds., *On Being the Church: Essays on the Christian Community* (Edinburgh: T&T Clark, 1989) 110–155.

Although all of these three confessions are fundamental for Reformed church polity, the Belgic Confession of 1561 is particularly important. From an ecclesiological perspective, Articles 27–32 of this confession are essential. They concern:

The holy and catholic church (Article 27)
The obligations of church members (Article 28)
The marks of the true church (Article 29)
The government of the church (Article 30)
The officers of the church (Article 31)
The order and the discipline of the church (Article 32)

In the Belgic Confession, Jesus Christ is presented as the eternal king (Art. 27), the only universal bishop (Art. 31), the only head of his church (Art. 29 and Art. 31), and the only master (Art. 32). From this perspective, it has to be considered that the – elected – office-bearers do not receive *magisterium* but *ministerium*. They do not or cannot act *suo jure*. They do not have complete ecclesiastical power. They are servants, not lords. Indeed, the golden rule of the acts of the Synod of Emden of 1571, the first synod of the Reformed Church in the Netherlands, prohibits one church or office-bearer from lording it over another.[6] This rule has been included in successive texts. Even today it is an essential part of the ecclesiology and church order of the Protestantse Kerk in Nederland (Protestant Church in the Netherlands), which is found in an instrument entitled the *Kerkorde en ordinanties van de Protestantse Kerk in Nederland.*[7] Generally speaking, these observations about the sources and forms of Reformed church order are reflected in the *Statement of Principles of Christian Law* (Principles I.2.1–3).

2 The subjects addressed by church order

Although there are a variety of approaches among Reformed denominations around the globe when it comes to which church order is valid, the focus of what follows is the Dort Church Order of 1619. Many Reformed church orders are in one way or another inspired by either the literal text or the spirit of the Dort Church Order of 1619. This church order is important insofar as it was the result of a process that started – for the Reformed Church in the Netherlands – with the Synod of Emden of 1571. Between 1571 and 1618/1619 four more general synods were held with the approval of the relevant civil authorities. Moreover, after 1618/1619 the civil authorities did not support convening any further general synod for almost 200 years. This meant the text of the church order remained unchanged, regardless of whether some rules had become outdated or whether new or more detailed rules were needed.

6 See www.kerkrecht.nl/node/5945 [accessed 26 April 2018].
7 See www.protestantsekerk.nl/thema/kerkorde [accessed 26 April 2018].

In any event, the Dort Church Order of 1619 and many of its successors in Reformed churches in the Netherlands and around the globe have the same pattern. The first article in each of these documents contains a small introduction about the importance of good order in the church, an implicit reference to 1 Corinthians 14:40. Thereafter, four matters are treated with a section on each – namely, offices; general assemblies; doctrine, sacraments, and other ceremonies; and discipline and admonition. These cover two main Reformed confessional areas: doctrine (*doctrina*) and discipline (*disciplina*). The Protestant Church Order is composed in a completely different way. It contains a theological constitution, the so-called Roman articles, and 14 organic ordinances. In general, these approaches to the subjects addressed by Reformed church order are echoed in the *Statement of Principles of Christian Law* (Principle I.4.1).

3 Whom does the church order bind?

The confessions and church order not only bind the office-bearers, including when they are gathered in assemblies (consistory, classis assembly, particular or provincial synod, and general synod), but also church members. Although the first of the four sections of the Dort Church Order of 1619 is on offices, this church order also binds the church members. They are more objects than subjects, although – and this was new in the context of sixteenth-century canon law – they had the right to elect their elders and deacons. Nevertheless, the Reformed church polity and the Dort Church Order of 1619 are addressed to office-bearers when these are gathered in general assemblies; the church order is also binding on those church assemblies when they act corporately. So, the Dort Church Order binds not only office-bearers but also church members. In general, these elements of Reformed church order are echoed in the *Statement of Principles of Christian Law* on the structure and effect of norms (Principles I.4.2–9).

4 The foundations and purposes of church order

The Reformed tradition has a range of ideas about the foundations of and reasons for church order. As seen previously, the foundations of church polity are the Bible and the confessions. However, a church order may be modified not only for theological or ecclesiastical reasons but also due to political, economic, or societal developments.

The Genevan reformer John Calvin (1509–1564) was and remains an important figure in the development of Reformed church polity. Having studied law and theology, he was positive about both law in general and church polity in particular. He may thus be contrasted with Martin Luther (1483–1546), who was excommunicated and burnt the Roman canon law books (12 December 1520) and the *ius circa sacra* to civil power, then in later years understood that some form of church polity was necessary. By way of contrast, Calvin composed the *Ordonnances ecclésiastiques* of 1541 and the revision of 1561, which he drafted for the Genevan church. Moreover, together with Guillaume Farel (1489–1565), he composed the *Articles concernant l'organisation de l'église et du culte à Genève* of 1537 – a draft church order for Geneva. This draft church order never came into force, but the *Ordonnances ecclésiastiques* of 1541 and the revision of 1561 did. Together with the French *Discipline Ecclésiastique* of 1559, they influenced the Reformed church polity in the Netherlands, and the Netherlands experience influenced Reformed churches in England and France as well as (Netherlands/ Dutch) overseas contexts.

Calvin's church polity may be understood as characterised by a *via media* between, on the one hand, the canon law system of the sixteenth-century Roman Catholic Church and, on the other, the system of ecclesiology and church polity of the Anabaptists. For Calvin, in his *Institutes* (Book 4), a church order, or system of church polity, is not simply a set of rules or regulations like any other, but concerns the church of Christ as *creatura Verbi*. As Mary-Ann Plaatjies van Huffel states:

> The Calvinistic system of church polity is based upon the following principles, which have exerted great influence in the development of Protestantism: (i) the autonomy of the church, or its right of self-government under the sole headship of Christ; (ii) the parity of the clergy as distinct from a *jure divino* hierarchy whether papal or prelatic; (iii) the participation of the Christian laity in church government and discipline; (iv) strict discipline to be exercised jointly by ministers and lay-elders, with the consent of the whole congregation; and (v) union of church and state on a theocratic basis, if possible, or separation, if necessary to secure the purity and self-government of the Church.[8]

Mary-Ann Plaatjies van Huffel then lists further 'Reformed church principles that may bind Reformed Churches together globally'. Though conceding that the list is not exhaustive, these principles include the necessity and nature of Christian discipline, the right to appeal, and the power of major assemblies with regard to misconduct and that denominational ties serve ecclesial well-being and church assemblies have restricted powers and responsibilities. She also maintains that Reformed church polity 'is not constituted by holding one of these principles; it is in manifesting them all'. However, Reformed churches 'in different contexts' may emphasise 'different nuances of the principles'. Nonetheless, and generally speaking, these ideas about the purposes of Reformed church order are summed up in the *Statement of Principles of Christian Law* (Principles I.3.1–4).

5 *The use of principles of law in the Reformed Church tradition*

Every Reformed Church has a book of church order. In Dutch, it is usually entitled *kerkorde* – literally 'church order'. Although there is diversity among

8 M-A. Plaatjies van Huffel, 'The Relevance of Reformed Church Polity Principles Revisiting the Concept': https://sun.academia.edu/MaryAnnPlaatjiesvanHuffel [accessed 1 May 2018].

Reformed denominations, in one way or another they all adhere to the principles of the Dort Church Order of 1619, or at least they are led by its spirit, with the possible exception of the *Nederlandse Gereformeerde Kerken* (Netherlands Reformed Churches). As a result of a schism in 1967, this denomination sought to limit the scope of its own rules as much as possible in its *Akkoord voor Kerkelijk Samenleven* (Agreement of Living Ecclesiastically Together).[9] This denomination expressly did not call the instrument a 'church order'. Other Reformed denominations, not only in the Netherlands but also in other countries globally, share in common the fact that their church orders are revised versions of the early seventeenth-century church orders. Some have only revised the language used, so they still use the literal text, whilst others contain more extended revisions in terms of the substance or content of the rules in their own regulatory instruments.

In the Reformed tradition a book of church order is considered to be an instrument to assist ecclesiastical practice, but it does not constitute the fullness of all ecclesial life itself.[10] The church order is not the spiritual foundation of the church. Also, it does not inspire the church in the sense of guaranteeing spiritual richness in the church, but it is an expression of an inspiring and inspired church and therefore a necessary and indispensable tool. As ecclesiology is given in the Three Forms of Unity, mainly in the Belgic Confession of 1561, the church order as a consequence or transformation of its confessional ecclesiology is limited to more practical topics/issues. The church order needs to help the church and not limit it.[11] That implies that the aim of the Reformed church order is not to strive for 'ecclesial perfection'. Essential for Reformed church order is whether it has the capacity to express Christ's sovereignty over and in his church and to maintain good order within the church.[12] Also, Reformed church order needs to assist everyone in the church, office-bearers and church members, as they serve in their vocations and functions as defined by the church order. The authority of the Reformed church order is not so much about formal but informal authority. This does not mean that every office-bearer or church member can ignore or downplay the church order. It means that just having a set of rules is considered not enough and that it is not simply a law book. A book of church order is a book of binding rules, though, a spiritual order with practical regulations formulated on the basis of Scripture and the confessions. Indeed, Article 1 of the Dort Church Order 1619 highlights this '[t]o maintain good order in the Church of Christ'.[13] With a view to achieving this aim, it continues: 'it is necessary to have in it offices, assemblies,

9 See file:///C:/Users/Gebruiker/AppData/Local/Packages/Microsoft.MicrosoftEdge_8wekyb3d8bbwe/TempState/Downloads/AKS%20(Akkoord%20Kerkelijk%20Samenleven)%202015.pdf [accessed 27 April 2018].

10 D. Nauta, *Verklaring van de Kerkorde van de Gereformeerde Kerken in Nederland* (Kampen: J.H. Kok N.V., 1971) 12.

11 Ibid., 15.

12 Ibid., 14.

13 See: http://kerkrecht.nl/node/440 [accessed 26 April 2018]

supervision of doctrine, sacraments and ceremonies, and Christian discipline, concerning which [matters the following articles] appropriately deal with'.[14]

The Reformed church order does not include the *potestas ecclesiastica externa* (power outside of the church). This is the realm of civil authorities. Rather, church order concerns the *potestas ecclesiastica interna*. However, the Reformed Church also has a strong tradition of divine law thinking. It distinguishes between *ius divinum positivum* and *ius divinum permissivum*. This means that *ius divinum* is either positive or immediate and direct or permissive or mediate and indirect. The latter concerns those affairs that are indifferent, over which God has allowed civil or ecclesiastical authority to make decisions. So, *ius divinum positivum* is the eternal, unchangeable, godly law. The *ius divinum permissivum* is the law that is attributed to the church and is changeable and flexible. By contrast, the *ius divinum positivum* concerns the essentials of the church, and the *ius divinum permissivum* concerns *adiaphora*; namely, things to which God's church is indifferent.

Indeed, one issue in debate about Reformed church polity is whether the Dort Church Order 1619 should be considered sacrosanct, absolute, and unchangeable. Some consider that it is; others do not. The problem in making (the Dort) church order absolute is that this leads to the petrification of the church and resistance to the concept that law is contingent or dynamic. This criticism is found in the work of the Protestant Swiss theologian Karl Barth (1886–1968) and in that of the Roman Catholic Belgian canonical jurist Rik Torfs, who criticises the static character of church law. Barth argued in 1955 that church polity is law that, with the function of serving others (*Dienstrecht*), is liturgical law (*liturgisches Recht*), exemplary law (*exemplarisches Recht*), and living law (*lebendiges Recht*).[15] Torfs points out the importance of the concept of law as a dynamic process. Moreover, he criticises jurists who talk about law without distinguishing between different kinds of law – for example legislation and jurisprudence. He does not seem to state than one jurist is more dynamic than the other. Moreover, he distinguishes four phases in the dynamic process involved in the relationship between theology and law: (1) finding the fundamentals of canon law or church polity, (2) the teamwork needed between theology and law in the elaboration of concrete legal rules, (3) the application of formulated legal rules, and (4) the critical analysis of church law and church polity.[16] By doing so Torfs emphasises the fact that law is a process and has different stages and so expresses the dynamics of church law.

Of relevance in this regard is the old juridical maxim *ius sequitur vitam* – law follows life. Law is not absolute but always needs to be understood in light of developments in the wider environment in which it exists. This should also apply to church law; namely, *ius ecclesiasticum sequitur vitam* – church law follows life.

14 Ibid.

15 K. Barth, *Die Ordnung der Gemeinde: Zur dogmatischen Grundlegung des Kirchenrechts* (München: Chr. Kaiser Verlag, 1955).

16 R. Torfs, 'Liefde en recht gaan hand in hand: Een denkoefening over de verhouding tussen theologie en recht', *Tijdschrift voor Theologie* 36 (1996) 270–289.

As a result, church polity needs to be seen as in a dynamic relation with theological and ecclesiastical, and societal and political, developments. This is, on the face of it, inconsistent with the historic view that the Dort Church Order of 1619 is absolute, sacrosanct, and unchangeable; others object to this and have made revisions of the text of this church order. Moreover, decisive for Reformed church polity is not what would be most historically acceptable but what God commands in his Word.[17] This is in accordance with what Calvin said in his *Institutes*: '[n]ow we have to speak about the order which and by which the Lord has wanted that his church would be governed'.[18] Similarly, he speaks of 'ordo gubernandae ecclesiae, ut nobis ex puro Dei verbo traditus est'.[19] This is reflected in Article 30 of the Belgic Confession as well as in Article 29 of the French Confession of 1561 (*Confessio Gallicana*):

> We believe that this true church ought to be governed according to the spiritual order that our Lord has taught us in his Word. There should be ministers or pastors to preach the Word of God and administer the sacraments. There should also be elders and deacons, along with the pastors, to make up the council of the church.[20]

On a frequent basis the tension between the historical and the dynamic positions has been and is discussed in debate in the synods of the Reformed churches today. This concerns not only the Reformed denominations in the Netherlands but also, for example, those in Australia, New Zealand, North America, and South Africa.[21]

17 H. Bouwman, *Gereformeerd kerkrecht: Het recht der kerken in de practijk*, Vol. 1 (Kampen: Kok, 1928) 29.

18 'Jam de ordine dicendum est, quo ecclesiam suam gubernari voluit Dominus', translated by H. Bouwman; Bouwman, *Gereformeerd kerkrecht* (1928), op cit., 1, 29 footnote 4.

19 'A Way to Govern the Church, as it is Handed over to us by the Pure Word of God', translated by H. Bouwman; Bouwman, *Gereformeerd kerkrecht* (1928), op cit., 1, 29 footnote 5; Calvijn, *Institutie*, book 4, chapter 3.

20 'Quant est de la vraie Eglise, nous croyons qu'elle doit être gouvernée selon la police que notre Seigneur Jésus-Christ a établie. C'est qu'il y ait des pasteurs, des surveillants et des diacres, afin que la pure doctrine ait son cours, que les vices soient corrigés et réprimés, et que les pauvres et tous autres affligés soient secourus en leurs necessités; et que les assemblées se fassent au nom de Dieu, esquelles grands et petits soient édifiés': https://reformed.org/documents [accessed 26 April 2018].

21 See for the process of revision of the Reformed church order in the Reformed churches liberated (*Gereformeerde Kerken vrijgemaakt*): www.kerkrecht.nl/sites/default/files/ActaGKv2011-2012.pdf [accessed 24 April 2019] and H.J.C.C.J. Wilschut, *De werkorde nagerekend. Kanttekeningen bij de conceptkerkorde voor de GKv*, s.l.: s.n., [2011]. See for the process in the Netherlands Reformed Church: Th. Klein, ed., *Veertig jaar orde in de hervormde kerk: Schetsen rond de hervormde kerkorde* (Zoetermeer: Boekencentrum, 1992); A. van den Beek, W. Balke and J.D.Th, Wassenaar, eds., *De kerk op orde? Vijftig jaar hervormd leven met de kerkorde van 1951* (Zoetermeer: Boekencentrum, 2001). See for the process of revision of Reformed church order in North America: L. van den Broeke, 'Flexibility or Fixed Idea: The Dort Church Order of 1619 as a Cultural Import', in H. Aay, J. Venema and D. Voskuil, eds., *Sharing Pasts: Dutch Americans Through Four Centuries* (Holland, MI:

II The principles of Christian law: empirical process

1 Principles that are not problematic for Reformed church order

From the perspective of the Reformed tradition of church order, most of the principles in the *Statement of Principles of Christian Law* (Rome 2016) are not problematic. This is unsurprising, needless to say, given the contribution from the Reformed perspective to drafting the *Statement*. As a result, only two simple but more detailed examples may be offered to illustrate how principles in the *Statement* reflect Reformed church order.

First, the principles on church membership provide that a church consists of those incorporated into it in accordance with its proper laws and customs; a church should serve appropriately all seeking its ministry regardless of membership; membership in a church, to participate in its government, may be based on any or all of baptism, baptism and confirmation or other mature demonstration of faith, and other conditions prescribed by law; the names of those belonging to a church may be entered into the rolls of membership subject to such conditions as may prescribed by law; and these names may be removed in accordance with law.[22] These clearly reflect Reformed church order: someone becomes a member by baptism or confession of faith or by moving from one church to another. An example with regard to baptism: '[t]he Covenant of God shall be sealed by Holy Baptism unto children of believers, including children legally adopted by members of the congregation. The session shall see to it that baptism is requested and administered as soon as feasible';[23] or with respect to confession of faith: '[m]embers by baptism and adults who have not been baptised shall be admitted to communicant membership upon public profession of faith with the use of the prescribed form. Before the profession of faith, the session shall examine them concerning motives, doctrine and conduct. Those who have not been baptised, shall receive holy baptism upon profession of faith'.[24] Usually, baptised members have fewer rights than full members. In some churches only full members have the right to be admitted to the Lord's table. In others, baptised persons who are not full members have that right, and in the case of

---

Van Raalte Press, 2017) 51–72. See for the process of revision of the church order in the Reformed Churches in the Netherlands: C. Veenhof, *Kerkgemeenschap en kerkorde: Kort overzicht van de strijd, gevoerd in de Afgescheiden Kerken tussen 1836 en 1840 over de Kerkgemeenschap en Kerkorde* (Amsterdam: Buijten & Schipperheijn, 1974); H. Bouwman, *De crisis der jeugd: Eenige bladzijden uit de geschiedenis van de kerken der Afscheiding* (Kampen: Kok, 1914); C. [Leon] van den Broeke, *Een geschiedenis van de classis: Classicale typen tussen idee en werkelijkheid 1571–2004* (Kampen: Kok, 2005) 207–239.

22 SPCL II.2.1–5.

23 Article 58 church order of the Reformed Churches of New Zealand; http://kerkrecht.nl/node/6240 [accessed 2 May 2019].

24 Article 59 church order of the Reformed Churches of New Zealand; http://kerkrecht.nl/node/6241 [accessed 2 May 2019].

adults, such persons may be elected as an elder or deacon. Also, the names of those belonging to a church may be entered on registers of membership; but the church may remove names following a prescribed process, be it disciplinary or not.[25]

Second, as to the principles on the laity, the law of a church should generally set out the basic rights and duties of its members; the laity should promote the mission of the church and bear witness to the Christian faith through their lives; a layperson should engage in collective ecclesial life, in proclaiming the Word of God, participating in worship, and receiving the sacraments and maintain Christian standards in their private lives as are prescribed by law; and they are encouraged to practise daily devotion, private prayer, Bible reading, and self-discipline, bringing the teaching and example of Christ into everyday life, upholding Christian values, and being of service to the church and wider community.[26] The principal focus of Reformed church polity might be the 'professional' office of pastors, elders, and deacons. However, it also contains what in German is called *Mitgliedschaftsrecht* – law concerning church members. This includes not only the rights of church members but also their duties. Reformed laypeople are expected to promote the mission of the church and to bear witness to the Christian faith through their lives in the world and in their ecclesial and private lives.[27] One example of this in Reformed church orders is the following: '[t]he consistory with the deacons shall give the congregation the opportunity to draw the attention of the consistory to brothers deemed suitable for the respective offices. The consistory with the deacons shall present to the congregation at the most twice as many candidates as there are vacancies to be filled. From this number the congregation shall choose as many office-bearers as are needed. Those elected shall be appointed by the consistory with the deacons. If necessary the consistory and the deacons may present to the congregation the same number of candidates

25 For example, article C45.2 of the church order of the Reformed Churches Liberated in the Netherlands (Gereformeerde Kerken vrijgemaakt) declares than the consistory may terminate the membership of a church member whenever they avoid every contact with the office-bearers. This decision needs the approval of the members of the local church; www.gkv.nl/kerkorde/c-het-leven-van-de-gemeente/ [accessed 23 April 2019]. See also article 5.2 of the *Generale Regeling Lidmaatschap* (General Regulations Church Membership) of the Protestant Church in the Netherlands: www.protestantsekerk.nl/thema/kerkorde [Accessed 23 April 2019]. This article provides that if a church member declares to the consistory or an office-bearer that they do not want to be a member any longer or no longer consider themselves to be a church member and are not willing to write this down, the consistory can ultimately take the decision to end the membership of the person.

26 SPCL II.3.1–5.

27 Article IV.2. of the church order of the Protestant Church in the Netherlands declares that all church members are called and entitled to apply their talents to the fulfilment of the assignment that Christ has given to his church: www.protestantsekerk.nl/thema/kerkorde [accessed 2 May 2019].

as there are vacancies'.[28] Another example would be that it is the consistory that calls a pastor, but only after election by the congregation – i.e. the full members.[29]

2 *The revision of draft principles to accommodate the Reformed church order*

Some of the candidate principles discussed by the Panel for inclusion in the final *Statement* in their draft form were problematic from a Reformed perspective, so changes were made to accommodate Reformed church order.

One example concerns the draft principle 'The faithful should not publicly manifest in word or deed, a position contrary to church doctrine'. This did not fully capture Reformed church order. In some cases, a church member or office-bearer can show evidence that a consistory, classis, or particular or general synod is wrong in doctrinal matters. Moreover, in that case an appeal is also possible. This dates back to Article 31 of the Dort Church Order of 1619. This article is still valid in many Reformed church orders around the globe. The following example may be offered: '[i]f anyone complains that he has been wronged by the decision of a minor assembly he shall have the right of appeal to the major assembly; and whatever may be agreed upon by a majority vote shall be considered settled and binding, unless it is proved to be in conflict with the Word of God or with the Church Order'.[30] Exactly the same text is used by the Canadian and American Reformed churches.[31] So, the candidate principle was changed to 'The faithful should respect, honour, and uphold the doctrine of their church'.[32]

A second example concerns the candidate principle: '[t]he administration of worship in the local church is subject to supervision by those regional authorities designated by law to provide this'. From a Reformed dimension this was not acceptable because of the emphasis on the local church. It is the consistory that exercises supervision of the administration of worship because it is the pastor in a collegial setting with the elders (and in some cases together with the deacons), rather than a single pastor, who have the final responsibility over worship. Two examples: '[e]ach year the churches shall, in the manner decided upon by the consistory, commemorate the birth, death, resurrection, and ascension of the

28 Article 3B of the Church Order of the Free Reformed Churches of Australia: https://synod.frca.org.au/ecclesiasticaldocs/ChurchOrder_of_the_FRCA_(2018).pdf [accessed 2 May 2019].

29 'De kerkenraad beroept onder aanroeping van de naam des Heren na verkiezing door de gemeente overeenkomstig de plaatselijk vastgestelde regeling' – Article 4 of the Church Order of the Christelijke Gereformeerde Kerken in Nederland; https://cgk.nl/project/de-kerkorde/ [accessed 2 May 2019].

30 Article 31 of the Church Order of the Free Reformed Churches of Australia: https://synod.frca.org.au/ecclesiasticaldocs/ChurchOrder_of_the_FRCA_(2018).pdf [accessed 2 May 2019].

31 Article 31 of the Church Order of the Canadian and American Reformed Churches: http://kerkrecht.nl/node/730 [accessed 2 May 2019].

32 SPCL VI.3.4.

Lord Jesus Christ, as well as His outpouring of the Holy Spirit';[33] and: '[t]he sacraments shall be administered only in a church service by a minister of the Word with the use of the adopted Forms, and under the supervision of the elders'.[34] However, a classis can oversee the consistory if something goes wrong.

A third example is the candidate principle: '[a] church is a community with a defined geographical area which may be international, national, regional, or local'.[35] This is problematic, as the Reformed churches around the world are part of what may be understood not as a global Reformed Church but as an international community of Reformed churches. Two hundred thirty-two of these are members of the World Communion of Reformed Churches,[36] whilst 32 Reformed denominations around the globe are members of the International Conference of Reformed Churches.[37] The World Communion of Reformed Churches includes not only Reformed churches but also Congregational, Presbyterian, United, Uniting, and Waldensian churches. The Communion works with its 232 member churches in over 105 countries (80 million Christians) on 'supporting theology, justice, church unity and mission'. Called 'to communion and committed to justice, the WCRC fosters church unity and coordinates common initiatives for mission, theological reflection and formation, church renewal, justice and dialogue'.[38] It is not a supranational Reformed Church; it does respect the autonomy of member churches. Similarly, the goal of the International Conference of Reformed Churches is to express and promote the unity of faith that the member churches have in Christ, to encourage the fullest ecclesiastical fellowship among the member churches, to encourage cooperation among the member churches in the fulfilment of the missionary and other mandates, to study the common problems and issues that confront the member churches and to aim for recommendations with respect to these matters, and to present a Reformed testimony to the world.[39] However, once again, it is to be stressed, as we shall see more fully later, that there is no such thing as an international Reformed 'church'. Reformed church orders do not demonstrate an international expression of church. For example, '[t]hree kinds of ecclesiastical assemblies shall be maintained: the consistory, the classis, and the general synod'.[40] This does not refer to any international synod whatsoever. The same goes for the church order of another Reformed

33 Article 53 of the Church Order of the Canadian and American Reformed Churches: ttp://kerkrecht.nl/node/730 [accessed 2 May 2019].

34 Article 51 of the Church Order of the Free Reformed Churches of Australia: https://synod.frca.org.au/ecclesiasticaldocs/ChurchOrder_of_the_FRCA_(2018).pdf [accessed 2 May 2019].

35 For the revised principle, see SPCL I.1.2.

36 See http://wcrc.ch/about-us [accessed 17 May 2018].

37 See www.icrconline.com [accessed 23 April 2019].

38 See http://wcrc.ch/wp-content/uploads/2015/04/Brochure-English.pdf [accessed 23 April 2019].

39 See www.icrconline.com/ [accessed 17 May 2018].

40 Article 29 of the Church Order of the Protestant Reformed Churches in America: www.prca.org/component/jdownloads/finish/11/128?Itemid=0 [accessed 2 May 2019].

denomination: '[t]here are the following kinds of church assemblies, the church council, classis, regional synod and general synod'.[41] So, the *Statement* accommodates the Reformed tradition by including among 'international organisations' those in the form of e.g. a 'communion' or a 'conference'.[42]

3 Principles in the statement that remain problematic for the Reformed tradition

At first sight some principles may seem to remain problematic for the Reformed tradition. Some in their final form are not a perfect reflection of Reformed church order. Nevertheless, a generous interpretation of them results in consistency with Reformed church order. What follows examines three sets of principles. They are taken in turn.

The first set of such principles is on international, national, and regional assemblies; the relationship between these and the local church; and assemblies.[43]

Section IV

3 National church structures

1 An ecclesial tradition may have a national organisation.
2 A church or other ecclesial community organised at national level may have such institutional structure as is prescribed by the regulatory instruments applicable to it.
3 The autonomy and functions of a national ecclesial entity, and its conference, synod, council, or other form of central assembly, may include the authority to legislate, administer, and adjudicate on matters within its competence.
4 A national ecclesial assembly or other such institution is composed of such members of the faithful as are elected or otherwise appointed to it in accordance with law.

4 Regional church structures

1 National ecclesial entities may have regional structures.
2 Regional ecclesial organisations may be in the form of a diocese, eparchy, synod, district, classis, presbytery, association, or other regional unit.
3 A regional ecclesial unit may have such institutions, in the form of a synod, council, classis, presbytery, or other assembly, as are prescribed by the law applicable to it.

41 Article 29 of the Church of the Gereformeerde Kerke in Suid-Afrika: www.cjbf.co.za/kerkorde/KOCO.pdf [accessed 2 May 2019].

42 SPCL IV.2.1.

43 SPCL IV.3 (national church structures), 4 (regional church structures) and 5 (the local church).

4 A regional institution exercises such authority and functions as are conferred on it by the ecclesial community to which it belongs or the constituent churches associated with it.
5 A regional ecclesial assembly or other such institution is composed of such members of the faithful as are elected or otherwise appointed to it by those competent to do so under the law.

5 The local church

1 Regional ecclesial units may be divided into or constituted by local churches or congregations existing at the most localised level of church life.
2 A church organised locally may be in the form of a parish, circuit, congregation, or other ecclesial unit.
3 A local church, its assembly and other institutions, such as a council, meeting, session, or other body, has such authority and functions as are lawfully inherent to it or conferred upon it by the institutions of the wider ecclesial entity to which it belongs.
4 The assembly of a local church is composed of those members of the faithful who are lawfully elected or otherwise appointed to it.
5 All ecclesial units at each level are interdependent.

At first sight this can be considered problematic among some Reformed denominations, with their (over)emphasis on the local church. This might become clear from a more or less general regulation in Reformed church orders as stated in one of them: '[i]n major assemblies only such matters shall be dealt with as could not be determined in minor assemblies: or such as pertain to the churches of the major assembly in common. In all assemblies only ecclesiastical matters shall be dealt with'.[44]

According to the Reformed tradition such assemblies are not permanent bodies. They consist of office-bearers delegated by the consistories of local churches. A local church is considered to be 'church' – but not the complete church. As these assemblies are not permanent bodies, they open when the delegates of the consistories of local churches convene, and at the end of the meeting the assemblies are closed. In the meantime, deputies are appointed to fulfil some tasks or to deal with urgent matters. Especially when it comes to the authority of general assemblies at the supra-local level versus the authority of the consistory of the local church in the field of admonition and discipline – and questions arise as to who has the authority to discipline an office-bearer – there is sometimes friction. According to Reformed church

44 See http://kerkrecht.nl/node/6208 [accessed 3 May 2019]. See also Article 30 of the church order of the Christelijke Gereformeerde Kerken in Nederland: https://cgk.nl/project/de-kerkorde/ [accessed 3 May 2019]; Article 30 of the church order of the Gereformeerde Kerke in Suid-Afrika: www.cjbf.co.za/kerkorde/KOCO.pdf [accessed 3 May 2019].

polity, local churches form a confederation on a voluntary basis. There is no central organised supra-local church.

In the past, disagreement about the relationship between the local and the supra-local church, in particular the authority of general assemblies, such as the classis (the regional level) and the particular (roughly the provincial level) and general synods (the national level), has led to schism. For example, in 1926 there was a schism over this matter in the Reformed Churches in the Netherlands, which led to the creation of *Gereformeerde Kerken in Hersteld Verband* [the Reformed Churches in Restored Cooperation], with the Revd Johannes G. Geelkerken (1879–1960) as its leader. In 1944 another schism occurred in the Reformed Churches in the Netherlands. This led to the creation of *Gereformeerde Kerken vrijgemaakt* [the Reformed Churches Liberated], with Professor Klaas Schilder (1890–1952) as its leader. Both schisms within two decades caused much ecclesial and personal discord. In the Reformed Churches in the Netherlands schisms led the general synod to attribute more authority to the general assemblies at the supra-local level (classis assembly, the particular or provincial synod, and the general synod), as was formulated in the church order 'entrusted by Christ', Article 28,[45] *Gereformeerde Kerkorde* (Church Order of the Reformed Churches in the Netherlands) of 1957. Article 28 continues by stating that the classis has the same authority over the consistory as the particular synod has over the classis and the general synod over the particular synod. This is an elaboration or extension of Article 36 of the Dort Church Order 1619.[46]

Moreover, something of Article 28 of the Church Order of 1957 is also expressed in the church order of the Christian Reformed Churches in North America; namely, each assembly exercises, in keeping with its own character and domain, the ecclesiastical authority entrusted to the church by Christ, the authority of councils being original, that of major assemblies being delegated (Article 27-a);[47] and the classis has the same authority over the council as the synod has over the classis (Article 27-b).[48] The Reformed Churches in New Zealand is the same in its treatment of the 'Authority of Major Assemblies'; it provides that each assembly exercises, in keeping with its own character and domain, the ecclesiastical authority entrusted to the church by Christ, the authority of sessions being original, that of major assemblies being delegated. The presbytery has the same authority over the session as the synod has over the presbytery (Article 35).[49] In the 'Church Order of Dordrecht as Revised

45 In some editions the number of this article is 26 or 32. The text of the article is in Dutch: '1. Deze vergaderingen hebben, elk naar eigen aard, een kerkelijk gezag, haar door Christus verleend. 2. Hetzelfde gezag, dat de classis heeft over de kerkeraad, heeft de particuliere synode over de classis en de generale synode over de particuliere'.

46 't'Selfde segghen heeft de Classis over den Kercken-Raet / 'twelck de particuliere Synode heeft over de Classe / ende de Generale Synode over de particuliere': www.kerkrecht.nl [accessed 17 May 2018].

47 See http://kerkrecht.nl/content/kerkorde-crcna-2010-art-27 [accessed 17 May 2018].

48 See http://kerkrecht.nl/content/kerkorde-crcna-2010-art-27-b [accessed 17 May 2018].

49 See http://kerkrecht.nl/node/6217 [accessed 17 May 2018].

by Synod 2003 of the Free Reformed Churches of Australia', Article 28 of the *Gereformeerde Kerkorde* of 1957 is expressed in this way: '[t]he classis has the same jurisdiction over the consistory as the synod has over the classis' (Article 35).[50] Moreover, similarly, the 'Church Order of the Canadian and American Reformed Churches' provides in Article 37: '[t]he classis has the same jurisdiction over the consistory as the regional synod has over the classis, and the general synod over the regional synod'.[51]

Another principle that could be problematic is the one that states that '[a] national ecclesial assembly or other such institution is composed of such members of the faithful as are elected or otherwise appointed to it in accordance with law'.[52] The Reformed churches in general are not national churches. They convene by their deputies in classis assemblies, particular/provincial synods, or general synods. These deputies belong to the faithful; however, they are office-bearers, not laypeople. The same applies, from a literal perspective, to the principle that '[n]ational ecclesial entities may have regional structures'.[53] This suggests that every church is a national ecclesial entity. This is not so for Reformed churches. Although national ecclesial entities may be divided into regions, this principle suggests a central organised (top-down) church. This contradicts Reformed ecclesiology and polity. The same objection from the Reformed perspective concerns the principle 'Regional ecclesial units may be divided into or constituted by local churches or congregations existing at the most localised level of church life'.[54]

The second set of principles that remains problematic from the Reformed perspective concerns the related matter of (international) oversight. As we saw earlier, there is no notion of an international church in the Reformed tradition. The tradition is cautious about any supra-local expression of church. The relevant principles are as follows:

Section III.4

The exercise of oversight

1 Oversight is an essential of ecclesial order.
2 Oversight is exercised by such authority as is designated by law.
3 A church may have a system of international oversight or leadership.
4 A minister has such international functions of oversight or leadership as are permitted by law.
5 International church offices include those of pope, patriarch, primate, president, moderator, or general secretary.

50 See http://kerkrecht.nl/node/1894 [accessed 17 May 2018].
51 See http://kerkrecht.nl/node/736 [accessed 17 May 2018].
52 SPCL IV.3.4.
53 SPCL IV.4.1.
54 SPCL IV.5.1.

6 Those who exercise international oversight or leadership are appointed or elected to that office by competent ecclesial authority.
7 A church may assign to such an office a coercive jurisdiction or a moral or persuasive authority.

Whilst there is no international Reformed Church, some Reformed denominations that share the same confession meet each other in international conferences, such as the International Conference of Reformed Churches (ICRC), which was founded in 1982 in the Netherlands.[55] Nevertheless, the principle that 'a church may have a system of international oversight or leadership' is for the Reformed tradition problematic, at least when it would mean a hierarchical system of oversight or leadership. However, the principle includes a 'may'; therefore, this aspect of it is not problematic. This may be contrasted with the principle that 'a minister has such international functions of oversight or leadership as are permitted by law'. This principle does not include a 'may'. No Reformed minister has 'international functions of oversight or leadership'. By contrast, a minister could exercise some international leadership when appointed to the executive board of the World Council of Churches or the International Council of Reformed Churches, but not in the form of hierarchical oversight. Once more, though, this principle includes the words 'as are permitted by law'. If a Reformed Church minister has the authority to exercise such international oversight or leadership, he or she can only exercise such authority 'as . . . permitted by law'. That would be consistent with Reformed church order.

4 Are some principles more important than others?

From a Reformed perspective it is difficult to consider whether some principles are more important than others. One could say that the first article of almost every Reformed church order that is based on the Dort Church Order of 1619 can be considered the most important article in the sense that it provides the ecclesiological and church polity introduction to subsequent articles. For example, '[i]n accordance with the apostolic injunction (1 Cor. 14:40) that in the Church of Christ all things are to be done decently and in order, the Reformed Churches of New Zealand, in this *Church Order*, regulate their organisation and activities, so that they may fulfil their calling according to the Scriptures and the Reformed Confessions. The main subjects treated in this Order are the Church's Offices, Assemblies, Worship, and Discipline';[56] its importance is clear.

55 See www.icrconline.com/ [accessed 26 April 2018].

56 Article 1 of the Church Order of the Reformed Churches of New Zealand: http://kerkrecht.nl/node/6183 [accessed 3 May 2019]. See also Article 1 Dort Church Order of 1619; http://kerkrecht.nl/node/440 [accessed 3 May 2019];

Article 1 of the church order of the Christelijke Gereformeerde Kerken in Nederland; http://kerkrecht.nl/node/265 [accessed 3 May 2019]; Article A2.2. Church Order of the Reformed Churches liberated (*Gereformeerde Kerken vrijgemaakt*) http://kerkrecht.

Moreover, there is another article that expresses, from the sixteenth-century context, the ecclesiological standpoint of the Reformed churches around the world. This is the famous first article of the first (Acts of the) Synod of Emden of 1571, the mother of all Reformed synods.[57] Among scholars in Reformed church polity this first article is called the *canon aureaus*, the golden rule.[58] It states that neither church nor office nor office-bearer (and/or person) lords it over another. This article, although not today the first in every Reformed church order, is still dominant in Reformed ecclesiology and practice. Usually this fundamental ecclesiological principle is considered something positive in prohibiting lordship or hierarchy. Sometimes, however, it is seen as an obstacle to renewal. This rejection of lordship and hierarchy needs to be understood against the background of the decline of the sixteenth-century Roman Catholic ecclesiology and hierarchy by the Reformed movement. By contrast, there is another fundamental principle in Reformed ecclesiology that also needs to be understood against the background of the sixteenth century. It is the rejection of independentism (against the Anabaptists). The last article of (the Acts of) the Synod of Emden of 1571 included the statement that church order can only be changed with the mutual consent of all the (local) churches.[59] In one way or another this principle is still present and valid in Reformed church orders; for example: '[t]his Church Order, having been adopted by common consent, shall be faithfully observed, and any revision thereof shall be made only by Synod'.[60] Both articles of the (Acts of the) Synod of Emden of 1571 are fundamental expressions of Reformed ecclesiology and are in consequence implemented in Reformed church polity today. Sometimes the balance between the two principles is challenged. This is clear from the discussion about the (lack of) balance between the local church and the supralocal church, as mentioned previously. Nevertheless, these two principles enjoy a certain weight, and one could state that the other articles in Reformed church orders are an elaboration of these principles.

nl/node/1103 [accessed 3 May 2019]; Article VI.1 of the church order of the Protestant Church in the Netherlands; www.protestantsekerk.nl/thema/kerkorde [accessed 3 May 2019].

57 See http://kerkrecht.nl/node/5945 [accessed 3 May 2019].

58 D. Nauta, J.P. van Dooren and Otto J. de Jong, eds., *De Synode van Emden Oktober 1571: Een bundel Opstellen ter Gelegenheid van de Vierhonderdjarige Herdenking* (Kampen: Kok, 1971) 89; M. Bouwman, *Voetius over het Gezag der Synoden* (Amsterdam: S.J.P. Bakker, 1937) 369ff.

59 "*Articuli hi ad legitimum Ecclesiae ordinem spectantes ita mutuo consensu sunt constituti, vt si vtilitas Ecclesiarum aliud postulet, mutari, augeri, et minui possint ac debeant; non erit tamen alicuius privatae Ecclesiae id facere, sed dabunt omnes operam vt illos observent, donec a Synodo aliter constituatur*/Deze Articulen de Wetterlijcke ende behoorlijcke ordre der Kercken betreffende, zijn alsoo met ghemeyn accoort ghestelt, datse, soo de nutticheydt der Kercken vereyschet, verandert, vermeerdert, ende vermindert moghen ende behooren te worden. Nochtans sal 't gheen besondere Kercke vry staen sulcx te doen: maer alle Kercken sullen arbeyden dese te onderhouden, tot dat in een Synodale vergaderinghe anders besloten wort': http://kerkrecht.nl/node/5997 [accessed 3 May 2019].

60 See http://kerkrecht.nl/node/6278 [accessed 3 May 2019].

III The value of the *Statement of Principles of Christian Law*

First, the value of the *Statement of Principles of Christian Law* for the Reformed tradition is that is helps that tradition obtain a better understanding of its own polity and theological foundations, the church polity of other Christian traditions, the importance of juridical ecumenism, and the interplay of both academic and practical expertise and experience. It can also help the Reformed tradition understand that church polity is more than a set of regulations or a book of pragmatic and efficient rules or, worse, that it is of no value at all. The *Statement* is an important 'business card' of juridical ecumenism. It would gain even greater importance if it could be discussed by ecumenical partners outside Europe – i.e. from the Global South – and by experts in Jewish law and Islamic law in order to have a wider, cross-cultural set of common principles of religious law.

Second, the principles in the *Statement* reflect the doctrinal or theological position in the Reformed tradition. The following principles are typical here: '[b]aptim is validly administered with water in the name of the triune God'[61] and '[t]he Eucharist and receiving of Holy Communion are central to ecclesial life'.[62] They demonstrate that Reformed church polity is also liturgical in nature, although many are not aware of this.

Third, the methodology used by the Panel is fruitful because it takes place in an ecumenical context. It connects with the statement of the German jurist Hans Dombois (1907–1997) that nowadays church polity can only be considered ecumenical church polity, whereas it was in the first millennium of church history more *epiclectic* in nature and in the second more transcendental in nature – *epiclectic* because the nature of the church in the first millennium was in general considered a unity in the Holy Spirit and transcendental because error led to theological reflection of the nature of the church and the application of it in a juridical format. According to Dombois transcendental church polity has lost of it credibility because it is no longer considered convincing.[63]

Moreover, as Leo J. Koffeman states, 'All kinds of legitimizing theology have to be abandoned'. It is time for an ecumenical approach to church polity. Comparison with other church polity systems reveals not only best practices but also the reverse side of each system: every church polity system is one-sided and has its strengths and weaknesses.[64] For example, many Reformed denominations within the presbyterial-synodical system (over)emphasise the autonomy of the local church and its consistory, but this may actually isolate it from other local churches and/or the supra-local church. Moreover, every system is theoretical in the sense that ecclesial practice varies within its own system. Comparison might

61 SPCL VII.1.4.

62 SPCL VII.3.2.

63 H. Dombois, *Das Recht der Gnade: Ökumenisches Kirchenrecht* 2. *Grundlagen und Grundfragen der Kirchenverfassung in ihrer Geschichte* (Bielefeld: Luther-Verlag, MCMLXXIV).

64 L.J. Koffeman, op cit., 34.103–243.

help to understand (better) one's own system and/or reflect upon one's own denomination and to learn or benefit from the strengths of other systems. In ecumenical discourse one's own system needs to be criticised and/or mirrored by others. For example, in 2004 the merger of the Netherlands Reformed Church, the Reformed Churches in the Netherlands, and the Evangelical Lutheran Church in the Kingdom of the Netherlands resulted in the foundation of the Protestant Church in the Netherlands. In the process towards this merger, the three denominations confronted the limitations and strengths of their respective ecclesial structures, norms, and governance.[65]

Conclusion

Participating in the ecumenical panel on the principles of Christian law is a fascinating and joyful journey. This is very much the case because one gets to learn more from the other (non-Reformed) traditions and to understand afresh through these perspectives one's own tradition. From the perspective of the Reformed tradition, most of the principles are not problematic. Some were, but these were generously adjusted. Only those principles with a view to supra-local oversight by supra-local office-bearers, hierarchy, and lordship and an overly heavy emphasis on a national church or international church can at first sight be considered problematic, especially through superficial lenses. However, a close reading of the principles makes clear that there is respect and space for the (variety within the) Reformed tradition. That is a gracious expression of juridical ecumenism.

65 See Chapter 12.

9 The Presbyterian tradition

John Chalmers

Presbyterian church polity has been adapted to serve as a form of church government in many different contexts around the world. This contribution to an understanding of the Presbyterian tradition is peculiarly Scottish, but since many Presbyterians across the world would describe the Church of Scotland as their 'mother church', it is to be hoped that the fundamental building blocks of Presbyterianism will be recognised in this short chapter. The primary elements of the primacy of the Word; the parity of ministry, authority, and discipline exercised through courts; and a built-in resistance to 'innovation' should become obvious.

I The roots of a Presbyterian polity

What began on 31 October 1517 with the publication of Martin Luther's Ninety-Five Theses, outlining his disquiet at many of the practices and teachings of the Roman Catholic Church, was the start of a sea change that rocked both church and society throughout Europe. Commonly referred to as the Protestant Reformation, this movement led to an almost unprecedented upheaval[1] in Church authority, structure, and governance. It is safe to say that no disruption of church life on anything of like scale has been experienced since. However, as the Protestant movement took root, it did not take on a consistent shape or form. Instead, across Europe, it was shaped not only by certain strong theological propositions but also by the social and political realities that stood in its way. By the time the Scottish Reformation Parliament of 1560 adopted a Protestant confession of faith and rejected papal jurisdiction and the mass, the movement, begun with Luther in Wittenberg, had been filtered and refined so that when it arrived in Scotland it came with a predominantly Calvinist theology, which eventually led to a Church of Scotland with a strongly Presbyterian ecclesiastical polity.

John Knox[2] emerged as the principal figure of the Scottish Reformation. He had spent time in Geneva with John Calvin, who, as a lawyer by training and a

1 With the exception of the East-West Schism of 1054.

2 John Knox (c. 1513–24 November 1572), Scottish minister, theologian, leader of the Scottish Reformation, and founder of the Presbyterian Church of Scotland.

legalist in outlook, brought to Protestant theology and governance a systematic approach that Knox seeded in Scotland. Calvin has sometimes been described as the epitome of rigour and cheerlessness; whether or not that is true, more than a little of that character found its way into early Presbyterianism in Scotland.

II Foundational principles

This background is important because it points us to the origins of three important historical documents – *The Confession of Faith* (1560), *The First Book of Discipline* (1560), and *The Book of Common Order* (1562) – that laid the foundation of the Reformed Church in Scotland. These documents defined, respectively, the creed, the government, and the worship of a church that was national in character and that bore the early marks of a Presbyterian structure. For the Church of Scotland, these documents are the earliest construction of a framework for a system of law, order, and polity as described in the preamble to Section I of the *Statement of Principles of Christian Law* (Rome 2016), hereafter the *Principles.*

The first of these documents, *The Confession of Faith and Doctrine believed and professed by the Protestants of the Realm of Scotland*,[3] was drawn up and completed in four days, and its principal author was John Knox. Its 25 chapters affirm the doctrinal tenets of the reformed faith, giving 'special prominence to those truths around which the struggle of the Reformation was chiefly waged in Scotland'.[4] It strongly emphasises the authority of Holy Scripture and describes the marks of the true Kirk of Christ as being 'first, the true preaching of the Word of God, in which God has revealed himself to us, as the writings of the prophets and apostles declare; secondly, the right administration of the sacraments of Christ Jesus, with which must be associated the Word and promise of God to seal and confirm them in our hearts; and lastly, ecclesiastical discipline uprightly ministered, as God's Word prescribes'.[5] These words express an early and particular understanding of servant law (Principle I.3) – in other words, law shaped by theological understanding, law conforming to the revelation contained in Scripture, and law serving the mission and witness of Christ.

The substance and content of *The Confession of Faith* are the foundation of the succeeding documents, *The Book of Discipline* and *The Book of Common Order*. Many of the main ideas contained in these documents would resonate with the descriptors contained throughout the *Principles* (2016). For example, these Presbyterian documents describe the distinguishing categories of church offices – namely, ministers, elders, and deacons (Principles III.1.1 and 1.2); they define the only sacraments to be recognised in the church to be baptism and the Lord's Supper (Principle VII, preamble); and they describe the need for election,

3 See www.creeds.net/reformed/Scots/scots.htm#Index.

4 J.A. Duke, *History of the Church of Scotland to the Reformation* (Edinburgh: Oliver and Boyd, 1937) 249–251.

5 The Scots Confession, 1560, Chapter 18.

examination, and admission of those who would be ordained to the ministry of Word and sacrament (Principles III.1.1, 1.3, and 1.4). So, whilst these sixteenth-century documents may be of little importance in the modern-day Church of Scotland, they nonetheless represent a major strand in the DNA of Scottish Presbyterianism. And since so many Presbyterian churches across the world regard the Church of Scotland as their 'mother church', the influence of these documents has reached the four corners of the earth.[6]

III Common roots and deep resentments

At this stage it is important to identify two other key strands that go into the making of Scottish Presbyterianism. The first is the clear self-understanding of the Church of Scotland as part of the one holy and catholic church under the headship of Christ alone (Principles IV.1.1 and VIII.1.1). In other words, Knox and the co-founders of the reformed Church in Scotland were at pains to show that they were not inventing a new church. One of the most celebrated principal clerks of the General Assembly of the Church of Scotland, the Revd Dr James T Cox, describes it thus: '[t]he fact that the Church of Scotland existed before the Reformation is of great importance in relation to its constitution'.[7] He goes on to describe how those things that were 'sound and valuable and not out of accord with Scripture, remained in force'. Included in those were the commitment to a parochial system (Principle I.1.3), access to spiritual support and care on a territorial basis (Principle II.2.2), and the provision of disciplinary supervision at the local, regional, and national level (Principle V). In relation to this particular study that, in the pursuit of ecumenical progress, is aimed at the discovery of common roots and shared principles of law and governance, Cox's view that 'there are principles of ecclesiastical law and procedure which have their roots in canons that existed long before 1560' is of great importance.[8]

In his introduction to the Constitution and Laws of the Church of Scotland,[9] James Weatherhead reaches back to the New Testament and to the early church fathers, identifying Romans 13 as the biblical foundation of Christian law (Principle I.3.4). He also quotes Justinian's *Institutes* as providing the three basic precepts of law; namely, 'to live honestly', 'to injure no one' (Principles II.3.4 and 3.5 and III.3.3 and 3.4), and 'to render to each his due' (Principle II.1.2). This acknowledgement of continuity of principle going back to the New Testament and the early church fathers is important; and the purpose of Christian law is best summed up by Weatherhead when he says that 'law cannot enforce an attitude

6 A useful summary of these publications is found in J.H.S. Burleigh, *A History of the Church of Scotland* (Edinburgh: Hope Trust, 1988) 153ff.

7 J.T. Cox, *Practice and Procedure in the Church of Scotland* (Edinburgh: Committee on General Administration: William Blackwood and Sons Ltd., 1976) 1.

8 Ibid., 2.

9 J.L. Weatherhead, *The Constitution and Laws of the Church of Scotland* (Edinburgh: The Board of Practice and Procedure, 1997).

of mind, [but] a certain attitude of mind, namely a hunger and thirst for justice, is basic to the enactment and judicial application of law'.[10] In other words, the continuing principle is the desire for rightness or, as expressed in Matthew 5:6, 'righteousness'; this is expressed in Principles I.4.9 and V.1.4.

The second important strand in the making of Scottish Presbyterianism is to note the way in which the interrelationship of church and state has shaped the character of the Scottish Church. I do not intend to unpack all of the implications of this relationship, but later we will come back to this topic because it has had much to do with the shaping of what might be described as the 'modern-day' Church of Scotland. At this stage, however, we note that in the early years of the Reformation, '[t]he governance of the civil and ecclesiastical realms overlapped; and since the first leaders of the Reformation of 1560 were among the magnates (i.e. the wealthy and powerful), burghers and senior nobility, their first General Assemblies, were naturally, gatherings of members of the same Estates that made up Parliament . . . suggesting that a single decision-making mechanism was separately, but only slightly differently, constituted for its spiritual and its secular tasks'.[11] It has been noted that 'in 1560 it might well appear that [this] true religion would have the support of the civil magistrate, and the Acts of Parliament so far as they went would support that hope'.[12] This is a description of church and state comfortably sharing the same nest, and it describes a state of affairs that would be the harbinger of witch hunts (quite literally), disputation, disruption, and schism.

In Chapter 25 of the Scots Confession there is an affirmation of the role and office of the civil magistrate. Civil magistrates, together with kings, princes, and rulers, are described as chiefly and principally being for the conservation and purgation of religion, appointed not only for the maintenance of civil policy but also for the conservation of true religion and the suppression of idolatry and superstition. A terrible example of the way in which the church's assembly and the civil authority of Parliament worked hand in glove is the 1640 Act of Assembly Against Witches and Charmers in which the general assembly invited Parliament 'carefully to take notice of charmers, witches, and all such abusers of the people, and to urge the Acts of Parliament to be execute against them . . . in the most behoovefull way'.[13] This is part of a sad chapter in Scottish Church and public life that contributed to the Great Scottish Witch Hunt (1649–1650);[14] more than 300 women were tried and executed for their supposed involvement in witchcraft. It may have been an aspiration of the Scottish reformers, inspired directly by Calvin, to create a Godly society in which church and state sang from 'the same hymn sheet', but corruption and abuse are the result of a relationship that has

10 Ibid., 2.

11 M.A. MacLean, *The Crown Rights of the Redeemer* (Edinburgh: St Andrew Press, 2009) 58.

12 J.H.S. Burleigh, op cit., 159.

13 Acts of the General Assembly of the Church of Scotland 1640: www.british-history.ac.uk/church-scotland-records/acts/1638-1842/pp44-45

14 See: https://en.wikipedia.org/wiki/Great_Scottish_witch_hunt_of_1649-50

no proper checks and balances. For a nation to call itself 'free' and 'democratic' it needs more than a freely elected government. It also requires its institutions – the law, the church, the fourth estate, and so on – to be free; that is, free to hold authority to account and free to be able to speak truth to power. In Scotland today, church and state no longer have their hands in one another's pockets, and Principle X.1.1 describes perfectly the relationship between the modern-day Church of Scotland and the state; but it has taken hard centuries and a long road to get to this place.

If the first of these two strands, expressed so cogently by Cox, highlights continuity and common rootedness and points towards a real measure of ecumenical hope, then the great sadness of this second strand is that it gave birth to a severely anti-Roman polemic that created a deeply sectarian division in Scottish public life. Professor John Burleigh notes that 'the extreme anti-papalism of these documents [*The Confession of Faith*, *The Book of Discipline*, and *The Book of Common Order*] savours of revolution rather than of reform. Continuity with the old Church is explicitly disavowed. It was a synagogue of Satan, by its doctrinal, ceremonial, administrative and moral corruptions disfiguring the face of the true Church'.[15] These harsh words, and the deeply negative tone, strain to the limits the argument for continuity of faith, far less continuity of church. Not for the last time would the Church of Scotland find itself stretched over the horns of a dilemma, believing almost contrary things about itself that had to be held in dynamic tension.

The deep distaste for the Roman Church expressed in these early documents was, of course, carried over into the Westminster Confession of Faith when it was drawn up in 1646. The Confession of the Westminster Divines was examined and approved in 1647 by the General Assembly of the Church of Scotland and was later ratified by Acts of Parliament in 1649 and 1690. It became the principal subordinate standard of doctrine[16] in the Church of Scotland, and as such it served to embed sectarian divisions that still persist in some forms to this very day. It took the General Assembly of the Church of Scotland until 1986 to pass an act declaring that the Church of Scotland no longer held to the anti-papalism prescribed in the Westminster Confession of Faith. This Declaratory Act dissociated the Church of Scotland from the anti-Roman Catholic statements in the Confession and no longer bound its ministers and other office-bearers to believe them.[17] This is a perfect example of Principle VI.1.2 (on the definition of doctrine) at work, where the church, using the authority of its law-making court to formulate, interpret, or modify its subordinate standards realises that times have changed and so belief and practice must also change. This, however, was not a

15 J.H.S. Burleigh, op cit., 177.

16 Article 1 of the constitution of the Church of Scotland declares that the Church of Scotland receives the Word of God, which is contained in the Scriptures of the Old and New Testaments, as its supreme rule of faith and life. Article 2 refers to the Westminster Confession of Faith as the church's 'subordinate standard'.

17 See www.churchofscotland.org.uk/__data/assets/pdf_file/0014/1823/1986_act_05.pdf.

sudden change. It was preceded by years in which trusting relationships between Presbyterians and Roman Catholics had been fostered at all levels, myths were debunked, and joint ventures in Christian worship and mission were forged and Presbyterians in Scotland began to put Principle VIII.2.1–5 (on ecumenism) into action.

This brief examination of the early years of the Scottish Reformation serves to highlight the origins of the later structure and polity of Scottish Presbyterianism that, with the Scottish Diaspora, found its way across the world.[18] The Church of Scotland was built, for good or ill, on a confession of faith that was foundational for both ecclesiastical and civil society in Scotland. That same confession was then the fixed point around which *The Book of Discipline* and *The Book of Common Order* were crafted; however, at the earliest stages of the Scottish Reformation the Church of Scotland could not be described as Presbyterian, just as John Knox could never be described as a Presbyterian.[19]

IV Hierarchy of courts and parity of persons

At the time of the Scottish Reformation priests became ministers and bishops served as superintendents (ministers with a regional remit) but it was not until 1592, under the significant influence of Andrew Melville, that a full Presbyterian system of government was adopted by the Scottish Church and Parliament. This structure included an ascending series of courts made up of ministers and elders – namely, kirk session, presbytery, synod, and general assembly – and this is reflected in the organisation of Section IV of the *Principles* on church governance. As well as establishing a system of local, regional, provincial, and national church government, this landmark moment gave free expression to the concept of ministerial parity. In this new structure there would be no hierarchy of persons, only a hierarchy of courts, with the lower courts subject to obeying and implementing the will of the higher courts and the higher courts being authorised to dispose of appeals and deal with disputes arising in the lower courts. This hierarchy of courts provides for the kind of oversight referred to in Section III of the *Principles* and orders the life of the church such that matters of discipline and dispute resolution (Principles V.2.4–5) can be handled with expediency.

These assemblies were to be populated by ministers and elders. Elders, once appointed, would occupy their position for life: 'their office, as it is ordinary, so it is perpetual, and always necessary in the kirk of God. The eldership [being] a spiritual function, as is the ministry. Elders once lawfully called to the office, and having gifts of God meet to exercise the same, may not leave it again'.[20] The

18 See http://flemish.wp.st-andrews.ac.uk/2015/11/13/migration-from-scotland-before-1700/. This reference provides one of many accounts of Scots establishing a Presbyterian presence across the seas.

19 J.H.S. Burleigh, op cit., 176.

20 Second Book of Discipline (www.swrb.com/newslett/actualNLs/bod_ch04.htm#CH06), Chapter 6:2.

spiritual nature of this office, whereby men[21] were ordained to the office of the eldership for life, is one of the distinguishing marks of Presbyterianism.

In Presbyterian polity the idea of parity in ministry is so strong that, in spite of obvious differences, it is held that there is no distinction in status between those who are ordained to office (whether to the ministry of Word and sacrament, the diaconate, or the eldership) and those who belong to what might be termed the 'ordinary' membership of the church. This derives from that great pillar of the Protestant Reformation, the doctrine of the priesthood of all believers.[22] The evangelical calling of the church was no longer to be the domain of the clergy alone; instead, each individual member of the body of Christ was to understand their calling as a part of the ministry of Jesus Christ exercised through the 'whole people of God', which is expressed in various ways in Principles II.3.2, II.3.5, and II.4.2. The proof text was an understanding of 1 Peter 2:9: '[b]ut you are not like that, for you are a chosen people. You are royal priests, a holy nation, God's very own possession. As a result, you can show others the goodness of God, for he called you out of the darkness into his wonderful light'.

So, in Presbyterianism, even within the ranks of the ordained ministry of Word and sacrament there is no hierarchy. There are different forms of ministry, and from time to time ministers may hold particular offices that require them to exercise the authority of the office (Principle III.2), but those who hold or preside over the courts (secretaries, clerks, conveners, and moderators) have no hierarchical ascendancy. Even the moderator of the general assembly, who enjoys the most honoured of positions, must remember the rule of *primus inter pares*, that they, like all others, serve the church only as first among equals. This principle is further reinforced by the practice of appointing moderators to serve for one year only; this is a convention rather than a law, but Scottish Presbyterians, being keen to emphasise that they are led by courts and not by individuals, have never broken that convention. The presbytery and not its moderator carries out the function of oversight equivalent to that of a bishop in Episcopal churches. The general assembly and not its moderator carries out the function of oversight equivalent to that of an archbishop in Episcopal churches. It is worth reflecting that Sections III, IV, and V of the *Principles* are short on detail relating to the hierarchical positions that are the backbone of the many church traditions, and perhaps this is because of the need to accommodate Presbyterians, Baptists, and others who invest authority in courts or committees and who eschew the practice of investing authority in individuals or even in the offices they hold.

21 Not until 1966 and 1968, respectively, were the offices of the eldership and ministry of Word and Sacrament opened up to women in the Church of Scotland. In the case of the ministry of Word and Sacrament, the inclusion of women was achieved by a simple amendment to what was Act XXV, 1968; this inserted the words 'Women shall be eligible for ordination to the Holy Ministry on the same terms and conditions as are at present applicable to men' (see J.L. Weatherhead, op cit., 60).

22 See www.britannica.com/topic/The-Protestant-Heritage-1354359/The-priesthood-of-all-believers#ref466232.

The *Principles*, however, may not go far enough in accommodating the idiosyncrasies of Presbyterianism. Just as Anglicans and Roman Catholics have their 'high' and 'low' church wings, so, too, do Presbyterians. In the Presbyterian tradition a 'high' view of ministry would recognise the particularity (not the status) of the ministry of Word and sacrament and would not countenance anyone, other than a person ordained to that office, celebrating the sacrament of the Lord's Supper; this is reflected in Principle III.3.2. A 'low' church view, however, might describe those ordained to the eldership as 'ruling elders', whilst those ordained to the ministry of Word and sacrament would be described as 'teaching elders', and some would argue that authority to preside at the sacraments should be extended, at the very least, to those 'ruling elders', if not to the wider membership itself.[23]

The *Principles* provides (in VII.3.5) for the Eucharist to be 'presided over by such persons as are lawfully authorised'; presently it is the case that only those ordained to the ministry of Word and sacrament are 'lawfully authorised', within the Church of Scotland, to preside. This view, however, has recently been challenged, and a committee of the general assembly has been charged with examining whether presiding at the Lord's Supper might be opened up to be celebrated by anyone of 'the faithful'.[24] If a review brought about such a change in practice, it could be argued that Principle VIII.3.5 still applied, albeit to a wider category of authorised presidents; however, the effect this would have on ecumenical agreements would, no doubt, be far-reaching. Whilst nothing is settled in this review, the wide range of difference in our understanding of Section VII of the *Principles* on the rites of the church remains the biggest barrier to the fullest possible ecumenical progress. In some respects, therefore, this section of the *Principles* is the weakest in terms of the contribution it makes to the ecumenical conversation. Of course, the *Principles* highlights a shared belief that the Holy Communion is instituted by Christ (Principle VII.3.1), and with the exception of Principle VII.3.6, Presbyterians would recognise the descriptors used in this section. Nonetheless, these remain secondary issues when compared with the level of theological disagreement that keeps us from sharing full communion across our denominations. It is, however, to be hoped that identifying commonalities in our observable practice might be a stepping stone towards dealing with our deeper differences in understanding how Christ is present at the holy table.

So, in reviewing some of the theological principles that lie behind Presbyterian practice and procedure we make two important observations. The first is that it is hard to overstate the importance of parity of persons in Presbyterian polity. The Merriam-Webster online dictionary defines the doctrine of the priesthood of all believers as 'a doctrine of the Protestant Christian Church [where] every

23 A discussion on this matter was opened in the Report of the Panel on Review and Reform to the General Assembly in 2017; see www.churchofscotland.org.uk/__data/assets/pdf_file/0005/39569/Panel_on_Review_and_Reform.pdf Section 5.7.

24 Ibid.

individual has direct access to God without ecclesiastical mediation and each individual shares the responsibility of ministering to the other members of the community of believers'. This foundational principle of universal priesthood was strongly expressed in the years immediately following the Reformation in Scotland. During the reigns of Charles II and James VII (1660–1688), Presbyterianism was for a time outlawed in Scotland and replaced by episcopacy. The reaction to this and to the doctrine of the divine right of kings was fierce resistance. It gave birth to the Covenanters,[25] and in this period of history much blood was spilled in the defence of Presbyterian government. So, to this day many people within the Church of Scotland tradition would avoid the use of terms such as 'clergy' and 'laity'. This factor,[26] common in Presbyterian churches across the world, sets distinct challenges for those who work in the pursuit of ecumenical alignment.

A very practical example of this difficulty was the experience of the mainstream churches in Scotland, who, in the 1990s, following what many regarded as the 'ecumenical century' of the Christian Church, established the Scottish Church Initiative for Union (SCIFU). This involved the Church of Scotland, the Methodist Church, the Scottish Episcopal Church, the United Reformed Church, and the Scottish Congregational Church, with the Roman Catholic Church in Scotland and the United Free Church as observers. Together they sought to find a way of combining the polities and practices of these five churches in Scotland. After seven years of intensive work the initiative brought to its respective national bodies a roadmap for the creation of maxi-parishes[27] within an organic union, but in 2003 the General Assembly of the Church of Scotland firmly rejected the plan, largely on the grounds that proposals to accommodate bishops within presbyteries were unacceptable. For the Church of Scotland this was nothing new. The final report did not explore in any detail commonalities in the legal structures of each denomination; rather, it focussed on the idea of a church shaped, in all its parts, for mission. The real cause of its failure may, in fact, have had less to do with the role of bishops and more to do with the fact that ecumenical engagement in mission was already possible without the need for institutional alignment.

The *Second Book of Discipline* (1578) describes the principal function of these Godly men as being 'to hold assemblies with the pastors and doctors (who are also of their number) for establishing of good order, and execution of discipline'.[28] Some 250 years later, in an essay on the warrant, nature, and duties of the ruling elder, Samuel Miller described this function in slightly more subtle terms; but still

25 The Covenanters were those who signed the National Covenant in 1638. They signed this covenant to confirm their opposition to the interference by the Stuart kings in the affairs of the Presbyterian Church of Scotland.

26 J.L. Weatherhead, op cit., 38.

27 The report was published in the Volume of Reports to the General Assembly of the Church of Scotland 2003 (Edinburgh: The Church of Scotland Board of Practice and Procedure) 27/8ff.

28 Second Book of Discipline (www.swrb.com/newslett/actualNLs/bod_ch04.htm#CH06), Chapter 6:9.

there is more than a hint that this 'Godly man' is understood to be something of a spiritual law enforcement officer. Miller says, 'It is their duty to have an eye of inspection and care over all the members of the congregation; and, for this purpose, to cultivate a universal and intimate acquaintance, as far as may be, with every family in the flock of which they are made "overseers" '.[29]

Perhaps it is this model of the supervision of the morality and behaviour of the flock of God that has given Presbyterianism a reputation for strict discipline and ensured an ongoing body of legislation focussed on ecclesial discipline, the basics of which are mirrored in Section V of the *Principles* on discipline. At its most severe this tendency towards policing the moral practice of the faithful could be described as one of the less endearing qualities of the Presbyterian DNA, and whilst it may largely be a thing of the past, there is little doubt that the influence of Calvin's thinking and practice has given Presbyterianism a reputation for judgementalism. This is no better illustrated than in some of the poems of Scotland's national bard, Robert Burns. Published in the latter part of the eighteenth century, poems such as 'The Unco Guid' and 'Holy Willie's Prayer' describe a 'holier-than-thou' attitude from which most modern-day Presbyterians would recoil. The discipline captured in this practice represents a legalistic interpretation of Principle II.3.4 on the Christian standards to be upheld in the private lives of the faithful. But, thankfully, today in Presbyterian traditions across the world elders are now better understood as the local councillors of the Kirk, with a duty of care for the local congregation and a responsibility for creating its vision, developing its mission, and growing its outreach. This has been a welcome move towards an understanding of law as described in Principle I.3.1 and 3.2, but the major peculiarity of Presbyterianism remains the practice of ordaining men and women to a role and function that most other denominations would see as belonging to the ranks of the laity. This factor has, perhaps, constrained the use of the terms 'clergy' and 'laity' in the construction of the *Principles*, and this may well have been somewhat frustrating for those representing other traditions.

The last word, in this section, on the origins and the nature of law and order in the practice and procedure of Presbyterianism should, however, belong to John Calvin, who, in *The Institutes of the Christian Religion*, alludes to 1 Corinthians 14:40:

> First, then, let us understand that if in every human society some kind of government is necessary to insure the common peace and maintain concord . . . this ought especially to be observed in churches, which are best sustained by a constitution in all respects well ordered, and without which concord can have no existence. Wherefore, if we would provide for the safety of the Church, we must always carefully attend to Paul's injunction, that all things be done decently and in order (1 Cor. 14:40). But seeing there is such

29 Samuel Miller, *The Ruling Elder in the Presbyterian Church* (Glasgow: M. Ogle and Son, 1831) 166.

> diversity in the manners of men, such variety in their minds, such repugnance in their judgments and dispositions, no policy is sufficiently firm unless fortified by certain laws, nor can any rite be observed without a fixed form. So far, therefore, are we from condemning the laws which conduce to this, that we hold that the removal of them would unnerve the Church, deface and dissipate it entirely. For Paul's injunction, that all things be done decently and in order, cannot be observed unless order and decency be secured by the addition of ordinances, as a kind of bonds.[30]

In all of reformed writing, there can be no clearer apologetic for law and order in ecclesiastical life. Calvin would have endorsed the *Statement of Principles of Christian Law* (2016) because it endorses the need for church life that is scripturally grounded, doctrinally orthodox, well ordered, and well disciplined; but like everyone else he would have wanted those things to be understood on his terms.

V Law and legalism

The problem for Presbyterians, as with all those who would describe laws for the good ordering of the Christian Church, is that law should be distinguished from legalism. Too often in the story of Presbyterianism the application of the law has betrayed a fundamental belief in the doctrine of 'salvation by grace alone'. Legalism, as Weatherhead points out, 'is a wrong attitude to law, and should have no place in the faith and life of church members, or in the enactment and application of the law of the Church'.[31] This wonderful expression underlines the rightness of the Principle on 'the servant law' (I.3.1).

Given the complex history, the politics, and the underpinning theology of Presbyterianism it is quite remarkable that, for the most part, the *Statement of Principles of Christian Law*, drawn up by the Panel, sits fairly comfortably within Presbyterian polity. However, there are two significant matters of constitutional substance that must direct the way in which the *Principles* is read within Presbyterianism in general and within the Scottish Presbyterianism in particular.

VI Autonomy and church authority

The first matter relates to the importance of the autonomy of church authority in relation to four touchstone issues, these being doctrine, worship, discipline, and government. In Section I of the *Principles*, 'Systems of Law, Order and Polity', Presbyterians across the world would recognise the description of their institution as autonomous in nature, constrained only in relation to the law of God, as revealed in Holy Scripture and by the Holy Spirit.

30 Calvin, *Institutes*, Book IV, Chapter X, Section 27.

31 J.L. Weatherhead, op cit., 9.

In relation to the need for independence in matters of church governance, Scottish Church history reveals the deep scars and the great damage done when church and state have no clear separation of roles. That same church history bears witness to the trouble that can result from the interference of the state in matters to do with the doctrine, worship, discipline, and government of the Kirk. So, it would be hard to exaggerate the importance of 'autonomy' in both personality and practice as expressed in the *Principles* on the institutional church (I.1.1) and church-state relations (X.1.1).

In Scotland, during the nineteenth century, two new Presbyterian denominations were formed around the principle that the church should be in control of its own house. Throughout the eighteenth and early nineteenth centuries there had been growing anger and division about the way in which church and state were so intertwined. A church nested in the pocket of the state (as described earlier) was no longer seen as relevant. It did not represent the aspirations of an ever more enlightened Scotland, and there was a growing resentment amongst many ministers, elders, and ordinary members that the church relied too much on the patronage of the landowners and the heritors.[32] Worse still, there was anger that these patrons could influence the choice of the minister being called to serve in the parish.

This led in 1843 to a huge split in the Presbyterian household of the Church of Scotland known as the Disruption. The Free Church of Scotland was formed when more than 450 ministers resolved to leave the national church and constituted themselves within a General Assembly of the Church of Scotland Free. Its principal purpose was the disestablishment of the church and the right to be free of interference by civil authorities in relation to four touchstone issues: all matters of doctrine, worship, discipline, and government. In 1847 a similar denomination, the United Presbyterian Church of Scotland, was created out of the many congregations that, throughout the previous century, had seceded over the self-same issue of patronage. So, in Scottish Presbyterianism the question of autonomy was a defining issue. Writing just a few years after the Disruption that had brought the Free Church to birth, Principal John Cunningham of St Mary's College in St Andrew's wrote, 'Never perhaps, in the history of any Church has so great a voluntary sacrifice been made for so slender a principle – but yet not too slender for the Scottish Ecclesiastical conscience to apprehend and exalt it into a question of life and death'.[33]

This description is not meant, however, to trivialise the principle of autonomy. This was the all-important issue when, after more than 50 years of separation, the Presbyterian churches in Scotland decided to begin their own 'ecumenical' movement towards national church unity. Times had changed; the modern church and

32 The heritors were landed proprietors who had a liability to contribute to the upkeep of the parish church. See W. Mair, *A Digest of Laws and Decisions Ecclesiastical and Civil* (Edinburgh: Blackwood and Sons, 1895) 421.

33 J. Cunningham, *Church History of Scotland*, Vol. ii (Edinburgh: James Thin, 1882) 535.

the modern state knew their respective places, and the primary reason (patronage) for separation was a thing of the past.

To make way for the reunion of the churches a 1921 Act of the UK Parliament was passed known as the Church of Scotland Act.[34] It confirmed that within the Church of Scotland there would be 'no limitation of the liberty, rights and powers in matters spiritual' – which accords with the *Principles* (I.1.1). This Act of Parliament and the attached Schedule, known as the Articles Declaratory of the Constitution of the Church of Scotland in Matters Spiritual, are the basis of the relationship that the Church of Scotland now has with the state. Once again, this is echoed in the *Principles* (X.1.3(3)), and it recognises the personality of the Church of Scotland as being derived from Jesus Christ and not subject to any civil authority; this is also reflected in the *Principles* (IV.1.1). Within these articles appended to the 1921 Act, Article IV is a masterpiece. It states: '[t]his Church, as part of the Universal Church wherein the Lord Jesus Christ has appointed a government in the hands of Church office-bearers, receives from Him, its Divine King and Head, and from Him alone, the right and power subject to no civil authority to legislate, and to adjudicate finally, in all matters of doctrine, worship, government, and discipline in the Church, including the right to determine all questions concerning membership and office in the Church, the constitution and membership of its Courts, and the mode of election of its office-bearers, and to define the boundaries of the spheres of labour of its ministers and other office-bearers. Recognition by civil authority [see Principle X.1.3(2) and 1.3(3)] of the separate and independent government and jurisdiction of this Church in matters spiritual, in whatever manner such recognition be expressed, does not in any way affect the character of this government and jurisdiction as derived from the Divine Head of the Church alone [see Principle IV.1.1], or give to the civil authority any right of interference [see Principle X.1.3(5)] with the proceedings or judgments of the Church within the sphere of its spiritual government and jurisdiction'. This statute stills stands in UK law. The Church of Scotland continues to be recognised as a discrete legislature within the United Kingdom, and the General Assembly of the Church of Scotland remains the supreme court when dealing with the four touchstone issues of doctrine, worship, government, and discipline. Principle I.1 expresses precisely the self-understanding of the Church of Scotland in defining itself as having institutional freedom and autonomy in respect of these defining characteristics.

The importance of the Church of Scotland Act 1921 cannot be overstated, as it opened the way, finally, in 1929 for the three Presbyterian denominations of the nineteenth century – the Church of Scotland, the Free Church of Scotland, and the United Presbyterian Church of Scotland – to be restored (with few exceptions) to one denomination.[35] Autonomy or the lack thereof was a principle over

34 See www.legislation.gov.uk/ukpga/Geo5/11-12/29.

35 The history of the Disruption is well documented in J.H.S. Burleigh, *A History of the Church of Scotland*, cited above; and the story of the reunion is best related in D.M. Murray, *Rebuilding the Kirk* (Edinburgh: Scottish Academic Press, 2000).

which Presbyterians splintered, and its restoration was the principle around which they were able to reunite.

The status of the Church of Scotland's independent jurisdiction has been challenged on a number of occasions – in 1936, in the case of *Ballantyne and Others v. Presbytery of Wigtown and Others*; in 1995, in the case of *Logan v. Presbytery of Dumbarton*; and most recently in 1997, in the case of *Helen Percy v. Board of National Mission*.[36] The arguments in each of these cases have been complex and nuanced. In particular they concern the question of who has the authority to determine the jurisdictional boundaries between church and state. The *Principles*, in the section about church governance, 'on systems of church polity' (IV.1.4), is accurate from a Presbyterian perspective in describing the limits of ecclesiastical authority as being determined by church law; but these limits, when tested to the full, may from time to time be determined by the civil authorities. Nonetheless, for the most part the independent jurisdiction of the Church of Scotland, with reference to the four touchstone issues and in relation to those who hold office within the church, remains intact. Not surprisingly, Scottish Presbyterians have worked hard to preserve this position and, no doubt, will continue to do so.

The latest issue to test the relationship between church and state in Scotland has been the introduction of legislation to permit same-sex marriage. However, before introducing the Marriage and Civil Partnership (Scotland) Act 2014,[37] the Scottish government went to great lengths to craft legislation that did not compel either the Church of Scotland (as a denomination) or its individual ministers (acting as celebrants) to conduct marriages to which they were opposed on grounds of soul and conscience.[38] If ever there was an example of the principle of Christian law on the institutional autonomy of churches (Principle X.1.3(5)) in operation, this was it.

VII The authority of scripture

The second major constitutional question is a more difficult area, where unification around a principle is harder to establish. In the context of the *Principles*, it is indisputable that '[c]hurch laws should conform to the Law of God, as revealed in Holy Scripture and by the Holy Spirit' (Principle I.3.4), but how does one establish the authenticity of what Scripture reveals and what the Holy Spirit inspires?

Presbyterians in some traditions will have closely worded confessions that determine the 'party line' that must be endorsed by each of its members, office-bearers, and ministers; the *Principles* allows for closely drafted doctrinal standards

36 See M.A. Maclean, op cit., 137ff for an overview of the cases that have tested the limitations of the legal jurisdiction of the Church of Scotland. This includes the most recent case of *Helen Percy v. Board of National Mission*, which extended over seven years and stretched the question of the Kirk's jurisdiction to its limits.

37 See www.legislation.gov.uk/asp/2014/5/pdfs/asp_20140005_en.pdf.

38 The law in this matter was crafted to apply to all religious denominations in Scotland.

to be applied (VI.3.1). Other Presbyterians, however, like the Church of Scotland, describe themselves more loosely. Article I of the Articles Declaratory of the Constitution of the Church of Scotland in Matters Spiritual identifies the Church of Scotland as being part of the Holy Catholic Church. It describes the Kirk as Trinitarian; it acknowledges the salvific work of Christ's cross and resurrection; and it gives a central place to the 'Word of God which is contained in the Scriptures of the Old and New Testaments as its supreme rule of faith and life'. These two words 'contained in' are, however, of acute importance. For most people in the Church of Scotland, this distances the church from any sense that the words of Scripture are co-terminus with the Word of God. Instead, the Word of God is regarded (as a matter of theology rather than law) as being more dynamic and more fluid than that. It is in the Word made flesh; it is *contained in* the written Word; and it is in the Word proclaimed.

This approach is consistent with the statement in Article II that describes the Westminster Confession of Faith as a 'subordinate standard'. It allows for the inclusion in Article V of 'liberty of opinion in points which do not enter into the substance of the Faith' (see Principle VI.3.6) and in the same article provides that the '[c]hurch has the inherent right, free from interference by civil authority, but under the safeguards for deliberate action and legislation provided by the Church itself, to frame or adopt its subordinate standards, to declare the sense in which it understands its Confession of Faith, to modify the forms of expression therein, or to formulate other doctrinal statements, and to define the relation thereto of its office-bearers and members, but always in agreement with the Word of God and the fundamental doctrines of the Christian Faith contained in the said Confession, of which agreement *the Church shall be sole judge*' (see Principle VI.1.2).

In this way the Church of Scotland, often regarded as the mother of Presbyterian churches, opens its membership to a wide range of views. So, the Church of Scotland could subscribe to Principle I.3.4 insofar as its application is not prescriptive of any one way of regarding or understanding the authority of the Word of God. This has been particularly important in a church that, since its reconstitution in 1929, has wrestled with a variety of contemporary issues where some believe that the message of Scripture is 'self-evident' whilst others argue that Scripture is either silent or unclear or indeed wrong. Nuclear deterrence as a political theory; sanctity of life issues; the role of women in the leadership of the church; and the place of lesbian, gay, bisexual, and transgender people are just some of the issues that have caused heated debate but have not led to schism (on any significant level) because the church has structured its legislation so as to *include people in* rather than *leave people out*. It has been a remarkable thing to note that throughout many of our most controversial discussions our ecumenical and worldwide partnerships have, with few exceptions, remained intact and undamaged.

So, autonomy of jurisdiction and liberality in the understanding of Scripture are amongst the fundamental principles of the constitution and law that mark the nature of the Church of Scotland. As these principles are sometimes disputed within our own polity, it is easy to see how they might form a barrier on the road to ecumenical convergence. However, more importantly, there may be lessons to be learnt from the way in which Presbyterian governance has evolved within the Church of Scotland. Earlier, reference was made to the way in which the post-Reformation Church of Scotland was, within itself, a contradiction in terms. On the one hand it emphasised its historic continuity as part of the holy catholic church, whilst on the other hand it vigorously castigated the pre-Reformation Church as a 'Synagogue of Satan'. Some would say, 'You can't have it both ways' – perhaps it is in the nature of Presbyterianism to defy such logic!

Far from providing a definitive understanding of Presbyterianism in general, this chapter does not even claim to provide a definitive understanding of Presbyterianism as practised in the Church of Scotland. The views expressed here are the views of the author, derived from a particular way of understanding the history of the Scottish Church. Nonetheless, this chapter highlights some of the distinctive marks that have given Presbyterianism (in general) and Scottish Presbyterianism (in particular) their underlying character. The most positive of these (so far as this writer is concerned), which lend themselves to optimism that the *Statement of Principles of Christian Law* might contribute positively to ecumenical progress, are around the things that have demonstrated the ability of Presbyterian law, order, and polity to evolve and change in response to changing circumstances.

This has never been easy. Sometimes change has meant costly sacrifice, as in the determination of those who, in past centuries, left behind the security of their living to bring an end to a flawed relationship between church and state. Sometimes change has been at the cost of repentance for past wrong, as in the movement from legalistic oversight to duty of care for the flock. Sometimes change has come about because the system has allowed a reassessment of realities and, with that, a change in belief and direction. This has been the case in relation to anti-papalism, the role of women in the church, and, more recently, the place of women and men who may be in civil partnerships or same-sex marriages in the diaconate and in the ministry of Word and sacrament.

This latter issue, which has deeply divided denominations across the world, has been accommodated in the Church of Scotland by a new piece of permissive legislation enacted by the general assembly: the Ministers and Deacons in Civil Partnerships and Same Sex Marriages Act (2015).[39] This Act is designed to provide space for both the *traditional* wing of the church and those who belong to what might be called the *progressive* wing of the church. On the one hand, this Act affirms '[t]he historic and current doctrine and practice of the Church in relation to human sexuality (including marriage) and their application to the ministers and deacons of the Church' (which broadly echoes Principle VI.1.1 regarding how doctrines themselves may generate norms of conduct), whilst on the other

39 See www.churchofscotland.org.uk/__data/assets/pdf_file/0004/27940/2015_Act_1.pdf.

hand the act provides that the 'historic and current doctrine and practice of the Church in relation to human sexuality [and] their application to the ministers and deacons of the Church . . . are points on which there is liberty of opinion in accordance with Article Declaratory V' (echoing Principle VI.3.6). It is interesting to note that the Ministers and Deacons in Civil Partnerships and Same Sex Marriages Act (2015), in Section 7, says, 'The provisions of this Act give effect to the strongly held religious convictions of significant numbers of the followers of the Church of Scotland'; in so doing it is citing the non-conflict principle as defined in the UK Equality Act 2010.[40] It will be interesting to see whether this view holds up in law if it is ever challenged or whether the provisions of Principle X.1.3(2) will be stretched to the breaking point.

This piece of legislation, approved under the procedure contained in the Barrier Act,[41] was passed into law, most probably, because the majority of those responsible for the ordering of the Church of Scotland were more interested in recognising and honouring the diversity of views within the church rather than exhausting everyone in a contest that no one could win. Some argue that the church is acting here like a vegetarian restaurant that offers steak on the menu. Others, however, are comfortable that the Kirk's polity has allowed it once again to hold in dynamic tension people who subscribe to very different interpretations of Scripture.

Conclusion

The *Statement of Principles of Christian Law* has usefully bottomed out some of the areas of church practice and procedure that will only ever be contained in one place if we learn to live with and accommodate our differences. Presbyterians may be precious about their courts, but it is possible to conceive of ways in which they could accommodate others forms of leadership. Presbyterians may well think that the eldership is a key way to develop the ministry of the whole people of God, but it is not hard to think of how the strength of a Kirk session could be combined with other forms of corporate governance. And the idea of a church that embraces the widest possible spectrum of belief is, for many, a key requirement in a context in which spiritual experience is more relevant to the lives of ordinary people than the survival of religious institutions.

The production of the *Statement of Principles of Christian Law* was only possible because the process demanded working together, thinking together, and forming friendships across cultural and religious differences. So, perhaps the process, as much as the *Principles* itself, is the tool that should be copied if progress

40 See www.legislation.gov.uk/ukpga/2010/15/pdfs/ukpga_20100015_en.pdf, p172.

41 The Barrier Act (see www.churchofscotland.org.uk/about_us/church_law/barrier_act) was passed into the law of the church in 1697. It provides for the widest possible consultation before innovative statutes can become the law of the church. The Ministers and Deacons in Civil Partnerships and Same Sex Marriages Act (2015) was therefore a long time in the making and had to be approved by two general assemblies and by the majority of presbyteries.

is to be made on those areas of ecumenical discourse that currently appear to be insurmountable. Perhaps, too, there is something to be learnt from the way in which Scottish Presbyterian practice and polity have evolved from narrow, dogmatic and sectarian beginnings to embrace such a wide range of belief and practice. By acknowledging our past mistakes and making room for difference the churches may begin to square some of the complicated circles of ecumenical dialogue.

10 Baptist church polity

Paul Goodliff

The dominant church polity for Baptists is congregationalism, and it is from this that flows much of the particular way that Baptists order their life. It is often supposed that the distinctive Baptist practice is believer's baptism (sometimes misnamed 'adult' baptism, but there are no particular reasons why a believing older child or teenager with a real and personal faith should not be baptised). However, this a result of the prior commitment to a community comprised of those who have a real trust and faith in Christ and who together form a 'gathered' or 'believer's' church that is Trinitarian and belongs to the one, holy, catholic, and apostolic church. What follows explores this in light of the *Statement of Principles of Christian Law*.

Whilst there is a 'genetic' strain in Baptist life that finds its origins in the Radical Reformation and the Anabaptists, the primary source for Baptist life in Britain – and the many places to which this form of Baptist life was exported through the long period of missionary endeavour associated with the British empire – is the Puritan emphasis within the Church of England in its immediate post-Elizabethan period. Early Baptists were desirous of a more thoroughgoing Protestant and Reformed Church. Concluding that such progress as they demanded within the Church of England was unlikely, they separated themselves and formed the kinds of congregations that might approximate more closely to their New Testament ideals from the early seventeenth century onwards. Like their Puritan cousins, most owed more to Geneva than to Wittenberg, and they certainly did not idealise Munster and its political radicalism, but they carried with them into their new congregational polity a conviction that the primary source of their beliefs was the Bible. As we shall see, as Baptists developed their theology and practices, they found a place for reason and tradition as well but, like their 'low church' Anglican brethren, placed Scripture above those other two members of Hooker's triad of revelation, reason, and history. Baptists, therefore, have a place among the 'Separatists', or the 'Dissenters', of the period of their earliest origins.[1] Today in Britain they could be described as most strongly associated with the polity and

1 Also identified with the 'Non-conformists' of the later seventeenth century and the 'Free Church' tradition of the nineteenth and twentieth centuries.

beliefs of evangelicalism, although by no means universally so; there remains a strongly liberal element within Baptists in England and Wales, although this is not true of Scotland and Northern Ireland. The same is true of the United States, for instance, where 'Southern Baptist' is a dominant tradition within the southern states at least; and in Canada, Australia, and New Zealand, Baptists would be similarly of a more conservative kind of Christian, albeit not universally so. Baptists are now present in most nations and are often influenced by the dominant Christian tradition within the society in which they practise their Baptist life. So, Hungarian Baptists owe much to their Reformed origins and Georgian Baptists have sought to self-identify in some regards as a form of Orthodox Christianity. Elsewhere, especially in places where Baptists have suffered more recent oppression from a dominant historic church, either Orthodox or Roman Catholic, Baptists have self-identified over against that tradition, including its juridical tradition.[2]

I Baptist polity

These historical and theological trajectories ensure that whilst there are a variety of Baptist approaches to church law, order, and polity, it is nevertheless possible to identify some common themes. Scripture (and therefore revelation) would be the primary source of church polity, and a widespread claim would be that Baptists are a 'biblical' family of churches. This claim is not limited to Baptists, of course, but amongst those other ecclesial traditions that make similar claims (Pentecostals, for instance) there is often some 'Baptist DNA' in their origins (early Pentecostals were often disaffected, or excluded, Baptists, for instance), making this claim to scriptural primacy one of the most significant drivers of 'baptist' polity.[3] This is not intended as a form of 'bibliolatry', however, where the Bible assumes a divine status. For instance, the Declaration of Principle for the Baptist Union of Great Britain (the nearest equivalent to a creed or statement of faith) says that the basis of this union is '[t]hat our Lord and Saviour Jesus Christ, God manifest in the flesh, is the sole authority in all matters pertaining to faith and practice, as revealed in the Holy Scriptures'. It is evident that the writers of this late nineteenth-century statement were aware of the charges that Baptists believed in the Bible rather than in Christ and were clear that whilst Scripture may reveal Christ, it remains the Lord Jesus Christ who is the authority. So, the source for the polity of the church is Christ revealed in Scripture. The declaration continues: 'and that each Church has liberty, under the guidance of the Holy Spirit, to interpret and administer

2 cf. J.H.Y. Briggs, ed., *A Dictionary of European Baptist Life and Thought, Vol. 33 Studies in Baptist History and Thought* (Milton Keynes: Paternoster, 2009). For instance, the entry on 'Georgia, Baptist history in', 219–221.

3 The use of 'baptist', without the capitalisation, is a feature of the influential Baptist theologian of the late twentieth century, James McClendon: *cf.* J. McClendon, *Systematic Theology, Vol. 1. Ethics* (Nashville, TN: Abingdon Press, 1986). I use it here to indicate the wider family of baptistic churches, rather than the specific denominations that describe themselves as 'Baptist'.

His Laws'. Here we unavoidably begin to introduce hermeneutical questions and hermeneutics; that is, the interpretation of (usually) ancient texts. Whilst Scripture may have the priority in determining polity and theology, it is applied with the assistance of reason and the traditions of the church.[4]

An example of this is the way in which governance of the church is worked out. From Scripture, early Baptists saw how the whole Jerusalem Church gathered to appoint deacons (Acts 6:16) and sought to apply this to their own practice. Deacons were (mainly) men who were appointed by the whole church and set apart for that office. The distribution of alms was an early task delegated to them, reflecting the Lucan account (Acts 6:1–6). Over the centuries, Baptist deacons evolved into those men and women charged with the oversight of the church in all matters not retained by a church meeting (the whole gathered congregation, which remains the ultimate decision-making body). 'Reason' applied to the biblical origins, together with the demands of secular charity law and contemporary organisational good practice (themselves a form of 'tradition'), has seen the task of a Baptist 'diaconate' (the group of deacons acting together) transformed from one of alms distribution to one of modern-day charity trustees.[5] This brings a tension between the ecclesial aspiration for the final authority in the church being the will, or mind, of Christ, discerned by the whole congregation in a church meeting, and the demands of secular charity law, where responsibility lies with the trustees – and, with legal responsibility, a desire for proper oversight and management. Increasingly, Baptists then take on a more 'Presbyterian' form of governance, with the trustees effectively being the final authority. This is especially so where contemporary social practices mean that gathering the whole congregation in a church meeting (given that it is often comprised of many members with little or no commitment personally to Baptist principles in this post-denominational age) – or even that part that would be deemed quorate – proves impossible. A rational response is to delegate to the diaconate/trustees much greater powers of governance than earlier Baptist polity would accept and to integrate a contemporary 'tradition' of proper charity governance with a scriptural mandate that becomes almost devoid of its original intention. To say that Baptists seek to be 'simply biblical' in the sources of their polity or church law would be disingenuous, for Baptist unions will have their own constitutions, bylaws, and memoranda of understanding, as will associations and churches.

To further complicate matters, Baptists, with their strong commitment to congregational independence, have always balanced that with a commitment to interdependence through voluntary associating, which is of the *bene* of the church, if not its *bene esse* (contra a *prima facie* interpretation of Principle IV.5.5 of the *Statement of Principles of Christian Law*: '[a]ll ecclesial units at each level

4 cf. H. Dare and S. Woodman, *The 'Plainly Revealed' Word of God? Baptist Hermeneutics in Theory and Practice* (Macon, GA: Mercer University Press, 2011).

5 Baptist Union Corporation: *Help, I am a Charity Trustee*, accessed at www.baptist.org.uk/Articles/368670/BUC_Guideline_Leaflet.aspx.

are interdependent'). Historically, in England and Wales, this was expressed through a commitment to the association to which, geographically, the church belonged. As churches planted other Baptist congregations, relations continued until, at quite an early stage, in the 1650s, formal associations emerged, such as the Abingdon Association led by Benjamin Cox and John Pendarves (the latter the first recorded minister of Abingdon Baptist Church) or the London Baptist Association, to which they wrote in 1653 'agreeing with the same church in principles and constitutions'.[6] Other early associations emerged in the Midlands, South Wales, and the West of England. As Baptist churches grew in number, so a pattern of largely county associations developed by the twentieth century. This pattern was rationalised in the late 1990s to 13 'regional' associations. Churches delegate to these associations responsibility for an early stage in the recognition of a call to ordained ministry and the allocation of mission grants to churches, amongst other things. So, whilst churches can recognise whomsoever they wish as their pastor or minister, for that person to be accredited by the wider union of churches, there is a regional stage of discernment. Churches, similarly, raise their own financial resources, but should they seek wider support in the form of a national grant towards the costs of ministry, the responsibility for agreeing to this is shared. The congregational polity is not removed, but for some aspects of life, together with other Baptist churches, the final authority becomes an association of churches.[7] In line with Principle IV.4, Baptist associations in England have councils (4.3), with delegated powers from the churches (4.4), and are composed of those elected to serve them from their member churches (4.5).

This is true also for the national body, the Baptist Union of Great Britain (hereafter BUGB, now popularly called 'Baptists Together'), which through its council and committees – populated largely by delegates appointed by the associations – accredits ministers, distributes financial resources, and represents churches ecumenically. Its annual assembly is now largely an inspirational rather than deliberative body and comprises delegates from churches, colleges, associations, and accredited ministers, but it would still be the body that approved major changes in governance or polity (even though, as a registered civil charity, Baptists Together has its own trustee board).[8] Elsewhere, Baptists act collabora-

6 B.R. White, *The English Baptists of the Seventeenth Century* (Didcot: The Baptist Historical Society, 1996) 83–84.

7 For instance in the granting of funds to support the costs of ministry or mission projects or the commending for training of those considering accredited ministry; see BUGB: *Called to Pastoral Ministry*, accessed at www.baptist.org.uk/Articles/368854/Called_to_Pastoral.aspx. For home mission grants, accessed through associations, see for instance http://centralba.org.uk/grants/.

8 'The Baptist Union has a Trustee board made up of twelve members elected by the Council. The role of the trustees is to provide strategic direction for our Union, ensure appropriate policies are in place and operated effectively, to oversee the Union's structure and to ensure compliance with statutory and regulatory requirements': www.baptist.org.uk/Groups/220798/Trustee_Board.aspx. For the Baptist union's constitution, see www.baptist.org.uk/Articles/366062/BUGB_Constitution.aspx; and see Part 1.5.

tively in more formal ways, with the Nigerian Baptist Convention, for instance, ordaining all its new ministers at an annual meeting of its equivalent assembly;[9] this is clearly reflected in the *Statement* (Principle IV.3.1).[10]

Whilst an association or union cannot change the polity of the member churches,[11] those aspects of corporate life – routinely, recognition of ministers and the raising and distribution of a 'common purse' – that have become mainly the responsibility of the ecclesial bodies beyond the local church, are generally accepted without demur by the churches, giving the governance a 'mixed' polity rather than pure congregationalism. Other matters, such as ethical questions about the use of nuclear weapons or the degree to which Baptists should embrace ecumenical relationships, are also debated by the wider Baptist groups but are less likely to be unquestionably adopted by the churches. Currently, this would be seen in the way in which churches may or may not become involved in local ecumenical instruments, even though the BUGB is fully committed to ecumenical life, or the acceptance – enthusiastically, mutedly, or not at all – of women's ordained ministry by local churches, even though the union has strongly advocated women's ministry at every level. The tensions between a simple congregational polity and the advantages of collaborative work between churches reflect the way in which Scripture, reason, and tradition are interwoven. Even in matters where *some* might argue that Scripture is uncompromisingly clear – the matter of the ethical status of same-sex relationships expressed in sexual relationships, for instance – Scripture, whilst important, might not have the final word without a careful hermeneutic applied to it. Baptist churches that subscribe to the principle of Christ's 'laws' being revealed in Scripture fiercely maintain their right to 'interpret' them at the congregational level, and some do so, in this matter, by allowing same-sex marriages to be solemnised in their buildings, their minister presiding. The majority of churches would take a different stance, and one suspects that the factors of reason and tradition play here a much larger role than Baptists might proclaim through their conciliar statements.[12]

As to Principle IV.5, 'The local church', Baptists reflect the following: 5.1 – regional associations are constituted by congregations 'at the most localised level of church life'; 5.2 – in the form of a congregation; 5.3 – the 'local church . . . meeting . . . has such authority and functions inherent to it' (but not 'conferred' on it by any 'wider ecclesial entity'); 5.4 – the assembly of a local church is composed of those members of the faithful elected to it (i.e. all church members); and 5.5 – Baptist polity encourages 'interdependence' rather than the exercise of

9 See www.nigerianbaptist.org/about-us/policies-and-practices/ [accessed 3 September 2018].

10 SPCL IV.3.1: '[a]n ecclesial tradition may have a national organisation'.

11 Decisions of the assembly of the Baptist union, or its council, offer 'advice, encouragement or exhortation to member bodies of the Union' (Constitution 6.2).

12 Unless a church changed its rules to specify that it would re-register for the solemnisation of equal marriage, there is unlikely to be any reference to this in its rules. I am not aware of any church that has re-registered for equal marriage changing its constitution to enable it to do so; those would be matters for church meeting to approve.

external or hierarchical authority. Local Baptist churches have an interdependent relationship with associations (IV.4) and the national union (IV.3), without that being one of imposition of policy or practice.

As we shall see, many 'principles of law, order, or polity' subscribed to by Baptists remain rooted in and adopted or implemented at the local congregational level, which, for Baptists, is the fundamental unit of the church universal. The role of the equivalent of the diocese or the presbytery or the synod in other forms of ecclesial polity is much more limited for Baptists but by no means absent. The Baptist Union of Victoria, Australia, notes: '[t]he numbers coming together for Gatherings has increased . . . reports from other states reflect a similar trend'.[13] Baptists are Congregationalists who have traded absolute independence or autonomy for the mutual benefits of associating together, as the strapline of the association – which I led as its regional minister team leader in the early years of the twenty-first century – 'Better Together', stated; the strapline today states: '[w]alking together in ministry and mission'.[14] This is both a pragmatic application of reason and a reflection of the traditions of the Baptists from earliest times and, finding no contradiction in Scripture, is the basis for the way in which church polity is distributed between congregations and the larger bodies to which they belong.

II The *Statement of Principles of Christian Law*: empirical process

To be comprehensive, discussing each principle of the *Statement of Principles of Christian Law* (2016) would be both tedious and prolix. So, I adopt the approach that those principles that widely and easily 'reflect Baptist polity' will be briefly explored as unproblematic. I shall take at least one from each section of the *Statement*.[15] Greater attention can then be paid to those principles that are more problematic or that require greater hermeneutical exploration before they can be said to more fully reflect 'Baptist polity'. In the drafting of the principles, some required greater attention, in the work of the ecumenical panel, to accommodate to Baptist polity and doctrine, and these include many of those more problematic principles.

1 Churches and systems of law, order, and polity

Those elements of the systems of law and polity agreed in Section I that fully reflect Baptist polity include the following: '[a] church has a distinct membership . . .

13 See www.buv.com.au/about-us/buv-churches [accessed 3 September 2018]. A gathering is a regional council.

14 See http://centralba.org.uk.

15 M. Hill and N. Doe, 'Principles of Christian Law', 19 *Ecclesiastical Law Journal* (2017) 138–155.

which may be . . . organised in . . . congregations' (Principle I.1.3); '[a] church has amongst its objects the advancement of the mission of Christ which includes proclaiming the Gospel . . . and serving the wider community' (Principle I.1.5); all three principles on the forms of ecclesial regulation (Principles I.2.1–3); '[c]hurch laws should conform to the law of God, as revealed in Holy Scripture and by the Holy Spirit' (Principle I.1.4), which is almost a paraphrase of the first principle in the Baptist Union Declaration of Principle quoted earlier; and '[l]aws may be binding or exhortatory' (Principle I.4.3). This last principle reflects, for instance, BUGB guidance on same-sex relationships; a binding aspect is the prohibition in its ministerial recognition rules against any same-sex act as conduct unbecoming of a minister,[16] whilst the BUGB council recently urged churches to refrain from registering their premises for same-sex marriage, though stopping short of prohibiting this (which would have contradicted the foundational principle of congregational competence and autonomy). This is a careful balance between what can be regulated and what can only be encouraged. Similarly, and in keeping with the same area of regulation, after the enactment by Parliament of the Civil Partnership Act 2004, the BUGB council approved guidance for ministers that effectively prohibited them from participating in any formal blessing of such a union, although it did not prohibit attendance for personal or family reasons. This reflected guidance extant in its ministerial recognition rules that had sought, 20 years previously, to define the ministerial status of those ministers who were gay or lesbian. This guidance firmly welcomed those who were same-sex attracted (homosexuality *per se* was not a bar to ministry) but described any same-sex genital practice as conduct unbecoming – as indeed it prohibited any heterosexual genital practice for those who were not married as husband and wife – and sought to prohibit any advocacy of the view that same-sex relationships might be equivalent to marriage. In other words, it sought to avoid homophobia, distinguishing between orientation and sexual practice, whilst still upholding the traditional Christian teaching that prohibited homosexual practice. In the absence of any recent deliberation by the council upon the ethical character of homosexual sexual practice, the ministerial recognition committee extended that extant guidance to the new context. However, as opportunity arose to revise the guidance, not least in the light of the introduction of same-sex, or 'equal', marriage under the civil Marriage (Same Sex Couples) Act 2013, the BUGB council approved a revision of its rules regarding the presidency of a minister at a ceremony of blessing or entering of such relationships. Instead of a general presumption that ministers may not do so, it prescribed those circumstances in which a minister may preside over such a blessing or marriage ceremony without fear of any disciplinary sanctions – namely, where the local church required their minister to do so and where the minister's own conscience allowed it. This reflected a change in the balance between the local congregation's autonomy and the wider union's

16 Appendix 4.3. Ministerial Recognition Rules, Oct 2016, issued by The Baptist Union Council: www.baptist.org.uk/Articles/482804/MRC_Rules_updated.aspx.

regulations for its ministers, privileging the local church in accordance with Baptist foundational ecclesial doctrine. Rather than imposing any policy made by the wider union, even where this might have a wide degree of agreement, the competence of the local congregation to 'interpret His Laws' was upheld. This also provides a recent example of how later law may abrogate earlier law (Principle I.4.5).

2 *The faithful*

Section II of the *Statement*, on the faithful, is largely consistent with Baptist polity. Baptists place a special emphasis upon the principle that 'all the faithful should be equal in dignity' (Principle II.1.2). For instance, New Zealand Baptists hold that 'Baptists do not have a hierarchy of position within their churches or denomination. We believe all members are equal';[17] and they enshrine this in their widespread insistence upon there being no ontological distinction between laity and clergy, the difference being more one of being set aside for a particular ministry or function within the church.[18] There are exceptions, however. For example, the National Baptist Convention of the USA – a black majority Baptist denomination – holds to some restrictions on the degree to which an un-ordained person can minister: '[a]n un-ordained pastor cannot carry out the responsibilities of the Pastor'.[19] There are no sacramental actions reserved for the clergy, nor any action that only a minister may perform. That Baptists will celebrate a call to ordained pastoral ministry in a way that they might not necessarily celebrate a call to being a nurse, school teacher, or engineer might seem to undermine the principle of equality, and it must be noted that there is a form of vernacular clericalism in Baptist churches, just as there is in most traditions. This contradicts Principle II.1.2 in its implementation, rather than being a principled negation of it. In practice, at the local congregational level, whilst all have equal dignity in discernment and authority exercised through age and experience, some might appear 'more equal than others'. The wise intervention of an aged member who has held office as a deacon and church secretary over many years might seem to count for more than the naive observation of a young Christian, full of the enthusiasm of the newly converted and baptised; but in principle, both carry an equal voice and weight. Here we need to admit that principles might be evident as much in the breach in observance.

17 See www.baptist.org.nz/general/Being-a-Baptist/ [accessed 3 September 2018].

18 cf. R. Hayden, *Baptist Union Documents* (Didcot: Baptist Historical Society, 1980) 85. In its report on ordination, the writers noted that in 1923 the Annual Assembly of the Baptist Union affirmed the doctrine of the priesthood of all believers and '[b]y the ministry we mean an office within the Church of Christ (not a sacerdotal order) conferred through the call of the Holy Spirit and attested by a particular Baptist Church' and '[b]y Ordination we mean the act of the Church by which it delegates to a person ministerial functions which no man can properly take upon himself'.

19 See www.nationalbaptist.com/resources/church-faqs/pastor-clergy-faqs.html [accessed 3 September 2018].

For Baptists, membership of the church is a key principle, and Baptists aspire to a 'believer's church', where membership is tested through confession of faith and demonstrated through baptism. It is sometimes said that for Baptists, believer's baptism functions similarly to the embracing of the Christian life expressed through confirmation in paedo-baptist polities – it is a rite of passage and a personal commitment to what has hitherto been adopted by others on behalf of the individual, either by godparents or others. It distinguishes the merely nominal from the personally committed. So, seeking membership of the church through the practices of the local congregation – applying for membership granted by a church meeting – is the customary way in which a person becomes a member of a Baptist church (as reflected in Principle II.2.1) and is based upon 'baptism . . . or other mature demonstration of faith' (as echoed in Principle II.2.3). The removal of a name from the register of those who are members of a local church is mostly routine, when the person transfers to another church because they have moved address or have died, for instance, but there will be proper processes of enquiry and discernment when the removal of a name is for reasons of profound immorality, loss of faith, or other serious concern (Principle II.2.5).

Again, the function of the laity (and this is not to distinguish them from 'the clergy') to 'promote the mission of the church, and to bear witness to the Christian faith through their lives in the world' (Principle II.3.2) is almost the same as the third section of the (admittedly) short BUGB Declaration of Principle; namely, '[t]hat it is the duty of every disciple to bear personal witness to the Gospel of Jesus Christ, and to take part in the evangelisation of the world'. This is a fine aspiration but one probably as notable in its breach as in its observance, although every disciple will bear witness to Christ in some form or other – sometimes to the detriment of the reputation of the Gospel. The principle of Christian law that '[l]ay persons are encouraged to practise daily devotions, private prayer, Bible reading and self-discipline' (Principle II.3.5) is similarly important for the kind of piety that is associated with Baptist practice, but I doubt it is regularly observed. It remains important, however, insofar as Baptists do not really accept the existence of a 'professional elite', like monks, nuns, or celibate priests in a Roman Catholic context. Instead, they aspire to every member being a participant in a Baptist equivalent, a Baptist church as a kind of secular monastic community of the fully committed, even if the emphasis must be upon aspiration, rather than admitting any success in such an endeavour.

Public ministry by laypersons in Baptist polity is a matter of custom, rather than something that is found in formal written rules. Still, in some congregations, participation in public worship by those who are not accredited ministers is rare; the minister is expected to lead most of the service, but this is an increasingly outdated model. However, in most British settings, laypeople, suitably recognised by the church meeting, will lead public prayers, read Scripture, preach, and preside at the Eucharist on occasion. Indeed, in order to affirm the equality of ministers and laity, in some Baptist churches where the minister will normally preside at the Eucharist, at least once a year they will customarily be replaced by a recognised layperson in order to declare that this is not a clericalized sacramental or priestly act.

3 *Ordained ministry, governance, and discipline*

Given the very different theologies about ministry held by the various traditions, it is surprising how little Baptists would find difficult in the third section of the *Statement* on ordained ministry. The principles of ordination (III.1.), ecclesiastical office (III.2), and the functions of ordained ministers (III.3) are all widely accepted by many Baptists. We shall return later to questions of sacramental language, and there will be many Baptists in the United States who would find language of ordination problematic – preferring the language of 'induction into an office' of pastor than 'ordination to a ministry' – but this is not so in Britain. It has not always been the case, and after an early 'high' view of ordination and being set apart for pastoral ministry until the eighteenth century, there was a period in the later nineteenth century and early to mid-twentieth century when ordination was rare. This can be dated to the rejection of ordination by the influential Charles Haddon Spurgeon in 1854, and by 1880 references to ordination had become infrequent. The 1957 report, *The Meaning and Practice of Ordination among Baptists*, reflected a desire to reinstate the practice that had long fallen by the wayside. It explains that having made their protest against the excesses of the Oxford Movement – the 'high church' initiative within the Church of England – Baptists, along with other Free Churchmen, are able today to see these questions of church order from a new perspective. There is also a moving away from the sometimes excessive individualism of the nineteenth century.[20] Something of this 'Spurgeonic' mood can be detected still in more conservative Baptist traditions, but it is now almost universal in Britain that at the time when ministry is first exercised, following appropriate formation and training and the acceptance of a call to be the minister in a particular Baptist church, a service of ordination will be held.[21] Indeed, in contradiction to the nineteenth-century rejection of a sacramental view of ordination, research into Baptist ministers' understanding of ordination and ministry reveals a widespread re-emergence of a sacramental view.[22]

Even in the principles in the *Statement* concerning the exercise of oversight there is little that is problematic from the perspective of Baptist polity. That oversight is an essential of ecclesial order (Principle III.4.1) is incontrovertible,

20 *The Meaning and Practice of Ordination among Baptists* (London: Baptist Union of Great Britain and Ireland, 1957) Introduction.

21 cf. BUGB, *Gathering for Worship* (Norwich: Canterbury Press, 2005) 121–131. The report that triggered the reintroduction of ordination was Baptist Union of Great Britain and Ireland, *The Meaning and Practice of Ordination*, 1957: cf. note 17 above.

22 P.W. Goodliff, *Ministry, Sacrament and Representation. Ministry and Ordination in Contemporary Baptist Theology and the Rise of Sacramentalism* (Oxford: Regents Park College Centre for Baptist History and Heritage, 2010).

although Baptists would disengage it from being essentially a clerical function (more on that later), and there would be no 'international' oversight exercised. It remains true, however, that there may be international oversight for some traditions, but for Baptists this is absent. There is a network of Baptist unions and conventions – the Baptist World Alliance – and it has a general secretary, but the general secretary carries no responsibility for oversight of any of its member bodies. Nevertheless, the existence of the Baptist World Alliance reflects the principle of Christian law that '[a]n ecclesial tradition may have an international organisation' (Principle IV.2.1). The alliance has a constitution that respects the autonomy of member churches commensurate with Baptist polity.[23]

Church governance at national, regional, and local levels has already been discussed previously, and the principles outlined in Section IV of the *Statement* are largely consistent with Baptist polity, provided the priority of the local church is always borne in mind. For Baptists, '[a] church organised locally' is unavoidably a 'congregation' to use what are presented as permissive categories in Principle IV.5.2 in ways that are not true for an episcopal form of polity. The assembly of the local church is *de facto* the local congregation, its members meeting in council at a church meeting – and this will be comprised of 'those members of the faithful who are . . . appointed to it' – and the meeting is comprised of all the members of the congregation. As a result, Principle IV.5.2 requires a nuanced reading for Baptist polity.

The principles on church discipline, in Section V of the *Statement*, generally reflect Baptist polity, although there will be some particular expressions of these principles. Matters of discipline for church members are exclusively for the local congregation, and the body that might exercise discipline – for instance in cases of gross immorality, such as adultery – will be the church meeting (although the diaconate or trustee body might do so in some cases where expulsion from membership is not anticipated or required). However, those who are accredited for ministry by the Baptist Union of Great Britain are subject to the ministerial recognition rules, under which a national tribunal (the ministerial recognition committee) exercises that function. A similar function is exercised by the national credentials committee of the Canadian Baptists of Western Canada.[24] There is a form of tiering in terms of original and appellate jurisdiction (as reflected in Principle V.3.4) insofar as, in theory, an appeal might be made to the BUGB council or its trustee body if there was a case of a gross miscarriage of justice. Where an appeal is made against decisions about the employment of a regional minister, it will be the national ministerial recognition committee that might hear the case. Every effort is made to ensure due process (see Principle V.4), and the ministerial recognition rules specify offences where sanctions may be applied. However, in general, at the level of the local congregation, and in cases of misconduct or

23 In its constitution there is no mention of authority over member churches: www.bwanet.org/images/pdf/AboutUs/BWA_Constitution_and_Bylaws_2018_Final.pdf.

24 CWBC Ministerial Protocol Manual. https://cbwc.ca/wp-content/uploads/2017/09/MPM-2017.pdf [accessed 3 September 2018].

immorality by lay members of a congregation, the only source applied would be Scripture. Matters of criminality would be referred to the secular courts, and it would only be in relation to those offences that society no longer deems criminal, but that the church understands to be incompatible with a holy lifestyle (such as adultery or fornication), that ecclesial sanctions such as rebuke, exclusion from participation in the Lord's Supper (the ban), or removal from membership (a form of excommunication) would be applied.

4 Doctrine, worship, and ritual

In the first century of Baptist life – that is, the seventeenth century – Baptists described their beliefs in confessions of faith typical of the period, equating to the (Anglican) Thirty-Nine Articles (1571) and (Presbyterian) Westminster Confession (1647). The London Confession of 1644 articulated the beliefs of seven London Particular Baptist churches and dealt with much the same material. Whilst there was no legal power to enforce the adoption of these confessions, they reflected the widely held convictions of Baptists. Some Baptists continue with detailed statements of faith; the Doctrinal Basis of the Baptist Union of Victoria of 1888 contained nine brief statements supplemented by a set of 'Principles and Ideals' but recognises that '[i]n adopting the Congregational Principle of Church government, with no formal creed, with no external authority, and no defined ecclesiastical polity, and each member having equal rights and responsibilities the Baptist Church is largely dependent on the reality and vigour of the spiritual life of its members'.[25] Russian Baptists adopted a long confession written for the group, centred on Ivan S. Prokhanov, in the mid-twentieth century, and this long document, *Religious Doctrine of the Evangelical Christians*, is as expansive as any continental confession, covering all aspects of faith. Others, such as the Baptist Union of Great Britain and Ireland (as it was then), from 1911 adopted the Declaration of Principle with just three brief statements – one on the authority of Christ and the liberty of the church to 'interpret and administer His Laws', the second on baptism, and the third on the duty to evangelise. It hardly carries the same theological weight as a statement of faith or confession. However, the trust deeds of many British Baptist churches offer a summary of their faith that is often expressed as 'that faith commonly called evangelical'. This would embrace, for example, the historic creeds, Reformation doctrines of salvation, and Protestant understandings of the sacraments.[26]

The principle in Section VII of the *Statement*, concerning the proclamation of the faith (Principle VI.2), would be generally consistent with Baptist polity; but whether all who are ordained would see preaching as inherent to their ministry (Principle VI.2.3) is questionable. British Baptists ordain youth specialists, and

25 W.L. Lumpkin, *Baptist Confessions of Faith* (Valley Forge: Judson Press, revised ed., 1969) 417–420, at 417.

26 cf. P.W. Goodliff, 'Baptist Church Polity and Practice', 168 *Law and Justice. The Christian Law Review* (2012) 5–21.

they would not necessarily be expected to preach, but this is the exception, and the norm is that Baptist ministers are undoubtedly 'preachers'.

Baptists do not often discipline on doctrinal matters (Principle VI.3). However, BUGB would exercise discipline over its ministers for one area of doctrine – baptism. Ministers baptising infants, except under the circumstances of ecumenical chaplaincies, would be subject to discipline, with the most serious sanction being the removal of their accreditation. All accredited ministers are expected to subscribe to the Declaration of Principle, as are member churches, and refusal to do so would result in removal (as under Principle VI.3.1). There has been only one disciplining of a church by BUGB for its beliefs and practices in the past 50 years, and that was the removal of a church that had abandoned all semblance of congregational government and was acting in authoritarian ways that appeared cult-like.[27]

As in so many other ways, the congregational government of Baptist churches lends itself to variety in worship. Baptist service books have been published since the 1960s,[28] their publication often proposed by the BUGB council;[29] and this is reflected in Principle VI.4.3. However, they have never been formally 'authorized' for use, nor do they carry any expectation that they are a requirement for worship, and many churches would have a limited awareness of their existence; Principle VI.4.3, therefore, requires a nuanced reading. A similar nuanced interpretation of Principle VI.5.2 is required for the entirety of it to be interpreted as consistent with Baptist polity. It states: '[o]rdained ministers are particularly responsible for the conduct of public worship' – this would find wide agreement among Baptists – but that ministers must do so 'in accordance with the authorized forms of service' would be problematic. There are no denominational 'authorized forms of service', as this is a matter for congregational discernment. Nevertheless, insofar as ministers conduct worship in ways their church meeting has tacitly authorised, the principle does reflect Baptist polity. However, if this were understood in the ways that the Church of England synod authorises orders of service and requires its clergy to use them, this would be foreign to Baptist polity.

Considerable time was taken in the formulation of the principles on the rites of the church to enable them as fully as possible to reflect Baptist polity. So,

27 cf. I.M. Randall, *The English Baptists of the 20th Century* (Didcot: Baptist Historical Society, 2005) 429–430.

28 E.A. Payne. and S.F. Winward, *Orders and Prayers for Church Worship: A Manual for Ministers* (London: Baptist Union of Great Britain, 1960); A. Gilmour, E. Smalley, and M. Walker, *Praise God: A Collection of Resource Material for Christian Worship* (London: Baptist Union of Great Britain, 1980); *Patterns and Prayers for Christian Worship: A Guidebook for Worship Leaders* (Oxford: Oxford University Press, 1991); and the current service book, C.J. Ellis and M. Blyth, eds., *Gathering for Worship. Patterns and Prayers for the Community of Disciples* (Norwich: Canterbury Press, 2005).

29 *Patterns and Prayers for Christian Worship* was commissioned by the General Purposes and Finance Committee in 1988.

there is little to disagree with in the principles as they stand. However, there is one that is controversial and remains a difficulty in many ecumenical discussions, and that is Principle VII.1.10 – Baptism cannot be repeated. Now, many Baptist churches will offer baptism by full immersion to those who have undergone a rite of infant baptism in a tradition that is paedo-baptistic. For those traditions, such as the Church of England, this is a matter of deep concern.[30] Any limitation on the liberty of Baptist churches to baptise believers, regardless of any previous rite of initiation, proved to be too far a compromise for the BUGB council to do anything other than 'receive' the report. For some Baptists infant baptism is no baptism at all, and therefore they would agree that baptism is unrepeatable – their baptism is the first to be enacted. To their paedo-baptist fellow Christians it looks precisely like a repeated baptism (and so, again, no baptism at all). Some progress was made at an ecumenical conversational level in this regard, as reported in *Pushing at the Boundaries of Unity*, but this was never implemented at the level of the local church, nor warmly accepted by the council, and therefore the practice remains seemingly in contradiction of Principle VII.1.10. Note that a believer's baptism cannot be repeated, and so, under some interpretations of the validity of an infant baptism, Principle VII.1.10 remains valid.

Likewise, the principles on the Eucharist are largely uncontroversial, although Baptists would tend not to distinguish between the Eucharist and receiving Holy Communion (Principles VII.3.4–5). The whole service is denominated by Holy Communion (or the Lord's Supper). It is worth noting that a formal practice called 'confession' (Principle VII.5) is unknown in Baptist churches, although informal pastoral conversations with a minister or other recognised person may well include the disclosure of sin and the granting of assurance of forgiveness through prayer.

5 Ecumenism

Baptists have never been the most enthusiastic of ecumenists, and some Baptist unions still distance themselves from their national ecumenical instruments. So, whilst BUGB is a full member of Churches Together in England (CTE), the Conference of European Churches (CEC), and the World Council of Churches (WCC), the Baptist Union of Scotland is not a member of the Scottish national ecumenical body, Action of Churches Together in Scotland, or any other body. This accords with the principle of participation (Principle VIII.5). Therefore, the most problematic part of Section VIII of the *Statement* is the second principle, on the nature of ecumenism and the ecumenical obligation (Principle VIII.2). Baptists might agree that visible unity is a good thing but struggle to know how to implement that vision given the congregational character of Baptist polity and, in many places, a history of oppression from the presiding national or state church.

30 cf. The report of Church of England-Baptist conversations, *Pushing at the Boundaries of Unity. Anglicans and Baptists in Conversation* (London: Church House Publishing, 2005).

Baptists in England may be more enthusiastic than most, but that is a very recent development. Until the early eighteenth century there were legislative attempts, often vigorously applied, to severely limit the freedom of Baptist churches. At the church where I was minister from 2015–2018, Abingdon Baptist Church, there is an annual endowed 'Schism Sermon', remembering the failed attempt by Parliament to limit all teaching in England at any level to members of the Church of England, never passed into law because Queen Anne died the night before she was due to assent to the relevant bill. Such providential events seemed worthy of annual remembrance to an earlier generation of Abingdon Baptists, even if they are not quite sure what to make of it today! Many Baptist churches would make it almost a statement of belief not to 'promote the ecumenical movement'. Moreover, when the Baptist union joined the new ecumenical instruments in 1989 (Churches Together in England and Churches Together in Britain and Ireland – the successor bodies to the British Council of Churches), whilst the vote in the union was strongly in favour, almost a quarter of churches represented voted against. By November 1989 thirteen churches had left BUGB over that decision and a further 65 had asked the union to note that they disassociated themselves from the decision.[31] This reflects Principle VIII.3.1, that the authorising of ecumenical engagement is 'in the keeping of the competent authority of a church'. In this regard, it was only BUGB that could join the ecumenical instruments, but the churches as independent congregations maintained their right to withdraw from such authorisation. The way the story unfolded reflected a deeper theological rift between those who were anxious to maintain their conservative evangelical identity, and encourage the union to walk in that direction (these tended to dissociate themselves from ecumenism), and those who wished to promote a more progressive, if not outright liberal, direction that embraced women's ordained ministry and, currently, affirmation of faithful and loving same-sex partnerships.[32]

6 Church property and church-state relations

In matters of finance and property (treated in Section IX of the *Statement*), Baptists engage with civil law in a more obvious way than in most other regards. In Britain, the purchase of Baptist churches and manses and their maintenance are the responsibility of the local congregation. However, such property is generally held in trust by a Baptist trust body, such as the London Baptist Property Board or the Baptist Union Corporation. Permission for the sale of such property needs to be sought from the trust body, as must any major refurbishment or development (especially where a building is a listed building under civil law, reflecting its historical and architectural merit). The disposal of the assets of a Baptist church when it closes is also organised in appropriate legal fashion, often with a proportion returning to the association and the remainder going for the use of the wider

31 I.M. Randall, op cit., 444–451.
32 Ibid., 442–451.

union's purposes, which often means the granting of loans or grants for a new church building. There is no provision for any national or regional appraisal of buildings (see Principle IX.2.4), but a local church, as the competent ecclesiastical authority, will generally undertake an annual survey of the manse, with a view to appropriate maintenance and regular reviews of the state of the church building. Otherwise, most of Section IX of the *Statement* would be generally consistent with Baptist polity.

Local churches raise their own funds, from which they pay a stipend to their minister(s) (reflected in Principle IX.5.2) – in most cases the greatest annual expenditure – and contribute to the finances of the BUGB 'common purse', which sustains the national and regional bodies, contributes to the funding of ecumenical instruments, and makes grants to churches and associations (through the 'Home Mission Fund').[33] Such arrangements are broadly reflected in the *Statement* (Principle IX.4.4). The Baptist Union of Victoria has a similar scheme.[34]

The relationship of Baptists to the state has been one born in conflict. Early Baptists in England were seen as political rebels when the state and the Church of England were synonymous, rejecting as they did the oversight of bishops in the prevailing episcopal polity. Differences were expressed about the degree to which Baptists could be magistrates (that is, those administering civil law), with some Baptist statements of faith prohibiting them[35] because their enforcement powers implied the bearing of arms.[36] As Baptists sought to become integrated into the political life of the nation, such prohibitions were relaxed, but there remains a strong separation of church and state in Baptist practice. So, from the end of the nineteenth century, for instance, Baptist churches began to be registered for the solemnisation of marriage, so that today most would be so registered. However, when requirements for re-registration were introduced for churches wishing to offer a service for same-sex marriage, a response to some who wished to ensure that under no circumstances they be required to do so (although this was very unlikely under the Marriage (Same Sex Couples) Act 2013) was to suggest that they de-register from providing any marriage service because of its implied action as an agent of the state (Principle X.1.3(4)), although in some other regards (for instance under charity law to operate as a charity) registration is acceptable. The principle in the *Statement* on the 'fundamental institutional autonomy of a church in carrying out its lawful objects and its freedom in these areas from intervention by the State' (Principle X.1.3(5)) is of paramount importance for Baptists. With an increasingly bureaucratic and

33 See http://centralba.org.uk.

34 It is called 'Grow, Give, Go'; see www.buv.com.au [accessed 3 September 2018].

35 A Short Confession of 1610, written by John Smyth and following Mennonite policy, stated: '[n]either hath [Christ] called his disciples . . . to be . . . magistrates': W.L. Lumpkin, *Baptist Confessions of Faith* (Valley Forge: Judson Press, 1959) 112.

36 cf. P.W. Goodliff, 'Natural Law in the Baptist Tradition', in N. Doe, ed., *Christianity and Natural Law: An Introduction* (Cambridge: Cambridge University Press, 2017) 140–161 at 156–160.

interventionist state, developing regulation in areas such as safeguarding, data protection, health and safety, food hygiene, and charity law, the relationship of church and state becomes increasingly problematic. Those who make such regulations might have good intentions, but the implementation of and compliance with them by laypeople in smaller congregations sometimes place impossible strains on the life of the church. It is distinctly possible those churches with a congregational polity, such as Baptists – being regulated by civil law in areas as if they were large charities with professional management – will signal their closure for no other reason than an inability to fully engage with increasing burdens of regulatory compliance.

In similar fashion, the tradition of human rights has remained strong in Baptist churches. It is often suggested, indeed, that the very idea of equal human rights originated with Baptists in England and then New England.[37] The principles in the *Statement* on human rights (Principles X.2.1–2), therefore, clearly reflect the Baptist position. The same can be said for engagement with social responsibility (Principle X.2). So, for instance, Nigerian Baptists have protocols to avoid abuses associated with the costs of burials and marriage engagements and the cultural abuse of widows;[38] and New Zealand Baptists campaign on behalf of their near-neighbours in Western Papua and 'hold the expectation that the New Zealand Government will recognize the sovereignty of the Indigenous peoples of Western Papua, and uphold their human rights'.[39]

Baptists have also engaged with the provision of ministry in public institutions like hospitals, universities, and prisons throughout the past century. In 1914, the Baptist Union of Great Britain and Ireland, with sister Free churches like the Congregational union, lobbied the government for permission to provide Baptist military chaplains to the Army and Royal Navy, and after some strong opposition from within the cabinet, this was granted, establishing the United Navy, Army and (subsequently) Air Force Board. Most of these posts, especially in National Health Service trusts, the prison service, and the military, are publicly funded (as is envisioned in Principle X.4.4), and some Baptist churches will seek funding in the form of grants for their own provision of youth work or social services to provide spiritual care. The separation of church and state is interpreted by some Baptists to mean that no state funding should ever be sought for its own work (and most churches would refuse to apply for grants from the National Lottery on the grounds of a moral suspicion of gambling) but most would make use of legitimate funding, such as the recovery of value added tax on the costs of redevelopment work upon a church that is under civil law a listed building, whilst such funds are available from the Department for Digital, Culture, Media and

37 Ibid., 152–156.

38 See www.nigerianbaptist.org/about-us/policies-and-practices/ [accessed 3 September 2018].

39 The Baptist Churches of New Zealand, *The West Papua Position Statement*: www.baptist.org.nz/news/61/22/West-Papua-postion-statement/ [accessed 3 September 2018].

Sport. This accords with the idea in the *Statement* about the 'institutional separation' of church and state and cooperation between church and state (as found in Section X, preamble, and Principle X.1.1).

III An evaluation of the principles of Christian law

In working ecumenically to formulate the principles of Christian law, the Baptist participants have recognised how much we have in common with the other Christian traditions, drawing as we all do upon the Scriptures and church fathers and, for Baptists, even when in disagreement, the Western Catholic tradition. So, for instance, with regard to the principle that '[a]ll ecclesial units at each level are interdependent' (Principle IV.5.5), Baptists would insist upon the voluntary nature of that interdependence, rather than any regulatory insistence. Moreover, a Baptist church may well be a member of its association and of BUGB, but it retains its freedom to withdraw from either or both. There are churches that are members of their association for historical reasons but have withdrawn from membership of BUGB on theological grounds or disagreement with policies about ecumenical engagement; and there are churches that are members of the union but not of their associations because retention of their buildings requires such membership. Given freedom to retain their buildings many of those churches probably would have chosen to leave both association and union. Despite those caveats, most Baptist churches in membership with the union would understand that despite the principle of congregational autonomy, there is an ecclesial and theological mandate for interdependence between local congregations and the bodies that enable wider fellowship and resourcing. Those bodies receive their funding from the local church, and in response the local congregation avails itself of the resources the regional or national body provides (arrangements for the deployment of clergy, legal and financial advice, and collaborative mission especially).

Many principles in the *Statement* concerning ministry, sacraments, and the responsibilities and privileges of the faithful (Sections II, III, and VII) are generally acceptable but all need to be read through the lens of congregational polity and its emphasis upon the equality of clergy and laity. Indeed, strictly speaking, ministers carry no ontological distinctives, and there is nothing reserved for the ordained Baptist minister that no other recognised member of a congregation might do (such as presidency at the Eucharist, baptizing, or preaching). There are continuing debates about whether baptism and the Lord's Supper are sacraments (in the Augustinian sense) or ordinances, and the nature of ordination itself is variously interpreted, but Baptists practise all three and interpret their significance in ways that are shared with many others, including evangelicals within the Church of England, many Methodists, and most Pentecostals.

The provision in the *Statement* of the permissive word 'may' means that in many cases where Baptists would interpret or hold the principles differently to others, they can affirm a principle simply because it is a point of fact. So, the principle that 'a church may make provision for a further rite accompanying or following baptism which may be styled confirmation or profession of faith' (Principle VII.2.1) is accurate from a Baptist perspective – a church other than a Baptist church may indeed do so – but Baptists have no need to do so because in believer's baptism, the act of baptism itself is an affirmation of faith. Again, the principle that '[c]o-operation between a church and the State may be exercised on the basis of . . . the establishment of . . . a church and the State' (Principle X.1.3) is factually true – the Church of England is so established – but no Baptist church would or could be so established because of the Baptist principle of separation of church and state, argued, for instance, by Nigel Wright.[40]

The great strength of the *Statement of Principles of Christian Law* for Baptists is that the principles act as a reminder of just how much we have in common with our ecumenical partners, and for those Baptists like myself who are committed to the ecumenical journey, this is a profoundly helpful resource. Where a few Baptists remain suspicious of Roman Catholicism, as if they remain stuck in a seventeenth-century time framework, most in England undoubtedly have rejected the idea that the Roman Catholic Church is not a true church, or worse, an institution opposed to Christ. Through participation in local Churches Together groups – whether formally instituted, such as the one in Abingdon, through a local covenant or informally, such as the churches of Bicester, and focussed upon collaborative mission – the presence of Roman Catholics in full participation has allayed many of the historic fears (widely shared until comparatively recently amongst most Protestant denominations). The degree to which the Roman Catholic participants in the principles of the Christian Law project have, like Baptists, found it possible to be in agreement about so much strengthens the arguments that counter the cool response to ecumenism from some Baptists. This is a project that has a vernacular character matching the ecumenism as practised on the ground throughout England.

Conclusion

The presence of Baptist participants on the ecumenical panel that formulated the *Statement of Principles of Christian Law*, throughout its work since 2013,[41] has ensured that there is a widespread ability for Baptists to affirm those principles. Since agreement with the substance of a principle was demanded of every participating tradition through those who, by their participation, reflected their tradition, there are no principles in the *Statement* that Baptists would reject *prima facie*. However, as we have seen, some principles require a particularly nuanced interpretation before they might be affirmed as reflecting Baptist polity, and

40 N.G. Wright, *Free Church, Free State* (Milton Keynes: Paternoster, 2005) 204–220.
41 Sequentially, Revd Dr John Weaver, Revd Dr Peter Stevenson, and Revd Dr Paul Goodliff.

Baptists working alone would have voiced them differently utilising the particular terminology derived from the dissenting reaction to the Catholic and Protestant character of the Church of England. That the ecumenical imperative recognised increasingly throughout the 'ecumenical century' of the past hundred years has been implemented in fresh ways in this Christian Law project is a matter of rejoicing, even for a tradition with as many 'soft' regulations as that of Baptists.

11 Pentecostal church polity

Paul Rochester

The Pentecostal tradition cuts across many forms of denominational Christianity. Theological differences existed amongst the early Pentecostal groups at the beginning of the twentieth century. The new groups that came out of the Holiness/Methodist movement were formed by people who placed great emphasis on the Scriptures. They possessed a deep desire to live out what the Bible teaches and to experience the power of God as described in the New Testament. One such person was 'the American' Charles Parham (1873–1929), who focussed on glossolalia (the phenomenon of speaking in another language or tongues, or the gift of tongues) as evidence of the baptism of the Holy Ghost. The Azusa Street Revival in Los Angeles, California, which broke out in 1906, was led by a former student of Parham named Joseph Seymour (1870–1922). The revival started spontaneously and continued in an unstructured fashion for many years, with many different expressions and leaders. However, many of the groups went on to form denominations, putting in place organisational structures, governance, and leadership models that, in many respects, resonate with the regulatory entities (polity documents, etc.) that are listed in the preamble to Section 1 of the *Statement of Principles of Christian Law* (2016). Whilst, for example, the Church of God churches placed an individual in charge – sometimes called the general overseer – they tended to adopt a democratised process for making decisions through general assemblies. The principles with respect to the international functions of leadership and organisation through a recognised authority (Principles III.4.3–6) help to explain the role of the general overseer and the general assemblies as a lawful authority within the Church of God. This formal mechanism for developing policy and religious belief continues to evolve, and for one denomination, which will be explored in more detail in the case study to follow, the current system in place addresses areas such as biblical doctrine and polity, finance and stewardship, and administration.[1]

1 *Ministry Policy Manual* (Cleveland, TN: White Wing Publishing House, 2015), Section One, Organizational Structure, The Role and Duties of the Assembly Committees.

I The varied nature of Pentecostalism

A precise definition of 'a Pentecostal Church' is something of a challenge. Not surprisingly, the baptism and work of the Holy Spirit – key tenets of the Pentecostal tradition – are a matter of contention. Some groups hold to speaking in tongues as the initial evidence of baptism of the Holy Spirit, whereas others focus on the fruit of the Spirit. Despite the differences in this particular area of doctrine, in several other areas there are similarities. The statement of faith for the denomination featured in the case study later refers to speaking in tongues and bearing the fruit of the Spirit as New Testament signs of being filled with the Holy Spirit. Yet its denominational objects, with a wider reach, make no specific mention of speaking in tongues as they are usually written in broader terms.

Speaking in tongues is therefore one of the significant characteristics of the classical Pentecostal movement. Other characteristics include the work of the Holy Spirit and experiencing the presence of God, with a strong emphasis on holiness. Worldwide mission was also a strong trait, seen as vital to ushering the return of Jesus Christ. The characterisation of glossolalia and the gifts of the Spirit are heavily based on the teaching from the Acts of the Apostles and passages in Corinthians.[2] However, many charismatics as well as Christians from the Anglican, Catholic, Evangelical, and Orthodox traditions, who are not part of the mainstream Pentecostal denominations, 'speak in tongues' and encourage the gifts of the Holy Spirit. The Pentecostal ecclesiology of speaking in tongues as the initial evidence of being baptised in the Holy Ghost is a theological position that has proved divisive and continues to raise questions in Pentecostal circles. The charismatics have also grown considerably, with established denominations operating across the UK.[3] Some charismatic groups may interpret the experience of the Holy Spirit differently, referring primarily to the fruit of the Spirit as a sign of the baptism of the Holy Ghost.[4] In general, the picture of Pentecostalism in the UK today remains mixed, with many new independent churches, some of them of African origin.

In the UK, occasionally, there is a tendency to refer to Pentecostalism in the context of black-led churches. Whilst many black-led churches in the UK are from the Pentecostal stream, Pentecostalism should be considered more broadly. The largest Pentecostal churches in the UK are probably Elim and the Assemblies of God, which, it would be fair to say, are white-led churches, though they boast

2 Acts Chapters 2, 10, 19 speak about the outpouring of the Holy Ghost at Pentecost, the conversion of Cornelius, and on John's disciples with signs of speaking in tongues. In Corinthians Chapters 12–14, the Apostle Paul lists the gifts of the Holy Spirit, including speaking in tongues. Whilst addressing particular concerns about the operation of the gifts in the Corinthian church, he provides instructions on the gift of speaking in tongues.

3 A. Davies, 'Heritage and Hope: A Story of British Pentecostalism', in J. Aldred, ed., *Pentecostals and Charismatics in Britain: An Anthology* (London: SCM Press, 2019) 3–34 at 3–6.

4 W.K. Hay, *Pentecostals in Britain* (Waynesboro, GA: Paternoster Publishing USA, 2000) 57–62 (denominational positions on tongues).

strong multicultural congregations. For example, the Assemblies of God, with over 550 churches in Great Britain, describes itself as a 'Pentecostal movement'.[5]

Church of God denominations, which have emerged from the holiness movement, share many similarities in terms of doctrine and organisational structure, whereas Elim and the Assemblies of God, whose historical journeys have followed similar paths, may look different.[6] Over time, doctrinal differences in areas such as divorce and remarriage have aligned, and there is less blue water between denominations. The Church of God denominations have, however, remained very strong in promoting the message of holiness. Despite this emphasis on holiness there are perennial discussions about the Arminian and Calvinist positions. Arminian theology is usually characterised as law-based with a focus on salvation by works, whereas Calvinism, emerging from Reformed theology, places emphasis on the sovereignty of God and salvation by grace alone, without works. Church law is also very important in respect of establishing doctrinal positions, but invariably we see different viewpoints because of personal interpretations of Scripture and conscience. Pentecostalism's emphasis on personal conviction and following the leading of the Holy Spirit can reinforce this situation. The younger generation poses different challenges, as they are less committed to denominational forms of Christianity and are more likely to make lifestyle choices as opposed to seeking to understand and follow what a denomination might teach.

Leadership structures vary among Pentecostal denominations. The appointment of bishops is one difference. Church of God denominations tend to operate under a leadership structure that includes bishops serving as presbyters, national and regional overseers, and, in some cases, pastors. Elim and other denominations do not appoint 'bishops' but use the office descriptor of 'senior minister' at all levels and that of 'director' for ministry leaders at the national level.

The tithe is another area of differences. The independent Pentecostal churches, some of which are mega-churches, may use church law to exert greater influence and control over members in respect of tithing and financial giving. A factor here could be the relatively short time they have been in existence and the need to fund their developing ministries. Similarly, governance and ministerial formation and accreditation in Church of God denominations are usually managed centrally, giving greater scope for the senior leaders to exert control. Civil law may also drive the creation of church law; for example, in recent times, civil charity law has strengthened the hands of senior leaders within the denomination, enabling them to push forward more stringent requirements applicable to local churches, which then form the basis of new church laws.

How churches respond to contemporary issues may also differ, especially in such areas as same-sex marriage, transgender, and gender-neutral issues. Some Pentecostal churches may hold strong and entrenched positions, whilst others

5 UK websites for Elim: www.elim.org.uk/; Assemblies of God: www.aog.org.uk/; New Testament Church of God: https://ntcg.org.uk; and Church of God of Prophecy: https://cogop.org.uk/.

6 W.K. Hay, op cit., 166.

may take a more liberal approach. At a time when equality and valuing diversity have risen to the top of the social and political agendas, it is worth noting the suggestion that Pentecostalism has had a positive effect on inter-racial worship and the role of women in leadership and ministry in the church. Harold Hunter suggests that positive movements in respect of women did not lead to the radical change in gender equality within the Church of God of Prophecy (which is discussed as a case study later) that may have been expected at the outset. It could be argued that the communal aspects of the outworking of the Holy Spirit led to greater integration between white and black members.[7] However, some denominations have gone much further than others in seeking to break down inter-racial barriers and to promote the role of women in ministry.[8] There is evidence that some Church of God denominations in North Carolina, at the beginning of the twentieth century, were very active in ordaining women and sending them on missions overseas.[9] The growth in the internationalisation of Pentecostalism could have therefore been a contributing factor in securing greater diversity. However, as Pentecostal groups established formal structures and procedures, there was a reversion to more restrictive practices in respect of women ministers. Whilst the institutionalisation of the Pentecostal groups had positive effects, it could be argued that it reduced the flexibility and spontaneity of the fledgling groups.[10]

II The growth of Pentecostal polity

There is no set pattern to describe the juridical aspects of Pentecostal denominations, although across the variety of denominations there will be similarities, which is discussed in more detail later. In this respect the *Statement of Principles of Christian Law* could be a useful way to consider how Pentecostal churches are organised. For instance, Pentecostal streams from Cleveland, Tennessee, which have their general or international headquarters in that part of the United States, follow similar formal structures in terms of organisation and governance.[11]

The Welsh revival and that at Keswick (1903–1905) played a part in the development of the Pentecostal movement in the United Kingdom. The Apostolic Church and Elim were offshoots of the Welsh revival and, more predominantly, the Sunderland conventions (1908–1914), the latter leading to a growing

7 A.M. Lord, 'Network Church: A Pentecostal Ecclesiology Shaped by Mission' (Thesis submitted to Birmingham University, May 2010) 63.

8 H.D. Hunter, 'International Pentecostal Holiness Church', in Yung-Chul Han, ed., *Acts of Pentecost* (Seoul: Han Young Theological University, 1998) 15–16: www.pctii.org/iphc.html.

9 A. and R. Kowalski, *What Made Them Think They Could?* Vol. 1 (Ten Case Studies of Early Pentecostal Women in Missions – 1906–1925).

10 A. Davies, op cit., 10.

11 Each of the Church of God denominations has its own governing documents but will share information informally. The Church of God of Prophecy has its *Ministry Policy Manual*, which is discussed later.

Pentecostal stream of Christianity in the United Kingdom.[12] The Apostolic Church held an Apostolic Faith convention in London in 1914. However, much earlier than this we saw individuals who spoke in tongues and experienced the baptism of the Holy Ghost. William Hutchinson started the first purpose-built Pentecostal church in Britain in Bournemouth, known as the Apostolic Faith Church, in 1911. That work grew, but Welsh assemblies left the Bournemouth parent body to form the Apostolic Church due to church government, property, and accountability issues. That denomination grew by accepting as members other congregations that had experienced the Pentecostal revival.

In 1937, a constitution providing a framework for committees and procedures to support missional and discipleship activities was established for the Apostolic Church.[13] The first Elim church is reported to have started in Belfast in 1916. As a result of structural changes brought about by the amalgamation of the Elim Evangelistic Board, Elim churches, and Elim missions, a new body was formed called the Elim Evangelistic Alliance, and the first Elim church in England was established in 1921. The growth in Pentecostalism led to the need for more formal structures, and Elim as a denomination formalised its work under the leadership of George Jeffreys (1889–1962). The Assemblies of God was formed in the United Sates in 1914 and emerged around the 1920s in the United Kingdom. Jeffreys' brother Stephen split from Elim to help form the denomination.

The growth of Pentecostalism in the United Kingdom and the United States, it can be argued, necessitated robust structures. Some leaders during the early years saw the democratisation of congregations as essential to growth, whilst others took the contrary view. A lack of formal structures was often driven by a desire to be true to the work of the Holy Spirit and to allow room for His work. However, church governance regarding the ownership and use of church buildings, and recognition and accountability of ministers, were pressing issues. The *Statement of Principles of Christian Law*, as to proper oversight of the administration of church property (Principles IX.2.2–3), would apply here, as regulations were required to clarify ownership and regulate the maintenance and use of church property acquired for worship. Doctrinal matters also required attention, as the groups sought to discern God's will and adjudicate on doctrinal positions. Unsurprisingly, doctrinal disagreements were divisive, with the potential to lead to splits, and ministers who sought reform faced opposition. The growth in denominations resulted from people taking different stances on certain doctrinal issues and, in some cases, financial irregularities and disagreements on organisational matters. For example, at the 1939 Elim conference, Jeffreys, the then president, urged reforms in respect of the introduction of district presbyteries. He probably wanted this to give more flexibility in what local churches preached.

12 W.K. Hay, op cit., 9–16.

13 Ibid., 20. In Bradford (1937) a new constitution was adopted that brought the churches under a general council of apostles and prophets, which met twice a year.

As stated previously, the Sunderland conventions, held annually at Whitsun, were instrumental in developing the Pentecostal movement in the UK. They ran from around 1908–1914 and provided an opportunity to preach and discuss the baptism of the Holy Spirit and how to respond to this new experience. Revd Alexander A. Boddy, the Anglican vicar of Sunderland, organised the conventions and produced a regular magazine, *Confidence*,[14] which contained articles and messages from the conventions, facilitating debates about tongues as a sign of baptism of the Holy Spirit and other issues. Whilst some of those at the Sunderland conventions were reluctant to set up Pentecostal denominations – as there was an aversion to encouraging sharp differences on baptism of the Holy Spirit – many did go on to establish Pentecostal denominations.[15]

For example, Assemblies of God and the Pentecostal Missionary Union formed a mission arm in 1925. The Assemblies of God adopted a distinctive approach to Elim, in terms of its organisation, which was based on a decentralised network of churches. The Assemblies of God network functioned on the basis of a set of fundamental beliefs, a fellowship of churches, and oversight by district presbyteries and general presbyteries made up of local pastors and elders. There were also efforts to centralise some matters such as spiritual leadership; however, some business matters were delegated to small local groups.[16]

Another significant development was the formation of the Church of God, inspired by the Methodists and the Holiness movement at the end of the nineteenth century. The Church of God was officially formed in the United States in 1907, but the name was used as early as 1886. Holiness and discussions around a second cleansing experience post conversion (known as sanctification, usually accompanied by great emotional and physical manifestations, such as tears and rolling on the floor) were very much part of the distinguishing mark of early Church of God churches. Leaders were primarily chosen on the basis of discernment and evidence of a divine calling, which was recognised through anointed preaching and teaching. Many leaders at the heart of Pentecostalism, at the beginning of the twentieth century, had tertiary education at a university or college level. The movement grew internationally, and it can be argued that many of its members were drawn from lower socioeconomic groups. Whilst the Church of God faced early challenges, it grew through good organisation and strong leadership.[17]

Growth in the United States and other countries was very encouraging, to the extent that by the 1920s the Church of God was carrying out missional activities in over 55 countries. The Caribbean countries saw a major growth in Church

14 Consortium of Pentecostal Archives: http://pentecostalarchives.org/digitalPublications/England/Independent/Confidence/Unregistered/1923/FPHC/1923_01_03.pdf#search=%22free%20churches%22.

15 More information is available on the following website: www.revival-library.org/index.php/pensketches-menu/british-pentecostal-pioneers.

16 W.K. Hay, op cit., 31.

17 Ibid., 32.

of God missions. It was by this route that the Church of God was established in Britain. West Indian migrants to Britain (the Windrush generation) included Church of God members. On arriving in Britain, they faced racism, as many were not accepted in white-led churches. As a result, many of these migrants set up Church of God churches. The number of Church of God churches grew significantly in the 1950s. Indeed, in the mid-1950s, in the United States, there were discussions about greater affiliation between Elim and the Church of God, but this never led to concrete proposals.

In summary, the development of regulations in Pentecostal denominations was driven by the need for doctrinal clarity, church governance, finance propriety, accountability structures for leaders and the laity, and the ownership and management of church property. To this extent, in terms of subject coverage, the *Statement of Principles of Christian Law* neatly summarises the principles of early Pentecostal polity.[18] Indeed, there are numerous records of minutes and manuals that address the ecclesiology of various Pentecostal churches, and these point to formal structures within the different groups that allowed them to address the matters outlined previously and grow in an organised fashion. However, there are questions about the degree to which the Pentecostal churches are 'Free churches', insofar as some groups adopted an episcopal approach, which could have been influential to an institutional approach to governance.

III Contemporary Pentecostal polity: a case study

This section outlines the sources of norms and the subjects they address in the Church of God of Prophecy, which is used as a case study, and discusses the extent to which these are reflected in the *Statement of Principles of Christian Law*. The name 'Church of God of Prophecy' was adopted by the then general overseer, M.A. Tomlinson, in 1952 following a court case in Cleveland, Tennessee. The court instructed the denomination to use the suffix 'of Prophecy' for business and legal purposes. It is argued by some that the court's instruction to use the suffix 'of Prophecy' recognised that the Church of God is fulfilling biblical prophecy.[19] To be clear, this court ruling only applied to external, not internal, affairs.[20] The church had been known as the 'Church of God' from its formation, as far back as 1903, until 1943, under the leadership of A.J. Tomlinson. There are many issues that could be highlighted here in explanation of the name, but suffice to say, for the purposes of this case study, the belief underlying

18 SPCL III. 3.1–4, 4.3–5: ordained ministry; IV. 1.1, 1.6: church governance; VI. 1.1–2, 2.1, 2.5: doctrine and worship; and IX. 2.4, 3.3: church property.

19 A.L. Varlack Sr., *Foundations – Church of God of Prophecy: Concise History, Polity, Doctrine, and Future* (Cleveland, TN: White Wing Publishing House, 2010) 24–28.

20 247 S.W.2d 63 (1952), *Church of God et al. v. Tomlinson Church of God et al.* Supreme Court of Tennessee.
March 7, 1952 (www.leagle.com/decision/1952310247sw2d631309).

the name is that 'Church of God' is the name Jesus gave his church, and the Church of God is seen as part of the continuation of the church organised in the Acts of the Apostles.

1 *The organisational structure of the church*

The Church of God of Prophecy operates on an international basis under a hierarchical structure, which includes a general overseer, general presbyters, national overseers, regional overseers, and local pastors. This structure includes plurality of leadership that is actively promoted and practised at all levels. As of 2016, the Church of God of Prophecy was present in over 130 nations and all 50 states of the United States.[21] Most of the members of the church are concentrated in North America, Latin America, and Africa.

The organisational structure of the Church of God of Prophecy exists and operates at three interdependent levels: international, national/regional/state, and local. The international level of the church organisation functions on a worldwide basis and currently provides a global network of support and interaction for the church's ministries in the United States of America and more than 130 other nations. The national/regional/state level provides more focussed leadership and support directly within the context of the nations, regions, and states. The local level is 'the heartbeat of the Church' and provides caring congregations around the world where the church's mission is carried out daily. These local bodies of believers form the framework within which the church meets its objectives of worship, evangelisation, equipping believers, and preparation for Christ's return.[22] The church's organisational structure is reflected in the *Statement* (Principles I.1.1–3 and 5 and IV.5.1). Members are not elected or appointed but voluntarily join local churches based on their salvation experience and a desire to be part of a Christian fellowship following God. It is a community that works on the basis of laws agreed to at the international, national, regional, and local levels. Leaders at all levels must apply church laws, and church membership is based on the acceptance of a church covenant and the commitment to accept and apply prominent teachings. Accepting, transferring, and removing church membership happens at the local church. The laws cover worship, admonition, discipline, and doctrine, amongst other things.

The denomination in the United Kingdom has a centralised system where, for example, the UK corporate office is the registered office and the charity's board of trustees is primarily constituted by the national overseer, six regional overseers, laity, and leaders, some of whom are professionals with management, human resource, and finance skills. All the local churches report to the corporate office

21 *Ministry Policy Manual* (Cleveland, TN: White Wing Publishing House, 2015), Section One, Organizational Structure, Preamble.

22 *Ministry Policy Manual* (2016), Section One, Organizational Structure.

and receive their charitable status through registration of the corporate office (Church of God of Prophecy Trust) with the civil Charity Commission.[23]

The Church of God of Prophecy is therefore regulated by its memorandum and articles of association and its *Ministry Policy Manual* – hereafter the *Manual* (2016) – which consists of a range of rules, rights, duties, and principles as well as recommendations, guidance, and advice. Whilst these regulations, as reflected in the *Statement* on the forms of ecclesial regulation (Principle I.2.1), are drawn from a variety of sources, including to an extent canon law, the Scriptures are seen as the primary source. The law of the church orders its activities but is shaped by theology, Scripture, and the Holy Spirit; these ideas are also reflected in the *Statement* (Principle I.3). The *Manual* (2016) is updated and re-published every two years following the meeting of the international assembly (previously general assembly). The Church of God of Prophecy believes that where God's law and governance are observed, so the church is present.[24]

The international assembly is the highest decision-making body in the church. After each international assembly, which is open to all members, minutes are written and published. Those minutes refer to any changes in church law as set out in the latest edition of the *Manual*, and subsequent reprints of it reflect those changes. The international assembly is organised and moderated by the general overseer in partnership with the general presbyters. The international assembly includes doctrinal and business sessions at which church law can be developed or changed. Every member has a say in these discussions and the discernment and decision-making process. There was a proxy system, discontinued in 2012, where local churches could provide expressions, for consideration, on matters to be discussed at the international assembly. This system sought to involve local churches in the discernment and decision-making process, recognising that it was not possible for everyone to travel to the assembly, and broadly reflects Principle IV.2.[25]

The *Manual* (2016) consists of three sections. Section One deals with organisational structure. There are norms on the international assembly, international presbyters, general presbyters, plurality of leadership, and international offices. At the national, regional, or state level, there are provisions on, for example, trans-local ministry and overseers. At the local level, there are rules on local church ministry, including organising and disbanding a new local church as directed by a national overseer; church membership; church discipline; and the local church conference. The provisions concerning ministry policies deal with, for example, ministerial competences (e.g. pastors and overseers), recommending members

23 Link to Charity Commission for Church of God of Prophecy Trust: http://apps.charitycommission.gov.uk/Showcharity/RegisterOfCharities/CharityWithPartB.aspx?RegisteredCharityNumber=287868&SubsidiaryNumber=0. The church is registered in accordance with UK law and in line with the church and so reflects SPCL X.4.

24 *Ministry Policy Manual* (2016), Section One, 6: Dynamics of Theocratic and Hierarchical Government.

25 *Ministry Policy Manual* (2016), Section One, Organisational Structure, 4: Assembly Business Procedures Revision.

for ministry, lay ministers, licenced ministers, elders (e.g. deacons and bishops), 'general instructions' (e.g. tithing by ministers, their 'secular work', observing ordinances, and marriage), ministerial discipline (including restoration following disciplinary process), and the roles of the general overseers and general presbyters. Section Two provides information and resources, including the statement of faith and information on biblical principles, beliefs, and practice. Section Three, which contains forms related to aspects of the life of the church, such as membership transfer and acknowledgement and pastor endorsements, broadly fits into Principles IV.3–5 of the *Statement.*

2 *The importance of understanding God's law and government*

The Church of God of Prophecy stresses the importance of understanding God's law and government. The background is as follows. An initial group met on 19 August 1886 at Barny Creek meeting house, Monroe County, Tennessee. At the outset, the group desired to resist man-made creeds and laws and to take the New Testament, or law of Christ, as the only rule of faith and practice. The Church of God, therefore, uses the concept of 'theocratic government' at the heart of its system of polity; this simply means that God rules. This is critical in understanding how church law is formed in the Church of God of Prophecy. At that time, it was also recognised that people have freedom to follow conscience and equal rights and the importance of the 'Church of God' coming together to transact business. This early group sought to complete the Reformation based on the principle that holiness and love had to be held in proper balance as a true characteristic of the church that Jesus Christ organised.

The group faced many challenges and potential splits and barely survived. But in 1902, at the home of W.F. Bryant, in Cherokee County, North Carolina, the group was renamed the Holiness Church at Camp Creek, having been previously known as the Christian Union. In 1903, the small church ordained two new ministers, including A.J. Tomlinson, and obligations were agreed to work together following the New Testament pattern in the Acts of the Apostles. The church followed the tenets of Wesleyan theology on holiness, with a strong spiritual focus. The church was committed to searching Scripture and to putting into practice the things learnt. A hallmark of the church was its eagerness to understand the Word of God and its willingness to conform to it. This is an important factor when considering juridical structures in the context of the Church of God of Prophecy because Scripture is seen as the bedrock of church law. There was a strong commitment to study the Scriptures and to apply revelation knowledge and learning to the life of the denomination worldwide. This is summed up in the *Manual* (2016), which is broadly in line with the *Statement* (Principle I.3):

> At all levels, efforts are made to retain a dynamic flexibility to avoid stagnation. In increasingly complex and ever-changing societies, the ability to remain relevant to people's needs is dependent upon the ability to respond to societal change in a positive manner without compromising truth. God is

> dynamic, not static. He is a God who moves and acts in the affairs of mankind. The Church is committed to be a mobile and pilgrim people who move when He moves and who stop when He stops. Therefore, the organizational structures currently serve its mission, but they are subject to review and revision as God's Holy Spirit may direct.[26]

As seen previously, the Church of God of Prophecy relied heavily on providing a written record of meetings of the international assemblies. There was a strong emphasis on leaving a record for future generations to understand how God worked through the denomination and to provide a foundation on which to continue building. This practice continues today. The need for a written record must also be viewed from the perspective of the belief that the Church of God is the continuation of the true church that Jesus Christ established, continuing the mission of the early church as described in the Acts of the Apostles. There is also a clear link to the written record in the Bible and the need to contextualise how God works with his people. Whilst the oral tradition has its place, there was an emphasis on keeping copious records following the Old Testament pattern of a written record of the law, its requirements, and God's dealing with his people and passing these on to future generations. Reference to the Acts of the Apostles and a written record of the Holy Spirit's work also apply. The minutes of the first assembly in 1906 end thus: 'It seemeth good to the Holy Ghost and us, being assembled together with one accord, with the Spirit of Christ in the midst, and after much prayer, discussion, searching the Scriptures and counsel, to recommend these necessary things and that they be ratified and observed by all local churches'.[27] This statement has guided ways in which doctrine and polity have been considered and developed over the years. The church leaders viewed the assembly as a judicial body only to consider the Word of God; to seek interpretation and understanding in the context of contemporary challenges; and to record deliberations and rulings.[28]

3 Leadership within the church

The Church of God of Prophecy operates a 'plurality of leadership' model at the international, national, regional, and local levels. The Questions and Subjects Committee, which had an international membership, considered plurality of leadership and reported to the 88th Assembly (1994). The report was duly accepted, and since that time we have seen changes in the leadership structure within the Church of God of Prophecy. For example, the general presbyters working with the general overseer to oversee the work globally is a direct result of that change. We see this model replicated in shared discernment and decision-making, including the appointment of bishops, pastors, and national workers in the countries the

26 *Ministry Policy Manual* (2016), Section One, Preamble.

27 Minutes of the Annual Assembly of the Churches of East Tennessee, North Georgia and Western North Carolina, held 26–27 January 1906, At Camp Creek, N.C., 10.

28 A.L. Varlack Sr., op cit., 49.

general presbyters oversee. Ministerial licensure and discipline rest in the hands of the international presbytery. Those overseers who serve in the international presbytery oversee countries and the states of the US. They have a variety of responsibilities that have been developed over time.[29] All ministers are licenced by the international office. Bishops are approved for licence by the general overseer and the general presbyters. They are usually ordained at the international assembly but can also be ordained at the national level by general presbyters with national overseers. Pastors are approved by the national overseers and their plurality team after completing the accreditation process, which includes completing theological and practical ministry courses and successful attendance at a ministerial panel.

The biblical references for leadership draw on Moses's approach to leadership and New Testament teaching. There is a real sense that, in Jesus Christ, New Testament teaching moved away from 'types and shadows.' So, leaders are no longer viewed in the context that Moses was seen in in relation to Jesus Christ as a type or shadow (Hebrews 3:1–7). Jesus Christ is the head of the church, with everyone coming under his leadership. There is a need to avoid raising any person above others and to discourage any potential attitudes of superiority. The *Statement* on ministers fashioning their lives after Jesus's example (Principle III.3.3) reflects the Church of God of Prophecy's focus on Christ being the head of the church and our example for ministry.

The principle of the body, with all its parts having roles to play, is taught and encouraged. Distinctions are drawn in relation to a person holding an office, a position, and carrying out functions that are attached to that office. For example, a person can be appointed to the office of bishop, hold a position of regional overseer, and carry out the functions of a regional overseer. The appointment of a regional overseer is the responsibility of the state/national overseer. Regional overseers have oversight for a group of churches in a geographical region, which includes caring for the people and churches, establishing churches, teaching, and watching in spiritual matters. The role of regional overseers includes a significant amount of administration to ensure local churches meet the requirements of the Church of God Prophecy Trust and regularly report, across a range of areas, to the corporate office.[30]

29 Licensing and ordaining of ministers (*36th Assembly Minutes,* 1941, 92; *88th Assembly Minutes,* 1994, 153). Disciplining of ministers (*82nd Assembly Minutes,* 1987, 56; *54th Assembly Minutes,* 1959, 128, 256; *58th Assembly Minutes,* 1963, 126, 256). Disbanding of churches (*71st Assembly Minutes,* 1976, 134). Restoring ministers (*82nd Assembly Minutes,* 1987, 47). Dealing with ministers who preach contrary doctrine (*54th Assembly Minutes,* 1959, 128). Dealing with ministers who usurp authority (*58th Assembly Minutes,* 1963, 126). Handling certain matters pertaining to marriage (*78th Assembly Minutes,* 1983, p. 137; *80th Assembly Minutes,* 1985, 139). Establishing procedures and policies for ministerial licence (*88th Assembly Minutes,* 1994, 153).

30 *Ministry Policy Manual* (2016), Ordination of Licensed Ministers, Bishops. The biblical office is seen as divine, the position of the office relative and the functions discretionary. Looking at 1 Timothy 3:1 it is suggested here that the word 'ministry' could be translated as 'office' – hence the language used is 'desiring the office of a Bishop'. Other Scripture references include Luke 1:8–9; Romans 11:13, 12:4; and 1 Timothy 3:10,13.

At all levels, plurality of leadership is practised and singular forms of leadership are discouraged. There are questions based on New Testament practice where, for example, Paul, James, and John assume more singular leadership roles. However, the plural aspect of leadership is clearly preferred in the Church of God of Prophecy. Although the word 'elder' was commonly used in early church government and on many occasions in relation to the apostles, elders are not appointed or licenced. An elder's role is seen more in the sense of 'quality of life' than as a ministerial licence and can therefore apply to people who are not licenced ministers. However, all licenced minsters should have eldership characteristics.[31]

Church law governs the appointment and accreditation of ministers. In earlier times, ministers were appointed and licenced for ministry primarily on the basis of the call of God in their lives. The call is usually evidenced by being used by God to preach and teach in local churches. Over recent years, ministerial accreditation has significantly changed, with more formal requirements, although the divine call remains central to the process. This begins with a local church conference setting forth the candidate for a ministerial licence as a lay minster. A lay minister's licence is issued, and they learn on the job. Formal training to certificate level is required, and ministerial courses, which include practical ministry, must be completed. Academic study in ministerial formation is therefore balanced by 'divine calling' without negating the importance of education. For ordained ministers to have credibility with secular government and to seek posts within, for example, prison and health care chaplaincy, they must be educated to at least diploma level. Church law brings clarity to the process so that those wishing to pursue licenced ministry understand the requirements, and it gives confidence to statutory bodies that wish to engage with the churches in the delivery of social projects and in fostering social cohesion. Candidates are supported in discerning their call and must attend a panel before going forward for a full licence. There is a post-licence consolidation period, with an internship of at least six months. This usually includes ministry at a local church other than that of the candidate.[32]

As seen previously, there is a detailed process to accredit and support ministers. The *Manual* (2016) covers all aspects of ministry, including the call, the different licences, and the relevant competences, accreditation, and ordination. The procedure for ongoing appraisals, with relevant forms, is also covered in the *Manual* (2016), in addition to the disciplinary process for ministers, tithing requirements, and responsibilities for services, such as marriage. The *Statement* (Principles III.1.1–6) expresses adequately most aspects of the way ordination takes place within the Church of God of Prophecy. The minister is set apart to carry out the functions of their office. There are certain training requirements to meet before ordination, and ordination is carried out by a competent authority. As seen previously, the *Statement* (Principles V.1.2 and 1.4), in relation to ecclesial discipline,

31 *Ministry Policy Manual* (2016), Section One, Organisational Structure, Ministry Policies, V, Elders, 98.

32 *Ministry Policy Manual* (2016), Section One, Organisational Structure, Ministry Policies, II, Recommending a member for Church Ministry, 75–82.

appears in the *Manual* (2016) in respect of church discipline for both the laity and ordained persons within the Church of God of Prophesy.

4 Local churches and membership

The local church is at the heart of the denomination. Its organisation is set out in the *Manual* (2016), along with the roles of officers, including trustees, who are responsible for charity and managing church property.[33] All local churches must hold quarterly business meetings attended by only church members. The local church conference is usually chaired by the pastor, supported by the clerk and treasurer. Standing agenda items must include the minutes from the last meeting and the treasurer's report. Administrative decisions are agreed by consensus, but spiritual matters, such as setting a person forth into the ministry, with one accord. Meetings can either be quarterly to follow the reporting cycle – for local churches to report to the national office – or called for a specific purpose. Business conferences at all levels are important functions of the church. There is specific wording that is repeated at the outset of a local business conference to formalise the meeting. This is as follows: 'The local church . . . is now in business conference to transact any business, which may properly come before it'.[34] These arrangements are broadly reflected in the *Statement* on the local church (Principle IV.5).

Church membership is based on a salvation experience, water baptism, and the local church giving the person the right hand of fellowship. Candidates for membership are taught the teachings of the church, founded on Basic Bible Beliefs, of which there are 29.[35] As part of the service to receive new members, candidates for membership must accept the church covenant. It is stressed that church membership is about acceptance into a local church and the commitment of its members to work together in fulfilling God's will for each person. Membership of the body of Christ is the work of the Holy Spirit whereby new converts are baptised into the body of Christ (1 Corinthians 12:12). Baptism of the Holy Spirit is a separate experience that can happen before or after the water baptism and the new members' service. The covenant for church membership is based on the following:

> Do you sincerely promise in the presence of God and these witnesses, to accept this Bible as the word of God, believe and practice its teachings, rightly dividing the New Testament as your rule of faith, government,

33 *Ministry Policy Manual* (2016), Section One, Local Church Ministry, Deeds for Church Property, 39–41.

34 *Ministry Policy Manual* (2016), Section One, Organizational Structure, V. The Local Church Conference.

35 The teachings include abstinence from strong drinks and smoking tobacco/drugs, refraining from membership in lodges/secret societies, marriage, divorce, and remarriage. Candidates are encouraged about the importance of walking in the light as the church receives greater understanding and grows in closeness to Jesus Christ. Loyalty to the international assembly is also taught.

practice and discipline, and to walk in the light to the best of your knowledge and ability so help you God?[36]

These arrangements are generally reflected in the *Statement* on church membership (Principles II.2 and 3).

A church member has a right to fully participate in the life and business/administration of the church, including the process to 'disfellowship' a person who is living in sin and unwilling to repent. Church membership is seen in legalistic terms and treated very seriously, although some churches take more nuanced positions. There is much that could be said about disfellowship in respect of fairness and consistency. However, in general the norms of the Church of God of Prophecy on the functions of members are reflected in the *Statement*.[37]

5 Church discipline

The degree to which local churches comply with the polity and doctrine of the Church of God of Prophecy in respect of church discipline varies. Up until the early 1980s a stricter regime existed, but there is now more flexibility, in line with the *Manual* (2016) Section One preamble. The leadership of the relevant area – national and regional bishops – plays a key part in determining how local churches enforce church discipline and whether more flexible approaches are needed. Church laws draw on the passage in Matthew 18 in which members with an offence to resolve are called to do so themselves before involving one or two others or eventually taking it to the church. The Corinthian passage (1 Corinthians 5:1–7) about purging the things that are not right to protect the whole is also practised.[38] At the heart of disfellowshipping members is the principle of loving action to correct and help rather than punish.

The *Manual* covers the process for dealing with a member who has fallen into sin and refuses to repent to make restitution: '[b]efore dealing with such a one, biblical attitudes must be prevalent in the lives of those seeking to bring about reconciliation. Such attitudes are love, patience, and humility'.[39] The following three matters must be considered: the glory of God, the purity of the church, and the spiritual good of the member. Two classes of 'offence' are described: private or public. A private offence is one in which a church member has a conflict with another, and the Matthew 18:15–17 passage applies. If the matter reaches the church, then restoration becomes the responsibility of the church, in line with 2 Thessalonians 3:14, 15.[40] A public or general offence – defined as bringing

36 *Ministry Policy Manual* (2016), Section One, Organisational Structure, Local Church Ministry, III. Church Membership, 56.

37 SPCL II.3 reflects Church of God of Prophecy norms.

38 *Ministry Policy Manual* (2016), Section One, Organisational Structure, Local Church Ministry, V. The Local Church Conference, 62–64.

39 *Ministry Policy Manual* (2016), Section One, IV Church Discipline.

40 *Ministry Policy Manual* (2016), Section One, IV Church Discipline, Objects of Church Discipline, A and B.

reproach of the body through persistent sin, spreading false doctrine, or causing division – should be dealt with immediately by the church and involves the ministry confronting the individual before, if that fails, bringing the matter to the church (1 Timothy 6:3–5, Romans 16:17, Titus 3:10). These approaches are covered by the *Statement of Principles of Christian Law* (Principles V.2.1–5). The Church of God has such a system, which is a fundamental part of its church law. The ministry has a key part to play, but it also requires participation from the local churches, including laity. In this system the local church and ordained ministers are treated as the competent authority. The aim of church discipline aligns with the *Statement* (Principle V.5.5) and seeks to glorify God, protect the integrity of mission, and promote the spiritual benefits of members, including safeguarding the vulnerable (Principle V.1.4). There is also an informal resolution process (as in Principle V.2.1), which pastors usually oversee, and it is hoped that most disagreements can be resolved in this way.

6 Doctrine and ritual

The international assembly, as a judicial body, rules on matters of doctrine, as those believers assembled sense and understand the leading of the Holy Spirit. It is important to note that the Church of God of Prophecy teaches the dynamic nature of theology, which has implications for its polity and practice. However, not everyone subscribes to the idea of the dynamic nature of theology, and, as such, some individuals are less willing than others to accept changes in church doctrine and polity. This presents a challenge for the general overseer and the leadership team at the international office, who seek to lead with an eye on ministry in a changing world. This does not imply changes to the foundational teachings, however – the leading of the Holy Spirit and the discernment of God's will are critical to decision-making.

For example, a key issue in the early 1920s was divorce and remarriage – the Questions and Subjects Committee received questions and prepared a response for presentation and discussion at the assembly. The resultant changes to church teaching on marriage and divorce are now covered in the *Manual* (2016),[41] as is performing a marriage: 'Marriage ceremonies should be performed in harmony with the teachings of the Bible'.[42] Because of their roles and offices, only pastors (who hold a minister's licence) and bishops are authorised to perform marriages.[43] In special circumstances ordained ministers who are not pastoring can request a permit to

41 *Ministry Policy Manual (2016),* Section Two, Important Information and Resources, Biblical Principles, Beliefs and Practices, 172.

42 'The minister should thoroughly acquaint himself with the Church's teaching regarding Marriage, Divorce and Remarriage (The Biblical Institution of Marriage and the Recommendations therewith) as presented, amended, and passed by the 94th International Assembly 2006, and be guided by its provisions and any guidelines set forth or authorized by the General Presbytery for its implementation' (94th Assembly Minutes, 2006, pp. 152–177; see Ministry Policy Manual, 2008, Appendix 3).

43 *95th Assembly Minutes*, 2008, 13.

perform a marriage, subject to the approval of the general presbyter or general overseer.[44] This church law clearly reflects the *Statement* on marriage (Principle VII.1.4): marriage is instituted by God and therefore important, hence the need for an authorised person to perform the marriage meeting the requirements of relevant civil law on marriage.

Today, the assembly has the following three standing committees: the Biblical Doctrine and Polity Committee, the Administrative Committee, and the Finance and Stewardship Committee. These committees are appointed by the general overseer, in consultation with the general presbyters. They operate and convene outside the international assembly but report to the assembly. Committee membership includes representation from the global church. The committees consider issues and topics in agreement with the general overseer assembly and the general presbyters.[45] Moreover, 'In order to give further clarification to our decision-making process, we recommend that reports concerning policies, procedures, and finances presented by Assembly standing committees be accepted by overwhelming consensus'; however, 'All matters of a doctrinal nature must be accepted by "one accord" '.[46] These norms appear in the *Statement* on defining doctrine (Principle VI.1).

Church law in the context of foundational biblical doctrine has always been important. For many years, up to the early 1980s, the doctrinal positions were described as the 'Twenty-Nine Teachings'. They are now called Basic Bible Beliefs and include theological positions on foundational salvation experiences, such as being born again, justification, sanctification and baptism with the Holy Spirit, the second coming of Christ, and Christian conduct – for example wearing gold for ornaments, drinking alcohol, and smoking tobacco.[47] Over the years there have been ongoing reviews of the various doctrinal positions. For example, at the 2018 assembly, the Biblical Doctrine and Polity Committee reported on work it had been doing on issues such as a statement of faith, the office and role of deacons and deaconesses, reaffirmation of the dynamics for theocratic and hierarchical government, and the practice of foot washing; the assembly minutes for that assembly are yet to be published at the time of writing. These arrangements are adequately summed up in the *Statement*.[48]

Along with many other Pentecostal denominations, the Church of God of Prophecy does not celebrate the Eucharist in every service. Local churches are encouraged to have a Holy Communion service at least once a quarter, and this is stated in the *Manual* (2016), although it encourages more regular observance of

44 *Ministry Policy Manual* (2016), Section One, Ministry Policies, VI. General Instructions, H. Performing Marriages, 105.

45 *Ministry Policy Manual* (2016), Section One, Organisational Structure, I.B, The Infrastructure of the International Assembly, 11–18.

46 Ibid., 10: it cites the *93rd Assembly Minutes*, 2004, 333.

47 *Ministry Policy Manual* (2016), Section Three, Important Information and Resources, Biblical Principles, Beliefs and Practices, 159–172.

48 SPCL IV, Preamble.

the ordinance. This should include foot washing, but this practice varies across churches in the Church of God.[49] Some Pentecostal denominations do not practise foot washing at all. More could be said about observing the ordinances; to help local pastors, this is covered as part of the internal training courses, which they can choose to attend. Licenced ministers are required to serve Holy Communion, but, again, there could be lapses in the application of this ruling. This is a function that may differ across denominations. Baby dedications and water baptism follow similar patterns. All these ordinances are supported by scriptural text referenced in the *Manual* (2016) to facilitate observance. For example, the Lord's Supper is described as a sacred ordinance instituted by Christ, which we believers are called to observe in remembrance of him. Scripture texts include Luke 22:14–22, 1 Corinthians 11:23–25, and Acts 2:46,47. The *Manual* states:

> No one should approach the Lord's Table with unforgiven sin in one's heart, and all should consecrate themselves in prayer before and upon every occasion of this observance. The Lord's Supper consists of 'the fruit of the vine' (unfermented grape juice, as is our practice), representing the blood of Christ, and unleavened bread, representing His broken body on the cross. The Church encourages the Lord's Supper to be observed at least once a quarter, but to do so more often is certainly compatible with scriptural teaching.

These norms in the Church of God of Prophesy are reflected in the *Statement* (Principles VII.3.1–9); the emphasis on Christ instituting the ordinance matches Principle VII.3.1. However, the principle of the centrality of Holy Communion to ecclesial life (Principle VII.3.2) is not as strongly followed in the Church of God of Prophesy; as we have seen, the *Manual* (2016) provides a minimum requirement to hold a Lord's Supper service once a quarter. Moreover, the *Statement* on admission to the Eucharist (Principle VII.3.9) is less explicit than the *Manual* (2016), which expressly forbids a person from approaching the Lord's table with sin.

7 *Property and finance*

Financial giving is an area of church law that is important to both the mission and the development of denominations. Tithing and giving are taught as part of the Basic Bible Beliefs. Probably less than 20% of pastors are full-time. Pastors' salaries are generally paid by the local church (in the UK, via the corporate office). This means that unless a local church can pay a reasonable salary, the pastor may need to take secular employment. The *Manual* (2016) does state that overseers should

49 *Ministry Policy Manual* (2016), 104: 'The pastor of the local church should ensure that the ordinances of the Lord's Supper and Feet Washing are conducted at least quarterly (*57th Assembly Minutes*, 1962, p. 134).'

discourage ministers from secular work when the local church can pay a competitive salary. Whilst this financial model has been used for many years, in some countries it is being reviewed. It is increasingly problematic for pastors to manage secular employment with ministerial responsibilities, especially today, given the increasing administrative burden of complying with requirements of civil government or statutory bodies.

Complying with the financial management responsibilities arising from stricter secular government requirements falls to pastors, who are supported by treasurers and clerks. Local churches are required to have a finance and stewardship committee to work with the pastor to manage finances.[50] This includes setting an annual budget and providing oversight for the operational income and expenditure. This committee reports to the local church conference. Church law governs the disbursement of funds in accordance with directions of the international assembly and state, regional, and national conventions. There are also norms on managing indebtedness whereby permission is required for significant projects. There is a financial manual, which pastors must be familiar with and apply in their local churches. Each local church must send an annual budget to the national/corporate office and submit information and reports at regular intervals throughout the reporting year. The end-of-year financial information that is required from each local church is extensive and feeds into the consolidated annual report for the charity, the Church of God of Prophecy Trust. This report is audited by a professional accountancy body in line with UK charity and company law.

This brief financial outline reflects the norms set out in the *Statement* (Principle IX.3). In the Church of God of Prophecy, at all stages, responsibility for financial management is shared and full transparency is required. Competent authorities exist and play important roles for the professional auditing of the charity's accounts. As part of that process, auditors visit several local churches each year. The financial manual and the *Manual* (2016) both ensure that the local churches comply with state laws so that the charity can meet its civil legal obligations.

8 Relationships with other Christians

The Church of God of Prophecy recognises that it is not independent of other Christians. It has a history that is connected to the work of God and his church throughout the centuries. The Church of God is firmly rooted in reformed theology and the ministries of Luther, Calvin, and Zwingli. Historically, the Church of God is also linked to the Reformation and denominations such as the Anabaptists, Mennonites, Baptists, and Quakers.[51] Discussions will of course continue about the degree to which the Church of God has built on these traditions and the areas of difference that have resulted from the search for a deeper relationship

50 *Ministry Policy Manual* (2016), Section One, V.H, The Role of the Local Church's Finance and Stewardship Committee.

51 A.L. Varlack Sr., op cit., 151.

with the Holy Spirit and the desire to follow him. There is so much about God's work in his world, much of which is a challenge to fully comprehend. There is, therefore, a perennial effort to grapple with biblical truth and how to apply it today. The Church of God's faithfulness to Scripture, which by no means is unique, involves the challenge of wrestling with Scripture regardless of how difficult that proves. The statement of faith has been partly developed precisely to support wider engagement with other Christian denominations, as it brings clarity to the Church of God's foundational beliefs. It is written in the form of a creed. The *Manual* states: 'The beliefs stated in the document express our solidarity and commonality with Christians within the Church throughout the world, whilst preserving some of our theological distinctives'. In turn, the statement of faith asserts: 'We believe in one holy, universal Church, composed of all true believers in Jesus Christ, offering fellowship and calling for service to men and women of all races, nations, cultures, and languages. We believe in the spiritual and ultimate visible unity of the Church'.[52] The statement of faith, with revisions, was presented to the 99th International Assembly, 2016. We await the approved version. There are no further specific references in the *Manual* about ecumenism, although local churches are expected to engage with the communities they serve, including other Christian denominations and faith groups. This approach does link to the *Statement*'s treatment of ecumenism (Section VIII), but there is probably scope for the *Manual* (2016) to develop this area to be more specific about intentions.

Conclusion

The chapter identifies the high-level developments of classical Pentecostalism in the UK and provides some comments on the current state of play. It has sought to show some of the main differences between Pentecostal denominations and the challenges these pose for defining Pentecostalism as a single phenomenon. There are denominational similarities and differences; but, interestingly, organisational structures and the use of church law indicate a high level of commonality. The case study on the Church of God of Prophecy, which is a useful benchmark of the denominations to emerge at the beginning of the nineteenth century, also shows a high degree of conformity with the *Statement of Principles of Christian Law*. This, in my view, is understandable given that Pentecostal denominations, like others, believe in the supremacy of Scripture and aim to faithfully interpret and apply God's word to ecclesial life. Comparisons with the *Principles of Christian Law* and the case study have proved useful and demonstrate that denominations probably share more in common on church law than is generally thought to be the case. Whilst the principles are about norms of conduct, they do give direction and clarity about what makes good church law. In respect of the

52 *Ministry Policy Manual* (2016), Report of the Biblical Doctrine and Polity Committee to the 99th International Assembly, 157–158.

Pentecostal denominations, many have beginnings that are rooted in the established denominations, so organisational models and structures will undoubtedly have some similarity. The norms in respect of the ordinances, save some of the fundamental theological issues based on the interpretation of Scripture and how communion and baptism are understood, share similarities. The use of church law can strengthen denominations and support growth, especially where that growth involves exponential growth in local churches. Without church law it would be difficult to manage whilst maintaining some form of conformity. Where denominations operate under a centralised model there can be clearer benefits, but even a looser network of churches could benefit. The *Principles of Christian Law* are very extensive and cover a wide range of areas that must be considered in church life. They have benefit for churches that operate nationally and internationally. One key area is the link between church law and civil government and law; how can church law be helpful, and where does it pose problems? The exercise raises several questions of this sort, which require much further thought, especially from the angle of ecumenism and breaking down barriers.

12 The polity of the United and Uniting Churches

Leo J. Koffeman

This chapter explores one aspect of the experiences of United and Uniting Churches: finding common principles of church law. It starts with a discussion of the churches themselves and then presents some telling examples from interconfessional unions. Diversity is key to these churches. After some observations about the relation between principles and process in church unification processes, it focusses on a case study of the unification process that gave birth to the Protestant Church in the Netherlands. This chapter concludes with some observations on the value of the *Statement of Principles of Christian Law* (2016) for United and Uniting Churches.

I United and Uniting Churches

The website of the World Council of Churches (WCC) lists 19 church families. One of them is the family of United and Uniting Churches.[1] At this moment, 41 of the member churches of the WCC belong to this family. It is debatable whether it is also possible to speak of these churches as representing an ecclesial 'tradition' in the same way we speak of the Roman Catholic, Anglican, and Reformed traditions. Indeed, the United and Uniting Churches have never decided to institute a separate Christian world communion – like the Lutheran World Federation or the World Methodist Council – although this has been considered time and again. They do not have an office with staff in Geneva or elsewhere. However, since 1967 (Bossey) representatives of these churches have been invited by the Commission on Faith and Order of the WCC to meet, about every seven years, in a consultation. The ninth and latest consultation took place at Chennai (India) in December 2015. A continuation committee, elected by each consultation, has the task of preparing the next consultation, in close cooperation with the staff of the Faith and Order Commission. The fact that Faith and Order has continued this support for decades, despite major staff

1 See www.oikoumene.org/en/church-families/united-and-uniting-churches [accessed 26 April 2018].

reductions, reflects the significance it ascribes to church unification from the perspective of the goals of the ecumenical movement.

Some of the United and Uniting Churches, like those in Germany, have chosen not to participate in any of the 'traditional' Christian world communions. Others, like the Church of North India, are members of three or more such communions. A Christian world communion that includes more than half of the United and Uniting Churches is the World Communion of Reformed Churches (WCRC). In addition, several of the United and Uniting Churches do share the Reformed heritage without being part of the WCRC. This high level of participation of Reformed denominations in unification processes is understandable if we consider that Calvin himself emphasised the need to accommodate church polity to 'the varying circumstances of each age and nation'.[2] This has deeply influenced the Reformed ethos regarding ecclesial institutions. In principle, they are temporal in character and flexible. This is expressed in a well-known Reformed rallying cry: *ecclesia reformata semper reformanda secundum verbum Dei.*

The word order in the title 'United and Uniting Churches' has been chosen deliberately. First, it embraces churches that have completed a unification process in a form of 'organic union',[3] and churches involved in such processes are also welcome to share their experiences. Second, the word order seeks to express that a unification process is never completed. After having reached full organic union, United Churches still need to deepen their concept of unity in practical church life; in that sense, they continue to be uniting. Third, it is a matter of experience that such churches often get involved in new unification processes. To express this, some of these churches – for instance in Australia, South Africa, and Sweden – have chosen the name 'Uniting Church [X]' at the occasion of their unification.

Most characteristic of the church family of United and Uniting Churches is its diversity. Some churches, particularly in Germany, have been united since the early nineteenth century due to the political situation at that time. In 1817, the Prussian king Friedrich Wilhelm III saw the third centenary of the Reformation as an appropriate occasion to bring churches of the Lutheran and Reformed traditions together into what is known as 'the Old-Prussian Union'. In the twentieth century, quite a few church unifications were a consequence of decolonisation; for instance, in Southern Asia and Africa the division of churches along traditional European lines (Anglican, Baptist, Congregationalist, Methodist, and Reformed) was seen as no longer relevant in light of the huge responsibility of the churches to participate in the building of a

2 J. Calvin, *Institutes of the Christian Religion* (1559), trans. Henry Beveridge (Peabody, MA: Hendrickson Publishers, 2008) IV.V.30.

3 See L. Newbigin, 'Union, Organic', in N. Lossky, J.M. Bonino, T.F. Stransky, G. Wainwright and P. Webb, eds., *Dictionary of the Ecumenical Movement* (Geneva and Grand Rapids: WCC Publications, 1991) 1028–1030.

new nation. Recently, the *Leuenberg Agreement* (1973),[4] which bridged the doctrinal division between Pre-Reformation, Lutheran, Reformed, and (later) Methodist churches, facilitated several unifications in Europe (e.g. Netherlands, France).

Diversity is also a characteristic of United and Uniting Churches with respect to their systems of church polity. Many of them have a Reformed/Presbyterian system of church government, with either a presbyterial-synodical or a congregationalist structure. However, some United and Uniting Churches – for instance in India and Pakistan – have included an Anglican denomination in their unification, and so they maintain episcopal elements in their church order. But they are exceptions: it is evidently difficult for episcopal churches that maintain the historical episcopate to unite with non-episcopal churches.[5]

II Principles and processes

As a result, it may be understood that the United and Uniting Churches do not represent an ecclesial 'tradition' in the 'traditional' sense. They do not have sources and forms of church polity that can be clearly distinguished from that of other ecclesial traditions. They do not necessarily have similar views or procedures regarding the role of church law. They do not necessarily share among themselves the same foundations and reasons for the law, nor do they all use the idea of a principle of church law.

What binds these churches together is that all the churches in this family, which have gone through (or are at the moment going through) a process of church unification, were challenged to find such common principles of church law *in the unification process itself.* Precisely which issues are on the agenda in this respect depends on the partner churches involved in the negotiations. In the search for organic unity, differences in church polity must be bridged, and this necessarily puts important questions about church law on the agenda for negotiation. It is only natural that churches primarily insist on those aspects of church polity that seem to be indispensable from the perspective of their own history and identity, and those aspects will often be characterised as 'principles'. In the process of negotiation, it must become clear what exactly makes such issues so fundamental, which in fact means that discussions will take place at a deeper theological level in order to find some sort of agreement.

Two examples may illustrate this. After three decades of negotiations, the (united) Church of South India was inaugurated in 1947; it was the first among the United and Uniting Churches that brought together an Anglican Church with other episcopal churches – i.e. a Methodist Church – and churches from the

4 See www.ekd.de/en/Leuenberg-Agreement-304.htm.

5 See, for more information on the united and uniting churches, M. Kinnamon, 'United and Uniting Churches', in Lossky et al., *Dictionary*, op cit., 1032–1036.

Reformed tradition (both Presbyterians and Congregationalists). Of course, the issue of 'bishops' became key to the process:

> This plan brought together the local Anglican church and some non-episcopal churches in one episcopal church, but without calling into question the authenticity of the previously exercised ministry of the non-episcopal churches and without demanding re-ordination.[6]

The historical episcopate is what connects Anglicans with, for instance, Roman Catholics and Scandinavian Lutherans. Giving up the office of bishops would mean that the Anglican tradition might also lose its bridging position between Catholicism and Protestantism. The solution was that the South Indian Anglicans accepted the existing offices in the other churches, and that from the outset new priests in the United Church of South India were ordained by bishops. Acceptance of the existing offices in the other churches was only possible from the perspective of the existence of *episkopè* as a vital function in the church, irrespective of the name of the offices. The church is a member of the Anglican Communion.

Comparing the way in which the Church of South India dealt with episcopal office with the *Statement of Principles of Christian Law*, it is telling that there is no mention of bishops or the episcopal order in the *Statement*. It is only touched upon in the principle that '[o]versight is an essential of church order' (Principle III.4.1). 'Oversight' is connected to (if not synonymous with) *episkopé*, a key topic in ecumenical ecclesiology.[7] In maintaining the episcopal office, the Church of South India not only accepted the need for *episkopè* as a common principle but also went a step beyond this principle.

Another example concerns the United Reformed Church, a church in the United Kingdom that is the result of three unifications, in 1972, 1981, and 2000, respectively. The 1981 unification was particularly challenging, as the church that had resulted earlier from a union between the Congregational Church in England and Wales and the Presbyterian Church of England was enriched with the entry of the Reformed Association of Churches of Christ, a church that did not recognise infant baptism. Meanwhile, some Congregationalists were not baptised at all because only faith was seen to be necessary. Susan Durber speaks of a growing ecumenical consensus in Britain in the 1970s 'that infant and believer's baptism could be held together if the two groups could give a serious account of both the sacramental action of God and the importance of the response of faith'. Although Baptists 'could not include themselves because of a continuing scepticism about the sacramental theology of baptism' – Baptists did, however, join the (united) Church of North India in 1970 – the Churches of Christ could 'since they, whilst being believer Baptist, also held a highly sacramental understanding

6 D.N. Power, 'Episcopacy', in Lossky et al., *Dictionary*, op cit., 359–361, at 359.

7 See *The Church – Towards a Common Vision*, Faith and Order Paper 214 (Geneva: WCC, 2013) par. 52f.

of baptism'.[8] The Basis of Union of the United Reformed Church, one of its legal texts, refers to baptism as both God's action and requiring a response of faith. Also key is that baptism is an act of the church, and that what the church does it can only do once; anything that might be interpreted as 're-baptism' is not allowed. The Basis of Union also covers 'conscientious scruples by both ministers and candidates, but ministerial scruples were not to prevent baptism taking place in the candidate's local congregation'.[9]

If we compare this agreement with the *Statement of Principles of Christian Law* regarding baptism, we immediately recognise some principles as pertinent to the unification process described earlier; namely, baptism is divinely instituted, baptism constitutes incorporation of a person into the Church of Christ, and baptism cannot be repeated (Principles VII.1.1, 3, and 10). However, in fully recognising infant baptism and believer's baptism, the United Reformed Church has found agreement beyond the principle that baptism in a church may be of infants or adults to the extent prescribed by its law (Principle VII.1.6).

III Case study: the Protestant Church in the Netherlands

Unification processes such as those dealt with previously clarify the role of common principles of law in church union negotiations. This can further be illustrated in a case study of the birth history of the Protestant Church in the Netherlands (PCN). Several church order issues that had been regarded as 'matters of principle' for the churches involved were resolved during the union negotiations. In fact, some of the 'principles of Christian law' were discovered in the process itself, whilst others seemed to be less relevant and in some cases a common principle with a higher degree of concreteness was formulated.

The PCN was born on 1 May 2004 as the fruit of a merger of three churches after a process that took about four decades.[10] Two of the churches, both belonging to the Reformed tradition, were reunited. This concerned the two major Reformed denominations in the Calvinistic tradition in the Netherlands, the Netherlands Reformed Church (NRC) and the Reformed Churches in the Netherlands (RCN). In the nineteenth century, two consecutive splits from the NRC, in 1834 and 1886, had resulted in two separate church communities. These two groups united in 1892 into the RCN. From 1990, the unification process also included the Evangelical Lutheran Church in the Kingdom of the Netherlands

8 S. Durber, 'Baptism, Unity and the United Reformed Church', 62.1 *Ecumenical Review* (2010) 4–13 at 7 and 8.

9 D.M. Thompson, 'The Freedom of the Spirit: The United Reformed Church in the United Kingdom', in A. Plaisier and L.J. Koffeman, eds., *The Protestant Church in the Netherlands: Church Unity in the 21st Century. Stories and Reflections,* Church Polity and Ecumenism – Global Perspectives IV (Zürich: LIT Verlag, 2014) 77–89 at 84.

10 See L.J. Koffeman, 'How the Protestant Church in the Netherlands was Born', in Plaisier and Koffeman, *The Protestant Church*, op cit., 11–37.

(ELC), a small church in terms of membership numbers but, of course, representing a different and internationally important branch of Protestantism. So, the process of *re*-unification also became a process of unification.

1 The declaration of consensus

In 1986, a few years before the entry of the ELC into the unification process, a joint meeting of the synods of NRC and RCN agreed on a declaration of intent along with a declaration of consensus. The conclusion was quite clear: there were no theological reasons for continuing to go separate ways. Shortly after that, the ELC joined the process. Its synod gave a positive reaction to both documents, without going into details. The ecclesiological points of reference for the shaping of the PCN appear in these documents.

The purpose of the declaration of consensus was to lay the foundations that would facilitate a reunion of the NRC and RCN. Its main thrust was to raise and confirm the awareness that the common confessional roots of the two churches contained a common obligation, as formulated in an 'agreement shown' document. The final part, on 'shared questions', reflected on five issues that, from an historical perspective, made the differences between the NRC and the RCN particularly clear. Each of them had a certain impact in terms of church polity. These questions continue to be important for both churches and can never be completely resolved. The declaration attempted above all to analyse the questions and to clarify the strengths and weaknesses of the answers that had been given in the two churches over a period of about a century – in theology, but even more in church practice. The renewal of the church could manifest itself in joint answers to these questions, however provisional they needed to be.

The five issues addressed in the declaration of consensus are: (1) church discipline, (2) plurality, (3) church membership of non-baptized people, (4) the relationship between the local congregations and the denomination, and (5) the public statements of the church. Each has its roots in history. In 1816, the first king of the Netherlands, Willem I, imposed a new church order – the General Regulations – on the NRC, the former state church and, until 1848, the established church in the Netherlands. The idea was to strengthen the national character and unity of the church and so strengthen the nation itself. In practice, it meant that the church was supposed to include and represent 'the Dutch people' and to be the national church and, thus, a 'people's church' (*volkskerk*); Roman Catholics, although about half of the population, were not regarded as true patriots! Under the General Regulations, however, the church itself had no power to deal with doctrinal discipline, and its administration was closely connected to the civil government. This changed after the 'liberal revolution' of 1848, which led to a stricter separation of church and state, although many of its members would still see the NRC as the national church (cf. Principle X.1.3(1)). Still, for more than a century the church itself was unable to replace the General Regulations with a new church order due to internal tensions. This only succeeded after the

Second World War, in 1951, and was stimulated by experiences of the need to speak out against the Nazi regime.

The splits from the NRC, in 1834 and 1886, that resulted in the birth of the RCN were directly caused by resistance against these 'liberal' characteristics of the NRC in the nineteenth century. The ideal of those who formed the RCN was a strictly Reformed confessional body consisting of 'local churches' that were to a great extent uniform in doctrine and practice. This common conviction was key to the whole concept. Christians with a strong awareness of the contents of 'Scripture and Confession' were to form the heart of the local church. They would also participate in several newly founded Reformed organisations – such as school associations, a political party, a trade union – in order to influence life in society to the best of their capacities (cf. Principle X.3.2). The RCN itself would not deal with political issues in any way.

What follows deals in more depth with the five issues addressed in the declaration of consensus. In each case, after a brief historical background, there is a discussion of how these issues were expressed in the church order of NRC and RCN around 1986. Next, I indicate how the churches have found legal common ground, in terms of church law, in the relevant provisions of the 2004 Church Order of the Protestant Church in the Netherlands. Then connexions are made with the *Principles of Christian Law*.

2 Church discipline

The declaration of consensus is quite clear in its view of doctrinal discipline in the church: '[w]hat the RCN has pursued too vigorously – unity in confession – was not looked after sufficiently in the NRC'. Whereas the members of the RCN had to deal with the consequences of their radical approach, the NRC had been too non-committal. However, the 1951 church order of the NRC had reintroduced doctrinal discipline. The NRC Constitution stated: '[i]n accordance with the nature of their vocation, the offices, assemblies, organs and services [of the church] . . . are bound to move forward on the [basis] of the church's confession' (Art. X.4); '[t]herefore, for the sake of the right implementation of the mandate of its office-bearers . . . the church is called to exercise oversight, according to the standard of the Word of God, over its members, and particularly over the proclamation, catechesis and the training and education of the servants of the Word [i.e. the ministers]' (Art. X.5); '[t]he church averts that which contradicts its confession' (Art. X.6).

In the NRC ordinances (bylaws), this was elaborated in regulations that were designed to guarantee a very careful process in matters of doctrinal discipline. The purpose was to avert 'what might impair the foundations of the church in that it excludes obedience to Holy Scripture and disrupts the communion with the confession of the fathers' (Ordinance 11–14–1, cf. Ordinance 11–15 and 11–16). If there are reasons to assume that this is the case, it is the regional assembly (*provinciale kerkvergadering*) that is to commence an investigation through its visitation committee. If 'fraternal discussion and pastoral exhortation' have no effect on the minister concerned, it is up to the regional assembly to decide whether a next step should be taken. If it so decides, the regional assembly is to invite the minister for another conversation, together with five members of the national committee for church and theology. The latter writes a report with advice on how to proceed. If necessary, the minister will again be invited for an exchange of views. If the regional assembly concludes that the minister's teaching might indeed 'impair the foundations of the church', it shares this view with the general synod of the church. The minister is again given the opportunity to defend himself in writing and in the meeting of the general synod. If the general synod confirms the view of the regional assembly, it gives the minister a period of six to nine months to reconsider their position before they can finally be removed from office. It is telling that this procedure was never applied in its entirety during the five decades these regulations were in force. As a result, no minister or professor of theology had been removed from office for reasons of doctrinal discipline.

In turn, the rules in force in the former RCN may be traced back to the Dort church order (considered earlier in Chapter 8) adopted by the general synod of the Dutch Reformed Church in Dordrecht (1619), which was applied in most provinces of the Netherlands during the seventeenth and eighteenth centuries, until king Willem I replaced it with his General Regulations. A central aspect of the RCN church order was the obligation for all office-bearers of the church to 'show consent to the confession of the church' by way of signing a form prescribed by the general synod (cf. Art. 26). On this basis, doctrinal discipline was possible.

If office-bearers acted in contradiction to their consent to the confession of the church or made themselves guilty of gross neglect or abuse of their office, or in another way deviated from sound doctrine or godly conduct, they would be suspended in performing their office or removed from it immediately (Art. 116).

Since the birth of the RCN in 1892, several ministers and professors of theology have been removed from office according to these rules, which has led to two major splits from the church, in 1926 and 1944. The second of these, which took place during the darkest years of the Nazi occupation, was so traumatic that, after the Second World War, the church became very reluctant to apply doctrinal discipline at all, although a few elements of such procedures were used in the 1970s.

The view of the declaration of consensus – that 'what the RCN has pursued too vigorously . . . was not looked after sufficiently in the NRC' – formed the basis for the way the church order of the PCN dealt with doctrinal discipline. Because the church order itself was not regarded as the problem in the NRC, but rather the way it functioned, the rules of the NRC were basically maintained, whereas the RCN obligation on officer-holders to indicate their consent to the confession of the church (by signing a form) was abolished. However, assent to the doctrine of the church – as part of the liturgical act of installation of an office-bearer to a particular office – was maintained. As is the case in the NRC, ordination candidates must sign a pledge to accept church doctrine.

Article I-11 of the PCN constitution provides: '[t]he church averts that which contradicts its confession'; and Article XII-1 deals with oversight: '[o]versight, grounded in the compassion of Jesus Christ, takes place to the glory of God, to preserve the congregation and to save those who err'. Oversight has different aspects, from mutual care in the congregation to visitation, pastoral dialogue, and admonition. Doctrinal discipline is an instrument of last resort:

> With a view to the right administration of Word and sacraments, the church exercises oversight of proclamation and catechetical instruction, as well as the education and training of ministers. . . . If necessary, the church shall proceed to apply the means entailed in ecclesiastical discipline, according to the rules laid down by ordinance.
>
> (Art. XII, 6 and 7)

The relevant rules are found in PCN Ordinance 10, Articles 13–15. These rules reflect well some of the *Principles of Christian Law* and in fact corroborate the value it has. To mention some: '[a] church as an institution has the right to enforce discipline and to resolve conflicts amongst the faithful' (Principle V.1.1); '[t]he purpose of discipline is to glorify God, to protect the integrity and mission of the church, to safeguard the vulnerable from harm, and to promote the spiritual benefit of its members' (Principle V.1.4); '[d]iscipline is exercised by competent authority in accordance with law' (Principle V.1.5); '[a] church has a right to enforce its own doctrinal standards and discipline' (Principle VI.3.1); '[o]rdination candidates and others may be required to subscribe, assent or otherwise affirm their belief in or loyalty to the doctrine of their church' (Principle VI.3.3); '[a]ny person who offends church doctrine may be subject to disciplinary process' (Principle VI.3.5). Only time will tell what doctrinal discipline might mean in an ever more pluriform church. In any event, the PCN clearly considers that 'a church has the right to determine the limits of permissible theological opinion, and to interpret its own doctrine and doctrinal standards' (Principle VI.3.6).

3 *Plurality*

Different theological opinions can be permissible, albeit within certain limits. This brings us to the second issue dealt with in the declaration of consensus – plurality. The declaration states that in both churches a large diversity exists in a wide range of areas of life and faith, such as spirituality, political commitment, interpretation of Scripture, and theological views. It emphasises that the unity of the church is not based on such matters, but only on the means of grace: the communion of the Word of God and the sacraments. In this communion, differences must be put in their proper perspective: the Lord who binds us together is stronger than what divides us. An important question here relates to the territorial system of establishing congregations: is it acceptable to build congregations on the basis of criteria other than the fact that a number of people live in the same area?

The church order of the RCN made no exception at all regarding the territorial system. The same was the case in the original NRC church order in 1951. But that NCR church order was later amended, and it became possible, although under strict conditions, to form a new congregation based on minority views in a certain territorial area next to an existing congregation or to become a member of a preferred neighbouring congregation. This tendency was accepted and strengthened in the process of drafting a church order for the PCN and, after 2004, in several changes made in this church order. Plurality is taken as a fact of church life. Members of the church can easily move to another congregation within or outside the area where they live. The territorial system only functions as a kind of bottom line.

This recognition of plurality is expressed in a rule that cannot be found in the church order of either the NRC or the RCN, but it is part of the church order of the PCN: '[i]n implementing its mandate, the general synod does justice to the diversity that exists within the church' (Ordinance 4–25–1). A similar rule concerns the role of the regional bodies, the 'classical assemblies' (cf. Ordinance 4–15–1). However, the *Principles of Christian Law* seems not to deal with the issue of plurality. It might be useful, therefore, to try formulating additional principles on this. Yet plurality seems implicit in the principle 'A church has a distinct membership, or other body of persons associated with it, which may be organised *in territorial or non-territorial* units such as provinces, districts, or congregations' (Principle I.1.3, emphasis added).

4 *'Members by birth'*

Membership issues played an important role in the negotiations about unification. The different concepts behind the regulations of NRC and RCN, respectively, had a strong impact on the relevant rules in the respective churches. As a *volkskerk*, the NRC intended to include as many people as possible. This was expressed in the constitution of the NRC in the following provision:

> To a Reformed congregation, assembled around Word and sacraments, and, therefore, to the Netherlands Reformed Church, brought under its oversight and bound to service to each other and to the world, belong, in virtue of the covenant of grace: those, who have become confessing members of the church through public confession of faith, those whose incorporation in the communion of the church has been validated by Holy Baptism, *and those who were born from Reformed parents.*
>
> (Art. II-1, emphasis added)

The words in italics imply that non-baptized children (and their children) were registered as so-called 'members by birth'. For the RCN this was in complete opposition to its tradition of connecting church membership with a clear decision: only 'confessing members' and their baptised children could be members of the church. This was so self-evident that it was not even stipulated in the RCN church order. If someone moved from one place to another, they would ask the local church for a certificate about their confessional standing to be given to the church council of the new domicile. It was only in the technical bylaws about membership registration that the issue of membership was dealt with. Non-baptized children could be co-registered with their parents but in no way as members of the church.

In this case, too, the declaration of consensus sought to bridge the gap by referring to the intent behind the regulations. What about the responsibility of the churches for the non-baptized? The line between pastoral responsibility and evangelisation becomes less clear. However, registration as a member only makes sense if some kind of contact is possible. Part of the problem is the decreasing potential of many of the congregations in a time of secularisation, which implies that the possibilities to maintain personal contacts beyond worship services have diminished.

On this basis, the differences in the rules of the respective churches could be reconciled in the church order of the PCN. As a result, its Article III opens with a basic principle: '[b]y the grace of God and in virtue of his covenant congregations are assembled around Word and sacraments' (Art. III-1). The subsequent paragraphs connect membership with baptism:

> To a congregation – and thus to the Protestant Church in the Netherlands – belong those whose incorporation in the fellowship of the Church has been confirmed by holy baptism and who as such have been registered as members of the congregation. . . . Those who receive baptism are called to public profession of Jesus Christ and to responsibility in the congregation.
>
> (Art. III-2 and 3)

But that is not the whole story: '[m]indful of the faithfulness of the God of the covenant, a congregation includes in its community the non-baptized children of congregation members as well as those who show solidarity with the congregation' (Art. III-1). On this basis a new category comes into play: 'those who show solidarity with the congregation', also known as 'friends'. It recognises the fact that an increasing number of people are interested in local church life without taking any steps towards formal membership. They may have been baptised once somewhere. In many cases they are not, but they do participate in church services or other activities. If they want, they can be registered in a separate registration to make continuing contact with the congregation easier.

In these stipulations we can easily recognise the value of some of the *Principles of Christian Law*. There should be no doubt about the significance of baptism for church membership, not, primarily, in administrative terms but from a theological perspective: '[b]aptism constitutes incorporation of a person into the Church of Christ' (Principle VII.1.3). Yet more needs to be said, as the section on 'Church Membership and Others Forms of Belonging' rightly shows (Principles II.2). Of course, '[a] church is made up of those incorporated into it in accordance with its proper laws and customs' (Principle II.2.1); but, moreover, '[a] church should serve, in appropriate ways, all who seek its ministry regardless of membership' (Principle II.2.2). However, the next principle might cause misunderstandings:

> Membership in a church, for the purposes of participation in its government, may be based on any or all of: baptism; baptism and confirmation or other mature demonstration of faith; and such other conditions as may be prescribed by law.
>
> (Principle II.2.3)

It may not be clear if these 'other conditions' should be understood as additional or alternative conditions. For instance, does this principle leave room for 'friends' to be acknowledged as members and to have voting rights within a congregation? To the extent that the principle is cast in permissive terms – with its inclusion of the word 'may' – and on the basis that it envisages membership in accordance with 'other conditions prescribed by law', the principle would seem to do so. In other words, this is a matter for the interpretation of the principle in the nuanced and particular circumstances of the PCN church order itself.

5 The relationship between the local congregations and the denomination

Law, including church law, is also about the division of powers. Within the wider Reformed tradition this has always been a hot issue. Congregationalists emphasise the autonomy of the local congregation. In the Netherlands, the NRC and the RCN always rejected congregationalism; they both opted for the presbyterial-synodical system, which tries to balance the powers of local congregations and supra-local assemblies. For centuries, the ELC organised itself basically along the same lines. Unlike, for instance, the Scandinavian Lutheran churches, it has never had an episcopal system, although the position of the chair of the ELC synod (which has been maintained within the PCN) has some episcopal characteristics – for example all ordinations of ministers are executed by the synod chair.

As far as the NRC and RCN are concerned, nineteenth-century history has sharpened the issue of the relationship between the local congregations and the denomination. King Willem I's intervention led to a top-down system of government in the NRC. By way of contrast, the RCN deliberately called itself the 'Reformed Church*es* in the Netherlands': each local congregation is a full-grown church. Once more, it adopted the old Dort church order. This church order contains the 'golden rule' of Reformed church polity (stemming from the Synod of Emden 1571); namely, the anti-hierarchical principle: '[n]o church shall lord it over other churches, no minister over other ministers, no elder or deacon over other elders or deacons' (Art. 84). This rule was also part of the RCN church order, though in slightly different wording:

> (1) In implementing their mandate, the office-bearers will hold themselves aloof from lording over each other, and they will lead everything towards

> submission under the Lordship of the only Lord, Christ. (2) The same applies to one church towards the others.
>
> (Art. 136)

The RCN developed the Dort church order in the direction of a stronger emphasis on local autonomy. Dort had already stipulated: '[m]ajor assemblies [i.e. regional and national assemblies] will deal only with those matters which could not be concluded in the minor assemblies or which concern its churches in common' (Art. 30). The RCN church order was more precise in this respect:

> Apart from matters which concern its churches in common, major assemblies will deal only with those matters which could not be concluded in the minor assemblies and which, therefore, are raised by these minor assemblies by way of a question, an instruction, an objection or in any other way, as well with matters in which a member of a local church or a minor assembly has appealed to it.
>
> (Art. 30)

Whereas Dort could be interpreted as unclear about who could take the initiative to raise a subject in a major assembly, the RCN church order leaves this exclusively to the minor assemblies. However, the clause about 'matters which concern its churches in common' seems to leave some room for the exercise of discretion by the major assembly. During the twentieth century, and particularly during the flourishing period between 1950 and 1975, many new 'common' initiatives were taken at the national level: mission and evangelism, pastoral care for specific groups (the military, prisons, the deaf, etc.), education, and many other services developed rapidly. In the early 1970s, the National Service Centre had hundreds of employees.

With the acceptance of the 1951 church order, developments in the NRC went in the opposite direction. It included some of the old Dort stipulations with slightly different wording. The 'golden rule' was formulated like this: '[s]o that no congregation shall lord it over the others, no office over the others, and no office-bearer over the others, the government of the church is executed in assemblies in which the offices convene' (Art. V-1). Dort was also recognisable in this rule: '[m]ajor assemblies will deal only with those matters which could not be concluded in the minor assemblies or which according to the order of the church belong to the work of the major assemblies' (Art. V.3). However, the functions of the regional assemblies and most of all the general synod, as elaborated in the ordinances, had a wide scope: '[i]t is in particular the task of the general synod to give leadership . . . to life and work of the church in its different fields of work and to take up whatever can further the life of the church' (Ordinance 1–11–1). The NRC also developed a large national staff.

The declaration of consensus speaks of the one-sidedness of both churches in this respect. However, the NRC has always been aware that the national church exists in its congregations. At the same time, the RCN has learnt that modern times require a clear overarching organisation. The whole and the parts need each other continuously. This should provide a basis for discontinuing the separate existences of both churches.

The issue of the relationship between the local congregations and the denomination caused severe tensions within both the NRC and the RCN in the final phase of the unification process. It was clear from the outset that not everybody would stay within the united church, an unfortunate experience shared with most of the 'organic unions' all over the world. The ELC joined without further divisions. The situation in the NRC was very different from that in the RCN. In the NRC, congregations had no option to leave the NRC as legal entities: in terms of civil law the NRC was one church, and congregations constituted its institutional parts. In the RCN, according to its status under civil law as a 'body in which churches are united', each local church council could decide that the congregation would leave the denomination, taking local church properties with them. Within the RCN eight out of about 850 congregations used their civil legal right to opt out; provisionally they constituted the 'Continued Reformed Churches in the Netherlands'; nevertheless, within a year, one of them joined the Protestant Church in the Netherlands. In the NRC, altogether about 60,000 members (out of some 1.5 million) decided to leave the church, most of them in groups, thus splitting local congregations. In quite a few cases civil law procedures were invoked to claim church properties. The transitory regulations in church law included a procedure for this kind of situation. National committees of the Protestant Church in the Netherlands – so-called committees of special care – had been installed to try and maintain communication as much as possible with those opposing the unification. The mandate of these committees included the authority to transfer church properties to those leaving the church in cases in which that would be necessary to start a separate community. In view of these regulations, civil courts rejected all the claims, urging those involved to deal with these committees first before suing the church in civil courts.[11] Under civil law, the relationship between the local congregations and the denomination in the PCN was the same as that which had applied to the NRC.[12]

The PCN church order includes the 'golden rule' in a clause that combines elements of the NRC and the RCN church order:

> So that one office shall not lord it over another, one office-bearer over another, or one congregation over another, but so that all things shall be

11 Article 2:2 of the Civil Code says: '(1) Religious communities and their independent subdivisions and bodies in which they are united, have legal personality. (2) They are governed by their own charter insofar the rules thereof are not in conflict with law' (cf. Principle IX.1.2). This implies that, in cases like this, civil courts will in principle only apply a marginal check. If church law is applicable, its rules should be applied first.

12 In terms of Art. 2:2 of the Civil Code, NRC and PCN congregations were regarded as 'independent subdivisions of a religious community', whereas RCN congregations were regarded as 'religious communities' and its synod as a 'body in which they are united'.

> aimed at obedience to Christ the Head of the Church, the leadership in the church is entrusted to ecclesial assemblies.
>
> (Art. VI-1)

It also states: '[t]he major assemblies will deal only with those matters which according to the order of the church belong to the work of the major assemblies, or with those which cannot be concluded in the minor assemblies' (Art. VI-11). But two developments are important in this respect. In the last decades of the twentieth century and, even more so, in the first decades of this century, the financial strength of the churches decreased in accordance with a decline in church membership. This had a direct impact on the size and capacity of the Protestant National Service Centre (in which the three churches had brought together their staff in 1998, six years before the official unification). More had to be left to the congregations. At the same time, diversity within the church grew, in all respects. New forms of congregational life – like 'missionary congregations' – developed and were facilitated in additional church order regulations. Additional rules were adopted regarding forms of cooperation between congregations; the election of local office-bearers; the shape, size, and frequency of meetings of the local church councils; and so on. A new worship book and a new hymn book were adopted, each including a large variety of liturgical orders and songs; traditional orthodox congregations can find what is to their liking as well as more evangelical, charismatic, liberal, or ecumenical congregations. In practice this means that the possibilities for local congregations to find their own way of worshipping and of organising themselves nowadays are larger than they have ever been in both the NRC and the RCN.

How does this relate to the *Principles of Christian Law*? Clearly, this set of principles cannot take an unambiguous position about a top-down, or rather a bottom-up, structure of a church. Both options must be accommodated. This is clear in the following wording: '[r]egional ecclesial units may be *divided into or constituted by* local churches or congregations existing at the most localised level of church life' (Principle IV.5.1, emphasis added). A similar balance can be found in the same paragraph:

> A local church, its assembly and other institutions, such as a council, meeting, session or other body, has such authority and functions as are *lawfully inherent to it or conferred upon it* by the institutions of the wider ecclesial entity to which it belongs.
>
> (Principle IV.5.1, emphasis added)

Finally, the balance is expressed in these words: '[a]ll ecclesial units at each level are interdependent' (IV.5.5). However, it would be worth considering more fully whether the 'golden rule' could be adopted as another principle of Christian law, beyond the principle that 'Christ is the ultimate head of the Church universal in all its manifestations' (Principle IV.1.1).

6 The public statements of the church

The fifth and final question dealt with in the declaration of consensus regards the role of the church in its relation to the state. For decades after its birth in 1892, the RCN had kept political and social issues out of the agenda of its general synod: '[t]he church assemblies will only deal with ecclesial matters' (Art. 29). This rule was also already part of the Dort church order: '[i]n the church assemblies only ecclesial matters will be dealt with, and so in an ecclesial manner' (Art. 30). In the RCN, it was up to the members of the church, cooperating in the relevant Reformed political party, trade union, or other association, to deal with such issues. During the extraordinary circumstances brought about by the Second World War, the general synod saw itself forced to express its concerns about the consequences of Nazi rule, but afterwards, until the 1960s, this division of responsibilities between the church and Christian associations worked quite well. Then, the unity of the RCN constituency in such issues started to fall apart.

Under the General Regulations, the NRC general synod was not supposed to deal with political and social issues. As mentioned previously, the Second World War also made a difference in this respect for the NRC: it had to speak out against the malicious measures of the Nazi regime regarding the Jewish population. The NRC church order of 1951 explicitly saw it as a task for the church to deal with hot political issues in public statements. The view of this church as the 'national church' still played a role in the background: '[t]he church, by virtue of its mandate addressing the government and the people with the appeal to order life according to God's promises and commandments, does so, if specific circumstances urge it, through its official assemblies, and so either by addressing the government and the people directly, or by means of a pulpit message or a pastoral letter' (Ordinance 4–19–1). On several occasions the general synod used this option – for instance in the 1970s and early 1980s – with regard to apartheid in South Africa[13] and nuclear armament.[14]

The issue of apartheid and that of nuclear armament were also urgent within the RCN. So, sometimes the general synod issued statements that went beyond its church order mandate, at least from the perspective of a substantial number of its adherents. For about eight years the synod discussed the need to change the church order so as to provide greater clarity. As a result, in 1989 a new clause was included in the church order:

> (1) The churches will participate in conversation about important problems of human society, and they will stimulate and support this conversation with the means available to it. (2) In particular cases, the churches will address the government and the people with their testimony.
>
> (Art. 130)

13 See E. Meijers, 'White Brothers-Black Strangers: Dutch Calvinist Churches and Apartheid in South-Africa', 38.4 *Exchange* (2009) 365–380.

14 See P.P. Everts, 'The Churches and Attitudes on Nuclear Weapons: The Case of the Netherlands', 15.3 *Bulletin of Peace Proposals* (1984) 227–242.

The declaration of consensus reflects this situation; due to changes in society, both churches have in fact developed similar views regarding public statements of the church. The constitution of the PCN includes a relevant provision in its foundational Article I:

> In its celebrations, words and actions the church continually confesses Jesus Christ as the Lord and Saviour of the world and thus calls for renewal of life in culture, society and state. Before people, powers, and governments, the church bears witness to God's promises and commandments, and in doing so it seeks a dialogue with other churches.
>
> (Art. I-6)

This rule is elaborated in the PCN ordinance about the confession of the church: the church promotes opinion-building with regard to social issues, and it may express its views or present a testimony on such issues (cf. Ordinance 1–3).

The *Principles of Christian Law* also deals with these matters in the section of 'Church-State Relations': 'a church should cooperate with the State in matters of common concern, but each is independent in its own sphere' (Principle X.1.1); '[t]he faithful may participate in politics save to the extent prohibited by church law' (Principle X.1.2); '[a] church should promote social justice' (Principle X.3.1); and '[t]he faithful should promote social justice and charitable work as regulated by their church' (Principle X.3.2). However, some questions must be asked in this context. As far as the church itself is concerned, are terms such as 'cooperation', 'independence', and 'promotion' sufficient? Could the 'prophetic role' of the church also be included in the *Principles*? Furthermore, regarding church members, is it imaginable that a church limits the participation of its officers in politics by, for instance, forbidding ministers to stand for a seat in Parliament? Could a church also prohibit participation of its common members in politics? Could it, for instance, forbid membership in a specific political party?

Conclusion

This case study of the Netherlands is illustrative of the way United and Uniting Churches have dealt with basic church polity issues. How does this contribute to the concept of the *Principles of Christian Law*?

First, the narratives from the Church of South India, the United Reformed Church, and the Protestant Church in the Netherlands show that theological ideas (which were of importance in bridging the gap between the churches participating in unification processes) can often be recognised in the *Principles of Christian Law*. However, in some difficult issues – for example those relating to the episcopal office and the relation between infant baptism and believer's baptism – such churches have found a consensus that goes beyond what the *Principles of Christian Law* is able to express.

Second, the *Principles of Christian Law* is based on empirical observation and comparison of existing church orders. In unification processes these (and often many more) common principles can be assessed, but this is only a start. The next step will always be normative in nature: which theological principles are decisive behind the still existing differences, and how can they be bridged theologically? Common theological statements pave the way for common legal principles to be included in a new church order.

Third, the *Principles of Christian Law*, as presented by the Panel of Experts, if supported and recognised in the ecumenical world, can help churches take steps forward in unification processes. It can help to overcome and relativise many so-called principled dividing issues. It can stimulate and deepen ecclesiological reflection. But it needs to relate to the fruits of ecumenical ecclesiological dialogue, as, for instance, presented by Faith and Order in *The Church – Towards a Common Vision*.

Conclusion

Grand Ecclesiarch Aetios (Dimitrios Nikiforos)

The 2016 *Statement of Principles of Christian Law*: A Landmark in the History of the Ecumenical Movement and a Pivotal Stepping-Stone to Christian Unity

> '*Our diversity in practice confirms our unity in faith.*'
>
> Irenaeus of Lyons, 'Letter to Victor', in Eusebius, *Ecclesiastical History*, 5.24.13

This famous sentence of Iranaeus,[1] the leader of the Christian community in Gaul towards the end of the second century, shows that the history of the Christian movement is not a triumphant march of unity and homogeneity through the centuries, one that was shattered at a certain point by divisions and schisms. On the contrary, from the very beginning, ecclesiastical history is marked by the struggle of the church to maintain unity in faith through diversity[2] – diversity in worship, liturgical texts, rites, calendars, fasting periods, regulatory instruments.

From the early centuries, each Christian community developed, out of Scripture and the Apostolic tradition, initially, its own customary,[3] and later – through the first local councils – written church law, applicable to the regional level. The ecumenical councils brought a consolidation and unification of these variant canonical traditions.[4] But still local and regional ecclesiastical

1 For Irenaeus of Lyons see J. Behr, *Irenaeus of Lyons: Identifying Christianity* (Oxford: Oxford University Press, 2013). The author notes (p. 2) that the one undivided '"Great Church" was catholic not because it was a universal monolithic institution, but because it embraced diversity'.

2 See D.T. Irvin and S.W. Sunquist, *History of the World Christian Movement,* Vol. 1 (Maryknoll, NY: Orbis Books, 2001) vii: '[t]he Christian movement is one that has continuously diversified itself through its expansion, all the while claiming to remain the same'.

3 See P. L'Huillier, *The Church of the Ancient Councils: The Disciplinary Work of the First Four Ecumenical Councils* (Crestwood, NY: St Vladimir's Seminary Press, 1996) 1, who talks about 'the existing customary law with its local variants'.

4 See S. Wessel, 'The Formation of Ecclesiastical Law in the Early Church', in W. Hartmann and K. Pennington, eds., *The History of Byzantine and Eastern Canon Law to 1500* (Washington, DC: The Catholic University of America Press, 2012) 1–23, at 2: 'the early documents pertaining to ecclesiastical law were mainly contained in letters and tractates whose purpose was to shape the particular communities to which their principles of church organization and norms of moral conduct and behavior were addressed'.

legislation survived, as, for example, the 2nd Canon of the Council in Trullo[5] shows in the case of the canon made by Cyprian of Carthage[6] 'and the council under him'.[7] This latter canon was 'confirmed' by Trullo Canon 2,[8] but with the qualification that it would 'remain in force only in the regions'[9] of Northern Africa.[10]

Similarly, in modern church law,[11] even within each Christian community, unity has never been understood as synonymous with uniformity.[12] Take the example of the Roman Catholic Church.[13] The 1983 Roman Catholic *Code of Canon Law* (CIC) in Canon 1 makes it absolutely clear that '[t]he canons of this Code regard only the Latin Church',[14] whilst the 1990 *Code of Canons for the Eastern Churches* (CCEO) explicitly states in Canon 1 that '[t]he canons of this Code affect all and

5 The Council in Trullo (or Quinisext Council), which took its name from the domed hall (Trullos) of the imperial place in Constantinople where it was convened by Emperor Justinian II in 691/2, adopted 102 canons with the goal to reorder church life, creatively re-formulating the Byzantine canonical tradition. See, for this council and its importance for ecumenism, G. Nedungatt, SJ, 'The Council in Trullo Revisited: Ecumenism and the Canon of the Councils', 71 *Theological Studies* (2010) 651–676.

6 For Cyprian of Carthage and the canon by 'the council under him' (255) see H. Ohme, 'Sources of the Greek Canon Law to the Quinisext Council (691/2): Councils and Church Fathers', in W. Hartmann and K. Pennington, eds., *The History of Byzantine and Eastern Canon Law to 1500* (Washington, DC: The Catholic University of America Press, 2012) 24–114, at 112–114.

7 Trullo Canon 2: '*καὶ τῆς κατ' αὐτὸν συνόδου*'.

8 For Trullo Canon 2 as a 'confirmation' canon of the Byzantine *corpus canonum*, see D.F. Wagschal, *The Nature of Law and Legality in the Byzantine Canonical Collections 381–883* – Durham theses (Durham University, 2010) 106–107.

9 Trullo Canon 2: '*ὃς ἐν τοῖς τῶν προειρημένων προέδρων τόποις, καὶ μόνον, . . . ἐκράτησε*'.

10 For the regionally restricted force of this canon see P. Menevisoglou, *Ἱστορικὴ εἰσαγωγὴ εἰς τοὺς κανόνας τῆς Ὀρθοδόξου Ἐκκλησίας* [*An Historical Introduction to the Canons of the Orthodox Church*] (Stockholm: Holy Metropolis of Sweden and all Scandinavia, 1990) 627.

11 For the notion 'modern church law' see N. Doe, 'Modern Church Law', in J. Witte, Jr., and F.S. Alexander, eds., *Christianity and Law: An Introduction* (Cambridge: Cambridge University Press, 2008) 271–291, at 271, who calls its study 'ecclesionomology' and defines it as 'the exploration of the internal laws and other regulatory instruments of Christian churches (as distinct from state laws on religion)'.

12 See Baroness Hale of Richmond, 'Secular Judges and Christian Law', 17 *Ecclesiastical Law Journal* (2015) 170–181, at 178: 'no branch of Christianity has a single document which governs everyone and everything everywhere'.

13 See J.D. Faris, 'An Overview of the Code of Canons of the Eastern Churches', in J.P. Beal, J.A. Coriden and T. Green, eds., *New Commentary on the Code of Canon Law* (New York, NY/Mahwah, NJ: Paulist Press, 2000) 27–44, at 27: '[i]t is not possible to retain an inaccurate conception of the Catholic Church as a monolithic, Latin entity, governed by a single body of legislation. To do so is to ignore a significant number of Christian faithful who take pride in their bonds of full communion with the See of Rome'.

14 See J.M. Huels, OSM, 'Introductory Canons', in J.P. Beal, J.A. Coriden and T. Green, eds., *New Commentary on the Code of Canon Law*, op cit., 49–55, at 49, who mentions that 'this initial canon sets forth the fundamental rule that this code pertains only to the Latin church *sui iuris*', without binding 'the members of the Eastern Catholic Churches, notwithstanding some canons that allude to them'.

solely the Eastern Catholic Churches, unless with regard to relations with the Latin Church, it is expressly stated otherwise'.[15] Of course, both the CIC and the CCEO are integral parts of the one *Corpus Iuris Canonici* of the Roman Catholic Church, but still 'there are areas of the codes that differ more significantly and contain norms that are unique to one or the other of the codes'.[16] In an analogous fashion, in contemporary Orthodox Christianity, the common core Byzantine corpus of the ancient canons remains intact, but each local autocephalous ('self-governed') church has also introduced various other regulatory instruments, such as its own church order constitution, statutes, guidelines, and new canonical precedents; and, in addition, an elaborate system of state ecclesiastical legislation applies to some of these churches.[17] Likewise, each of the 44 member churches of the Anglican Communion is autonomous and free to govern itself in accordance with its own legal system, without any mandatory body of Anglican global law and with no institution in the Communion competent to make juridical decisions binding on individual churches.[18]

However, the greatest confirmation of Christian unity in juridical diversity, or – if you prefer – of juridical diversity in Christian unity, is the 2016 *Statement of Principles of Christian Law* since it proves beyond any doubt that out of ten distinct global Christian legal traditions – Catholic (Roman and Eastern), Orthodox (Eastern and Oriental), Anglican, Lutheran, Methodist, Presbyterian, Reformed, Congregational, United, and Baptist – shared general propositions expressing fundamental ecclesial values common to all of them can be induced through comparison between the modern church law of these traditions. The outcome of this comparison is in full agreement with the perception of these church regulatory instruments as 'expressions of the eternal in the temporal. The temporal is the "how", the mode of application',[19] of the absolute truth about the order of church life that these regulatory instruments express. The mode of application differs from Christian tradition to Christian tradition because it conforms to the historical existence of each one of them. The 'eternal' is the essence of the church, the absolute truth of faith that finds its application in these regulatory instruments. The truth of faith is shared by all these Christian traditions because

15 See R. Metz, 'Preliminary Canons (cc. 1–6)', in G. Nedungatt, SJ, ed., *A Guide to the Eastern Code: A Commentary on the Code of Canons of the Eastern Churches* (Rome: Pontificio Instituto Orientale, 2002) 67–80, at 68–73, according to whom (p. 68), 'In the Catholic communion the Latin Church is the only Church under the category of *Western*; and it is governed by CIC. The other twenty-one Churches fall under the broad category of *Eastern* and are governed by CCEO'.

16 J. Abbass, 'CCEO and CIC in Comparison', in G. Nedungatt, SJ, ed., *A Guide to the Eastern Code: A Commentary on the Code of Canons of the Eastern Churches*, op cit., 847–896, at 848.

17 See D. Wagschal, 'Orthodox Canon Law: The Byzantine Experience', in A. Casiday, ed., *The Orthodox Christian World* (Abingdon: Routledge Press, 2012) 383–397, at 390.

18 N. Doe, *Canon Law in the Anglican Communion: A Worldwide Perspective* (Oxford: Clarendon Press, 1998) 339–342.

19 N.N. Afanasiev, 'The Canons of the Church: Changeable or Unchangeable?', 11 *St Vladimir's Seminary Quarterly* (1967) 54–68, at 62.

it has its source in Scripture.[20] For this reason, it explains the profound similarities between the regulatory instruments of these churches and justifies the existence of common juridical maxims across these ten Christian legal traditions.

These common maxims are contained in the 2016 *Statement of Principles of Christian Law*. Each of the words in the title of this document has not been randomly selected, but is the fruit of careful thought and reflects this text's nature, methodology, and purpose. The word 'Statement' reveals the truly ecumenical nature of this project. The names of other textual juridical categories could be used – which are more closely associated with the various regulatory instruments of the churches – such as 'Code', 'Constitution', 'Charter', 'Statute', 'Book', or 'Manual'. Nevertheless, the characterisation of this document as 'Statement' not only makes a direct connotation to the ecumenical movement, since 'common statements' are the cornerstones upon which the whole textual architecture of this movement has been erected, but also seals the fruitful (informal but substantial) partnership between the World Council of Churches' (WCC) Faith and Order Commission and the Christian Law Panel of Experts, who produced the *Statement* because the 'common statement' is the 'classic multilateral "convergence" genre of the WCC Faith and Order Commission'.[21]

The 2016 *Statement* is paradigmatic on how ecumenical conversation can be transacted through a text that is to be owned by more than one Christian tradition. In the preceding chapters of this volume, each of the contributors reflects not only on how their own tradition is not locked out of the *Statement* but also, on the contrary, on how through this document they can rediscover their own tradition and engage in the building of Christian unity without abandoning their existing identities, histories, and categories of ecclesial self-understanding.

This precious achievement was accomplished mainly through the methodology employed for the drafting of the *Statement*. The third word of the title of the *Statement*, 'Principles', offers illuminating hints about its method of production. Looking at the etymology of the world 'principle' – which comes from the Latin words *princeps* (first, chief) and *principium* (source, plural *principia*, foundations) – legal 'principles' are the origins, the beginnings, or fundamental standards of general applicability 'with a dimension of weight'[22] that 'reflect[s] and express[es a] legal system's underlying values or traditions'.[23] To reach these underlying values and origins of Christian jurisprudence, the members of the

20 See N. Doe, 'The Ecumenical Value of Comparative Church Law: Towards the Category of Christian Law', 17 *Ecclesiastical Law Journal* (2015) 135–169, 168: 'juridical unity is often based on the practice of churches to use a common source in shaping their laws (chiefly that of Holy Scripture)'.

21 D. Wagschal, 'The Common Statement Called into Question', 2 *Ecclesiology* (2005) 53–70, at 54–55.

22 R.M. Dworkin, 'Is Law a System of Rules?', in R.M. Dworkin, ed., *The Philosophy of Law* (Oxford: Clarendon Press, 1977) 38–65, at 38.

23 R. Cotterrell, *The Politics of Jurisprudence: A Critical Introduction to Legal Philosophy* (London: Butterworth & Co Publishers, 1989) 170.

Panel went back to the historical texts and formularies of Christianity. The contemporary regulatory instruments of the ten traditions were compared within a web of textual references or contexts,[24] which each of the Panel's members brought to the table, comprising the essential framework for each church's ecumenical interactions.[25] Through their mutual exposure and introduction to each other's juridical tradition as coherent wholes, the Panel was able to move to a more organically conceived rapprochement by developing a global compass of shared foundational maxims on church ministry and governance, doctrine and discipline, worship and ritual, property and finance, inter-church and church-state relations, based on a common frame of inter-textual connexions and references. This methodology could be called 'ecumenical maximalism'[26] because the Panel members were not encouraged to set aside their traditional expressions of faith to distil common principles; quite the opposite, the agreed shared foundational maxims were the product of sincere dialogue among the ten juridical traditions and were compared in voices that were as authentic as possible.

Even a quick look at these foundational maxims, these common principles, leads to the conclusion that they have the appearance of laws since they may be preceptive, prohibitive, or permissive in form.[27] Nevertheless, they are not themselves laws. The ingenuity of this whole project lies precisely in the selection of the concept of 'principles' to clothe these propositions. As was shown in the first chapter of this volume, the employment of 'principles' or 'maxims' has been constant in church law across the various Christian traditions from the very beginning.[28] This is an additional reason for these ten traditions to feel at home with the 2016 *Statement*: it does not appear as a competing regulatory document to their fundamental juridical instruments, one that poses the threat of replacing them. On the contrary, using the very familiar concept of 'principles', this text acts as the foundation of an overarching *ius commune ecclesialis*,[29] of polity and order, which then finds its particular expression within each of these traditions.[30]

24 N. Doe, *Christian Law: Contemporary Principles* (Cambridge: Cambridge University Press, 2013) 7: 'it is axiomatic that context is critical to understand law'.

25 See M. Hill and N. Doe, 'Principles of Christian Law', 19 *Ecclesiastical Law Journal* (2017) 138–155, at 139: '[e]ach Christian tradition contributes through its regulatory instruments to this store of principles'.

26 See this term in Wagschal, 'The Common Statement', op cit., 69.

27 See N. Doe, 'The Principles of Canon Law: A Focus of Legal Unity in Anglican – Roman Catholic Relations', 5 *Ecclesiastical Law Journal* (1999) 221–240, at 224: 'a rule is directed to a specific matter, it is prescriptive – preceptive, prohibitive or permissive'.

28 See also N. Doe and S. Pulleyn, 'The Durability of Maxims of Canon Law: From *Regulae Iuris* to Canonical Principles', in T.L. Harris, ed., *Studies in Canon Law and Common Law in Honor of R. H. Helmholz* (Berkeley, CA: Robbins Collection Publications, 2015) 303–336.

29 For the *ius commune* as source of canon law see R.H. Helmholz, *The Spirit of Classical Canon Law* (Athens, GA and London: The University of Georgia Press, 1996) 22–24, 28–31.

30 See N. Doe, 'The Common Law of the Anglican Communion', 32 *Ecclesiastical Law Journal* (2003) 4–16, at 9–10: '[t]he collective effect of similarities between individual legal systems and the shared principles which emerge from them, is the *ius commune*'.

Despite the fact that these common principles are not laws, still, as is clearly stated in the 2016 *Statement*'s title, they are 'principles of Christian law'. With this document, the category 'Christian law', which was considered non-existent until recently, is factually established as both a theological and juridical notion. The selection of the adjective 'Christian' – over the more obvious choices 'canon' or 'church' – as an attribute of the noun 'law' successfully serves the ecumenical orientation of this text. This is so not merely because only a few of the ten traditions compared ascribe the title 'canon law' to their regulatory instruments,[31] whilst others use titles such as 'church order' or 'church polity', but also because the phrase 'church [or ecclesiastical] law' implies mainly civil legislation that regulates church affairs.[32] What is even more important about the category of 'Christian law' is that it also encapsulates within itself the methodology followed by the Panel in drafting the *Statement*: the contemporary juridical instruments were compared within the broader context of the foundational theological texts and formularies of Christian civilisation.[33]

If the adjective 'Christian' underlines the theological dimension of the 2016 *Statement*, the noun 'law' highlights the juridical character of this text. Law has been called the 'missing link' in the ecumenical movement,[34] which has been doctrine-focussed thus far, even though the term 'law' is explicitly employed by all Christian traditions to generically describe their regulatory instruments.[35] The absence of Christian law from ecumenism can be explained through the belief – one that is widespread[36] – that the various regulatory instruments are 'borders' that define the 'limits'[37] of each church, erecting juridical walls that distinguish those within each Christian community from those outside of it. Nevertheless, the very existence of such a significant number of common principles of Christian law challenges this popular conception of church law as divisive because it shows that the various Christian legal traditions actually converge in their goals, and the means of executing these goals, in fulfilment of their mission to society at large.

31 Basically, the Roman Catholic, Orthodox, and Anglican traditions.

32 See, for example, in the Eastern Orthodox tradition, P. Rodopoulos, *An Overview of Orthodox Canon Law*, W.J. Lillie, trans. (Rollinsford, NH: Orthodox Research Institute, 2007) 21: 'Canon Law is different from Ecclesiastical Law, by which is understood the sum total of the laws passed by the Church and the State, through which the life of the Church is generally ordered'; and 22: 'State Ecclesiastical Law . . . is based on the State law concerning the Church'.

33 For this perception of 'Christian Law' see J.A. McGuckin, *The Ascent of Christian Law* (Yonkers, NY: St Vladimir's Seminary Press, 2012) 11–14.

34 See M. Reuver, *Faith and Law: Juridical Perspectives for the Ecumenical Movement* (Geneva: WCC, 2000) 5.

35 See N. Doe, *Christian Law*, op cit., 5.

36 See B.F. Griffin, 'The Challenge of Ecumenism for Canonists', 55 *Canon Law Society of America Proceedings* (1993) 17–38.

37 See G. Florovsky, 'The Limits of the Church', in B. Gallaher and P. Ladouceur, eds., *The Patristic Witness of Georges Florovsky – Essential Theological Writings* (London: T & T Clark, 2019) 247–256, at 256.

The 2016 *Statement*, without claiming to be the exclusive self-contained whole of the Christian tradition, nevertheless serves as a map to the tradition, an integral part of that tradition, and as the common fertile ground for the fruitful advancement of the ecumenical dialogue through a stable methodology.

This methodology is 'juridical ecumenism',[38] or juridical ecumenical maximalism, because these shared legal maxims, these common juridical principles, cultivate the understanding that the remarkable degree of similarities between the compared Christian regulatory traditions, without downplaying the doctrinal differences that divide them, links Christians in common action based on their common norms of conduct. Very much like *The Principles of Canon Law Common to the Churches of the Anglican Communion* (2008),[39] which functions as one of the 'bonds of affection' that hold together the 44 member churches of the Anglican Communion,[40] the *Statement of Principles of Christian Law* (2016) constitutes an instrument of church unity that contributes to Christian identity and cohesion.

In this spirit, in his keynote address at the 24th International Congress of the Society for the Law of the Eastern Churches (Rome, 16 September 2019), His All Holiness, Ecumenical Patriarch Bartholomew of Constantinople, who occupies the First Throne of the worldwide Eastern Orthodox Church, a canonist by training and founding member of the Society, characterised the 2016 *Statement* 'a means of unity and collaboration between Christians of different traditions, designed to fill the historical juridical deficit in the ecumenical enterprise'.[41] Moreover, in his address to the delegation of the Church of Rome on the occasion of the Thronal Feast of the Ecumenical Patriarchate (Feast of St Andrew the Apostle, Istanbul, 30 November 2019), the Patriarch highlighted that juridical ecumenism serves 'as a theoretical and practical framework to complement our long-ago established dialogue of truth and love, our commitment to always "speak the truth in love" ' (Eph. 4:15).[42]

38 See the definition of this term in N. Doe, 'Juridical Ecumenism', 14 *Ecclesiastical Law Journal* (2012) 195–234, at 234: 'the study and practical deployment of laws and other regulatory instruments on ecumenism'.

39 Anglican Communion Legal Advisers Network, *The Principles of Canon Law Common to the Churches of the Anglican Communion* (London: The Anglican Communion Office, 2008).

40 See N. Doe, 'The Instruments of Unity and Communion in Global Anglicanism', in I.S. Markham, J.B. Hawkins IV, J. Terry and L. Nuñez Steffensen, eds., *The Wiley-Blackwell Companion to the Anglican Communion* (Chichester: John Wiley & Sons, Ltd, 2013) 47–66.

41 Ecumenical Patriarch Bartholomew, 'The Society for the Law of the Eastern Churches 50 Years Later and the Ecumenical Movement – Keynote Address (Rome, *Pontifical Oriental Institute*, September 16, 2019)': www.scribd.com/document/426106379/HAH-Keynote-Address-15-09-2019-24th-Congress-of-the-Society-of-the-Law-of-the-Eastern-Churches [accessed 17 February 2020].

42 Ecumenical Patriarch Bartholomew, 'Address to the Delegation of the Church of Rome on the Occasion of the Thronal Feast of the Ecumenical Patriarchate (Phanar, 30 November 2019)' www.christianunity.va/content/unitacristiani/en/dialoghi/sezione-orientale/chiese-ortodosse-di-tradizione-bizantina/relazioni-bilaterali/patriarcato-ecumenico/altri-documenti-ed-eventi/2019-address-of-patriarch-bartholomew-on-feast-of-st-andrew.html [accessed 17 February 2020].

At a private audience at the Apostolic Palace with the members of the Society for the Law of the Eastern Churches (Vatican City, 19 September 2019), His Holiness Pope Francis of Rome, head of the Roman Catholic Church, concurred with the position of the Ecumenical Patriarch, proclaiming for the first time in papal history that 'canon law is not only an aid to the ecumenical dialogue, but also an essential dimension'.[43] He also underlined that the current theological dialogue between the Roman Catholic and the Eastern Orthodox Church has 'a canonical dimension too, since ecclesiology finds expression in the institutions and the law of the Churches',[44] on the basis of their common canonical heritage.

Since church law/order/polity receives Christian theological truth about the nature and structure of the church, and it then particularises it in its various regulatory instruments,[45] it is understood as 'applied ecclesiology'.[46] Today, through the previously mentioned inspiring words of the two visionary primates, each Christian tradition is invited to consider its ecclesiology in light of juridical ecumenism.[47] This volume serves as an apt response to this invitation. It penegyrically seals the conclusion of the first phase of the work of the Panel of Experts, whose achievement is the drafting of the 2016 *Statement of Principles of Christian Law*, and it symbolically marks the promising beginning of the second phase of the work of the Panel, whose main aspect will be the reception of the *Statement*.

Reception should be sought both at the inter-Christian level and at the domestic level of each church. At the inter-Christian level, the facilitation of the discussion ideally will take place under the auspices of the WCC, especially in the context of its 2022 assembly meeting in Karlsruhe (Germany), through the careful planning not only of the examination of the *Statement*'s compatibility with the Christian traditions represented in and beyond the WCC[48] but also of the possibility for the future adoption of the *Statement* by the WCC.

However, it is equally important that action be taken by the members of the Panel at the domestic level of each of the compared ten Christian legal traditions, with the official submission of the 2016 *Statement* to the governing bodies of

43 Pope Francis, 'Address to Participants in the Conference Promoted by the Society for the Law of the Eastern Churches (Clementine Hall, Thursday, 19 September 2019)' www.vatican.va/content/francesco/en/speeches/2019/september/documents/papa-francesco_20190919_diritto-chieseorientali.html [accessed 17 February 2020].

44 Ibid.

45 See M. Hill QC, 'Legal Theology', 32 *Journal of Law and Religion* (2017) 59–63, at 60.

46 See N. Doe, 'The Category "Legal Theology" and the Study of Christian Laws', 32 *Journal of Law and Religion* (2017) 64–70, at 65.

47 See R. Ombres, 'Ecclesiology, Ecumenism and Canon Law', in N. Doe, M. Hill, and R. Ombres, eds., *English Canon Law: Essays in Honor of Bishop Eric Kemp* (Cardiff: University of Wales Press, 1998) 48–59, at 49: 'assuming that the law of the church is the application of its ecclesiology, then the resulting canon law will be affected by considering ecclesiology in the light of ecumenism'.

48 See, for example, from the perspective of the Religious Society of Friends (Friends Church), F. Crammer, 'The Statement of Principles of Christian Law: A Quaker Perspective', 20 *Ecclesiastical Law Journal* (2018) 290–304.

these churches for testing, deliberation, and, finally, reception, at least as an auxiliary source of their internal regulatory system. The *Statement* could be a powerful aid both for the advancement of the bilateral theological dialogues between the various churches – as emphasised by Pope Francis and Ecumenical Patriarch Bartholomew – since the mutual recognition of the regulatory instruments of each tradition is often a prerequisite for full ecclesial communion,[49] and for the further development of interfaith relations, especially between Judaism, Christianity, and Islam, through the drafting of a similar statement of principles of religious law common to the Abrahamic faith traditions.[50] Moreover, the *Statement* could inspire renewal of the internal legislation of each Christian legal tradition, either in the form of amendments that would reflect the convergence of – currently divergent – regulatory instruments of the churches or in the form of new legislation in implementation of certain principles from the *Statement*, or even in the articulation of common principles within a particular tradition.[51]

In any event, as it is assessed and celebrated in this volume, the *Statement of Principles of Christian Law* (2016) stands out as a monumental document of the ecumenical movement and as a decisive step in the quest for Christian unity. Without destroying the legitimate juridical diversity among the various churches, it transcends the mere habit of separation, learnt from centuries of being out of communion, highlighting the common rule of faith as an authentic expression of the shared Christian identity.

49 See, for example, paragraph 16 of the 2007 *Ravenna Agreed Statement* between the Roman Catholic Church and the Eastern Orthodox Church: 'Ecclesial Communion, Conciliarity, and Authority: The Ravenna Document', in J. Chryssavgis, ed., *Primacy in the Church: The Office of the Primate and the Authority of Councils*, Vol. 1 (Yonkers, NY: St Vladimir's Seminary Press, 2016) 405–420, at 411: 'in order for there to be full ecclesial communion, there must be, between our Churches, reciprocal recognition of canonical legislations in their legitimate diversities'.

50 See, for example, 'A Statement of Principles of Religious Law Common to Judaism, Christianity and Islam', in N. Doe, *Comparative Religious Law: Judaism, Christianity, Islam* (Cambridge: Cambridge University Press, 2018) 398–408.

51 See, for example, N. Doe, 'The Contribution of Common Principles of Canon Law to Ecclesial Communion in Anglicanism', 8 *International Journal for the Study of the Christian Unity* (2008) 93–111.

Appendix I
Faith and Order Commission and church law

Leo J. Koffeman

In Chapter 1 of this book, Norman Doe refers in outline to the discussion in the Faith and Order Commission of the World Council of Churches, in the 1970s, on the role of church law in the ecumenical enterprise. Unfortunately, the discussion led to the conclusion that too little resources were available to transform it into a successful study project for the global ecumenical movement. What follows takes a closer look at that discussion in order to give more background and context to the present project on the principles of Christian law. To what extent was that which was intended in the 1970s different from the scope of the present project? And what can we learn from that earlier discussion? Pivotal to an understanding of the position of the Faith and Order Commission is the outline for further study as presented to the commission meeting in Accra (1974) in the document entitled *The Ecumenical Movement and Church Law*.[1] This outline was accepted, which means that it indeed reflected the intentions of the Faith and Order Commission. It was four years later – in Bangalore in 1978 – that the director of Faith and Order had to report that not much progress had been made and that the limited resources available would not justify any expectations for the future of this project. Because of the content and importance of the Accra document, it is published here again in full (section A). Next, in section B, I will present some important steps in the history that led to this document, followed by a few observations regarding some relevant developments after Accra. I intend to conclude with some evaluative comments.

A Accra 1974

THE ECUMENICAL MOVEMENT AND CHURCH LAW

I Why Church law is becoming an ecumenical problem

The ecumenical movement is striving for "the visible unity of the Church in the one eucharistic fellowship". Inevitably, sooner or later, this effort will raise issues

1 'The Ecumenical Movement and Church Law', in G. Gassmann, ed., *Documentary History of Faith and Order 1963–1993* (Geneva: WCC, 1993) 283–288. See https://archive.org/details/wccfops2.166.

of church law. The churches differ in their order and their constitution. But so far not much attention has been paid to this aspect of the search for unity.

On the whole, the ecumenical discussion on the unity of the Church has concentrated on issues of doctrine and worship as the most obvious causes for the division of the Church. With the advance of the ecumenical movement, the debate will need to include more and more constitutional and legal issues. Wherever churches consider concrete stops on the way towards the unity of the Church, they face, inevitably the question as to how their different orders can be brought closer to one another. Therefore, if the churches are to go beyond the present state of their divisions, the ecumenical movement needs to provide them with some help in dealing with the legal issues arising from their mutual encounter.

At this stage we cannot visualize the structure of legal organization of the one Church, which is the ultimate goal of the ecumenical movement. But in working towards that goal, we are faced by intermediate problems of a legal nature in the life of the various churches. When trying to solve these problems, the separate churches should be aware of their commitment to the ecumenical cause and try to work out solutions which will further or at least not hinder the process of convergence towards unity which has already started.

In order to achieve this, the ecumenical movement and especially its Commission on Faith and Order needs to make a conscious effort to help member churches in this particular field by engaging in a serious study of the legal aspects of inter-church cooperation and eventual church union. For even if the ultimate goal may still seem very distant, there are at present several features in the progress of the ecumenical movement which make it urgent to take up these kinds of questions within the framework of the Faith and Order Commission. Several factors point in that direction:

1 The growing ecumenical fellowship among the churches has made practically inoperative certain statements or rules in the various churches, e.g. condemnations, rules against contact with heretics, etc. This raises the question of the continuing validity of these statements and rules.
2 Ecumenical fellowship has led to new structures and regulations not foreseen in the traditional legal system of the different churches, e.g. representative systems which did not exist before, new financial arrangements, etc. Some churches have put explicit references in their constitution to the ecumenical movement or their membership in the World Council of Churches, National Councils or other ecumenical bodies.
3 Agreements reached in ecumenical dialogue call for juridical implementation. They may imply changes in the constitutions of the churches, e.g. references to confessions of faith, etc., or changes in the discipline of the churches, e.g. rules concerning ordination, intercelebration, intercommunion, etc.
4 When dialogue leads to closer collaboration, often new ecumenical structures come into being. What is their juridical significance? Can the competence of decision which a church has be transferred to such "para-constitutional" bodies?

5 Implementation of ecumenical agreements and common action of the churches at the international level require freedom of decision and action on the part of the individual churches. How far have the churches – especially churches in close relationship with a state – the freedom to decide as a church and to dispose of its resources in order to give priority to solidarity with the rest of the churches?

Against the background of such considerations, it is recommended that the Faith and Order Commission undertake a study of issues of church law with the aim of identifying and clarifying differences and to provide a forum where concerted action can be worked out.

II The underlying issues

To raise the question of the ecumenical significance of church law is to call attention to a whole range of underlying issues which must be kept in mind. Whatever its theological position, confessional allegiance, or institutional past, every Christian community has some concrete social and legal form. It has both an inner structure of its own and occupies a "social space" acknowledged by the larger society. In some way, every Christian community relates both its internal legal structure and its external legal form to its understanding of the Gospel. The way these elements are related differs from one situation to the next. So does the way in which churches conceive of these relationships.

These considerations point to what one might quite simply call the concrete presence of God's people in history. No Christian body, whether institutionally or anti-institutionally oriented, can avoid it. To own property, to receive and pay out money, to gather as a voluntary society, to have both an internal and an external legal form. It is in fact the vehicle for worship, witness and service. It is the structure in and through which a church responds, or fails to respond, to the ecumenical challenge. Thus the practical and theological importance of "church law in the ecumenical perspective" can hardly be overstated.

Many differences in the structures and legal systems of the churches have their roots in different confessional traditions. In order to reach a full understanding of the differences, the different confessional approaches need to be analysed and adequately described. In fact, it can be argued that the confessional heritage persists most powerfully in the different ways in which the churches are constituted and perpetuate the inherited order. The differences concern not only the actual order which the churches have, but also the general orientation by which their legislation is inspired. A very careful analysis is required in this respect. No exhaustive list of the different approaches can be given here, but the importance and the weight of the confessional differences need to be underlined. There are differences even as to the role attached to law as such in the life of the Church. While the Roman Catholic Church tends to understand the Church as an institution which can be described in juridical terms, Lutheran and many Free Churches are inclined to visualize the Church as "spiritual institution" and to deal with the juridical questions at a non-theological level. While some churches have a tendency to present their legal tradition in a systematic way, others feel that the nature of the church law is betrayed by a systematic approach. They hold the view that church law must constantly arise out of the sacramental fellowship. They reject the idea of a constitution of the Church.

Obviously the question of the law of the Church and its setting in the law of the civil community is inseparable from a full panoply of cultural and sociological considerations. To focus attention on legal structures is a way of making the inquiry tangible and pointed. Law and precedent can be studied in church canons, constitutions and by-laws as well as in the record of their practical application. The same is true of civil customs and codes. Their relation to society and culture is itself an open question. Even more so the question of the underlying essence of law. But laws and their application inside and outside the church do have a practical bearing on how a church understands itself and how it behaves.

Of special importance is the interaction between the church's own legal structures and its civil setting. We must ask how the legal situations of the churches affect their relations to each other and, more concretely, how each particular style of interaction affects the possibilities for cooperation in the wider ecumenical community. Many examples can be given. What does financial support from the state imply? Does it simply assure the salary of clergy or also preclude the use of funds for purposes outside the nation concerned? To what extent does the Church's status as one voluntary society among others enhance freedom and limit influence? What does it mean for the ecumenical commitment of a church if it does not possess the full right of assembly and association? What role do Church institutions play (schools, hospitals, etc.)? To what extent should churches be free to receive or reject financial help from abroad?

A basic dilemma arises when Church leaders and public authorities have different views of what church structures are for. In the eyes of the state, the Church may have legal standing because it is good for public morale. Under some circumstances, the Church may be happy to play this role, even if its own perspective on the role is different. At other times, a church may find itself in opposition to an officially-backed state religion. Or the Church may play a socially affirmative role in one respect and a prophetically critical role in another. A nation's past traditions, embodied in the Church's legal position, may be invoked against public policies being followed in the present. Each legal pattern, each structure of internal church organization, offers a range of possibilities while excluding others. Each makes possible certain kinds of ecumenical participation while inhibiting others. Societies the world over are changing rapidly. So are the roles open to churches within them. While on the one hand, new opportunities may arise, on the other hand, functions so far fulfilled may disappear. There is, for instance, a distinct possibility, especially in the Western world, that the position of voluntary associations will gradually be weakened as public administration and mass communication become more centralized and as social services become nationalized. Electronic information storage and retrieval limits personal privacy and places the affairs of voluntary associations under surveillance. Increasing religious pluralism undermines any claim the Church may have for special treatment. Institutions of every kind, governmental as well as churchly, inspire less confidence.

In such a fluid situation, we urgently need to study the range of possibilities open to the Church in different circumstances and different parts of the world. A comparative study, or typology, of existing and emerging forms of the Church in legal perspective would help us. The relation of such structures to theological self-understanding, their practical strengths and weaknesses, their kinds of responsiveness to ecumenical responsibility, could all be considered. Four fundamental questions might well underlie such a comparative survey.

1 How do the different churches conceive the relation between the notion of the people of God theologically considered and that people of God juridically embodied? Is this a question of the relation of church law to civil law, a question of the foundations of law as such, a matter of grace and law related or grace and law opposed? Or must the issue be formulated in some other way?
2 How do the different churches understand the content, style and functioning of their internal legal systems? How is the law applied? What role does ecumenical commitment play in these codes, written and unwritten, now? What issues are at stake as the different churches reconsider and reformulate their canons, constitutions, bylaws and guidelines?
3 Have the churches any common convictions about the sorts of relation to the civil community which best make for faithfulness to the Gospel and ecumenical responsibility to each other? Is there a trend towards "disestablishment" or is the tendency now the opposite? Is there any agreement about what "establishment" and "disestablishment" mean? Do the churches advocate the notion of the "secular state"? Do they agree what this means?
4 What do the churches see as the critical issues affecting their integrity and identity in modern societies? Do they feel that circumstances tend to force a certain identity upon them? Do they feel free to redefine and reexpress their identity as insight and circumstances demand? Are they able, in concrete terms, to affirm an ecumenical identity? How?

III The implications of the ecumenical movement for the legal systems of the Churches

The ecumenical movement has led to the recognition of partial communion already existing among the churches. The churches do not exist any more in isolation from the others. They recognize that the Holy Spirit has been at work in other churches. Much of their legislation does not reflect this recognition however. Each church needs, therefore, to examine itself to what extent the progress of the ecumenical movement calls for changes and revisions in its legal systems.

1 Though the ultimate goal of the ecumenical movement may still be in a distant future, each church should make clear its commitment to it. This may mean that it needs to give clear public expression to its intention to work

towards this goal. This implies the willingness to adopt results reached in ecumenical discussions.

2 The ecumenical movement has led to first and partial results. Some churches have united. Some churches have found bilateral agreements which have juridical implications. Such achievements should be examined and taken into account by all churches. All achievements in the ecumenical movement have consequences for all churches.

3 Many structures of ecumenical collaboration have been created in the course of the last decades. Does church law take sufficient account of them?

4 While the ultimate goal cannot be described in full detail, there are steps imposing themselves at this stage of the ecumenical movement. Each church must ask itself whether the partial insight already gained has found expression in its constitution and legal rules.

   i Rules governing the relations with Christians of other churches (mixed marriages, common worship, etc.).

   ii Role of the whole people of God in the decision-making processes of the Church.

   iii Freedom of action which is required if the churches are to participate effectively in the universal fellowship of all churches (church-state relations, synodical structures, etc.).

   iv Each church faces the question of representation. Who speaks for the church in dialogue and ecumenical assemblies? Who is entitled to take decisions?

IV The next step

It is not enough simply to state the problem. Steps must be taken to focus the attention of the churches upon it. This will not be easy. There may be in the churches, as in other institutions, a tendency to accept uncritically the prevailing juridical forms, and to resist change. Certainly the question is rarely asked whether the internal laws of a particular church, or the public or civil laws of the state in which it operates, contribute to, or hinder the progress of the ecumenical movement at the national or international level.

How can we encourage the churches to open these questions? We believe that the essential first step must be to devise a method by which individual churches can make a judgement, each upon its own situation. To pave the way for comparative studies, it is necessary for each to ask whether its legal framework is sufficiently flexible to allow the people of God to discharge their responsibilities fully in worship, witness and service not only denominationally but also ecumenically. Is a church free to act in cooperation and partnership – and, if it so desires, to go forward to organic unity – with other churches? A church must be encouraged to seek the answers to these questions by looking closely at the rules which govern its internal life – how far do these match up to the challenge of its ecumenical commitments? For example, if a church is to be represented in ecumenical bodies, does its existing constitution or juridical rules allow it to give sufficient authority to those who represent it in such bodies? In many cases there will be need to examine closely the particular relation which a church has to the state. In some cases a close relationship may be found to be of advantage to the particular church and in some measure also to the whole ecumenical cause. But in other cases a church may find itself possessed of constitutional, economic or other privileges, conferred or protected by the state, which in themselves either weaken its ability to reach out in mission and service to the wider community, or which are incompatible with the development of ecumenical cooperation. There may be in the particular juridical forms which the church has adopted – or in some parts of them – features which create obstacles to ecumenical cooperation and to the achievement of organic unity.

In opening these questions for study, the aim is not to establish everywhere a uniform juridical pattern. There are wide divergences now and we must expect wide divergences so far ahead as we can see. But no situation is static, and we believe that an increased awareness of the juridical issues may help in changing the circumstances towards a gradual convergence to exercise a prophetic ministry and to be able to respond fully to the claims of its ecumenical commitment both in the particular society and internationally. Putting the same point in another way, any church which makes changes either in its internal rules or in its public legal framework should always in future take ecumenical considerations fully into account.

Who is to suggest the method by which the churches can apply themselves to this task? We recommend that the Faith and Order Commission should establish a small committee to undertake the task. This should include theologians, legal, administrative and sociological experts with experience of different types of situations. Their first task would be to produce a working paper, which would include a series of questions to be put to the churches. We envisage that the working paper would then be circulated to member churches.

We think, however, that initially only certain selected member churches should be asked to respond. This would, in effect, constitute a pilot study. The answers from this pilot group would then be considered by the supervisory committee, giving an opportunity to check the effectiveness of the method, and allowing for modification of the questions before the churches generally were asked to participate.

It is suggested that the pilot group should include a range of situational types. Thus, taking first churches which are members of the World Council of Churches, we think that the initial list should include examples as follows:

1 A West European established national church, with the Free Churches of that country.
2 An East European Protestant church.
3 Some examples of Orthodox churches, including an East European case.

4 A range of Third World examples, illustrating:

 i situations where Christianity is predominant,
 ii situations where Christianity co-exists with other living faiths,
 iii situations where the Christian Church is numerically small.

5 Some North American examples, carefully differentiated.
6 Some examples of non-structured, independent Christian movements.

We think it important that the Roman Catholic Church should fully participate in the project. We hope that some studies might be based upon Roman Catholic experience in particular countries. It will also be important to receive comments from those concerned in canon law revision and in the preparation of the Lex Fundamentalis. We see this latter comment as invaluable in making any overall judgement on Roman Catholic experience.

In sending the working paper to the churches, the Faith and Order Commission would be asking them to engage in self-criticism or, as we should prefer to say, in selfstudy. We expect that each church would remit the task to a group comparable with the committee appointed by the Commission. We expect that at both levels – national and international – the work will often require calls to be made upon people who are not normally drawn into consideration of the ecumenical issues, and certainly not into international ecumenical issues. We see this as an important by-product of the study which we propose.

B Observations

1 Background

The document published here again is part of a thread in the history of Faith and Order that goes back to its early days. In his *Documentary History of Faith and Order 1963–1993*, Günther Gassmann, former director of Faith and Order, describes the work of Faith and Order on church law issues under the heading 'Institution, Law and State'.[2]

He recognises that, apart from doctrinal issues, social, political, cultural, and other factors play a role in the divisions between churches and their search for unity. In that context he refers to a report presented to the second world conference on Faith and Order (Edinburgh 1937), *The Non-Theological Factors in the Making and Unmaking of Church Union*, that introduced the term 'non-theological factors' into ecumenical language. The report was written by a North American preparatory committee, and it mainly deals with political and sociological issues like nationalism (1937!), race, language, and class, and so forth, in the North American context. Church polity is not addressed as an issue in itself,

2 Ibid., 206f.

but it is referred to sometimes in the context of North American denominationalism, where independency as a church polity is widespread: '[a]ll American Churches are congregational (i.e., independent) in polity'.[3] Political and economic divisions – for instance between radical and conservative groups – are seen as more important than traditional differences in theology and polity. The beliefs and polity of the numerically large 'African' denominations in the United States of America are substantially those of the white churches of the same name; the existing disunity has been occasioned solely by the fact of colour.

A comparable report was written for the third world conference on Faith and Order (Lund 1952). Apart from a report of a preparatory consultation, it contains three contributions by well-known authors. It is only the French philosopher and lay theologian Jacques Ellul who indirectly refers to church polity, in the context of conservatism, as a source of division. In his view, organisation is an element of conservatism tending to maintain separations between churches because administration is of its nature rigid: '[i]ts tendency is to lay down fixed patterns and definite, coherent rules difficult to amend and render flexible. It likes to manage and foresee everything, and to establish statutes and regulations; it transforms human relations into legal ones'.[4]

In this respect the preparatory document for the fourth world conference (Montreal 1963), *Institutionalism*,[5] is not different: it focusses on a sociological approach, and church polity is only referred to as an element of organisation. This world conference suggested a study of the relation between the work of the Holy Spirit and the nature of the church as an institution, and as a consequence an outline for a study on 'Spirit, Order and Institution' was accepted by the Commission in Aarhus (1964). A concluding report was presented to the commission meeting in Louvain (1971).

Subsequently, the Accra Commission meeting in 1974 decided to consider the role of church law in efforts towards the visible unity of the church. The Accra document was – at least partly – inspired by the report of the second consultation of united and uniting churches in Limuru (Kenya), 1970, saying, 'Study of legal aspects of church union should be continued. Several union negotiations have been frustrated or delayed because the legal problems involved in uniting have not been sufficiently foreseen. It must be borne in mind that unsolved legal questions can be used by dissenting minorities as a means of frustrating union. The Faith and Order Commission has not yet given much attention to church constitutions as an ecumenical problem. It is obvious, however, that this area is

3 *The Non-Theological Factors in the Making and Unmaking of Church Union*, Faith and Order Publications (old series) 84 (London /and New York, 1937), p. 11. See https://archive.org/details/wccfops1.096.

4 C.H. Dodd, G.R. Cragg and J. Ellul, *Social and Cultural Factors in Church Divisions*, Faith and Order Publications 10 (London, 1952), pp. 21f. See: https://archive.org/details/wccfops2.010.

5 *Institutionalism*, Faith and Order Paper No. 37 (Geneva, 1963). See https://archive.org/details/wccfops2.041.

becoming more and more important. A general study on church constitutions and law could be of considerable help to union negotiations. In the framework of this wider study the particular problems of constitutions in union negotiations should receive special attention'.[6]

Representatives of several union negotiations had noted that in such processes 'it is essential that early provision be made for dealing with legal and property matters, and that these should be listed and investigated, even though in some cases the solution of such problems may more profitably be found after union rather than before it. It is suggested that before organic union is undertaken negotiating churches study their constitutions to make sure that their constitutions give their highest authority (a) the right of dissolution, (b) the right to unite with another denomination to form a new united church. Negotiating churches are advised to see that the same rights are included in the constitution of the newly formed church so that it is enabled to unite legally with another church'.[7]

Experiences in church union negotiations had shown the relevance of such study. For instance, in Nigeria, internal tensions within the Methodist Church, including lawsuits, had caused delay in the 1960s. In North India, the Methodist Church in Southern Asia (Episcopal) withdrew from the union plan in 1970, but in 1972 that church's juridical council affirmed that the 1970 vote was 'beyond its legal authority', which opened the way for the Methodists to join later.

In his introductory notes to the *Survey of Church Union Negotiations 1965–1967*, Faith and Order staff member Gerald F. Moede also pointed to 'a general uneasiness, not to say, anxiety, with present and former structures of the church. It is increasingly realised and admitted that the structures of the past were historically conditioned, adequate perhaps for one era, but in no way holy in themselves. Thus the need for flexibility of structure, for imagination and experimentation, if the church is to exist as a reconciling force, if she is to truly serve in the world, is receiving greater attention'.[8] The question emerges: in the setting up of new structures that any church union involves, how is the impersonality, the bureaucracy, the indifference of the institution to be avoided? If order is sought, how can the deadening effects of institutionalisation be avoided? Can continual openness to the Holy Spirit be built into a structure?

In fact, this is a repetition of earlier complaints about the snail's progress towards union, which easily results in a loosening of institutional loyalty. During the fourth World Conference on Faith and Order (Montreal 1963), the question was raised as to 'whether the institutional patterns of our local churches and denominations are not increasingly obsolescent, in the light of our deepened understanding of the nature of the unity we seek, and because of the impact

6 'Statements and recommendations', *Mid-Stream* 9, 1970/2–3, pp. 4–12, p. 10.

7 'Notes from the Limuru Discussion', *Mid-Stream* 9, 1970/2–3, pp. 13–33, p. 29.

8 *Survey of Church Union Negotiations 1965–1967*, Faith and Order Commission Papers No. 52, reprinted from *The Ecumenical Review* Vol. XX No. 3 – July 1968, p. 3f. See https://archive.org/details/wccfops2.058.

of secular challenges to our common calling'.[9] The report reflects the findings of a study commission on institutionalism. In that report a distinction is made between 'order' and 'organisation': '[o]rder is in this context taken to denote the visible complex of institutions which is held to be essential to the continuous existence and identity of the Church as a community in history. Organisation, on the other hand, refers to the broad range of institutional elements which, under varying historical conditions, express some aspect or other of the community which is structured and sustained by that "order" '.[10] So, how can that 'order' find appropriate forms of 'organisation' in the present ecumenical age?

In short, discussions until Accra covered a wider area of research than church law. The so-called non-theological factors include social, political, and cultural issues. Particularly, the issue of church and state relations was pursued a bit further.

2 After Accra

At Bangalore in 1978 Lukas Vischer, the director of Faith and Order, reported to the commission that, concerning the study on church law, 'not much progress has been made on this proposal and, given the limited resources available to the Commission, the study will probably never get very far'.[11] One consultation had been held regarding the relation between church and state: how are churches to achieve greater freedom from the powers and authorities that seek to restrain them and at the same time serve with greater solidarity the society in which they live?

Gassmann is quite clear in his evaluation: '[l]imited financial and personnel resources and, consequently, the need to concentrate on a few major studies have prevented Faith and Order from implementing these initiatives in the areas of institution, church law, and church and state. But questions and conflicts in these areas have accompanied the ecumenical movement ever since, which confirms the foresight of those earlier initiatives and the need to take them up once again'.[12] Indeed, the importance of church law issues continued to be evident in church union negotiations after 1974. Let me present just a few examples:

1 In Sri Lanka a decision of churches engaged in the union negotiations was being challenged in the courts regarding the legality of the voting procedures, and in 1975 the constitutional court, by a majority of two to one, held that the bill was inconsistent with the constitution. The union of churches

9 P.C. Rodger and L. Vischer, eds., *The Fourth World Conference on Faith and Order: Montreal 1963*, Faith and Order Paper No. 42 (London, 1964), p. 81. See https://archive.org/details/wccfops2.046.

10 *Institutionalism*, p. 21.

11 *Sharing in One Hope. Reports and Documents from the Meeting of the Faith and Order Commission, Bangalore 1978*, Faith and Order Paper No. 92 (Geneva: World Council of Churches, 1979), p. 35.

12 Gassmann, op cit., 207.

continued to be held up by unresolved legal questions before the district court. At the end of the day, church union would not be implemented at all.

2 In Australia Presbyterians started lawsuits against unification around the same time.

3 In other cases, church union schemes failed to gain the support of congregations by the legally required majorities. Therefore, in 1981, for instance, in the United Kingdom, the Association of Churches of Christ was dissolved by a vote of the member congregations to allow the congregations that wanted to unite with the United Reformed Church to act in accord with their own convictions.

4 After the breakdown of apartheid two churches of the Dutch Reformed family in South Africa (one 'black', one 'coloured') decided to unite into the Uniting Reformed Church in Southern Africa, but in the end it was not clear for one of them whether it could legally unite, and fears were voiced about possible legal challenges to the union. A number of congregations broke away from the former 'black' church, and lawsuits would continue to waste time and money after the unification in 1994.

3 Evaluative comments

The report *The Ecumenical Movement and Church Law* suggests a study of the legal aspects of inter-church cooperation and church union was necessary because of the advance of the ecumenical movement. Study is needed of the continuing validity of existing statements and rules and the possible need for new structures and regulations not foreseen in the traditional legal system of the different churches, e.g. representative systems that did not exist before or new financial arrangements. Churches should examine to what extent the progress of the ecumenical movement calls for changes and revisions in their legal systems. The report mainly focusses on this need with a view to the new ecumenical structures that have come into being: what is their juridical significance? How does this development relate to the freedom to decide as a church and to dispose of its resources?

The Accra document is also characteristic of its historical context, in that it is quite positive about 'organic unity' of churches as one of the goals of the ecumenical movement. A lot has changed since Accra, in this respect. The merger of churches seems to be less desirable than it was in the early days of the ecumenical movement. Ecumenical dialogue, however, both in Faith and Order and in bilateral dialogue, has made serious progress in terms of ecclesiology. It can also be argued that – in spite of the fact that Faith and Order could not implement the study as suggested in Accra – many churches have revised their legal systems with a view to ecumenical cooperation and participation in the ecumenical movement.[13] A relevant example of soft law in this respect is the *Directory for*

13 See N. Doe, *Christian Law: Contemporary Principles* (Cambridge: Cambridge University Press, 2013) 274–309.

the Application of Principles and Norms on Ecumenism[14] of the Roman Catholic Church, approved by Pope John Paul II in 1993. Other examples are the documents in which churches – usually within one national setting – confirm their mutual recognition of baptism. A lot of study was also done after 1974 on the external legal form of churches and its relation to civil law, as this depends on the different church-state relations.

The Accra document also refers to cases in which certain statements or rules in the churches, like condemnations of other confessional positions, have in fact become inoperative as a result of the growing ecumenical fellowship. A well-known example in this respect – at that time a recent step forward – is the Leuenberg Agreement (1973), in which European churches from different Protestant backgrounds declared that the mutual condemnations pronounced by the Reformation confessions of faith regarding the Lord's Supper, Christology, and predestination were now inapplicable to the doctrinal position of these churches, so that pulpit and table fellowship were now possible. However, this agreement itself states: '[t]his declaration of church fellowship does not predetermine provisions of church law on particular matters of inter-church relations or within individual churches. The churches will, however, take the Agreement into account in considering any such provisions'.[15] Only more recently was church unification in some cases based on the Leuenberg Agreement.[16]

The Accra document proclaims: '[a]ll achievements in the ecumenical movement have consequences for all churches' and 'any church which makes changes either in its internal rules or in its public legal framework should always in future take ecumenical considerations fully into account'. In this respect much still has to be done, not least in the area of church law. Further study might prove me wrong, but it is my impression that churches do not often consider ecumenical progress when they must revise their legal systems anyway. For instance, when churches with a different background merge into one church, they, of course, should deal with differences regarding e.g. ordination; in such cases they usually look for the 'greatest common divisor', rather than considering the ecumenical discussion on ordination in its full scope.

A few remarks on methodology may be helpful as well. The Accra document suggests a comparative study, or typology, of existing and emerging forms of the church in legal perspective, including an analysis and description of the different confessional approaches; the confessional heritage persists most powerfully in the different ways in which the churches are constituted and perpetuate the inherited order. Therefore, law and precedent can be studied in church canons, constitutions, and bylaws as well as in the record of their practical application. The same is true of civil customs and codes. A comparative survey might deal with the relation between the notion of the people of God theologically considered and

14 See www.vatican.va.

15 *Leuenberg Agreement*, § 43. See: www.leuenberg.net/leuenberg-agreement.

16 See my 'The polity of the United and Uniting Churches' in this volume.

that of the people of God juridically embodied, with the understanding of the different churches regarding the content, style, and functioning of their internal legal systems, with the common convictions about the sorts of relations to the civil community (establishment, disestablishment, secular state?) and with the critical issues affecting the integrity and identity of churches in modern societies. The report suggests a pilot study, asking selected churches to engage in self-study, including people who are not normally drawn into consideration of the ecumenical issues, and certainly not into international ecumenical issues.

This approach is different from what the Panel is pursuing, in that it starts from individual churches rather than from church families and focusses on a description of existing differences rather than on common principles. However, as far as I can see, both approaches are complementary to a high degree. A comparative approach, focussing on the analysis and explanation of differences, was characteristic of ecumenical dialogue in its early history; only after Lund 1952 did a more 'synthetic' approach, focussing on theological commonalities, become leading. This is what the Panel aims at as well, but now in the area of church law.

Appendix II

Statement of Principles of Christian Law

Christian Law Panel of Experts
Rome 2016

These principles of law are derived from a comparative study of the regulatory instruments of churches of the members of the Panel of Experts from eight traditions worldwide, namely: Roman Catholic, Orthodox, Anglican, Lutheran, Methodist, Reformed, Presbyterian, and Baptist. The Panel of Experts found that: (1) there are principles of church law and church order common to these churches and their existence can be factually established by empirical observation and comparison; (2) the churches of each Christian tradition contribute through their own regulatory instruments to this store of principles; (3) the principles have a strong theological content and weight and are fundamental to the self-understanding of Christianity; (4) these principles have a living force and contain within themselves the possibility of further development and articulation; and (5) these principles demonstrate a degree of unity between the churches, stimulate common Christian actions, and should be fed into the ecumenical enterprise to enhance fuller visible unity.

A 'principle of Christian law' describes a foundational proposition of general applicability; is induced from the similarities of the regulatory systems of the churches studied; is derived from their juridical tradition; and may reflect their theological understanding.

Each of the Sections that follow, which articulates principles of law with regard to a range of areas of ecclesial life, opens with a short narrative. This narrative sets out a number of facts based on church regulatory systems which the Panel considers relevant to the area of ecclesial life treated, but which may not in the Panel's opinion represent principles of law.

The use of the word 'may' in a principle denotes the right or freedom of the entity in question to engage in the conduct specified, unless the context indicates otherwise.

Section I

Churches and their systems of law, order and polity

The word 'law' encompasses a variety of regulatory instruments and other norms including constitutions, canons, covenants, books of church order, and other polity documents.

1 The institutional church

1 A church as an institution may define itself by its autonomy, polity and objects.
2 A church is a community which may be international, national, regional, or local.
3 A church has a distinct membership, or other body of persons associated with it, which may be organised in territorial or non-territorial units such as provinces, districts, or congregations.
4 A church is autonomous in its system of governance or polity.
5 A church has amongst its objects the advancement of the mission of Christ which includes proclaiming the Gospel, administering the sacraments, and serving the wider community.
6 Communion amongst the faithful is an essential quality of ecclesial life.

2 The forms of ecclesial regulation

1 Laws are found in a variety of formal sources including codes of canon law, charters and statutes, constitutions and bylaws, and books of church order.
2 Customs may have juridical force to the extent permitted by the law of a church.
3 Ecclesiastical quasi-legislation, which includes guidelines and codes of practice, is designed to complement formal law and consists of rules that are nevertheless prescriptive in form and generate the expectation of compliance.

3 The Servant Law

1 Church law and church order exist to serve a church in its mission and in its witness to the salvific work of Christ.
2 Laws contribute to constituting the institutional organisation of a church and facilitate and order its activities.
3 Theology may shape law and law may realise certain theological propositions in norms of conduct and behaviour.
4 Church laws should conform to the law of God, as revealed in Holy Scripture and by the Holy Spirit.

4 The structure, effect and relaxation of norms

1 Church laws principally deal with ministry, government, doctrine, worship, rites, admonition and discipline, and property.
2 Church laws consist of various juridical formulae, such as precepts, prohibitions and permissions, and may be cast as principles and rules, rights and duties, functions and powers.
3 Laws may be binding or exhortatory.
4 All members of a church are subject to its laws as are its component institutions, to the extent that the law provides.
5 Later laws may abrogate earlier laws.

6 Laws are prospective and should not be retrospective in effect unless this is clearly provided for in the laws themselves.
7 Laws should be clear, stable, and coherent.
8 A church may have in place a mechanism for the enforcement and vindication of the rights and duties of the faithful.
9 A law may be relaxed, by competent ecclesial authority, by means of dispensation, economy or other form of equity for the spiritual good of the individual and the common good of the ecclesial community.

5 The interpretation of law

1 Laws should be interpreted by reference to their text, context, and precedent.
2 A church has authority to interpret its own law.
3 For the interpretation of law, recourse may be had to the purposes of the law, the mind of the legislator, and the faith and practice of the church.

Section II

The faithful

Some churches expressly use in their regulatory instruments the category 'member', others do not. However, each church has an identifiable group of the faithful associated with it. For the purposes of this section, the word membership denotes both juridical categories.

1 The people of God

1 The Christian faithful constitute the people of God.
2 All the faithful should be equal in dignity.
3 Baptism generates duties and rights for the faithful.
4 The faithful includes lay and ordained people.

2 Church membership and other forms of belonging

1 A church is made up of those incorporated into it in accordance with its proper laws and customs.
2 A church should serve, in appropriate ways, all who seek its ministry regardless of membership.
3 Membership in a church, for the purposes of participation in its government, may be based on any of all of: baptism; baptism and confirmation or other mature demonstration of faith; and such other conditions as may be prescribed by law.
4 The names of persons belonging to a church may be entered on one or more rolls or other registers of membership subject to such conditions as may be prescribed by law.
5 Names may be removed from such rolls and registers in accordance with the law.

3 The functions of the laity

1 The law of a church should generally set out the basic rights and duties of all its members.
2 The laity should promote the mission of the church, and bear witness to the Christian faith through their lives in the world.
3 A lay person should engage in the collective ecclesial life, in proclaiming the Word of God, participating in worship, and receiving the sacraments.
4 Lay persons should maintain such Christian standards in their private lives as are prescribed by law.
5 Lay persons are encouraged to practise daily devotion, private prayer, Bible reading, and self-discipline, bringing the teaching and example of Christ into every-day life, upholding Christian values, and being of service to the church and wider community.

4 Public ministry exercised by lay persons

1 Public ministry, a gift of God, is the fulfilment of a function assigned formally in a church to an office or other position exercised under authority on behalf of that church in the service of its mission and witness to the Gospel.
2 The law should enable the laity to exercise public ministry in those offices and other positions lawfully open to them.
3 Lay persons may be admitted to such offices and positions provided they are suitable, qualified, selected and admitted by competent ecclesial authority for such term as is prescribed by law.
4 Lay ministers and officers exercise such public and representative ministry within and on behalf of a church and perform such functions as may be prescribed and permitted by its law.
5 The authority to discipline, dismiss or reappoint a lay minister or officer depends on, and its exercise must comply with, the law of the church.

Section III

Ordained ministry

The churches set apart persons for ministry in a special rite, for most called ordination.

The following principles apply to ordained ministry and also address ecclesiastical offices which, depending on the church concerned, may be held by either ordained or lay persons.

1 Ordination

1 Ordained ministry is divine in origin and persons are set apart for it.
2 A church may distinguish between different types of ordained minister.
3 Candidates for ordination must be called by God and by the church to ordained ministry.

4 Vocation to and suitability for ordained ministry are tested by the church through a process of selection, examination and training by competent authority.
5 Persons are generally admitted to ordained ministry through ordination.
6 Ordination is administered by competent authority by means of the laying-on of hands and invocation of the Holy Spirit.

2 Ecclesiastical offices

1 An ecclesiastical office is a position constituted by law.
2 An ecclesiastical office exists independently of the person who occupies it.
3 An ecclesiastical office enables the discharge of functions of the particular ministry attaching to it.
4 An ecclesiastical office may be held by a person or persons with such qualifications as are prescribed by law.
5 An ecclesiastical office is filled by a variety of means, often by appointment or election.
6 The jurisdiction or other authority which attaches to an office is determined by or under the law.
7 Authority attaching to an office may be delegated to the extent provided by law.
8 The authority to exercise ecclesiastical office ceases upon lawful dissolution of the office, expiration of the stated term of office, attainment of the prescribed age limit, or the death, resignation, transfer, retirement or removal of the office holder.

3 The functions of ordained ministers

1 Ordained ministers must be duly authorised by their church to exercise ministry.
2 Ministers are to preach the Word of God, teach the faith, administer the sacraments, and provide pastoral care.
3 Ministers should fashion their ministry after the example of Jesus Christ.
4 Ministers must lead their private lives in a manner which befits their sacred calling.
5 Ministers may engage in such other occupations, including offices held beyond the local church, as are not forbidden by church law or competent authority.
6 Ministers are accountable for the exercise of their ministry to the competent authority in the manner prescribed by law.

4 The exercise of oversight

1 Oversight is an essential of ecclesial order.
2 Oversight is exercised by such authority as is designated by law.

3 A church may have a system of international oversight or leadership.
4 A minister has such international functions of oversight or leadership as are permitted by law.
5 International church offices include those of pope, patriarch, primate, president, moderator, or general secretary.
6 Those who exercise international oversight or leadership are appointed or elected to that office by competent ecclesial authority.
7 A church may assign to such an office a coercive jurisdiction or a moral or persuasive authority.

Section IV

Church governance

All the churches have institutions for their governance. Their functions may be legislative, administrative (or executive), or judicial. These institutions may exist at a variety of levels – local, regional, national or international – depending on the polity of the church in question.

1 Systems of church polity

1 Christ is the ultimate head of the Church universal in all its manifestations.
2 A system of government used by a church reflects its conception of divine law.
3 A church should have institutions to legislate, administer and adjudicate for its own governance.
4 An ecclesial institution has such power, authority or jurisdiction as is assigned to it by law.
5 An ecclesial institution must comply with the law and may be subject in the exercise of its functions to such substantive and procedural limitations as may be prescribed by law.
6 Ecclesial institutions may be organised at international, national, regional, and/or local level.

2 International ecclesial communities

1 An ecclesial tradition may have an international organisation in the form of a church, communion, federation, conference, alliance, or other global association.
2 An international ecclesial community has such institutional structure as may be constituted by or assigned to it under its doctrine and law.
3 An international ecclesial institution is composed of such persons on such terms of tenure as are assigned to it in accordance with its own juridical instruments.

3 National church structures

1 An ecclesial tradition may have a national organisation.
2 A church or other ecclesial community organised at national level may have such institutional structure as is prescribed by the regulatory instruments applicable to it.
3 The autonomy and functions of a national ecclesial entity, and its conference, synod, council, or other form of central assembly, may include the authority to legislate, administer and adjudicate on matters within its competence.
4 A national ecclesial assembly or other such institution is composed of such members of the faithful as are elected or otherwise appointed to it in accordance with law.

4 Regional church structures

1 National ecclesial entities may have regional structures.
2 Regional ecclesial organisations may be in the form of a diocese, eparchy, synod, district, classis, presbytery, association or other regional unit.
3 A regional ecclesial unit may have such institutions, in the form of a synod, council, classis, presbytery, or other assembly, as are prescribed by the law applicable to it.
4 A regional institution exercises such authority and functions as are conferred on it by the ecclesial community to which it belongs or the constituent churches associated with it.
5 A regional ecclesial assembly or other such institution is composed of such members of the faithful as are elected or otherwise appointed to it by those competent to do so under the law.

5 The local church

1 Regional ecclesial units may be divided into or constituted by local churches or congregations existing at the most localised level of church life.
2 A church organised locally may be in the form of a parish, circuit, congregation or other ecclesial unit.
3 A local church, its assembly and other institutions, such as a council, meeting, session or other body, has such authority and functions as are lawfully inherent to it or conferred upon it by the institutions of the wider ecclesial entity to which it belongs.
4 The assembly of a local church is composed of those members of the faithful who are lawfully elected or otherwise appointed to it.
5 All ecclesial units at each level are interdependent.

Section V

Church discipline

All the churches have a system of discipline, the administration of which is regulated by norms which deal with the purpose and scope of discipline and processes to enforce it.

1 Ecclesial discipline

1 A church as an institution has the right to enforce discipline and to resolve conflicts amongst the faithful.
2 The right to exercise discipline has a variety of foundations including divine and spiritual authority.
3 A church may exercise discipline in relation to both lay and ordained persons to the extent provided by law.
4 The purpose of discipline is to glorify God, to protect the integrity and mission of the church, to safeguard the vulnerable from harm, and to promote the spiritual benefit of its members.
5 Discipline is exercised by competent authority in accordance with law.

2 Informal dispute resolution

1 Ecclesiastical disputes may be settled by a variety of formal and informal means including administrative process.
2 The competent authority may settle the matter in a process short of formal judicial process in the manner and to the extent provided by law.
3 Anyone with a sufficient interest in the matter may challenge a decision by recourse to the relevant and competent authority.
4 Visitation is exercised pastorally by a regional or other competent authority in relation to the local church or other such entity in the manner and to the extent provided by law.
5 The aim of visitation is to monitor, affirm and improve the life and discipline of the entity visited.

3 Church courts and tribunals

1 A church may have a system of courts, tribunals or other such bodies to provide for the enforcement of discipline and the formal and judicial resolution of ecclesiastical disputes.
2 Church courts, tribunals or other such bodies may exist at international, national, regional and/or local level to the extent permitted by the relevant law.

3 The establishment, composition and jurisdiction of judicial bodies are determined by the law applicable to them.
4 Church courts, tribunals and other such bodies are established by competent authority, administered by qualified personnel, and may be tiered in terms of their original and appellate jurisdiction.
5 Church courts, tribunals and other bodies exercise such authority over the laity and ordained ministers as is conferred upon them by law.

4 Due process

1 Every effort must be made by the faithful to settle their disputes amicably, lawfully, justly, and equitably, without recourse in the first instance to church courts and tribunals.
2 Formal process is mandatory if church law or civil law require it.
3 Judicial process may be composed of informal resolution, investigation, a hearing, and/or such other elements as may be prescribed by law including an appeal.
4 Christians must be judged in the church according to law applied with equity, and disciplinary procedures must secure fair, impartial and due process.
5 The parties, particularly the accused, have the right to notice, to be heard, to question evidence, to an unbiased hearing, and where appropriate to an appeal.

5 Ecclesiastical offences and sanctions

1 A church may institute a system of ecclesiastical offences.
2 Ecclesiastical offences and defences to them are to be clearly defined in writing and a court, tribunal or other body acting in a judicial capacity must give reasons for its finding of breach of church discipline.
3 A church has a right to impose spiritual and other lawful censures, penalties and sanctions upon the faithful provided a breach of ecclesiastical discipline has been established.
4 Sanctions should be lawful and just. They may include admonition, rebuke, removal from office and excommunication. They may be applied to the laity, clergy and office-holders to the extent provided by law. Their effect is withdrawal from some of the benefits of ecclesial life. Sanctions are remedial or medicinal.
5 A church may enable the removal of sanctions.

Section VI

Doctrine and worship

Each church teaches as its doctrine on matters of faith and practice. The doctrine of a church is rooted in the revelation of God as recorded in Holy Scripture, summed up in the historical Creeds, conveyed in tradition, and expounded in instruments, texts and pronouncements issued by persons and institutions with lawful authority to teach.

1 The definition of doctrine

1 The doctrinal instruments of churches may have elements which themselves may generate norms of conduct.
2 The doctrines of a church may be interpreted and developed afresh to the extent and in the manner prescribed by law.

2 Proclamation of the faith

1 The proclamation of the Word of God is a fundamental action of the church and a divine imperative incumbent on all the faithful.
2 A church has the right and the duty to instruct the faithful and proclaim the Gospel.
3 Preaching is inherent to ordained ministry.
4 Authorised persons may deliver sermons or other forms of preaching for the glory of God, the edification of the people, and the exposition of church doctrine.
5 Biblical texts must be treated respectfully and coherently building on tradition and scholarship so that scriptural revelation may continue to illuminate, challenge and transform thinking and doing.

3 Doctrinal discipline

1 A church has a right to enforce its own doctrinal standards and discipline.
2 The faithful should be taught and encouraged to believe church doctrine.
3 Ordination candidates and others may be required to subscribe, assent or otherwise affirm their belief in or loyalty to the doctrine of their church.
4 The faithful should respect, honour and uphold the doctrine of their church.
5 Any person who offends church doctrine may be subject to disciplinary process.
6 A church has the right to determine the limits of permissible theological opinion, and to interpret its own doctrine and doctrinal standards.

4 The nature and forms of worship

1 The worship of God is a fundamental obligation of a church.
2 Worship enables an intimate encounter between a church corporately and the faithful individually with the presence of God.

3 Each church and those bodies within it which are competent to do so may develop liturgical texts or other forms of service for the public worship of God provided these are consistent with the Word of God and church doctrine.
4 The use of a particular form of service must be authorised.
5 Forms of service may be found in a book of rites or liturgy, a book of common prayer, a directory of worship or other instrument.
6 Service books may include rubrics or other directions to facilitate worship.

5 The administration of public worship

1 A church must provide for public worship.
2 Ordained ministers are particularly responsible for the conduct of public worship in accordance with the authorised forms of service.
3 Regular attendance at divine worship, particularly on the Lord's Day, is an expectation on the faithful.
4 The administration of worship in the local church is subject to supervision by those authorities designated by law to provide this.

Section VII

The rites of the Church

All the churches have rites of passage which mark the stages in the spiritual life of the Christian. Certain churches call some rites sacraments and others call them ordinances.

1 Baptism

1 Baptism is divinely instituted.
2 A church may call baptism a sacrament or an ordinance.
3 Baptism constitutes incorporation of a person into the Church of Christ.
4 Baptism is validly administered with water in the name of the triune God.
5 Baptism should be administered ordinarily in public in the presence of the faithful by an ordained minister but extraordinarily in cases of necessity by a lay person.
6 Baptism in a church may be of infants or adults to the extent prescribed by its law.
7 A church may impose conditions for admission to baptism.
8 A church should nurture the baptised person in the faith.
9 Baptism should be susceptible to proof.
10 Baptism cannot be repeated.

2 Confirmation and profession

1 A church may make provision for a further rite accompanying or following baptism which may be styled confirmation or profession of faith.
2 Candidates may undergo preparation and instruction prior to the administration of this further rite which should be administered in accordance with the practice of the church.

3 The Eucharist, Holy Communion or Lord's Supper

1 The Eucharist, Holy Communion or Lord's Supper is instituted by Christ.
2 The Eucharist and receiving of Holy Communion are central to ecclesial life.
3 The faithful should participate in the Eucharist regularly.
4 The faithful should receive Holy Communion regularly.
5 The Eucharist is presided over by such persons as are lawfully authorised.
6 The Eucharist should be celebrated in an authorised place.
7 A church should provide for the reception of Holy Communion by the sick.
8 The elements for the celebration of Holy Communion are bread and wine.
9 A church is entitled to make provision with regard to admission to the Eucharist.

4 Marriage

1 The foundation of marriage is a lifelong union between one man and one woman.
2 Marriage is instituted by God.
3 Marriage is for the well-being of the spouses.
4 To be married validly in the eyes of the church, the parties must satisfy the conditions prescribed by church law and should be instructed in the nature and obligations of marriage.
5 Marriage is celebrated in the presence of an authorised person.
6 Marriage should be registered.
7 A marriage is ended by the death of one of the spouses and may be dissolved when so determined by competent authority.

5 Confession

1 A church may practise private confession and absolution in the presence of an ordained minister to the extent that this is permitted by the law of that church.
2 The seal of the confessional is inviolable, save as may be provided by the law of a church.
3 A duty of confidentiality attaches to the exercise of ministry to the extent provided by law.

6 Funerals

1 The faithful who have died should be given a church funeral according to the norms of law.
2 Disposal of human remains may be either by burial or by cremation accompanied by the administration of any service authorised for lawful use in a church.

Section VIII

Ecumenism

Ecclesial communion between two or more churches of different traditions exists when a relationship is established in which each church believes the other to hold the essential marks of the Church universal. Full communion involves the mutual recognition of unity in faith, sacramental sharing, the mutual recognition and interchangeability of ministries, and the reciprocal enjoyment of shared spiritual and pastoral resources. Partial communion is an ecclesial relationship in which at least one but not all the elements of full communion is present. The extent and terms of ecclesial communion or other relationship between churches of two or more different traditions may be set out in a constitutional union, concordat, covenant or other instrument agreed between the participant churches. The establishment of ecumenical agreements is an exercise of autonomy by a church in the form of collaborative ecumenical norm-making which may be prescriptive or aspirational.

1 The church universal

1 There is one, holy, catholic and apostolic Church.
2 Christ bestows unity on the Church, the Body of Christ.
3 A church has such relationship to the Church universal as is prescribed in its doctrine and law.
4 The unity of the Church universal is impaired but not destroyed by the denominational division of churches.

2 The nature of ecumenism and the ecumenical obligation

1 Each church should promote visible unity amongst the separated churches.
2 Each church should promote the ecumenical movement through active dialogue and cooperation.
3 The purpose of ecumenism is greater ecclesial communion.
4 Ecumenical activity must be in accordance with the law of the ecumenical partners involved so that the discipline of each is respected.
5 The law of a church should protect the marks of the Church universal and define what ecclesial communion and reciprocity is possible.

3 Institutional structures for ecumenism

1 The regulation and authorisation of ecumenical activity are in the keeping of the competent authority of a church.
2 The competent authority of a church may be assisted by commissions and other advisory bodies in the ecumenical enterprise.
3 A church should provide for the ecumenical formation of the faithful.

4 Ecclesial, ministerial and sacramental communion

1 An agreement to establish ecclesial communion between two or more churches does not of itself affect the legal relationship between them and other churches not party to it.
2 The validity of an act performed in a church is determined by that church and recognition of such validity by another church is a matter for that other church.
3 Norms about ecumenism concerning the administration of the sacraments, mixed marriages and sharing property are supplementary to general rules which confine such facilities to the enjoyment of the faithful within the ecclesial tradition which created those norms.

5 Structural communion

1 A church is free to determine whether to participate in existing international, national, regional, or local ecumenical arrangements.
2 A church may incorporate in its own law the terms of an ecumenical agreement.
3 Ecumenical agreements may be varied only with the agreement of the participant churches.

Section IX

Church property

The juridical instruments of the churches all contain elaborate rules which apply to church property and finance, including the use and maintenance of church buildings and the offerings of the Christian faithful. The idea of Christian stewardship is fundamental.

1 The ownership of property

1 A church has the right to acquire, administer, and dispose of property.
2 A church and/or institutions or bodies within it may seek legal personality under civil law to enable ownership of property.

3 A church may have rules about the acquisition, ownership, administration, sale or other form of disposal of church property.

4 A church may have in place provision for its own dissolution or that of institutions or bodies within it and for the distribution of property on dissolution.

5 Property which vests in institutions is held on trust for the benefit of the church and its work and such institutions are required to exercise proper stewardship of that property.

2 Sacred places and objects

1 A church may dedicate or otherwise set aside a building or other space, prescribed objects, and other forms of property, to worship and other sacred purposes.

2 A place of worship, or other space, or sacred object, must be used in a manner which is consistent with its dedication.

3 Responsibility for the use, care, and maintenance of sacred places and objects, vests in a designated person or body.

4 Oversight of the administration of church property vests in competent ecclesiastical authority and a periodic appraisal of its condition may be the object of a lawful visitation.

3 The control of finance

1 A church has the right to make rules for the administration and control of its finances.

2 The civil law applicable to financial accountability must be complied with.

3 A church must ensure sound financial management including the framing and approval by competent authority of an annual budget.

4 A church should provide, with regard to each entity within it, for the keeping of accounts for approval by a competent authority.

5 A church must ensure that financial accounts are audited annually by qualified persons in order to promote proper stewardship in the church.

4 Lawful income

1 A church has a right to receive funds.

2 The faithful must contribute financially, according to their means, to the church's work.

3 The officers of a church should encourage the faithful in the matter of offerings and collect and distribute these as prescribed.

4 The local church and other entities may be required by competent authority to make a financial contribution to meet the wider institutional costs and needs of the church.

5 A church which invests money should do so prudently and in ventures which are consistent with the ethical standards of the church.

5 Ecclesiastical expenditure

1 A church should require the designated institutions or bodies within it to insure church property against loss.
2 A church should support and sustain those engaged in ministry according to their need and circumstance.
3 A church should make suitable provision for ordained ministers who are in ill-health and for those who retire.

Section X

Church and state relations

The churches have a wide variety of legal experiences in terms of their relationship to or institutional separation from the States in whose territorial boundaries they function.

1 Church-state relations

1 A church should cooperate with the State in matters of common concern, but each is independent in its own sphere.
2 The faithful may participate in politics save to the extent prohibited by church law.
3 Cooperation between a church and the State may be exercised on the basis of:

(1) The establishment of, or other formal relationship between, a church and the State;
(2) An agreement or civil legislation negotiated freely with the State;
(3) The juridical personality which a church or institutions within it may enjoy under civil law;
(4) The registration of a church in accordance with the provisions of any applicable State law;
(5) The fundamental institutional autonomy of a church in carrying out its lawful objects and its freedom in these areas from intervention by the State.

2 Human rights and religious freedom

1 All humans, having been created in the image of God, share an equality of dignity and fundamental human rights.
2 A church should protect and defend human rights in society for all people.

3 Social responsibility

1 A church should promote social justice.
2 The faithful should promote social justice and charitable work as regulated by their church.

4 Public institutions

1 A church may promote the teaching of Christianity in State schools.
2 Christian teaching provided in State schools by church entities and persons is a matter of cooperation between the relevant and competent church and civil authorities.
3 A church should avail itself of the opportunities under civil law for the provision of spiritual care in public institutions which include hospitals, homes, prisons, and the armed forces.
4 A church may seek financial assistance from the State in the provision of spiritual care in public institutions.

Bibliography

Aarflot, A., 'The Collegiality of Bishops: A Lutheran Perspective', 48 *Jurist* (1988) 359–375.

Aarflot, A., 'Jus in sacra', 4 *Lov og Rett* (1983) 75, 200–212.

Aarflot, A., 'Motifs and Perspectives in the Reform Process of the Church of Norway', in H. Askeland and U. Schmidt, eds., *Church Reform and Leadership of Change* (Eugene, OR: Pickwick Publications, 2015) 18–37.

Aarflot, A., 'Rettslig handleevne lokalt og sentralt i Den norske kirke; refleksjoner over rettssituasjonen etter den siste revisjon av kirkeloven', 56 *Lov og Rett* (2017) 195–214.

Afanasiev, N., 'The Canons of the Church: Changeable or Unchangeable?', 11 *St. Vladimir's Theological Quarterly* (1967) 54–68.

Agapius and Nicodemus, *The Pedalion (The Rudder)* (Athens, 1886), translated by Denver Cummings (Chicago: Orthodox Christian Education Society, 1957).

Alivizatos, A., *Η Οικονομία κατά το Κανονικόν Δίκαιον της Ορθοδόξου Εκκλησίας* (Oikonomia according to the Canon Law of the Orthodox Church) (Athens: Astir, 1949).

Anglican Communion Legal Advisers Network, *The Principles of Canon Law Common to the Churches of the Anglican Communion* (London: Anglican Communion Office, 2008).

Barth, K., *Die Ordnung der Gemeinde: Zur dogmatischen Grundlegung des Kirchenrechts* (München: Chr. Kaiser Verlag, 1955).

Beck, B.E., 'Conference Episcope', in M. Davies, ed., *A Thankful Heart and a Discerning Mind* (Milton Keynes; Lonely Scribe, 2010) 110.

Beek, A. van den, W. Balke and J.D.Th, Wassenaar, eds., *De kerk op orde? Vijftig jaar hervormd leven met de kerkorde van 1951* (Zoetermeer: Boekencentrum, 2001).

Beneševč, V., ed., *Ioannis Scolastici Synagoga L titulorum*, Tom. 1 (München: Verl. d. Bayer. Akad. d. Wiss. 1937).

Berman, H.J., *Law and Revolution II: The Impact of the Protestant Reformations on the Western Legal Tradition* (Cambridge, MA: Belknap Press Harvard University, 2003).

Blunt, J.H., *The Book of Church Law, being an exposition of the Parochial Clergy and the Laity of the Church of England* (1872)

Bouwman, H., *De crisis der jeugd: Eenige bladzijden uit de geschiedenis van de kerken der Afscheiding* (Kampen: Kok, 1914).

Bouwman, H., *Gereformeerd kerkrecht: Het recht der kerken in de practijk*, Vol. 1. (Kampen: Kok, 1928) 29.

Bouwman, H., *Voetius over het Gezag der Synoden* (Amsterdam: S.J.P. Bakker, 1937).

Briggs, J.H.Y., ed., *A Dictionary of European Baptist Life and Thought, Vol. 33 Studies in Baptist History and Thought* (Milton Keynes: Paternoster, 2009).

Broeke, C. [Leon] van den Broeke, *Een geschiedenis van de classis: Classicale typen tussen idee en werkelijkheid 1571–2004* (Kampen: Kok, 2005) 207–239.

Broeke, L. van den, 'Flexibility or Fixed Idea: The Dort Church Order of 1619 as a Cultural Import', in H. Aay, J. Venema and D. Voskuil, eds., *Sharing Pasts: Dutch Americans Through Four Centuries* (Holland, MI: Van Raalte Press, 2017) 51–72.

Broom, H., *Legal Maxims* (London: Sweet and Maxwell, 3rd edition, 1852).

Brundage, J., *Medieval Canon Law* (Longman: London and New York, 1995).

Burleigh, J.H.S., *A History of the Church of Scotland* (Edinburgh: Hope Trust, 1988).

Burn, R., *Ecclesiastical Law* (London, 2nd edition, 1767).

Calvin, J., *Institutes of the Christian Religion* (1559), trans. Henry Beveridge (Peabody, MA: Hendrickson Publishers, 2008).

Calvin, J.C., *Institutie of onderwijzing in de christelijke godsdienst*, translated by A. Sizoo, 3 vols. (Delft: W.D. Meinema 1949).

Campenhausen, Hans Frhr. von, *Kirchliches Amt und geistliche Vollmacht in den ersten drei Jahrhunderten* [Ecclesiastical Office and Spiritual Authority in the First Three Centuries] (Tübingen: Mohr, 1963).

Caparros, E., and H. Aubé, eds., *Code of Canon Law Annotated* (Montréal: Wilson & Lafleur Limitée, 2nd edition, 2004).

Carey, J., ed., *The Historic Episcopate* (London: Longman and Green, 1947).

Carosi, M.B., 'Some Notes on the Problem of *regulae iuris* in the History of Law', 10 *Annuario di emeneutica giuridica* (2005) 305–312.

Chiappetta, L., *Il Codice di Diritto Canonico: Commento Giuridico-Pastorale* (Bologna: Edizione Dehoniane, 3rd edition, 2011) 3 vols.

Christian Law Panel of Experts, Response to the World Council of Church Faith and Order Commission Paper, *The Church: Towards a Common Vision* (2013) (December 2015).

Christoffersen, L., 'The Argument for a Narrow Conception of "Religious Autonomy"', 4 *Oxford Journal of Law and Religion* (2015) 278–302.

Christoffersen, L., 'Church Autonomy in Nordic Law', in L. Christoffersen, K. Å Modéer and S. Andersen, eds., *Law & Religion in the 21st Century – Nordic Perspectives* (Copenhagen: DJØF Publishing, 2010) 563–592.

Christoffersen, L., 'Towards Re-Sacralisation of Nordic Law?', in M.T. Mjaaland, ed., *Formatting Religion: Across Politics, Education, Media, and Law* (Abindgon: Routledge, 2019) 175–204.

Conn, J., N. Doe, and J. Fox, eds., *Initiation, Membership and Authority in Anglican and Roman Catholic Canon Law* (Cardiff and Rome: Centre for Law and Religion and Angelicum University, 2005).

Cox, J.T., *Practice and Procedure in the Church of Scotland* (Edinburgh: Committee on General Administration: William Blackwood and Sons Ltd., 1976).

Cracknell, K., *Towards a New Relationship* (London: Epworth, 1986).

Cranmer, F., 'The Church of Sweden and the Unravelling of Establishment', 5 *Ecclesiastical Law Journal* (2000) 417–430.

Crifò, G., 'La Chiesa e l'Impero nella storia di diritto da Costantino a Giustiniano', in *Cristianesimo e istituzioni politiche da Costantino a Giustiniano*, a cura di E. dal Covolo e R. Uglione (Roma: LAS, 1997) 194–196.

Cunningham, J., *Church History of Scotland* (Edinburgh: James Thin, 1882).

Dare, H., and S. Woodman, *The 'Plainly Revealed' Word of God? Baptist Hermeneutics in Theory and Practice* (Macon, GA: Mercer University Press, 2011).

Davies, A., 'Heritage and Hope: A Story of British Pentecostalism', in J. Aldred, ed., *Pentecostals and Charismatics in Britain: An Anthology* (London: SCM Press, 2019) 3–34.

Davies, R.E., *Methodism* (Harmondsworth: Penguin, 1963).

Davies, R.E., and E.G. Rupp, *A History of the Methodist Church in Great Britain*, Vol. I (London: Epworth Press, 1965).

Dawson, J., *John Knox* (New Haven, CT: Yale University Press, 2015).

Dodd, C.H., G.R. Cragg, and J. Ellul, *Social and Cultural Factors in Church Divisions*, Faith and Order Publications 10 (London: SMC Press Ltd., 1952).

Doe, N., ed., *The Approaches to Public Matters and Private Matters in Anglican and Roman Catholic Canon Law* (Cardiff: Centre for Law and Religion, 2016).

Doe, N., ed., *Bishops in Anglican and Roman Catholic Canon Law* (Cardiff: Centre for Law and Religion, 2018).

Doe, N., 'Canon Law and Communion', 6 *Ecclesiastical Law Journal* (2002) 241–263.

Doe, N., *Canon Law in the Anglican Communion* (Oxford: Oxford University Press, 1998).

Doe, N., *Christian Law: Contemporary Principles* (Cambridge: Cambridge University Press, 2013).

Doe, N., 'The Common Law of the Anglican Communion', 7 *Ecclesiastical Law Journal* (2003) 4–16.

Doe, N., 'The Contribution of Common Principles of Canon Law to Ecclesial Communion in Anglicanism', in *The Principles of Canon Law Common to the Churches of the Anglican Communion* (London: Anglican Communion Office, 2008) 97–124.

Doe, N., ed., *Counsel and Consent: Church Government in Anglican and Roman Catholic Canon Law* (Cardiff: Centre for Law and Religion, 2016).

Doe, N., 'Ecclesiastical Quasi-legislation', in N. Doe, M. Hill and R. Ombres, eds., *English Canon Law* (Cardiff: University of Wales Press, 1998) 93–103.

Doe, N., 'The Ecumenical Value of Comparative Church Law: Towards the Category of Christian Law', 17 *Ecclesiastical Law Journal* (2015) 135–169.

Doe, N., ed., *The Formation and Ordination of Clergy in Anglican and Roman Catholic Canon Law* (Cardiff: Centre for Law and Religion, 2009).

Doe, N., *The Law of the Church in Wales* (Cardiff: University of Wales Press, 2002).

Doe, N., *The Legal Architecture of English Cathedrals* (Abingdon: Routledge, 2017).

Doe, N., *The Legal Framework of the Church of England* (Oxford: Clarendon Press, 1996).

Doe, N., ed., *Marriage in Anglican and Roman Catholic Canon Law* (Cardiff: Centre for Law and Religion, 2009).

Doe, N., 'Modern Church Law', in J. Witte, Jr. and F.S. Alexander, eds., *Christianity and Law – An Introduction* (Cambridge: Cambridge University Press, 2008) 271–291.

Doe, N., 'The Principles of Canon Law: A Focus of Legal Unity in Anglican-Roman Catholic Relations', 5 *Ecclesiastical Law Journal* (1999) 221–240.

Doe, N., 'The Principles of Christian Law Project in Context', *Quaderni Di Diritto e Politica Ecclesiastica* (2017) 3–25.

Doe, N., 'Richard Hooker: Priest and Jurist', in M. Hill and R. Helmholz, eds., *Great Christian Jurists in English History* (Cambridge: Cambridge University Press, 2017) 115–137.

Doe, N., ed., *The Teaching of Canon Law in Anglicanism and the Roman Catholic Church* (Cardiff: Centre for Law and Religion, 2016).

Doe, N., 'Towards a Critique of the Role of Theology in English Ecclesiastical and Canon Law', 2 *Ecclesiastical Law Journal* (1992) 328–346.

Doe, N., and S. Pulleyn, 'The Durability of Maxims in Canon Law: From Regulae Iuris to Canonical Principles', in T. Harris, ed., *Studies in Canon Law and Common Law in Honor of R.H. Helmholz* (Berkeley: The Robbins Collection, 2015) 303–336.

Dombois, H., *Das Recht der Gnade: Ökumenisches Kirchenrecht* [The Right of Mercy: Ecumenical Church Polity], 3 vols. (Bielefeld: Luther-Verlag, 1961–1983).

Dombois, H., *Das Recht der Gnade: Ökumenisches Kirchenrecht* 2. *Grundlagen und Grundfragen der Kirchenverfassung in ihrer Geschichte* (Bielefeld: Luther-Verlag, MCMLXXIV).

Duke, J.A., *History of the Church of Scotland to the Reformation* (Edinburgh: Oliver and Boyd, 1937).

Dulles, A., '*Ius divinum* as an Ecumenical Problem', 38 *Theological Studies* (1977) 681–708.

Durber, S., 'Baptism, Unity and the United Reformed Church', 62.1 *Ecumenical Review* (2010) 4–13.

Ellis, C.J., and M. Blyth, eds., *Gathering for Worship. Patterns and Prayers for the Community of Disciples* (Norwich: Canterbury Press, 2005).

Engelhardt, H., 'The Lawyer's Contribution to the Progress of Christian Unity', *The Ecumenical Review* (1969) 7–22.

Evans, G., *Law and Theology in the Middle Ages* (Abingdon: Routledge, 2002).

Everts, P.P., 'The Churches and Attitudes on Nuclear Weapons: The Case of the Netherlands', 15.3 *Bulletin of Peace Proposals* (1984) 227–242.

Fagerli, B., L. Nathaniel and T. Karttunen, eds., *Towards Closer Unity: Communion of the Provoo Churches 20 years* (Porvoo Communion of Churches, 2016).

Fanuelsen, O., 'A Distinct and Independent Ministry – the Deacon's Ministry in the Church of Norway: Answers and Questions on the General Synod's Decision (2011)', 13 *International Journal for the Study of the Christian Church* (2013) 312–326.

Fliflet, A., 'Den Norske Kirkes Private Autonomi', 6 *Lov og Rett* (2001) 40 323–345.

Fox, J., ed., *Render Unto Caesar: Church Property in Roman Catholic and Anglican Canon Law* (Rome: Angelicum University, 2000).

Friedner, L., 'Church and State in Sweden', in G. Robbers, ed., *State and Church in the European Union* (Baden-Baden: Nomos, 3rd edition, 2019) 641–656.

Friedner, L., 'Sweden', in *Encyclopedia of Law and Religion* (Leiden: Brill, 2015).

Gassmann, G., ed., *Documentary History of Faith and Order 1963–1993* (Geneva: WCC, 1993) 206–207.

Gassmann, G., 'The Ecumenical Movement and Church Law', in G Gassmann, ed., *Documentary History of Faith and Order 1963–1993* (Geneva: World Council of Churches, 1993) 283–288.

Gilmour, A., E. Smalley, and M. Walker, *Patterns and Prayers for Christian Worship: A Guidebook for Worship Leaders* (Oxford: Oxford University Press, 1991).

Gilmour, A., E. Smalley, and M. Walker, *Praise God: A Collection of Resource Material for Christian Worship* (London: Baptist Union of Great Britain, 1980).

Goodliff, P.W., 'Baptist Church Polity and Practice', 168 *Law and Justice. The Christian Law Review* (2012) 5–21.

Goodliff, P.W., *Ministry, Sacrament and Representation. Ministry and Ordination in Contemporary Baptist Theology and the Rise of Sacramentalism* (Oxford: Regents Park College Centre for Baptist History and Heritage, 2010).

Goodliff, P.W., 'Natural Law in the Baptist Tradition', in N. Doe, ed., *Christianity and Natural Law: An Introduction* (Cambridge: Cambridge University Press, 2017) 140–161.

Gullaksen, O., *Stat og kirke i Norge: kirkerett mellom teologi og politikk* (Oslo: Verbum, 2000).

Habermas, J., *Auch eine Geschichte der Philosophie: Band 2. Vernunftige Freiheit. Spuren des Diskurses über Glauben und Wissen.* (Frankfurt: Suhrkamp, 2019).

Hale, Baroness (Brenda), 'Religious Freedom and the Law', in F. Cranmer, M. Hill, C. Kenny and R. Sandberg, eds., *The Confluence of Law and Religion: Interdisciplinary Reflections on the Work of Norman Doe* (Cambridge: Cambridge University Press, 2016) 218–232.

Hale, Baroness (Brenda), 'Secular Judges and Christian Law', 17 *Ecclesiastical Law Journal* (2015) 170–181.

Hansson, K., *Norsk kirkerett* (Oslo: Aschehoug, 2nd edition, 1957).

Hardy, T., *Far From the Madding Crowd* (London: Folio Society, 1985; first published by Smith, Elder and Co., 1874).

Harnack, A. von, *The Constitution and Law of the Church in the First Two Centuries* (London: Williams & Norgate, 1910).

Hay, W.K., *Pentecostals in Britain* (Waynesboro, GA: Paternoster Publishing USA, 2000).

Hayden, R., *Baptist Union Documents* (Didcot: Baptist Historical Society, 1980).

Hegstad, H., 'Å være luthersk er å være økumenisk (To be Lutheran is to be Ecumenical)' (Oslo: The General Synod of the Church of Norway, 2011).

Hegstad, H., 'Evangelisk-luthersk kirke i en økumenisk kontekst', in S. Dietrich, T.S. Dokka, Trond Skard and H. Hegstad, eds., *Kirke nå – Den norske kirke som evangelisk-luthersk folkekirke* (Trondheim: Tapir Akademisk Forlag, 2011) 11–28.

Hegstad, H., ed., *Kirke nå – Den norske kirke som evangelisk-luthersk folkekirke* (Trondheim: Tapir Akademisk Forlag, 2011).

Heikel, I., ed., 'Eusebius Caesariensis: Eusebius Werke. Band 1. Über das Leben Constantins. Constantins Rede an die Heilige Versammlung. Tricennatsrede an Constantin', in *Die griechischen christlichen Schriftsteller der ersten drei Jahrhunderte* (Leipzig: J. C. Hinrichs'sche Buchhandlung, 1902).

Helmholz, R.H., *The Canon Law and Ecclesiastical Jurisdiction from 597 to the 1640s*, *The Oxford History of the Laws of England*, Volume 1 (Oxford: Oxford University Press, 2004).

Helmholz, R.H., *The Spirit of Classical Canon Law* (Athens and London: University of Georgia Press, 1996).

Hill, M., 'Canon Law: The Discipline of Teaching and the Teaching of the Discipline', in T Harris, ed., *Studies in Canon Law and Common Law in Honor of R H Helmholz* (Berkeley: Robbins Collection, 2015) 337–353.

Hill, M., ed., *Clergy Discipline in Anglican and Roman Catholic Canon Law* (Cardiff: Centre for Law and Religion, 2001).

Hill, M., ed., 'A Decade of Ecumenical Dialogue on Canon Law, A Report on the Proceedings of the Colloquium of Anglican and Roman Catholic Canon Lawyers 1999–2009', 11 *Ecclesiastical Law Journal* (2009) 284–328.

Hill, M., *Ecclesiastical Law* (Oxford: Oxford University Press, 4th edition, 2018).

Hill, M., 'Gospel and Order', 4 *Ecclesiastical Law Journal* (1997) 659–663.

Hill, M., 'The Regulation of Christian Churches: Ecclesiology, Law and Polity', 72.1 *Theological Studies* (2016).

Hill, M., and N. Doe, 'Principles of Christian Law', 19 *Ecclesiastical Law Journal* (2017) 138–155.

Hill, M., R. Sandberg, and N. Doe, *Religion and Law in the United Kingdom* (Alphen aan den Rijn, Netherlands: Wolters Kluwer, 2nd edition, 2014).

Hite, J., and D. Ward, eds., *Readings, Cases, Materials in Canon Law: A Textbook for Ministerial Students* (Collegeville, MN: The Liturgical Press, revised edition, 1990).

Hunter, H.D., 'International Pentecostal Holiness Church', in Yung-Chul Han, ed., *Acts of Pentecost* (Seoul: Han Young Theological University, 1998) 15–16.

Iversen, H.R., 'Det folkekirkelige i den danske folkekirke – organisation, baggrund, egenart og pejlemærke', in E. Berggren and M. Eckerdal, eds., *Ecclesiologica & alia: studia in honorem Sven-Erik Brodd* (Stockholm: Artos & Norma Bokförlag, Bibliotheca Theologiae Practicae, 2016) 125–140.

Jansen, J., *Korte verklaring van de kerkorde* [Short Explanation of Church Order] (Kampen: Kok, 3rd edition, 1952).

Kasper, Walter Cardinal, 'Canon Law and Ecumenism', 69 *The Jurist* (2009) 171–189.

Kent, J., *Wesley and the Wesleyans* (Cambridge: Cambridge University Press, 2002).

Kinnamon, M., 'United and Uniting Churches', in N. Lossky, J.M. Bonino, T.F. Stransky, G. Wainwright and P. Webb, eds., *Dictionary of the Ecumenical Movement* (Geneva and Grand Rapids: WCC Publications, 1991) 1032–1036.

Kirby, J.E., *The Episcopacy in American Methodism* (Nashville: Kingswood, 2000).

Kirkens embete & råd: hvem skal bestemme hva – og hvorfor?: utredning fra en arbeidsgruppe oppnevnt av Kirkerådet (The Church's Ministry and Council: Who Shall Decide – and Why? Report from a working group appointed by the National Council) (Oslo: Kirkerådet, 1987).

Kjems, S., 'The Significance of Church Tax – The Historical Background, the Concept and the Significance of Church Tax: The Case of the Established Church in Denmark' (Copenhagen: University of Copenhagen, 2018).

Klein, Th., ed., *Veertig jaar orde in de hervormde kerk: Schetsen rond de hervormde kerkorde* (Zoetermeer: Boekencentrum, 1992).

Koffeman, L.J., 'The Ecumenical Potential of Church Polity', 17 *Ecclesiastical Law Journal* (2015) 182–193.

Koffeman, L.J., 'How the Protestant Church in the Netherlands was Born', in A. Plaisier and L.J. Koffeman, eds., *The Protestant Church in the Netherlands: Church Unity in the 21st Century – Stories and Reflections*, Church Polity and Ecumenism Global perspectives IV (Zurich: LIT Verlag, 2014) 11–37.

Koffeman, L.J., *In Order to Serve: An Ecumenical Introduction to Church Polity* (Zurich: LIT, 2014).

Kowalski, A., and R., *What Made them Think They Could?* Vol. 1 (Ten Case Studies of Early Pentecostal Women in Missions, 1906–1925).

Laourdas, B., and L.G. Westerink, *Photii patriarchae Constantinopolitani Epistulae et Amphilochia*, Vol. 3 (Leipzig: Bibliotheca scriptorum Graecorum et Romanorum Teubneriana, 1985).

Leahy, B., 'The Role of Canon Law in the Ecumenical Venture: A Roman Catholic Perspective', 13 *Ecclesiastical Law Journal* (2011) 15–25.

Lord, A.M., 'Network Church: A Pentecostal Ecclesiology Shaped by Mission' (Thesis submitted to Birmingham University, May 2010).

Lumpkin, W.L., *Baptist Confessions of Faith* (Valley Forge: Judson Press, revised ed., 1969).

MacLean, M.A., *The Crown Rights of the Redeemer* (Edinburgh: St Andrew Press, 2009).

Macquarrie, J., *Christian Unity and Christian Diversity* (London: SCM Press, 1975).

Maddox, R., and J.E. Vickers, *The Cambridge Companion to John Wesley* (Cambridge: Cambridge University Press, 2010).

Maddox, R.L., *Responsible Grace* (Nashville, TN: Abingdon Press, 1994).

Maghioros, N., 'Autonomy, Individual Rights and the Law of the Church', 13 *Nomokanonika* (2015) 154–155.

Maghioros, N., 'The Concept of oikonomia in Inter-Orthodox Relations. The Preparatory Phase: 1902–1904', 24 *Kanon* (2016) 84–97.

Maghioros, N., 'Diritto e spiritualità nella tradizione dei canoni dei concili orientali (Evo antico)', 73 *Studia et Documenta Historiae et Iuris* (2007) 487–496.

Mair, W., *A Digest of Laws and Decisions Ecclesiastical and Civil* (Edinburgh: Blackwood and Sons, 1895).

McClendon, J., *Systematic Theology, Vol. 1. Ethics.* (Nashville, TN: Abingdon Press, 1986).

Meehan, A., '*Regulae iuris*', *The Catholic Encyclopaedia*, Vol. 12 (New York: R. Appleton, 1911).

Meijers, E., 'White Brothers-Black Strangers: Dutch Calvinist Churches and Apartheid in South-Africa', 38.4 *Exchange* (2009) 365–380.

Merwe, D. van der, '*Regulae iuris* and the Axiomisation of the Law and in the Sixteenth and Early Seventeenth Centuries', 3 *Journal of South African Law* (1987) 286–302.

Meyendorff, J., 'Contemporary Problems of Orthodox Canon Law', 17 *The Greek Orthodox Theological Review* (1972) 41–50.

Miller, S., *The Ruling Elder in the Presbyterian Church* (Glasgow: M. Ogle and Son, 1831).

The Mission of the Orthodox Church in Today's World, 2016: www.holycouncil.org/official-documents/-/asset_publisher/VA0WE2pZ4Y0I/content/mission-orthodox-church-todays-world?_101_INSTANCE_

Munsonius, H., *The Church and Its Law: An Introduction* (Leipzig: Evangelische Verlagsanstalt, 2019).

Murray, D.M., *Rebuilding the Kirk* (Edinburgh: Scottish Academic Press, 2000).

Nauta, D., *Verklaring van de Kerkorde van de Gereformeerde Kerken in Nederland* (Kampen: J.H. Kok N.V., 1971)

Nauta, D., J.P. van Dooren and O.J. de Jong, eds., *De Synode van Emden Oktober 1571: Een bundel Opstellen ter Gelegenheid van de Vierhonderdjarige Herdenking* (Kampen: Kok, 1971).

Newbigin, L., 'Union, Organic', in N. Lossky, J.M. Bonino, T.F. Stransky, G. Wainwright and P. Webb, eds., *Dictionary of the Ecumenical Movement* (Geneva and Grand Rapids: WCC Publications, 1991) 1028–1030.

Noailles, P., and A. Dain, *Les Novelles de Léon le Sage* (Paris: Belles Lettres, 1944).

Ombres, R., 'Canon Law and Theology', 14 *Ecclesiastical Law Journal* (2012) 164–194.

Ombres, R., 'Ecclesiology, Ecumenism and Canon Law', in N. Doe, M. Hill and R. Ombres, eds., *English Canon Law* (Cardiff, University of Wales Press, 1998) 48–59.

Ombres, R., 'Why then the Law?', 55 *New Blackfriars* (1974) 296–304.

Owen, D.M., *The Medieval Canon Law: Teaching, Literature and Transmission* (Cambridge: Cambridge University Press, 1990).

Paolis, V. de, 'Commentary on Canon 1501', in G. Nedungatt, ed., *A Guide to the Eastern Code: A Commentary on the Code of Canons of the Eastern Churches* (Rome, 2002).

Papastathis, Ch., 'Greece: A Faithful Orthodox Christian State, The Orthodox Church in the Hellenic Republic', 339–375: www.iclrs.org/content/blurb/files/Greece.2.pdf

Payne, E.A., and S.F. Winward, *Orders and Prayers for Church Worship: A Manual for Ministers* (London: Baptist Union of Great Britain, 1960).

Phillimore, R., *Ecclesiastical Law*, 2 vols. (London: Sweet and Maxwell, 1st edition, 1873; 2nd edition, 1895).

Pollock, F., and F.W. Maitland, *The History of English Law before the Time of Edward I*, 2 vols. (Cambridge: Cambridge University Press, 2nd edition, 1898; reprint Liberty Fund: Indianapolis, 2010).

Pound, R., 'The Maxims of Equity – I: Of Maxims Generally', 34 *Harvard Law Review* (1921) 809–836.

Power, D.N., 'Episcopacy', in N. Lossky, J.M. Bonino, T.F. Stransky, G. Wainwright and P. Webb, eds., *Dictionary of the Ecumenical Movement* (Geneva and Grand Rapids: WCC Publications, 1991) 359–361.

Rack, H., *Reasonable Enthusiast* (London: Epworth Press, 1989).

Randall, I.M., *The English Baptists of the 20th Century* (Didcot: Baptist Historical Society, 2005).

Reuver, M., *Faith and Law: Juridical Perspectives for the Ecumenical Movement* (Geneva: World Council of Churches, 2000).

Ridderbos, H.N., *Paulus: Ontwerp van zijn theologie* (Kampen: Kok, 1966).

Robbers, G., 'State and Church in Germany', in G. Robbers, ed., *State and Church in the European Union* (Baden-Baden: Nomos, 3rd edition, 2019) 109–124.

Rodger, P.C., and L. Vischer, eds., *The Fourth World Conference on Faith and Order: Montreal 1963*, Faith and Order Paper No. 42 (London, 1964).

Rupp, E.G., *Religion in England 1688–1791* (Oxford: Clarendon Press, 1986) 439.

Sagovsky, N., 'The Contribution of Canon Law to Anglican-Roman Catholic Ecumenism', 13 *Ecclesiastical Law Journal* (2011) 4–14.

Sandberg, R., *Law and Religion* (Cambridge: Cambridge University Press, 2011).

Schweizer, E., *Church Order in the New Testament*, trans. Frank Clarke (London: SCM Press Ltd, 3rd edition, 1979) 13.

Schwöbel, C., 'The Creature of the Word: Recovering the Ecclesiology of the Reformers', in Colin E. Gunton and Daniel W. Hardy, eds., *On Being the Church. Essays on the Christian Community* (Edinburgh: T&T Clark, 1989, 110–155 (45).

Shier-Jones, A., 'Conferring as a Theological Method', in C. Marsh and B.E. Beck, eds., *Unmasking Methodist Theology* (New York: Continuum, 2004) 82.

Skarsten, T.R., 'The Reception of the Augsburg Confession in Scandinavia', 11 *The Sixteenth Century Journal* (1980) 87–98.

Sohm, R., *Kirkenrecht I: Die geschictlichen Grundlagen* (Leipzig: Duncker & Humboldt, 1892).

Stein, P., *Regulae Iuris: From Juristic Rules to Legal Maxims* (Edinburgh: Edinburgh University Press, 1966).

Tanner, N., ed., *Decrees of the Ecumenical Councils*, 2 vols. (London: Sheed & Ward, 1990).

Thompson, D.M., 'The Freedom of the Spirit: The United Reformed Church in the United Kingdom', in A. Plaisier and L.J. Koffeman, eds., *The Protestant Church in the Netherlands: Church Unity in the 21st Century. Stories and Reflections*, Church Polity and Ecumenism – Global Perspectives IV (Zürich: LIT Verlag, 2014) 77–89.

Torfs, R., 'Liefde en recht gaan hand in hand: Een denkoefening over de verhouding tussen theologie en recht', *Tijdschrift voor Theologie* 36 (1996) 270–289.

Troianos, S., 'Θεσπίζομεν τοίνυν, τάξιν νόμον ἐπέχειν τοὺς ἁγίους ἐκκλησιαστικούς κανόνας . . .', 13 *Byzantina* (1985) 1193–1200.

Turner, J.M., *Conflict and Reconciliation: Studies in Methodism and Ecumenism* (London: Epworth, 1965).

Valiyavilayil, A., 'The Notion of sui iuris Church', in J. Chiramel and K. Bharanikulangara, eds., *The Code of Canons of the Eastern Churches: A Study and Interpretation, Essays in Honour of Joseph Cardinal Parecattil* (Alwaye: St. Thomas Academy for Research, 1992) 57–90.

Varlack Sr., A.L., *Foundations – Church of God of Prophecy: Concise History, Polity, Doctrine, and Future* (Cleveland, TN: White Wing Publishing House, 2010).

Veenhof, C., *Kerkgemeenschap en kerkorde: Kort overzicht van de strijd, gevoerd in de Afgescheiden Kerken tussen 1836 en 1840 over de Kerkgemeenschap en Kerkorde* (Amsterdam: Buijten & Schipperheijn, 1974).

Vik, I., and C. Endresen, 'Norway, Religion and the United Nations', in A. Stensvold, ed., *Religion, State and the United Nations: Value Politics* (Abingdon: Routledge, 2017) 170–184.

Vinding, N.V., 'State and Church in Denmark', in G. Robbers, ed., *State and Church in the European Union* (Baden-Baden: Nomos, 3rd edition, 2019) 87–108.

Weatherhead, J.L., *The Constitution and Laws of the Church of Scotland* (Edinburgh: The Board of Practice and Procedure, 1997).

Wessel, S., 'The Formation of Ecclesiastical Law in the Early Church', in W. Hartmann and K. Pennington, eds., *The History of Byzantine and Eastern Canon Law to 1500* (Washington, DC: The Catholic University of America Press, 2012) 1–23.

White, B.R., *The English Baptists of the Seventeenth Century* (Didcot: The Baptist Historical Society, 1996).

Wijlens, M., such as *Sharing the Eucharist: A Theological Evaluation of the Post-Conciliar Legislation* (Lanham, New York and Oxford: University Press of America, 2000).

Wilschut, H.J.C.C.J., *De werkorde nagerekend. Kanttekeningen bij de conceptkerkorde voor de GKv*, s.l.: s.n. (2011).

Witte, J., *Law and Protestantism: The Legal Teachings of the Lutheran Reformation* (Cambridge: Cambridge University Press, 2002).

Woestman, W., *Papal Allocutions to the Roman Rota 1939–2002* (Ottawa: St Paul University, 2002).

Wolf, E., *Ordnung der Kirche: Lehr- und Handbuch des Kirchenrechts auf ökumenischer Basis* [Order of the Church: Text- and Handbook of Church Polity on an Ecumenical Basis] (Frankfurt am Main: Vittorio Klostermann Verlag, 1961).

World Council of Churches, *Baptism, Eucharist, Ministry* (Geneva: WCC, 1982).

World Council of Churches, *The Non-Theological Factors in the Making and Unmaking of Church Union*, Faith and Order Publications (old series) 84 (London and New York, 1937).

World Council of Churches, *Sharing in One Hope. Reports and Documents from the Meeting of the Faith and Order Commission, Bangalore 1978*, Faith and Order Paper No. 92, Geneva, World Council of Churches [1979].
World Council of Churches, Faith and Order Commission, *The Church – Towards a Common Vision*, Faith and Order Paper 214 (Geneva: WCC, 2013).
World Council of Churches, Faith and Order Commission, 'The Ecumenical Movement and Church Law', Document IV.8 (1974).
Wright, N.G., *Free Church, Free State* (Milton Keynes: Paternoster, 2005).

Index

Made in the USA
Monee, IL
12 November 2026

907aa840-7158-43c3-ab69-bdac87c84b8aR01